# THE POLITICS OF PO
# STATE FORMATION, STATISTICS, AND
# THE CENSUS OF CANADA, 1840-1875

Inspired by recent developments in social theory and based on extensive archival research, this book provides the first systematic analysis of the developing knowledge capacities of the state in Victorian Canada. No government can intensively administer citizens about whom it knows nothing. As a result, the centralization of knowledge in the form of official statistics has been an important dimension of state formation. The census of population was the leading project for the production of social intelligence.

*The Politics of Population* provides a detailed account of the political and social context in which census making developed in Canada. It discusses census making as a political project, investigating its place in and impact on party politics and ethnic, religious, and sectional struggles. It also looks closely at census making as an administrative practice, identifying the main census managers and outlining the organization of five attempts at census making between 1842 and 1850, before describing how census making finally unfolded between 1852 and 1871. Curtis examines parliamentary debate and governmental reports, but he also follows census enumerators into the field and traces how what they saw was transformed into 'official statistics.' On the theoretical level, this book engages in a critical dialogue with scholarship on the history of statistics, studies of state formation, social studies of scientific knowledge, and work in the field of 'governmentality.'

BRUCE CURTIS is a professor of sociology at Carleton University.

# The Politics of Population

State Formation, Statistics, and the Census of Canada, 1840–1875

BRUCE CURTIS

UNIVERSITY OF TORONTO PRESS
Toronto Buffalo London

© University of Toronto Press 2001
Toronto Buffalo London

Printed in the U.S.A.

Reprinted in paperback 2002, 2013

ISBN 0-8020-4853-6 (cloth)
ISBN 0-8020-8585-7 (paper)

Printed on acid-free paper

**National Library of Canadian Cataloguing in Publication**

Curtis, Bruce, 1950–
　The politics of population : state formation, statistics, and the
　census of Canada, 1840–1875 / Bruce Curtis.

　Includes bibliographical references and index.
　ISBN 0-8020-4853-6 (bound).　　ISBN 0-8020-8585-7 (pbk.)

　1. Canada – Census – History – 19th century.　2. Canada –
　Statistical services – History – 19th century.　I. Title.

　HA37.C22C87 2000　　352.7′5′0971　　C00-931987-5

University of Toronto Press acknowledges the financial assistance to its
publishing program of the Canada Council for the Arts and the Ontario
Arts Council.

This book has been published with the help of a grant from the Humanities
and Social Sciences Federation of Canada, using funds provided by the
Social Sciences and Humanities Research Council of Canada.

University of Toronto Press acknowledges the financial support for its
publishing activites of the Government of Canada through the Book
Publishing Industry Development Program (BPIDP).

Well dey had some of dem dere questions what was harder to answer dan t'others. When dey come to ask la Cruche to 'splain what she did fer a livin' ... or when dey come to ask de Boy to name all o' his kids ... she's a tough 'un.

T'ain't all. 'Cause dey gots even a tougher question on der list. Ah, der now, Gapi, he din't know how t'answer neither. Yer natioonallity, dey asks ya. Cityzinship then natioonallity. Dere's a tough 'un to tell.

I be livin' in 'Merica, but I ain't no 'Mericans. Nope, 'Mericans, dem is what works in yer shops in 'a States, an' comes up'ere trottin' around on'a beach in'a summer wit' der white pants on talkin' henglish. An'er rich, dem 'Mericans, I ain't atall. Us here, I lives in Canada; which makes out dat I should otta be Canajuns, 's' how I makes 'er out.

... But can't be dat neither, 'cuz 'em Dysarts, 'n' em Carolls, 'n' em Joneses, what ain't none of our race, 's what lives in Canada 'n' all. If deys are Canajuns I cain't be none, us. 'Cuz deys 'r' henglish and us's, I'se French.

... dat don't work neider. Dem French Canajuns, dat's folks 'at lives in Qweebeck, dey calls 'em Canahiens, or well Qweebeckers. So how could I be Qweebeckers if I amn't livin' at all at Qweebeck? ... For the love of Gad, where be I livin' us here?

... In Acadie, I hear say, and I'se Acadjiens. So I set myself to answer der question about nationality like dis: Acadjiens, I tells 'em. ... but dey ain't wantin' to write dat der word in der list not at all, the idjits. 'Cause dey tries to tell me dat l'Acadie, dat ain't no country, 'n' Acadjien dat ain't no natioonallity, 'cause you wa'n't gonna find dat in no book o' Geehographie!

La Sagouine on the census.
(Translated from Antonine Maillet,
*La Sagouine. pièce pour une femme seule* [Québec: Poche, 1986]:191–2.)

# Contents

*Acknowledgments* ix

Introduction: The 'Eyes of Politics' 3

1. Making up Population 24

2. The First Experiments 46

3. Numbering Names 92

4. Calculating Canada in the 1850s 134

5. Setting up the Sectarian Census 171

6. The 'Reality of the Representation' 197

7. Facts, Figures, and Fundamentalism 235

8. The 'Pur Sang' Census 274

Conclusion: Administering the 'Knowable Community' 306

*Notes* 317

*Index* 379

# Acknowledgments

I'm not going to make a list. I started research for this book ten years ago and I'd have to begin by thanking Dean Read at Wilfrid Laurier University and the Social Sciences and Humanities Research Council of Canada and then go through seventy or eighty names before ending up at Carleton University and closing with some suitably affectionate words for Michèle Martin. You'd be bored or you'd stop reading after you found your name or didn't, and she knows anyway, so consider yourself thanked and your help gratefully appreciated, unless you're the critic who rejected the project and said I should start over, in which case start over yourself, I'm done.

Actually, I could make a counterlist. It would go like this: a hole in the ground where the house stood; the outline of the barn foundation; a well that goes dry in mid-August and then it's seventy yards to the lakeshore, which Harold Green says made your hands burn when you were a kid with a bucket; a dead apple tree and a patch of day lillies; stove parts; rusted out tin-ware vessels; rough-forged horseshoes, axeheads, harness rings, buckles, and hoops; hayrake teeth; bits of old medicine bottles and cheap willow ware; mica chips; rotten shoe leather; stone piles and a few plough lines; fence fragments eaten by red oaks; the bowl from a clay pipe with the initials 'T.D.' That's about what remains of the last attempt to scratch a living out of the piece of the Canadian Shield on which I spent a year writing this book. In the 1850s and later, a Canadian government agency tried to convince people that you could make a living here but almost no one made it out of a log cabin or their fifties. As for me, with a sabbatical, a salary, and a supermarket twelve miles away, the deep freeze meant I could cut across the lake and make it out to the car in only twenty minutes. Snow meant light-bounce and more gain from the solar panels. Howling northwesterlies made the stove draw better and the wolves that got the deer couldn't get me. I'd do it again if I had the chance.

– the Drader homestead in the former Bedford Township, Ontario, December 1999

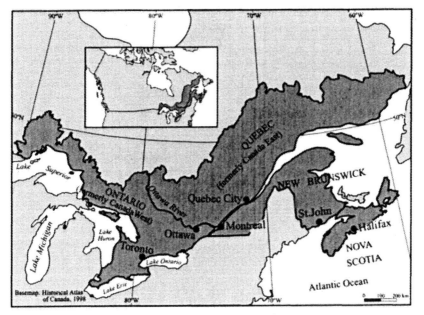

The four provinces of the Dominion of Canada, 1867

THE POLITICS OF POPULATION:
STATE FORMATION, STATISTICS, AND
THE CENSUS OF CANADA, 1840–1875

Introduction

# The 'Eyes of Politics'

Political administration has come to depend heavily on statistical knowledge of population, a leading source of which is the periodic census. This knowledge has become a backdrop for social-policy formation. Political regimes and lesser government agencies use it to assess the progress and consequences of administrative projects and to allocate both resources and the right to political representation. Supranational bodies draw on it to evaluate compliance with international protocols. Official statistical data are 'mined' by private corporations seeking opportunities for profit, scrutinized by epidemiologists looking for disease clusters, pored over by citizens eager for a sense of genealogical identity. Official statistical knowledges of population are essential components in the technologies of risk management and insurance that shape many of the ways in which contemporary social life is understood and governed.

Yet for many people, the production of official statistics in general, and the operations of census making in particular, are perceived as tedious and vaguely scientific, and as interesting only to technical experts. This book argues that a critical scrutiny of the making up of population through the census is of central importance to a great many historical and social-scientific debates and investigations. Census making involves identifying political subjects and centralizing knowledge. It entails the grouping of subjects together to form a 'population' whose elements may then be selectively disaggregated and made the objects of social policy and projects. As a practice that creates social equivalencies, census making is further bound up with the formation of states. It serves to increase the possibilities for intensive administration.

The study of census making is located in the larger field of the history of statistics, which Libby Schweber has aptly characterized as the 'laboratory for social theory.'[1] Such a characterization points to the fact that attempts to construct the abstraction 'population,' and to enlist representations of it in political projects, raise fundamental questions about the status of social knowledge. These questions are central to debates about the authority of science in the field of social studies of scientific knowledge. They preoccupy Foucauldian students of the 'governmentality'; for many, the 'discovery of population' marks the origins of modern government. The same questions are also pertinent to scholars writing about state formation; for them, the centralization of knowledge and the capacity to generate authoritative representations of social relations were central to the construction of the modern state. Some practices of census making have also engaged the many social historians and social scientists for whom census numbers are 'data,' elementary sources of evidence. A huge literature now exists in which particular census categories are examined critically. Oddly, however, empirical studies of census making as such are remarkably rare, and so are theoretically inspired interrogations of 'population,' which is the object of census making.[2]

As a practice that ties subjects and citizens to official identities, census making often generates political conflict. The development of equality of civil rights, and the importance of census returns for allocating state funds and for determining political representation, have politicized census making dramatically in the last several decades in countries such as the United States. Political demands for an objectively accurate census are on the increase, just as sociologists become more firmly convinced of the fundamentally elusive character of 'population' as a social construct. In this book, I undertake a theoretical reflection and detailed empirical investigation of the politics of census making in mid-nineteenth-century Canada; my purpose in this is to show that in political terms, census making is inescapably overdetermined. I argue that an empiricist concern with 'accuracy' is of little use in gaining critical purchase on census making. This is the case because making a census involves the application of what Michel Foucault called 'normalizing judgment' to social relations. Censuses discipline elements of the social in order to assign them to their 'proper places,' and 'propriety' is inescapably political.[3]

**Canada 'Goes Statistical'**

It has become a commonplace that there is no single history of statistics to be written; census making would seem to fall under the same rubric. As one author has put it, individual countries 'went statistical,' most of them in the period from the late eighteenth to the mid-nineteenth centuries, under circumstances peculiar to each.[4] These varied circumstances call for investigation in their own right. The historical sociology offered here focuses on the British North American colonies known as the Canadas (the southern parts of the current Canadian provinces of Quebec and Ontario) and, later, on the newly sovereign Dominion of Canada, in the period 1840 to 1875. It draws on one of the world's best surviving nineteenth-century 'manuscript' census archives in order to track a number of hotly contested attempts to make up population and to enlist population in political projects.

The general cultural and political transformations associated with the rise of 'statistical thinking' are examined in what is now a very large literature.[5] My analysis of the Canadian case centres on the concrete social struggles that surrounded the construction of a statistical agency of state and its operations. Census making became one particularly contentious area of practice. The Canadian case is illustrative of more general developments in the emergence of statistical knowledge of population and its implication in political struggle, social administration, and social science. The period covered in the book is one in which 'statistics' as a form of knowledge became increasingly removed from its origins in historical, geographical, and literary description. Discursive elements were purged from the visible surfaces of statistical practice, and statistics came to be seen primarily as knowledge in numerical form.

Numerical statistics developed in many different venues, both inside and outside the state system, and in conjunction with a variety of projects and interests, both intellectual and administrative. In the period of which I write, census makers contested and eventually defeated other methods for defining the object 'population.' The authoritative, scientific practice of census making emerged during a time of political conflict and proto-social-scientific experimentation. It came to assert forcefully the state's sovereign authority to configure and represent social relations. As we shall see, census making in Canada was directly linked to larger projects and networks of statistical internationalism. In a particular context, Canadian census makers attempted to apply 'population' models worked out elsewhere. Thus, the unusually rich Canadian census archive provides a unique opportunity to investigate census making as an experimental science and to draw the links among knowledge forms, state power, and social imaginaries.

The period between 1840 and 1875 in Canada marked the transition from colonial dependence to national sovereignty. It opened with attempts by British Radical and liberal politicians and administrators to reconstruct colonial government in the wake of the insurrectionary struggles of 1837–38 – struggles that signalled the failure of British colonial policy, which itself was a response to the American War of Independence. The territory that became the Canadian colonies was ceded by France to England at the end of the Seven Years' War. It contained perhaps 60,000 European colonizers, and feudal social relations prevailed. When civilian rule was established after a period of military occupation, English criminal law was instituted, but French civil law continued, along with the feudal seigneurial system.

In 1791 the territory was divided along a northwest-southeast axis, and two new colonies, Upper and Lower Canada, were thereby formed. The western or upper colony, roughly west of the Ottawa River, was intended to serve as a refuge for antirepublican American immigrants, and English criminal and civil law prevailed in it. The eastern or lower colony remained the home of the bulk of the conquered French population, and French civil law and feudal social relations were preserved in much of it. In contrast to England, where Catholics suffered civil disabilities until 1829, the Test and Corporation Acts were not extended to French-speaking Canada. French Canadians did not experience the dramatic social and political-economic transformations of the French Revolution.

Conditions in the two new colonies led to intense political conflict. A complex movement for colonial independence resulted in an armed insurrection in Lower Canada in 1837, echoed in a muted fashion in Upper Canada. Armed border incursions took place in 1838, and insurrectionary activity in Lower Canada was suppressed by bloody military force. An investigative commission was sent out from Britain to determine how to make the Canadas governable, and as a result, the colonies were reunited in 1841. The Act of Union provided for equal sectional representation in an elected Legislative Assembly for the two colonies, which were now called Canada West and Canada East. It imposed Canada West's high public debt on the new colony – a provision the imperial government attempted to render more palatable by a major new loan guarantee for the completion of the St Lawrence canal system.

The representation provision proved to be highly contentious. It was firmly entrenched by the requirement of a two-thirds majority vote for any change, and it was intended to speed up the assimilation of the French-speaking majority, whose separate cultural identity and political and religious institutions were seen by English liberals and tories as inimical to 'British improvement.' At the time of the union, there were roughly 650,000 inhabitants in Canada East and perhaps 420,000 in Canada West. Equal sectional representation was intended to give the overwhelmingly English-speaking members from Canada West and the small English-speaking minority in Canada East control over the Parliamentary agenda. But events did not unfold that way.

In the early part of the union period, the Canadas were a proving ground for experiments in representative democracy and centralized political administration. Reformers sought to propagate practices of 'self-government' (i.e., government of the self and moral regulation) both inside and outside the state system and to monitor their development and progress. Liberal 'freedom' was a value in its own right for some, but self-government was also closely linked to attempts to promote the Canadas as a site for British immigration and capitalist investment. 'British' institutions of freedom were promoted to undermine colonial aspirations for republicanism, and to assimilate the French-speaking majority (or to submerge it in a sea of immigrants), and to sustain a new civic religion that would marginalize if not eliminate the civil pretensions of the Catholic church.[6]

The changing character of colonial governance brought about changes in the nature of political and administrative knowledge. Rule in the colony had originally been organized locally, based on the dominance of individual large landed proprietors, whose personal and experiential knowledge of their own domains was sufficient for administrative purposes as long as administrative projects undertaken were limited in scope. As a centralized administration began to seek to rule the colony directly, and as the intensity of its projects increased, knowledge about local conditions accumulated at the centre of government. While reputable and powerful men at the local level remained important sources of intelligence, and while the centralization of intelligence provoked resistance, standardized forms of knowledge, bereft of observational idiosyncracies and applicable to all domains, acquired a heightened importance after 1840.

The development of knowledge in the form of statistics was thus favoured by the transition to representative government. This knowledge become pertinent administratively; and as Cline Cohen has shown, as an element in a broader cultural transformation it was also widely embraced as popular recreation and promoted as wholesome personal discipline. By the mid-1850s, Canadian politicians were awash in statistical information; it tended to frame their positions in political debate. Statistics was becoming what Gian Domenico Romagnosi called the 'eyes of politics' – a way of focusing and extending the administrative gaze.[7]

The development of the colonial administrative apparatus, including the production of statistics, was shaped by party and political economic conflicts and by the failure of the assimilationist agenda. Despite the provisions for equal sectional political representation, party divisions proved not to follow ethnic lines in the united colony; struggles for internal colonial governmental autonomy, or 'responsible government,' dominated the political agenda until a shift in British policy led to cabinet government in 1848. In any case, neither imperial nor colonial politicians managed to assimilate French Canadians. There was no frontal assault on feudal property relations, which continued in existence until a compromise of 1854 allowed for their commutation. Repeated initiatives aimed at forcing eastern peasant farmers to govern and to tax themselves for local improvements by joining in representative municipal bodies foundered until after feudalism was abolished. Attempts to create a secular polity through elementary schooling were subverted by the Catholic clergy; clerical control over secondary education in Canada East was solidly established in the 1840s. Fundamentalist, ultramontane sections of the Catholic hierarchy encouraged the immigration of religious orders from Europe and the formation of new Canadian orders. As feudal relations of dependence declined, an insurgent church rose to a hegemonic position. As well, French became an official language of Parliament, and dimensions of social life on the two sides of the Ottawa River continued to differ markedly. For instance, two systems of weights and measures – a pre-1824 imperial system and a prerevolutionary Paris system – existed in the eastern section. All of this made uniform state-forming initiatives, including the making of census observations, difficult technically and volatile politically.

With the granting of cabinet government in 1848, a resurrected liberal political alliance pushed for social reform and economic development. Colonial politics and the colonial economy, however, were shaken by the concurrent breakup of the old British imperial system. The repeal of the Corn Laws and the Navigation Acts and the coming of free trade ended the colonies' privileged access to imperial markets and threatened the heavy commitments they had made to transportation infrastructure. The influx of Irish immigrants fleeing famine in their homeland contributed to the formation of an urban proletariat. A major political crisis erupted in 1849 when the Baldwin–Lafontaine Reform government passed legislation providing for compensation to those in

Canada East whose property had been destroyed by troops during the insurrectionary period. The legislation made no distinction between participants and non-participants. Its proclamation was greeted by a mob attack on the carriage of the governor general, the burning of the Parliament buildings in Montreal, and attempts to sack the houses of Reform MPPs.

The Rebellion Losses riots, the perception among English farmers and capitalists that the government was the captive of the 'French rebels,' economic crisis, and the failure of the Reform alliance to push for radical democratic reforms shaped Canadian political and economic life at midcentury. A movement for annexation to the United States gained considerable support. The Reform party was split when its English-speaking left wing joined in the formation of the agrarian radical 'Clear Grit' party, which drew some of its planks from the English Chartist movement. The colony's creditors became uneasy about the government's ability to meet its debt, even as more funds were being sought to pursue ambitious railway construction projects. Statistical demonstrations of growth and prosperity became political resources, and control over the statistical apparatus became an issue in party politics. An interest in economic advertising came to influence statistical practice, including census making.

The Union itself was under attack by French-Canadian liberal-conservatives, who were demanding representation by population in the late 1840s. Yet British immigration was shifting the population balance dramatically – something that made census making more important politically. The colonial finance minister tied the colonial credit to the capitalization of the Crown Lands, which were thrown open for settlement. The immigrant stream was diverted southwards for a time after a head tax was imposed after the famine immigration; when it resumed, new settlers overwhelmingly chose to settle in the western section. The 1852 census showed that Canada West's population was greater than that of Canada East; slightly over 950,000 of the 1,800,000 colonial inhabitants were now said to be in the west. A census in 1861 showed a continuation of this trend. Politicians from the east, many of whom had opposed the representation provisions of the Act of Union, now opposed representation by population, perceiving it as an assimilationist initiative.

No government could muster the two-thirds majority to change the representation provisions, and in the later 1850s, as governments whose majority was based in the east passed social legislation affecting the west, the issue became increasingly controversial. There were repeated changes in government as alliances formed and fell apart; in 1858 an east-west Liberal coalition seemingly about to pursue representation by population was finessed from office after only three days. Finally, in the early 1860s, a peculiar alliance of western Liberals and eastern Conservatives carried a project for the Confederation of the British North American colonies. The Dominion of Canada, comprising New Brunswick, Nova Scotia, and the two Canadian provinces (now called Ontario and Quebec), came into existence in July 1867. Representation by population applied to the new House of Commons, and the political significance of census making was transformed dramatically.

The period covered in this book thus ends with the new Canadian federal government asserting its sovereign powers by standardizing a wide range of administrative practices across the national territory. Scientific census making in 1871 took place at the same time as other dimensions of administrative infrastructure were being organized: a national currency, a unified system of weights and measures, an extensive inspectoral system, an extension of national police powers, and other such assertions of territorial sovereignty.

**Census Making and Liberalism**
In the early 1840s, census making and a detailed knowledge of population were relatively minor elements in the colonial governmental project, even though imperial politicians and administrators active in the Canadas often had close ties to innovative census-making practice in England. At first, the making of a census was driven mainly by the administrative practice of distributing school monies. Census making acquired a heightened importance in the later 1840s and 1850s, in part because population distribution came to be seen as a defensible criterion for deciding where to place administrative agencies and how to allocate government monies. In addition, even as the colonial state system grew rapidly and administrative projects were increasing in number and scope, administrative incursion into some domains by means other than census making was being blocked. Access to vital events was now seen as particularly important, yet this access was impeded by a variety of social conditions and by the absence of administrative infrastructure. Given the developing colonial market economy (which was being spurred by a railway construction boom in the first part of the 1850s), the absence of a system of civil registration in Canada West was held to be menacing to relations of property by creating uncertainty around inheritance. Also, religious voluntarists were sharply critical of the control that the Catholic church

had over the registration of vital events in Canada East. Census enumeration seemed to promise powerful insights into this domain.

Demands for census making also emerged out of rising ethnic, religious, and cultural antagonisms. Beyond the question of representation by population, the destiny of French-speaking people – a minority since 1850 as a result of immigration from the British Isles – became an object of struggle in its own right, with liberals fighting a losing battle against an insurgent ultramontane Catholic church. Census results fuelled attempts to fashion ethnic and religious imaginaries.

Finally, colonial census making was regularly demanded by imperial authorities. Control over the production of knowledge shifted away from imperial officials in the Union period and by 1867 the official documentary system was overwhelmingly in Canadian hands. That being said, imperial officials still could (and did) exert pressure on their Canadian counterparts. In the late 1840s the colonists were urged to adopt an English census-making template; in 1851 and again in 1861, they were pressured to carry out an enumeration in concert with the imperial government and other colonial administrations. Colonial officials were pushed to adopt the census-making procedures advocated at the 1857 International Statistical Congress, and to submit Canadian census materials for approval to the census section of the 1860 Congress.

For all the demands they faced for census making, Canadian politicians and administrators were unable to execute a colonywide census in the 1840s. Despite a considerable expenditure of energy and money, the censuses of 1852 and 1861 were remarkably confused. Later I will show that the first 'scientific' census of Canada, that of 1871, was in fact a fundamentalist Catholic ethnic-national project – a fascinating instance of 'feudal' science in the nineteenth century.

There were three broad reasons for the uneven success of Canadian census-making projects. *First,* the state system lacked the administrative infrastructures that were necessary for governments to make contact with and discipline distant social relations in the ways demanded by census making. This was especially the case in French Canada East. This absence was partly a product of extensive political opposition to liberalism and to representative self-government. Ongoing attempts by colonial administrations to force liberal freedom downwards in society disorganized the census-making process. The local authorities empowered to conduct the census in one local government enactment might no longer exist in the law in force when the moment to enumerate arrived. As a protection of liberal freedoms, time limits were placed on the inquisitorial powers of census officers, with the result that local delaying tactics could render census making illegal. Peasant census informants in French Canada East, already subject to heavy church tithes and arcane feudal exactions, saw representative local governmental bodies as '*machines à taxer*' and refused to cooperate with enumerators. Attempts at a common census of both sections of the colony failed in 1842, 1848, and 1850. A census planned for 1847 was abandoned.

For a common enumeration to go forward at all, colonial politicians had to abandon the liberal plan for a decentralized system of autonomous, local self-government in this domain. Control over the process of census making had to be centralized. To enumerate the eastern section in 1844, the central government resuscitated a law of 1831 from the discredited preinsurrectionary regime. It extended its control to both sections of the colony before the 1852 census. However, because the central authority remained heavily dependent on the autonomous activities of its local allies, and because it adopted a confused version of the English census template, it could not put consistent observational protocols into effect in either 1852 or 1861. Local census managers retained control over the initial compilation and publication of census results. Effective central control over all aspects of census making was first exercised for the 1871 census, as the newly sovereign national state's authority was asserted broadly.

The *second* force accounting for the uneven development of colonial census making relates to the reliance of the census on the elaboration of techniques of inquiry and analysis, as well as on the existence of a workable prior representation of the object of investigation – a point on which I elaborate in the following chapter. Before the mid-1860s, Canadian census making was not guided by a unifying political or administrative project capable of generating a transcendental vision of social relations, that is, a coherent imaginary of people, places, and identities. Colonial officials attempted in 1852 and 1861 to apply the Queteletian model recommended to them by the Colonial Office, but it was unworkable in colonial social conditions. Canadian officials had neither the insight nor the political independence to abandon it before 1871. Other projects that propelled census making, such as the assessment of men's property in land or attempts to advertise the colony's flourishing condition to promote colonization, configured social relations in ways whose practical administrative utility was highly limited. Disciplined social observation was not encouraged by making a census for advertising purposes.

The officials charged with managing the colonial censuses had narrow intellectual horizons and limited expertise. For instance, the managers of the 1852 and 1861 censuses did not command an abstract conception of property relations sufficient for them to separate property in general from the physical location of proprietors' households. This meant that if an individual owned land in more than one enumeration district, either all property and produce were reported as if they existed in one enumeration district; or the individual was reported as living in more than one enumeration district; or only the property and products produced in the district where the individual's residence was located were reported. Also, political party patronage tended to trespass on the terrain of social scientific inquiry, and census making was prey to accidents: the manager of the 1861 census died suddenly in the midst of its compilation.

On the other hand, the execution of the 1871 census in Canada offers a striking refutation of the Weberian thesis that there is a close affinity between scientific rationalism and the ethics of Protestant religion.[8] Here it was a fundamentalist Catholic project that provided the internally coherent imaginary of social subjects, territory, and time of the sort needed to sustain systematic social observation. It was the disciplined organizational skills and the intellectual sophistication of the ultramontane intellectual J.-C. Taché that sustained scientific census making; and it was his shared and transcendental vision of French-Canadian Catholics as the world's most prolific people, charged with the mission of civilizing North America against the ravages of Protestant liberalism and capitalist luxury, that provided the foundation for what he conceived to be a statistical 'monument' and an exercise in genealogy.

*Third*, if science and religion had by 1871 combined in such a way that census making was effective, changes in social relations themselves – the very object of census making – facilitated the process of statistical appropriation and translation. Mass schooling, rising levels of literacy and numeracy, the spread of market relations with their accompanying metrological discipline, a greater popular awareness of the potential benefits of science, and related forces, all worked together to increase the degree of standardization in social relations and in people's understanding and experience. The categories mobilized to discipline social relations in the census had penetrated those relations to a far greater degree by 1871 than they had by 1841.

**The Statistical System, the Census, and Contemporary Historiography**
Remarkably little attention has been paid to the development of statistical activity in British North America. This period has been declared to be of little interest for statistical history, especially by those claiming that serious statistical practice begins with mathematization. Using a very

restrictive definition of 'statistical system,' M.C. Urquhart, for instance, concluded that 'in the pre-Confederation period the only activities that had some of the characteristics of a statistical service were isolated episodes connected with the taking of the periodic census.' R.H. Coats came to a similar conclusion about the absence of statistical practice before Confederation, describing Robert Gourlay's remarkable *Statistical Account of Upper Canada* [1822], for instance, as 'more "account" than "statistical", though he summarizes prices and wages well.' David Worton's recent book on the Dominion Bureau of Statistics and its antecedents in the period 1841–1972 devotes very few pages to the pre-Confederation years.[9]

All three of the last-mentioned authors regard Joseph-Charles Taché, Deputy Minister of Agriculture and Statistics from 1864 to 1888, a person who figures centrally in my account, as the founding father of Canadian statistics. All three participate in the revealingly schizophrenic canonization of Taché that prevails in the biographical literature. For while those doing the history of statistics have seen Taché as a dispassionate scientific worker, some historians of French-Canadian literature and culture see him as an imaginative, pious, and nationalist artistic figure. For the former, Taché's life began in an Ottawa office in 1865 and ended when he last walked out his office door. For the latter, if Taché's life did not end in 1865, his time as Deputy Minister of Agriculture and Statistics was at the very least a distraction from a literary career.[10]

Taché was a fascinating transitional figure in the history of statistics, as I will show in more detail in a later chapter; but one cannot understand the importance of his work by studying it in a narrowly selective fashion. Taché was influential in banishing literary description from the work of Canadian statistical observers, even as he drew on statistical observation for his own literary endeavours. He was a remarkable state servant and a disciplined administrator, but he was surrounded by a team of workers who have remained anonymous in earlier accounts. Taché's fundamentalist national-religious politics have been expurgated from accounts of him as a statistician, yet they formed an integral part of his social vision and they directly shaped his work as census maker. Taché improved on the efforts of a number of predecessors who also had attempted – with less assiduity and ability – to invest social relations in statistical forms. He consciously reworked some of their efforts at statistical production, and learned much about social science and social administration in the process; from this it follows that without a detailed knowledge of Taché's predecessors, an accurate appraisal of his own accomplishments cannot be made. Moreover, when one abandons the teleological assumptions of the historians of statistics cited above, it becomes obvious that Taché's conception of 'statistics' was by no means limited to knowledge in numerical form. Rather, numerical statistics was, for him, only one component of a broader field of political intelligence that included lists, directories, inventories, and genealogies of office, as Taché's work on the production of the colonial statistical compendium known as the Blue Book demonstrates. For Taché, as for Walter Crofton and William Hutton (his predecessors on the Canadian Board of Registration and Statistics), statistics was a kind of administrative activity and a form of knowledge that focused on 'putting things in their place.' One remarkable feature of Taché's work as a census maker was that he established clear observational protocols that lodged his politics in the deep structures of the census.

The broader literature on the history of statistics tends to trace out processes of political, administrative, and scientific development that propel statistical knowledge from a concern with making general inventories of the resources of a state, toward quantification and, much more recently, toward mathematization. The period covered in this book was premathematical in terms of statistical practice, but it contained many attempts by developing agencies of the Canadian state to invest social relations in statistical forms. The importance of census making stands out in part in relation to other attempts at statistical production.

Over the last several decades, the use of the 'manuscript' census has had a dramatic effect on the practice of English-language historiography generally and on English- and French-Canadian historiography in particular. In the late 1960s and early 1970s, a generation of social science historians, emboldened by emerging computer technology and by the scientific promise of statistical methods, seized upon routinely generated administrative records, especially manuscript census records, and used them as a resource for producing 'the new social history.'

The manuscript census seemed to offer new insights into everyday life and experience in the past. In 1973, E.A. Wrigley anticipated that its use would hail a period 'in which the history of the common man' would be written 'not through the eyes of his betters' but, on the contrary, would be 'drawn out from the workaday records of the past.'[11] The census, it was held, would allow us to see the past differently, through democratic eyes that saw true. Early contributors were not particularly interested in asking who was looking at what, through which lenses, and for what purposes. According to Michael Katz in his influential work on the social history of Hamilton, Canada West, the study of the census yielded 'hard knowledge,' in contrast to the rash speculations and literary accounts that sustained the dominant historiography of Great Men. Census data revealed the 'patterns made by the everyday lives of people,' and while Katz saw the data as subject to interpretation, he claimed that 'at rock bottom, they do provide a solid and enduring contribution' on which to base argumentation and debate.[12]

Such optimism has come to seem naive after the linguistic turn in the social sciences,[13] but the new social history did indeed transform historiographic practice dramatically, precisely by legitimizing the study of the 'common man' and by encouraging a productive cross-fertilization among history and other disciplines. Also, interrogations about the 'common man' reintroduced questions of class into North American historiography – questions that had been strongly marginalized during the depths of the Cold War. And the study of the 'common man' as the absent other in 'Great Man history' quickly propelled interrogations about *other* others – that is, women, children, people of colour, subaltern peoples, and so on.

Yet, the naively realist attitude of the new social historians toward the manuscript census has proved to be durable. Like their counterparts in other countries, most Canadian social historians who draw on census data have been deeply concerned about the 'accuracy' of that source. When they have asked questions about 'how the census was done,' they have usually done so in a workaday spirit and with the intention of achieving a better grasp of particular empirical problems. True, local skirmishes over what enumeration practices *mean* have sometimes developed. Some writers have attempted to rework census observations to make them more consistent internally. Calls for a systematic analysis of an individual census as a whole have been made, but such calls have gone unheeded in the Canadian literature.[14]

In presenting the first extensive historical sociology of Canadian census making and of the pre-Confederation statistical system, I face a peculiar situation: hundreds of studies have used census data as evidence, yet the topic of census making as an administrative practice of state and as an object of political struggle is almost completely absent from Canadian social history.[15] For Canadian historical sociologists, and social science historians more generally, this book presents a detailed investigation of the politics and practices of mid-nineteenth-century census making. I place census making in its changing political-economic context, identify the early census managers (two of whom are still virtually unknown), discuss the projects of government surrounding statistical production and census making, and, last but not least, trace out in detail the practices through which competing attempts were made to translate visions of social relations in Canada into authoritative numerical accounts. As I explain in Chapter 1, I attempt to study the census as 'science in the making,' rather than as 'made science,' as researchers are so often tempted to do.

With some incidental exceptions, I have chosen not to engage directly with studies in the Canadian historical literature that use census data in the support of empirical investigation. While this choice may be controversial, it is part of a necessary strategy. On the one hand, hundreds of empirical studies have drawn on manuscript and aggregate nineteenth-century Canadian census returns: dealing even with a selection of the issues raised in them would draw attention from the main point. Furthermore, in the absence of a detailed account of 'how the census was done,' attempts to evaluate the uses made of census results are unavoidably hobbled. I do make a number of general arguments about Canadian census returns as historical evidence. I show, for instance, that the censuses before that of 1871 did not mobilize consistent observational protocols or coherent observational practices. Aggregate returns are haphazard for these censuses, are shaped by editorial practices, and do not provide coherent accounts of social relations. I argue that unless researchers manage to reconstruct observational practices at the local level, such aggregate census returns should certainly *not* be invoked as factual evidence. I also show that the 'scientific' census of 1871 was a fundamentalist religious project and that its configuration of 'population' achieved scientific status in part for this reason. I show that the accepted proposition of 'underenumeration' in the mid-nineteenth-century censuses is dubious. If anything, the evidence suggests widespread *multiple recording* of names. I will articulate a number of other arguments as I write, and elaborate on them in my conclusion.

While the book will make it easier for researchers who use the Canadian 'manuscript' census in empirical work to evaluate it critically as a source of evidence, and while I document the development of a central part of the Canadian official statistical system, my theoretical concern is with the mutual constitution of state and knowledge forms and with the working out of the knowledge/power relations involved in investing social relations in statistical forms.

**Statistical Internationalism**

I end here with some remarks about the developing international statistical networks of the nineteenth century. While I agree with other contributors to the literature on the history of statistics that it is fruitless to seek a grand theory of census making in the needs of capitalism, or in the growth of state administration, or in the genius of scientists, we should be sceptical of claims that there are only national statistical histories. Such claims may serve as alibis for the failure to synthesize, or more simply as pleas for attention to particular cases. It is true that global statistical development and census making have been shaped by innovative local practices; however, local practices were shaped by international developments as well.

Well before 1840, the Canadians investigated in this book were tied into a trans-Atlantic network of intellectuals, politicians, and state servants for whom the articulation of a common set of procedures and protocols for census making was one element in a larger project of world making. Networks of intellectuals, administrators, and politicians had been attempting to coordinate and standardize an array of social practices at least since the middle of the eighteenth century. Standardization, in everything from language use to weights and measures, was held to increase liberty and wealth by allowing the free circulation of ideas and goods, and by turning the world into a knowable place subject to human mastery.

One highwater mark of this movement toward standardization came during the late Enlightenment and related to attempts to internationalize the metric system. These efforts were blocked in England by the outbreak of war with France, and in the United States by political opposition, but were generalized to the French client states in the early nineteenth century. The latter states were influenced as well by the example of the French Bureau de Statistique. In places such as Milan detailed, continuous population registers originate in the late eighteenth century.[16]

Exchanges multiplied in the early nineteenth century among activists working both within and without state systems, especially as the increasing intensity of administration multiplied observational resources. The period was marked by what writers have termed the 'avalanche,' the 'flood,' and the 'cult' of numbers.[17] Statistical production was also fuelled by competition among states for pride of place in the race for 'progress' and 'improvement.' Statistical resources became enmeshed in political and intellectual conflict. They contributed to the emergence of new objects of knowledge – 'things which stay together,' as they have been called – actionable ways of configuring social relations, such as rates of death and crime.[18] When published by state agencies, statistics served as political ammunition for medical doctors, 'friends of education,' the antislavery lobby, factory and prison reformers, free traders, and so on.

For example, in the early 1810s in England, John Powell's *Statistical Illustrations ... of the British Empire* claimed to demonstrate conclusively that the misery of the 'productive classes' was increasing under the existing administration of society, even as the mass of wealth grew dramatically. The proof was there for anyone to see in his hundred-odd pages of official tables of imports, exports, customs and excise duties, currency values, and prices of necessities. Policy demands resulted from such statistical demonstration.[19]

### Lambert-Adolphe-Jacques Quetelet

A central place in the growing international statistical networks of the nineteenth century was occupied by L.-A.-J. Quetelet (1794–1874), the polymathic Belgian intellectual and administrator who presided over the Belgian Central Statistical Commission from 1841. Quetelet was publishing on matters of vital statistics by the late 1820s, if not before, and was actively involved in the Brabant population census of 1829. In the early 1830s, his ideas about statistics and its place in the 'social physics,' which promised to reveal the elementary principles of social life, attracted a large audience. Quetelet's plans for census making were realized in the 1842 census of Brussels, which served as the trial run for the Belgian census of 1846, which he also directed. The procedures invented in these cases were taken as the leading standard for international census making throughout the second half of the nineteenth century and beyond.

Quetelet's plan emerged out of the enumeration of a compact city, where well-developed administrative divisions and a cadre of literate officials made it relatively easy to canvass quickly and thoroughly. This partly explains why his model held that enumerations should be conducted in a single day on the *de facto* principle. Quetelet pioneered the prior distribution of census schedules, one to a household, to be collected (and completed if necessary) by enumerators on the census day. Local administrators would inspect the returns and compile those parts of them of interest to the locality, before shipping them to a central office for general compilation.

While Quetelet did not invent the principle of nominal census enumeration, it was a standard feature of his plan, at a time when only household heads were named in most enumerations. Other census-managers justified the move to nominal enumeration as a control device to prevent enumerators from faking census returns, and it certainly served this purpose; but for Quetelet, it was clearly a method for augmenting scientifically useful knowledge. Generating information about individuals increased dramatically the possibilities for making comparisons and hence for identifying social regularities.

Quetelet was influential in the organization of the London Statistical Society. This society was a breakaway from the British Academy for the Advancement of Science, and emerged out of the academy's 1833 Cambridge meetings, to which Quetelet was the Belgian delegate. The society involved a large number of highly placed intellectuals and members of Parliament from its first meeting in 1834. It had close connections to the English Board of Trade, presided over by Poulett Thomson. Thomson encouraged the London society (as he had done the Manchester Statistical Society, formed the previous year) to concentrate its energies on the areas of inquiry not covered by his own statistical department. The statistical branch at the Board of Trade had recently been placed on a permanent footing, and served as the main source of official statistics in England in the 1830s.[20]

Poulett Thomson's brother, Poulett Scrope, and his secretary at the Board of Trade, Rawson W. Rawson, were members of the London society from the outset. Rawson served as the society's secretary and later became its president. He maintained an active correspondence with Quetelet in the later 1830s. The London Statistical Society's program for the 1841 English census, which would introduce nominal enumeration, proposed procedures described by Quetelet to Rawson. The program was accepted *in toto* by the government.[21]

Quetelet's American correspondents included, from at least 1839, Lemuel Shattuck of the American Statistical Association. Shattuck had sought advice from Quetelet about census organization in preparation for the 1845 census of Boston, which he managed and whose procedures were based on those of the 1841 British census. In 1850, Shattuck was part of the team assembled by the American census superintendent, J.G.G. Kennedy, to advise on procedures in preparation for the 1850 U.S. census, which would be modelled on the 1845 Boston enumeration.[22]

**The International Statistical Congress**
Quetelet played a leading role in the International Statistical Congress, which met nine times between 1853 and 1876. At the first meetings, at Brussels in 1853, Paris in 1855, Vienna in 1857, and London in 1860, there was active participation by high-level state servants and government ministers from countries throughout Europe and America. Those who attended pushed their governments to adopt a standard template

for census making on the Queteletian model and urged them to establish central statistical commissions to produce standardized information on a wide range of subjects. The congress was a voluntary organization; even so, its activities had a strong effect on international statistical practice. It provided a venue for government ministers from many parts of the world to discuss weights and measures, tariffs, monetary standards, public health, and, of course, census making. The recommendations of the census making section of the 1853 meeting, endorsed again in 1857, were copied by the British Colonial Office to all colonial governors late in the 1850s as the template to be applied to colonial social relations. By the fourth congress, in London in 1860, members of the Census Section were already debating many of the concepts – the 'moral density' of social relations, for instance – that would soon reverberate through social science.[23]

Canadian statistical development and census making practice were firmly situated in this network. Intellectuals and politicians close to the London Statistical Society accompanied the imperial commissioner, Lord Durham, on his mission to the Canadas in the wake of the 1837 insurrection. They attempted to employ the new methods of statistical inquiry to produce the detailed local knowledge they required to execute their plans for governmental reform; however, they were stymied by political opposition and by the absence of administrative infrastructure. Poulett Thomson was himself appointed governor of the Canadian colonies in 1839, charged with transforming the colonial state system for administering representative democracy. In 1842, Rawson W. Rawson took over the office of Civil Secretary in the newly united Province of Canada. Until colonial struggles for autonomy undermined the office, the Civil Secretary was the chief colonial information manager, gathering intelligence for transmission to the imperial authorities. Soon after Rawson took the post, modifications were suggested in the colonial Legislative Council to bring enumeration schedules for the 1844 census of Canada East into line with practice in Belgium – evidence, perhaps, of a first link, via Rawson, between Quetelet and Canadian census making.[24]

Later in the decade, in anticipation of an empirewide census in 1851, the British Colonial Office distributed to all colonial governors the outline of the Queteletian procedures to be followed in census making – an outline compiled by William Farr of the General Register Office. Governors were sent sample English enumeration schedules and copies of instructions to census administrators. In adopting the English model, Canadian census managers effected the transition from household to nominal enumeration a decade after the imperial government and at the same time as their American counterparts. Canadian and American census officials were in correspondence in the 1850s and 1860s, sharing sample forms and instructions and published census reports.

There was a Canadian delegation to the 1860 Statistical Congress, although it did not include the census manager. The delegation made a comparatively poor showing, in that it was one of the few from the colonies not to read a detailed statistical paper. The Canadians were present for discussions on sanitary statistics, on tariffs, and on weights and measures, but not for the census debates. Even so, Canadian census schedules and forms of instruction were submitted to the Census Section for approval, and the procedures adopted and the categories of information sought in the 1861 census of the Canadas would closely follow the recommendations made at the congress. The Canadian delegation's shabby performance at the congress heightened domestic pressure for a reorganization of the statistical apparatus.[25]

Finally, in preparation for the Canadian census of 1871, the census manager conducted a lengthy correspondence with officials in many other jurisdictions, seeking detailed information about enumeration and compilation practices, including sample schedules, forms, and instructions. The five published volumes of reports on the 1871 Canadian census provide evidence of one of the world's most sophisticated attempts at enumeration and analysis; the most recent innovations were adopted and new procedures were created. The investigation of Canadian census making has the potential to provide insights into the workings of an international statistical project.

**Organization of the Book**

Chapter 1 examines the constructed nature of 'population' and discusses the theoretical resources concerning state formation and the sociology of knowledge on which this book draws. It offers a limited endorsement of Michel Foucault's analysis of 'governmentality,' as well as some pointed criticism. Chapter 2 investigates the first experiments at census making under the Union, examines the organization of the first government statistical office, and identifies its secretary before discussing the 1849 Parliamentary representation debates. Chapter 3 concerns the attempt to centralize control over census making in the early 1850s and analyzes the practical working out of plans for the 1852 census. Chapter 4 deals with the consequences of the 1852 census results for sectional and ethnic-national conflict. The organization of the new statis-

Introduction: The 'Eyes of Politics' 23

tics agency is discussed, the biography of the new statistics secretary is provided, and the very uneven success of his attempts to produce a regular statistical overview of colonial conditions is considered in detail. The failure of his inquiries raised the stakes at issue in the 1861 census, even while the census became tightly connected to advertising the flourishing condition of the Canadas. Chapter 5 begins with an account of the virulent debate over comparative sectional development that raged in the late 1850s; it then traces out the preparations for the 1861 census, from the 1860 Statistical Congress to the appointment of census officers. Chapter 6 focuses on the execution of the 1861 census. It follows out the long and increasingly tenuous interpretive chains in the census-making process from government offices, to field encounters between enumerators and informants, to the compilation of results. Chapters 7 and 8 focus on the 1871 census. Chapter 7 examines the reorganization of the statistical apparatus and the creation of a census team in the Department of Agriculture and Statistics. The connection between census-making and political representation is shown to have heightened the importance of the practice; noteworthy in this regard is that census planning and design were guided by a fundamentalist Catholic ethnic-national imaginary. Chapter 8 examines the conflict that surrounded the census agency's attempts to define a field of matters of 'national importance' at the expense of local interests in knowledge. The controversy leading to the re-enumeration of Montreal in 1872 is detailed, and the chapter argues that the political project guiding the 1871 census was effectively buried in its deep structures – 'black boxed,' to employ a concept to be discussed shortly. The book concludes with some reflections on census making, statistics, state power, and social imaginaries.

# Chapter 1

# Making up Population

I have argued that Canadian census making was initially hindered by the absence of a coherent imaginary of social relations. It may seem peculiar to associate 'population' with the notion of constructed or imagined visions of social life. Both in everyday parlance and in social scientific discourse, 'population' is thought to be an empirically existing entity susceptible to scientific discovery. I suggest that this elementary realist misconception is a tribute both to the power of state institutions to frame social representations and to the credulity of social scientists in the face of their own theoretical conjectures, for 'population' is a theoretical, not an empirical, entity. Population is not an observable object, but a way of organizing social observations. The concept emerges out of projects that seek to configure social relations so that these may be known and mastered. It has come to sustain remarkably powerful ways of gaining purchase on dimensions of social life, by 'investing' social life in governmental and administrative forms.

When social relations are invested in the statistical form known as 'population,' equivalences are established among at least three conceptual elements: human bodies; virtual spaces within territories; and virtual time. Practical attempts to configure social relations as population typically seek to seize other aspects of social activity in addition to these three. However, at the outer limit of abstraction, population configures social relations as consisting of so many undifferentiated human atoms existing in virtual time and space. The equivalence of the bodies comprising population is to be found in membership in an authoritative community. I include in the concept of authoritative community any configuration of social relations that mobilizes an authoritative categorization, and the extent to which such authoritative categorizations have a practical impact on social relations themselves is an empirical question. In principle, the consequences of such categorizations depend on the extent to which occupants of categories can be induced or coerced to conduct themselves in terms of them, or on the extent to which their life chances are determined by such categorizations.

Where population is made up through a census, the authoritative community is typically a political institution. In the case of large-scale census of population, it is the state. Of course, subordination to the state is not the only way of positing common membership in an authoritative community. Other bases of authority, such as religious allegiance, have been used in the past to conceive of human beings as possessing an essential sameness. However, over the past two or three centuries, subordination to the authority of the state has come to constitute the most general form of social allegiance and belonging. In censuses of population, human bodies are conceived as equivalently subject to state authority. In a fundamental sense, population is both an artefact and a field of the exercise of state authority.

In practice, attempts to configure social relations as population abstract only from some of the many differences that exist among social beings. Such abstraction occurs in a variety of ways and to a lesser or greater extent, without approaching its theoretical limits. In the practice of census making, other forms of subordination typically intercede between the state and the individual subject. Such intercessions tend to be both practical and political in nature. First, because no large-scale census of population can be based on direct physical observations of equivalent bodies in time and space, it is practically necessary to generate and assemble opinions about such things. Typically, only some opinions are solicited, and relations of authoritative opinion-making thus tend to intervene between the state agency and the individual. For instance, the opinions solicited by census making are most commonly expressed by 'heads of household.' Assembling such opinions gives a gender-, age-, and often property-specific account of social relations.

Again, political projects may lead to population being shaped through intermediate relations of dominance and subordination. Thus, for example, when the census of population in Canada was perceived as tributary to the assessment of men's property in land, only the names of male heads of households were recorded in it. In the United States, the body of a slave was counted as only 60 per cent of a free white body, and until the 1860 census, slaves were not named but rather were numbered after the names of their masters. In the early nineteenth century, censuses of passenger ships under the English Passenger Act counted children as a fraction of adults; in this case the conception of bodily equivalence was shaped by practical considerations relating to food consumption and physical size. To repeat, the theoretical outer limit of population is the mass of undifferentiated human bodies. Empirical configurations of social relations as population cannot attain this limit.

Population also implies the localization of political subjects in space. The space in question is the territory of the authoritative community in which the relevant shared relations of subordination reign. This space may or may not have clear physical limits. For example, authoritative categorizations in medical science that yield disease populations may exist in a primarily theoretical space. The population census, however, configures social relations by tying human beings to virtual spaces within the physical space of political territories. The execution of a census of population typically depends on the capacity of state agencies to define territorial boundaries, to subdivide them in convenient ways, and to attach political subjects to such subdivisions. We shall see in a later chapter that in the Canadian case, projects for investing social relations in statistical forms were conditioned by the organization of administrative sub-units and by the development of resources for territorial mapping.

Once nominal enumeration techniques have been developed, making a census involves abstracting single spaces from all the locations practically or hypothetically occupied by individual social beings in the course of their daily existence and confining each of those beings to such single spaces. As Benedict Anderson has put it, 'the fiction of the census is that everyone is in it and that everyone has one – and only one – extremely clear place.'[1] Census making is inherently a *disciplinary* practice, as Michel Foucault employs that term. It seeks to tie individuals to places within an administrative grid and then to hold them steady so that they may become objects of knowledge and government.[2]

The process of attaching individuals to particular spaces is driven by political and social scientific convenience, as I will explain at length later in this work. However, the two basic types of population spaces are that of entitlement (the *de jure* model) and that of habitude (the *de facto* model). In other words, in actual configurations of social relations as population, human beings are typically situated either *there*, where they have some established right to be, or *there*, where they may reasonably be expected to be found habitually. Historically, census making has mobilized conceptions that fall between these polar types, or that confuse them. Both entitlement and habitude are social constructs, and elements of social imaginaries.

Mediate forms of social subordination have sometimes modified these principles in practice. For instance, in nineteenth-century French Canada, women's legal status was severely truncated; thus, census enumerators strove to attach men to their habitual spaces (where they were at the moment of enumeration) but to attach women to the space of their husbands or fathers (where they were entitled to be under the reigning Coutume de Paris). Again, in many censuses conducted according to a *de facto* principle, where some people were *found* was regarded as a perturbation of where they *ought to have been*: they were reassigned administratively to places considered more appropriate.

Furthermore, according to the particular hold on social relations that is sought by configuring them as population, objects, relations, or events may be assigned to one location for one purpose and to another location for another purpose. For instance, since the Second World War, hospital births have come to predominate in Canada, and births are recorded for many purposes of administration and management as if they had taken place at the mother's habitual residence. But hospital administrators, being interested in securing public funds for obstetrical services, record those same births as having taken place in their hospitals.[3] The practical interest guiding the configuration of social relations as population will shape both the ways in which they are categorized and the kinds of administrative spaces in which they are placed.

Finally, the process of making up population has a temporal dimension. The time mobilized in the configuration of social relations as population is virtual time, neither the present nor the past but rather, modally, the time of chance (where subjects were found to be) or the time of the law (where people were entitled to be), depending on the practical measures used to produce 'population.' In addition to these three fundamental elements of 'population' – common political subordination, and placement in administrative space and in administrative time – other aspects of social relations are usually also investigated and organized in the course of making up population. This work will investigate many of these, but for the moment it is pertinent to underline only that 'population' involves a specifically political imaginary of social relations.

### Political Science, Struggle, and Resistance

Census making is a political-scientific activity. It is a general condition of scientific practice that objects of knowledge and targets of intervention must be represented theoretically before they can be known scientifically. Representations, of course, may be more or less refined and consciously thought out, and while intervention necessarily takes place on the basis of representations, experimental science modifies its representations on the basis of its interventions.[4] The practical work of making a census involves attempts to translate prior conceptual postulates about the organization of social relations into a body of empirical knowledge. How 'population' is imagined or postulated tends to change from one census to the next, both as a practical consequence of past attempts to observe it and, to the continuing chagrin of social scientists, as a consequence of changing political and administrative interests.

At the same time, as a specifically *political* science, census making is commonly an object of political struggle and contest. The contending and conflicting social imaginaries sustained by social classes, groups, and political parties produce antagonistic or competing representations of social relations as population. Struggles over census making are to be found with respect to the legitimacy of representations of population as such, and also with respect to the legitimacy of the policy measures that result from those representations. Conflict and more or less coherent differences of interest also surround the encounters between census makers and census informants.

Conflicts over census making are important historically and interesting sociologically precisely because population is produced conceptually before being enacted practically. When incorporated into administrative policy and adopted as common sense, the results of census making shape trajectories of social development. They provide resources that sustain or run counter to political projects. The decision to count or not to count the homeless, the recasting of women's domestic labour as productive economic activity, and the construction of the category 'visible minority,' to take some contemporary Canadian examples, have practical political consequences for the distribution of resources, the valuation of social practices, and the shaping of collective identities. In the period examined in this book, similar struggles surrounded census making as an instrument for forging ethnic, religious, and national identities.

In many modern states, population experts have come to prefer techniques of sampling and estimation as a way of making up population, over the nominal census, which is often seen as an unreliable method for determining 'it.'[5] Here, social scientific practice is re-enacting a debate of the late eighteenth century, in which Enlightenment intellectuals sought a 'universal multiplier' which, when applied to a selection of recorded observations, would yield the 'true population.' As Dupâquier and Dupâquier have pointed out, 'population' was posited on the basis of sampling techniques before censuses were attempted. Dissatisfaction with the deductivism involved in determining the universal multiplier led to attempts to discover population inductively through enumeration techniques. These in turn did not provide access to the posited object in ways considered satisfactory for administrative projects, and so a return to ways of estimating population was made.[6]

Yet attempts to determine population *inductively*, through census making, have rarely involved enumerators actually counting anyone or anything directly. Even under the *de facto* model, the placement of people at a given moment cannot be directly observed. For most of modern history, census numbers have been the product of individuals considered to be knowledgeable telling stories about themselves, and others around them, to third parties, who attempt in turn to translate those stories into hieroglyphs in the cells of enumeration schedules. Other people then divine the essential significance of these marks and work them up into official representations, usually in numerical form. Census making typically involves the construction of lengthy chains of observations of observations.

**Science Studies and the Limits of Deconstruction**

With others who are sceptical of the pseudo-scientific pretension that privileges census returns as 'hard data' because of their numerical form, I share the delicious irony that such returns in mid-nineteenth-century Canada were typically worked-over oral history and third-hand hearsay. Yet in this book I do not offer a discursive-determinist account in which social relations are whatever our discursive resources allow us to apprehend them to be. Nor am I interested in 'data bashing,' the practice that deconstructs numbers in order to privilege other rhetorical devices in argument and investigation. I maintain that social science depends as much on systematic social observation as on theoretical reflection; no rigid separation of the two is possible. Systematic observation and the construction of social statistics, including statistics of population, offer the potential for practical purchase on some otherwise unknowable dimensions of social relations. The bodies of knowledge constructed through census making are invaluable resources for contemporary and historical sociological investigation. Their use has transformed the writing of sociology and of history in productive ways; I do not propose their abandonment. Yet it is not necessary to operate within the confines of a narrowly realist theoretical frame in order to defend systematic social observation. The problem of reflexivity – in this case that census numbers result from negotiated understandings on the part of interested observers – must be addressed directly, and the tactics employed to manage the essential uncertainty of social observations should not be concealed.

I reject the so-called hermeneutic circle or interpretive spiral, according to which my claim to demonstrate that the 'facts' of the census are interpretations of interpretations would itself be shown simply to be another interpretation. It is paradoxical, but as Stephan Fuchs demonstrates convincingly, inevitable, that deconstructionist investigations have to employ realist assumptions about their own use of evidence and analysis. There is no 'view from nowhere' that authorizes objective knowledge; that being said, no observer can both observe from an observation post and at the same time observe the observations he or she makes from that observation post. The deconstruction of observations involves realist assumptions about its own findings.[7]

I follow writers in the field of social studies of scientific knowledge so far as to argue that some constructed accounts of the world are more authoritative than others because they can enlist powerful allies in their support. I adopt the distinction made by Bruno Latour between 'made science' and 'science in the making.' Science in the making is messy, haphazard, uncertain, and characterized by conflict and debate. Competing or conflicting interpretations reign, and their partisans attempt to mobilize resources to strengthen their own positions while undermining those of their opponents. Made science is what results from the resolution of scientific debate. The facts of made science are hardened and rendered durable, in Latour's account, by their location in strategic positions in social networks. Made science is 'black boxed': that is to say, its dependence on particular modalities of investigation and its enlistment of supportive allies has receded into the background, while its claims have entered the realm of the taken for granted. Census numbers are routinely treated as made science by historians and social scientists; I follow the census as science in the making.[8]

In coming to grips with census making from the perspective of science studies, one useful concept is 'investment in [statistical] forms.' As foreshadowed in the work of Laurent Thévenot, the concept carries three connotations. *First*, it implies investment in the conventional sense of directing economic resources toward a particular end. *Second*, it preserves an earlier meaning of investment as a military practice of laying hold or seizing: armies invest castles and citadels, diseases invest cities, and statisticians and census makers invest social relations. *Third,* investment connotes the practices that surround investiture, that is, the imbuing of social relations with particular attributes. As Alain Desrosières has elaborated, the investment of social relations in statistical forms involves both cognitive and institutional transformations. Statistical knowledge depends on the establishment of relations of equivalence among categories of objects and on the routine execution of social observations; in the case of census making, both of these are practical accomplishments of agencies of state. Both are also bound up with the deeper cultural and epistemological transformation, characterized by Ian Hacking as 'the taming of chance,' through which an indeterminate world comes to seem to be ordered probabilistically. Successful statistical investments create 'things which hold together' – actionable objects such as birth and death rates, indices of poverty and sickness, and movements of population.[9]

Bruno Latour's work has been influential in the field of political sociology and the sociology of knowledge through its examination of the phenomenon of 'action at a distance,' which is a restatement of a long-established problem of central-local political relations. Latour has recast the question of how particular localities come to be the objects of effective action by distant authorities in terms of the technology of knowledge. He draws our attention to the role of 'inscription devices' – such as maps, tables, reports, and measurements – which translate observations of local conditions onto the two-dimensional surface of texts. Texts, unlike social relations and conditions themselves, can be transported. They are 'immutable mobiles' in Latour's terms – things that can go away and come back again unchanged. Accumulated at some central point, inscriptions can be ordered, scaled, compared, and rearranged. They can provide central sites with knowledge of conditions in many localities and hence can serve as resources in projects for the mastery of conditions in localities.[10]

This dimension of Latour's work helps us understand census making as an administrative practice of state. It encourages analysis of the technology of knowledge involved in making up population, both in the field encounter between enumerators and informants and in the census office. The statistical investment of social relations in localities makes it technically possible to transport those relations to distant sites where they can be worked up into administrative resources. Yet I suggest that careful critical attention be paid to Latour's analysis of knowledge/

power relations, as well as to Desrosières's distinction between cognitive and institutional transformation. One obvious weakness of Latour's account of action at a distance is its tendency to resolve political authority into the technical operations of inscription devices. This has increased its appeal for analysts who wish to avoid an engagement with structured relations of domination and exploitation in capitalist societies. Latour's model of social struggle is the scientific debate, and it is notable that he consistently avoids the use of the concept 'antagonism,' preferring to make reference to 'agonistic' encounters. Agonism implies competition for shared goals. Similarly, with Desrosières, cognitive and institutional transformations tend to be treated formalistically, in isolation from social struggles.

In Latour's account, centres of authority become authoritative because inscriptions are concentrated there. Yet such an account assumes the authority relations it seems to explain. Inscription devices do not spring up in localities like mushrooms, later to be harvested. They originate from authoritative sites. If social relations are in fact translated into text in localities, it is because observers manage to convince or compel informants to yield up accounts of such relations. Authority is already present in this encounter. Population as an artefact of statistical investment depends on *authoritative* categorizations; its historical sociology must attend to their bases. How, and to what extent, representations of population constructed by state agencies come to be authoritative is thus one question this book addresses. I suggest that in the Canadian case, the census became authoritative in part through efforts by state officials to defeat or limit the scope of other ways of determining population – an assertion of sovereignty over social relations. This part of my analysis culminates in an investigation of the re-enumeration of Montreal in 1872, when city officials attempted to contest the federal government's account of the city's population.

As a scientific activity, census making depends on the execution of the organizational and observational activity commonly known as 'infrastructural work.'[11] The concept refers to all the arrangements necessary to translate the imaginings of state officials about social relations into practical observations and measures of 'the population' and its activities. Infrastructural work involves the design and operationalization of conventions of observation, reporting, and recording – conventions that are intended to isolate relevant aspects of essentially transient and mobile social relations and to freeze them in the cells of a census schedule. At the same time, and especially because census making is based on the extraction of reports from human informants, infrastructural work involves the often mundane practices and arrangements whereby observers make contact with potentially knowledgeable informants. Encounters between census enumerators and informants engage both parties in practices of meaning making. I suggest that both the capacity and the willingness of informants to respond to enumerators in the ways presupposed in census design are directly related to prior infrastructural work – a point on which I will soon elaborate.

In brief, then, censuses are made, not *taken*. They do not simply report aspects of social relations existing in a pristine condition prior to the work of census making. Rather, census making configures social relations in keeping with particular political and cultural objectives and interests in order that such relations may be known and governed. In its pursuit of relevant knowledge, census making cannot but specify and discipline investigators and informants and their social relations. And the knowledge gained is inevitably reflexive, bound up with the conditions of its own production. Without a knowledge of those conditions, we cannot grasp the implications of census results.

**The Accuracy of the Imagination?**
The attribution of scientific authority to official statistics of population is as remarkable as the realist illusions that surround the concept 'population.' As Paul Starr points out, the results of census making are in principle neither replicable nor testable. Census making is thus deprived of one leading ground for claims to scientific stature available to those who work in the experimental and other observational sciences.[12] Even so, the notion that there is a knowable, empirical object called the population continues to be a commonplace in the social scientific literature that claims to investigate the 'accuracy' of census returns. Contributors to this literature typically operate in a realist frame and focus particularly on censuses in the United States. Perhaps because of the overwhelming importance of the census as an allocative mechanism in that country, they have tended to concentrate on the question of 'underenumeration' – that is, the tendency of census enumerators not to record the names of individuals whose existence is implied by their presence in other documentary systems. For many social historians working with census returns, it is a piece of accepted wisdom that census making 'underenumerates' population.[13]

'Population' is particularly bedevilled by the paradoxes that surround attempts to attach invariant meanings – in this case numerical values – to inherently variable social objects. As a 1972 American National Academy of Sciences report on 'missing' people in the 1970 U.S. census put it, 'social data are not simply out there for the asking but rather are structured in terms of purposes, assumptions, instruments, and interactions among people, which to varying degrees perturb, focus, and depend on the customary ambits of everyday life.'[14] To repeat, censuses are not 'taken,' they are *made*. They are made through practices that do not simply reflect but that also discipline and organize social relations. The possibilities for making a census depend in part on the extent to which 'the customary ambits of everyday life' are susceptible to capture by enumeration practices and instruments. Census making is especially vulnerable to the reactions of census informants.

In this literature on census making, 'accuracy,' which implies exactitude in the relationship between two objects, is in fact a misnomer for the way census returns are treated. It is true that some early and exuberant contributors argued that second or re-enumerations of population could provide measures of the accuracy of first enumerations, but this position is clearly untenable. Without an independent knowledge of the object of investigation, 'population,' we have no criteria for estimating the 'accuracy' of differing accounts of 'it.' The accuracy literature has thus tended to evaluate census returns either by looking at the internal coherence and consistency of observational practices, or by estimating the degree of coherence between census returns and other records, such as wills, assessment returns, city directories, or marriage licences.[15]

My quarrel is not with attempts to evaluate the internal consistency of observational practices, but rather with the equation of consistency with empirical accuracy. If one moves off a narrowly realist terrain to argue that population is a way of configuring social relations – that knowledge and power intertwine – 'accuracy' is not a useful concept. The concern with accuracy commonly leads researchers to posit the object 'population' as an empirical entity that only awaits adequate investigative methods to reveal itself in its fullness. The preoccupation with accuracy seeks truth in a correspondence theory of reality and representation, rather than attempting to evaluate constructions of population in terms of their practical utility for social projects. I suggest that the preoccupation with 'accuracy' is a poor way of attempting to gain critical insight into census making. It is a tactic for managing uncertainty that seeks to avoid rather than engage with the fact that population is a mobile abstraction that is responsive to the devices employed in attempts to freeze it.

In what follows, I adopt two critical stances with respect to census making. First, in keeping with one thrust of the existing literature, I approach census making in terms of criteria of systematic social observation. These criteria are based on the assumption that scientific census making involves the consistent application of clearly articulated observational measures and protocols to well-defined objects of observation. The degree of interpretive discretion allowed to observers and recorders should be clearly visible. It should be possible to examine the post-observational work of correction, categorization, summation, and abstraction and to scrutinize the decisional rules that guide it. Census making should not be allowed to remain 'black-boxed.'

Observational consistency in census making demands a high degree of intersubjective agreement between observers and informants – the disciplinary dimension of infrastructural work referred to above. Where the social practices that the census aims to record have not first been disciplined in this way, informants may be incapable of offering reports, either at all, or in the form in which such reports are sought by enumerators. For example, attempting to acquire reports of crop yields in standard measures from producers not engaged in market relations, or the ages of children from informants not tied to a system of civil registration, will seriously affect the degree of observational coherence. Census knowledge is reflexive knowledge; it is shaped by the conditions of its own production and is not simply a reflection of preexisting conditions. Thus, the criteria I adopt in evaluating census making are to be found, in part, in the character of social relations themselves.

Inconsistent and incoherent social observations can yield consequential representations of social relations. The *second* basis for evaluating censuses that I adopt in this book concerns their practical utility. For researchers seeking to use census materials, incoherent observations can provide insight, for example, into social understandings. For those interested in the politics of knowledge, incoherent configurations of social relations can be invoked in political projects just as well as coherent configurations. However, not all ways of configuring social relations as population and of attempting to observe such configurations offer the same practical possibilities for intervention and administration. The worth of census data is related to the projects in whose service they are enlisted. Censuses, in short, can be evaluated by looking at their form – that is, the extent to which practices of observation were consistently applied – and at their adequacy when it comes to allowing practical purchase on relevant aspects of social relations.

## State Formation

Census returns acquire authority through their implication in state power. Census making is inseparable from other practices whereby agencies of states come to claim successfully the authority to administer social relations and to elaborate collective representations of those relations. Census making is itself a practice of state formation, an assertion of sovereign authority over people and social relations. It seeks to tie people as state subjects and citizens to official identities within a determinate territory in order to rule them. It does so through the disciplining of social relations and the centralization of knowledge.

The literature on the history of statistics makes repeated reference to the origins of this form of knowledge in political relations, and in passing it often relates the nineteenth-century explosion in the production of statistics to the development of state administration; yet the mutual constitution of state forms and knowledge forms has rarely been a direct object of inquiry. For instance, official statistics are seen to be matters of state because they shape political identities; or the extraction of knowledge is seen to parallel other forms of state extraction, such as taxation.[16]

This book, in contrast, investigates census-making practices as practices of state formation. I offer a grounded account of the interactions among particular kinds of political, religious, ethnic, linguistic, and economic conflicts and struggles; attempts to form social relations in the political institutions and through the practices of liberal democracy; and the developing administrative capacities of state agencies. I argue that there is a close formal connection between liberal democratic political forms, state administration, and statistical knowledges of population. However, the limited translation of this formal connection into a factual one takes place through real social struggles that need to be examined empirically.

I adopt an approach to the study of state formation that is influenced by the way of problematizing 'the State' proposed by Philip Abrams and elaborated by Philip Corrigan and Derek Sayer. This work has been widely influential and quite productive, although it has also faced some telling criticism. For example, it has been called to account for assimilating all forms of regulation to state regulation, and charged with basing claims about state domination on an unsustainable dichotomy between reality and representation. I use this work advisedly, and my own position in subsequent debate has been elaborated more fully elsewhere. I offer only a brief outline here.[17]

I follow Abrams's work by consciously refusing to invoke the 'State' as an internally unified third-order object possessed of will and intention and capable of providing coherence to political relations and struggles. Abrams's work proposes a more empirically grounded account of state capacities and political projects. At any given historical moment, the extent to which, and the manner in which, political agencies monopolize capacities to exercise and to legitimize violence, to extract economic resources, to frame representations of social relations, and to administer the conduct of subjects is a set of empirical questions. Abrams refers to the organization of these capacities as the 'state system' – a concept I adopt.

For Abrams's notion of the 'state project,' used to suggest that capacities of the state system serve ultimately to legitimate the fundamentally illegitimate domination of subjects, I substitute a more capacious concept of political projects and a broader conception of domination and subordination. Abrams stressed that the state system may be characterized by internal relations of conflict and struggle. I suggest, in addition, that the boundaries of state systems are historically fluid. The capacities of the state system may be the object of political struggles and projects that have their origins elsewhere. Such projects may seek to extend, destroy, or reconfigure state capacities.

From Corrigan and Sayer, I draw on the notion of state formation as cultural revolution. Their work stresses that political forms are cultural forms and forms of subjectivity. Under capitalist democracy, political domination works through 'consent,' through its incorporation in the selves of the dominated. In Corrigan and Sayer's understanding of Marxism, domination is not limited to economic might or ideological distortion. Rather, effective domination implies cultural leadership: the fashioning of imaginaries of whence current conditions came; of why they are as they are; and of what the future may portend. In Corrigan and Sayer's account as well, domination comes to be incorporated into forms of selves and cultural forms, and not simply by means of habituation (although discipline plays an important part in their analysis). Attention to the ritualistic dimensions of rule invites us to study the historical anthropology of relations of domination. Given my position that 'population' is a way of configuring social relations, attention to the making of social meanings is particularly important.

In a related vein, I draw on Bernard Cohn's analyses of the forms of knowledge implicated in British imperialism. Cohn examined census making as an element in the formation of states, as an instrument of political domination, and as a potential base for political opposition. In conjunction with other practices, census categorizations framed the social relations of British domination in nineteenth-century South Asia and imposed particular kinds of identifications upon people, against their struggles of resistance. Cohn showed that the imposition operated so successfully in some cases of ethnic-religious identifications that the imposed categories were appropriated as elements of the self-identities of the subjugated. When later projects of domination led to attempts on the part of rulers to recategorize social relations, they were opposed in defence of the categories imposed earlier.[18]

More recently, Cohn has argued that the operation of power in European states from the eighteenth century onward was manifested through the operation of 'officializing practices.' Such practices involved the definition and classification of space, the separation of public and private domains, the counting and recording of information about populations, and the creation of standard languages and systems of writing. These practices sustained the British imperial investment of Indian social relations. They allowed the insertion of these relations into cultural and political forms that were intelligible to imperial projects, and they generated a vast amount of information upon which the capacity of regimes to govern came increasingly to depend. At the same time, they reified 'the State' as the natural embodiment of territory and history. Cohn situated census making as an element in larger processes of world making. I follow his general argument about the elementary importance of the centralization of knowledge, particularly statistical knowledge, in practices of state formation as well as his insistence on the importance of the public/private knowledge divide. The development of the practical capacity to situate, locate, identify, and know elements of territory and social relations is constitutive of modern state power. In state systems were administration becomes increasingly intensive, the possibility for central state agencies to rule distant localities depends on the centralization of knowledge.[19]

**Governmentality**

The central importance of the concept 'population' and of the practices made possible by it are stressed in Michel Foucault's later work. His interest in 'population' has been echoed repeatedly in what is now a large literature concerned with questions of 'bio-politics' and 'governmentality.' A number of investigations have dealt with the apparatuses of security – the disciplines and the expert knowledges implicated in the government of population. Studies have also focused on the constitution of 'risk populations' through particular kinds of investigative technologies and practices of representation, and have emphasized the remarkable possibilities both for administrative management and for informed individual self-government that emerge from risk and insurantial technologies. Other, more critical accounts point to the implication of statistical knowledges of population in neoliberal policies of prudentialism that aim to make individuals bear the burden of responsibility for their own fates. However, no one working in the field has yet subjected Foucault's use of the concept 'population' to sustained critical scrutiny. Nor has anyone attempted to use Foucault's analytics of government to investigate projects or practices for configuring social relations as population through census making.[20]

According to Foucault's various accounts, 'population' as an object of knowledge and an instrument of the arts of government appeared sometime in the eighteenth century, in a context characterized by demographic change, the increasing presence of money, and the growth of the agricultural economy. These forces were mutually reinforcing in ways 'with which the historians are familiar,' but whose analysis was not of interest to Foucault. Their operation was coterminous with the development of the science of political economy.[21]

In one early formulation of the question, Foucault pointed to what he called 'two great revolutions in the technology of power: the discovery of discipline and the discovery of regulation,' or respectively, anatomo-politics and bio-politics. He argued that the second of these technologies emerged especially in England in the second half of the eighteenth century and targeted not individuals as such, but rather population. 'And population,' he asked, 'what does that mean? It does not simply mean a numerous human group, but living beings penetrated, compelled, ruled by processes, by biological laws. A population has a birth rate, a death rate, an age curve, an age pyramid, a degree of morbidity, a state of health, a population may perish or may, on the contrary, expand.' The discovery of population had particularly important consequences for the form and object of political power. Bio-politics recast the relationship between the individual subject and power. It moved away from techniques of simple extraction toward the utilization of 'population as a machine for producing, for producing wealth, goods, for producing other individuals. The *discovery of population* is, at the same time as the discovery of the individual and of the malleable body, the other major technological nucleus around which the political procedures of the West were transformed.' It is through the transformations associated with the discovery of population, suggests Foucault, that 'power becomes materialist.'[22]

As a political object, population involved both a greater degree of abstraction in the conceptualization of human beings and more concrete and practical points of access for the arts of government. As Foucault put it in another formulation, population 'is not conceived as a collection of subjects of right, nor as a mass of hands destined to labour; it is analysed as a mass of elements which, on the one hand, belongs to the general administration of living beings (population then depended on the "human species": the notion, new to the period, is to distinguish the "human genus" [a more general category]) and, on the other hand, may provide a hold for concerted interventions (by the intermediary of laws, but also by changes in attitude, in ways of doing and living that may be achieved by "campaigns").'[23]

There are two particularly important consequences of this new conception of population. In keeping with the new science of political economy, population phenomena were held to depend on particular kinds of articulations of institutions, orders, forms and relations of production, and relations of domination. The fate of population, as a living process, was a result of configurations of such elements. Population had its own internal dynamics, which both limited the scope for and specified the conditions of intervention. As Foucault put it, 'the transition which takes place in the eighteenth century from an art of government to a political science, from a regime dominated by structures of sovereignty to one ruled by techniques of government, turns on the theme of population and hence also on the birth of political economy.'[24]

As such, the 'discovery' of population marks an important dividing line between rule predicated on the model of police, whose utopia is the completely regulated society, and liberalism, where rule is limited by attempts to respect the essential nature of things and aims at framing the freedom of autonomous political subjects. Some writers adopt a dichotomous view of police and liberalism, but I follow those like Alan Hunt who have suggested more caution with respect to the degree of discontinuity at issue. My position is that the accomplishments of police remain infrastructural to liberal regimes of government, which are themselves riven by the tensions, described by Barry Hindess, that surround attempts to create greater 'freedom' through more intense regulation.[25]

For Foucault, the second thrust of the new conception of population, as composed of articulations of equivalent human atoms, is that it makes the individual body and life stand forth as a political target and as a political anchorage point. In theory, rule no longer had to operate via the intermediary of the household head, although in practice, access to population phenomena was still through that figure. Campaigns and projects aimed at disciplining elements of individual conduct and subjectivity could work directly on the vital processes of population.

The government of population thus operates along two axes: one of individualization, the other of totalization. Within and without the state system there develop disciplines, techniques, and instruments that are implicated in projects for the formation of individual subjectivities. Individuals become the objects of projects that seek to change their conduct by effecting their bodily forces, by tying them to physical space or social categories, by colonizing their wills, and by developing selectively and encouraging pointedly their capacities for reflection and self-discipline. Along the other axis, individuals may be grouped together into categories within which their health, understandings, morals, and desires become the objects of particular governmental projects. Such totalizations may construct new subjectivities, and they may touch groups that are relatively small or that are as large as all the occupants of a national territory. Census making, I will argue, can usefully be examined from this perspective.

Foucault's concept of 'governmentality' thus broadens our understanding of domination and rule. This work presents richer conceptions of subjectification than can be found in much of the literature on state formation. It points to the production of disciplined and self-disciplining individuals; yet it also draws attention to totalizations, potential bases of social solidarity, and objects of rule without limiting solidarities exclusively to relations of class. 'Population' thus provides access to one of the universalizing moments of the class domination that is characteristic of capitalist societies. Ironically, Foucault's work offers those interested in employing Marxist analytic concepts a way of coming to grips with practices of social administration, even as it decentres the state. In this book I engage with Foucault's conceptions, drawing on his attempt to triangulate the operation of modern political domination around sovereignty–discipline–government. I show that this attempt offers some useful purchase on practices of census making. At the same time, however, I suggest that this triangle is not sufficiently capacious to accommodate a historical sociology of the making up of population.

One difficulty in using Foucault's work derives from my analysis of population as the configuration of social relations. While clearly aware that population involves authoritative categorization and while stressing, at times, that it is an abstraction which emerges out of a complex of particular empirical determinations (medical nosology, inspection, demographic estimations, and so on), Foucault tends nonetheless to write naturalistically about population. It is an object on which power can act. It flows from one place to the next, it increases or decreases, it changes its character. It is composed of processes that can be listed.

In fact, the 'natural' processes of population are themselves only further ways of configuring and apprehending social relations. Nature has no such rates; historically located human actors work up the social relations around them into such forms in pursuit of their own projects. I suggest that we hold consistently to an understanding of 'population' as the variety of ways in which social relations are subjected to authoritative categorization and configuration by state agencies. Writing naturalistically about population as a *thing* composed of elements and empirical processes is not helpful for the examination of political practices.

Furthermore, if my initial analysis is sound, authoritative configurations of the social relations of subjection, as large-scale population, are inherently state forms. It is thus misleading to suggest that they are 'discovered' by political authorities as objects of rule. This formulation implies that population exists as an object before the political authority that 'discovers' it; in fact, population is inextricably a category of state, at least insofar as political subjects are concerned. The capacity to configure social relations authoritatively as population is coincident with the formation of a particular kind of sovereign authority itself – the authority that imposes social equivalencies. I suggest that it would be more fruitful to approach the configuration of social relations as population, and the formation of liberal democratic states, as phenomena that are mutually constitutive.

At the same time, I argue that attempts, like those present in the early work of Peter Miller and Nikolas Rose, to make the state into a subcategory of a general will to govern are fundamentally mistaken. In one of their formulations, for instance, they propose that 'rather than "the State" giving rise to government, the state becomes a particular form that government has taken.' They then seek support for this position in the argument that 'population' is 'the terrain *par excellence*' of government. If population is a category of state, this argument cannot be sustained, although in following Abrams I am not suggesting that we must then see a hypostatized 'State' as the origin point of power and social struggle.[26]

Taking my position with respect to population forces one to confront

Foucault's confused and incoherent attempts to analyse the state. The substance of the confusion has been well documented in the governmentality literature, although many writers have been remarkably charitable toward Foucault in this matter.[27] Foucault attempts both to displace government from law and the state, by broadening it to include all forms of the conduct of conduct, *and* to make the state into the centre to which all forms of government ultimately refer. The state is treated both nominalistically, as the balance of political forces obtaining at a particular moment, *and* as a real entity capable of action and able to survive by dissolving its own boundaries and inscribing the conditions of rule in the subjectivities of those it dominates. The confusion has allowed writers from different perspectives to lay claim to Foucault's analysis for projects that are quite incompatible, usually by defining Foucault's 'real' position as one of the two main interpretations he presents.

My position is that one cannot triangulate power around sovereignty–discipline–government in the case of the configuration of social relations as population without an account of state formation and political administration – two domains in which Foucault's analytics are of far less help than they might be. Foucault's analysis of the state was sharply limited by his preoccupation with 'how to get rid of Marxism' – specifically, the theory of the state promoted by the French Communist Party. In this theory, the state appeared as the centre from which social power and domination emanated and as the main object of political struggle. Foucault's well-known proposition that political theory had yet to cut off the king's head was directed at this heavily economic-determinist analysis of the state. Even though the contemporary English-language literature of state formation was moving well beyond such an analysis in its engagement with the work of Antonio Gramsci, Foucault's attack on state-centred theory was imported acritically into English-language sociology by some writers. Foucault did not present a cogent political analysis of a decentred state, and as a consequence his work tended to flatten, if not eliminate, hierarchical structures of domination.[28]

In my view, the valuable part of Foucault's analysis is his attention to the creative potential of power/knowledge relations and his insistence that domination in capitalist democracy involves the articulation of liberal freedom with projects for rule. Yet I reject his refusal to analyse the state system as an organized set of capacities that are themselves objects of contest and struggle. In what follows, I pay particular attention to census making as a set of disciplinary practices and as an assertion of sovereign authority over territory. I attend to the ways in which census making is caught up with attempts to govern population by isolating problematic aspects of individuals and their social relations and by grouping social relations and practices to turn them into objects of administration.

**First and Effective Instances**
Studying the making up of population in ways that draw on Foucauldian concepts also confronts one with the challenging relationships between theoretical abstractions and empirical determinations. The notion, for instance, that the kingdom contained a certain number of people of given ages and 'qualities,' whose capacities could be enlisted in war or peace, who consumed and produced determinate amounts, and who could be enumerated, is already well articulated in works of the sixteenth century. Dupâquier and Dupâquier point out that urban censuses were common in fifteenth-century Italian states; they also point, as Corrigan and Sayer do, to the lists taken for the 1377 Poll Tax in England as authoritative political resources. From the fourteenth century onward in western Europe, individuals were subjected to an increasing weight of identifying practices. Eighteenth-century Swedish parish registers sustained nominal enumerations.[29]

Clearly, 'population' had emerged as a more or less defined abstraction well before the late eighteenth century, which is where Foucault claimed that it was 'discovered.' On the other hand, population did not approach its conceptual limit of undifferentiated atoms in virtual time and space until much later than that time. First instances are not necessarily consequential; proto-conceptual advances may wait on mundane empirical investigation to acquire substance, and a genealogical account of the emergence of population is not adequate. Unlike the confessional, for instance, one cannot see 'population' emerging in the fullness of its concept in response to local struggles and then migrating to other contexts in different circumstances. I follow Marx in arguing that the most general abstractions emerge out of the richest concrete material determinations – a position that encourages an interest in empirical investigation rather than a preoccupation with the Foucauldian history of 'population reason.'[30]

Nonetheless, I argue that the generalization of the nominal or every-person enumeration marked a heightened development of the abstraction 'population' and dramatically extended the possibilities for large-scale individualizing and totalizing initiatives. The two things that did the most to make 'every person' enumeration possible were the establishment of the social equivalencies predicated on political subordination and the development of technical enumeration instruments and social infrastructures. As a regular practice of government, the nominal enumeration appeared only toward the end of the first half of the nineteenth century and developed unevenly internationally.[31]

The chapters that follow examine the social and political struggles that surrounded the development of a Canadian statistical apparatus and present a detailed historical sociology of census making as a political science.

Chapter 2

# The First Experiments

The repeated efforts undertaken in the 1840s to conduct a census of the new, united Province of Canada are the focus of this chapter. Attempts at a common enumeration of largely anglophone Canada West and largely francophone Canada East failed in 1842, 1848, and 1850 because of local opposition and a lack of administrative infrastructure. A common enumeration scheduled for 1847 was abandoned, even as administrative and political demands for a credible colonial enumeration intensified. The distribution of inhabitants between the colonial sections became a matter of political conflict, and the colonial government was under pressure from its imperial counterpart to deliver population numbers. At the same time, the colony's official documentary system was expanding rapidly and politicians were increasingly demanding statistical information on topics of moment. In 1847 the weak Tory government in office took steps to organize a dedicated statistics office and gave a loyal, high Tory functionary the authority to oversee the colony's developing statistical resources. However, this official proved to be incompetent as an administrator, and his political partisanship did not encourage the development of dispassionate social observation and disciplined statistical practice.

One of the first enactments of the Parliament of the newly united colony was for the taking of a periodic census. The 1841 Census Act anticipated quinquennial enumerations modelled on existing practice in Upper Canada; however, no account of an 1841 Parliamentary census debate survives. A Foucauldian analysis would lead one to expect that the liberal politicians involved in governing the Canadas would be preoccupied with generating detailed analyses of population, but there were no visible demands from intellectuals, scientists, doctors, or state servants for a regular population enumeration. Census making figured initially as a necessary if minor adjunct to the more general liberal project, which was to install representative self-government in the colony in the wake of the insurrectionary struggles of 1837–8. A census would further the plan to introduce property registration and property taxation in Canada East; moreover, it would guide the allocation of school grants between the two colonial sections under the 1841 School Act. £50,000 in school monies constituted the single most important source of social spending.

The legislative agenda of the first Parliamentary session was largely that of the governor, Poulett Thomson, now Lord Sydenham, whose close connections to the London and Manchester Statistical Societies have been mentioned. Yet, the 1841 Canada Census Act embodied none of the innovations contained in the 1841 English census. The details of the Census Act were thus likely another result of the political score-settling that followed the insurrection. The triumphant anglo-Tory merchant faction took advantage of the discomfiture and demoralization of its Reform and francophone opponents by imposing Upper Canadian legislative provisions on the new united province.[1]

**The Imperial Interest**
Perhaps a census law was included on the first legislative agenda in response to the interest of the imperial authorities in developing the population and resources of the Canadas, for such matters had a geopolitical importance. For reasons relating to Anglo-American relations, the Colonial Office had a strong interest in the size, component parts, and geographical distribution of the Canadian population. The eighteenth-century strategy of keeping the Quebec territory French, feudal, and Catholic had been aimed at creating a bulwark against republicanism to the south; in the same vein, the initial division of Quebec into Upper and Lower Canada in 1791 had been aimed at creating a homeland for antirepublican refugees.[2] These kinds of concerns continued after the union of the Canadas. For instance, the Maine boundary dispute of the 1840s raised questions of settlement distribution, while potential conflict around the enforcement of the American fugitive slave laws made it interesting to determine the location and numbers of black residents in Canada.

Imperial immigration and colonization schemes propelled attempts to inventory colonial resources and conditions. Imperial and colonial government authorities, as well as private organizations, sought to identify areas fit for agricultural colonization, to ascertain average wages and prices and the demand for different kinds of labour, and to publicize the promise of particular localities as development sites. Also, the ongoing financial obligations of the imperial government toward Canadian aboriginals sustained an interest in their numbers, characteristics, and geographical distribution. After 1829, the administration of the Imperial Passenger Act led to an increasingly sophisticated monitoring of immigrant arrivals at the main ocean port of Quebec. The Canadian Emigrant Agent kept detailed lists of arrivals and delivered weekly reports that included such things as the age, sex, and occupation of immigrants. No system existed for tracking arrivals beyond the port of entry, however, and there was no means of recording immigration or emigration at other border points.

Furthermore, after the early 1820s the completion of the Blue Book – the annual report required of the colonial administration – demanded fairly detailed settlement returns, and Canadian officials frequently encountered other demands from their imperial counterparts for reports of various dimensions of population. In Britain in the 1830s and early 1840s there were intense political conflicts over the Corn Laws and free trade, and as one consequence colonial state servants found themselves being pushed by imperial authorities to provide accounts of such things as grain yields, agricultural prices, and settlement densities. In the absence of a census and other administrative resources, they were frequently unable to respond.[3] Throughout the 1840s, information-gathering practices in the colonies lagged behind those in England; the Blue Book continued to use the tripartite division of population into agricultural, manufacturing, and commercial categories – a division abandoned in English census making in 1841. So the Colonial Office was one source of pressure for a colonial census act; worth noting as well is that its efforts were not coordinated with those of the General Register Office until 1849.

## Population and Political Representation

The 1841 Canadian census provisions cannot be attributed to a constitutional requirement for the allocation of political representation because representation was not determined according to population distribution (as it was in the United States). Rather, each section of the colony was accorded the same number of seats in the Legislative Assembly, an arrangement firmly entrenched by the stipulation that a two-thirds majority was required for any change. The principle of equal sectional representation was initially promoted by anglophone capitalists eager for the immediate establishment of a pro-British majority in the Assembly and for the disenfranchisement of French Canadians. Lord Durham, in contrast, in analysing colonial reform in his *Report on the Affairs of British North America*, had pointed to other methods for limiting the political power of francophones and had correctly anticipated that ongoing immigration would soon create an anglophone majority.[4] It is a well-known irony that a principle meant to limit the power of Canada East in the Canadian union increased that power disproportionately after 1850. 'Representation by population' became a recurrent political demand after the mid-1840s, served as one basis of sectional political grievances, and led to calls for population enumerations. Yet these calls did not precede the initial census legislation. Indeed, the representation provisions in the Act of Union provoked an impasse in Canadian politics that was resolved only with Confederation in 1867. Severing the census from the process for determining political representation removed one potential source of pressure for consistency and exhaustiveness from Canadian census-making practice.

Neither of the former colonies of Upper and Lower Canada had based Parliamentary representation strictly on population distribution. In the west, a mixed principle of population distribution and property valuation guided the distribution of seats; in the east, geographic criteria predominated. In both sections, very unequal degrees of political representation prevailed, exacerbated by the kind of disenfranchisement caused by the establishment of limited numbers of polling places (sometimes only a single one).[5] This is not to say that the sectional representation contained in the Act of Union was seen as equitable; far from it. The point here is that opposition to the plan was not based on the notion that Parliamentary seats should be distributed strictly in keeping with population distribution. This point is worth dwelling on briefly, for it suggests that the dominant conception did not see population as a totalization of equivalent individuals distributed throughout territory as uniform space.

Word of the plan to give each section of the united colony the same number of seats provoked immediate protest in the press of Lower Canada. In the spring of 1840, *Le Canadien* of Quebec City published a list showing the varying relationships between population and political representation in different ridings. In Canada West, for example, Halton with 35,216 residents, Russell with 2,585, and Cornwall town with 1,515 were each accorded a seat. So, in Canada East, were Deux-Montagnes with 20,905, Megantic with 2,284, and Sorel town with 2,000.

The editor of *Le Canadien* objected to the representation plan not because of the internal distribution of seats but because of the fact of equal sectional representation. He hoped that the plan was the result of a miscalculation on the part of some imperial bureaucrat, which the government would correct. As he saw it, the problem was that calculations of Lower Canada's population were based on the census of 1831, which returned about 511,000, while Upper Canada's population was estimated as 400,000 in 1840. To be both honest and accurate, the editor pointed out, 'they should have taken the population figure for Upper Canada as it was in 1831, that is to say, 215,750, instead of 393,925.' A later Parliamentary return of religious affiliations in Upper Canada gave a population figure well below the estimated 1840 figure.[6]

Interestingly, the editor of the Quebec *Gazette* did denounce what he saw as inequities in the distribution of representation within the two sections, but not because of a violation of a principle of representation by population. Thus it was inequitable, for example, that Russell in Canada West and Dorchester or Beauce in Canada East should each have one seat because, although the populations of the three ridings were very similar, the Canada East counties were much larger geographically. The operative principle in these criticisms was not that equitable representation meant cutting up territory into units containing identical numbers of inhabitants.[7]

The 1841 Census Act did not respond to any clear or consistently planned governmental project. It was not a technology responding to a well-articulated rationality of government, as some Foucauldian accounts might suggest. It was most likely part of the package imposed by the triumphant British interest on the rebellious and backward Lower Canadians. It was not sufficiently interesting or important to attract the kind of Parliamentary opposition directed at the District Councils or School Acts. Still, population totals were invoked in debate at the moment of the Union. Where did these come from?

## Administrative Specification of Population in Upper Canada

The capacity of government to configure social relations as population, and the related statistical resources that it could command, differed sharply in the two sections of the united colony. In what had been Upper Canada, regular population enumerations were envisioned in 1793 under one of the colony's first local government acts (32 Geo. III c.II). The act specified that town, township, and parish clerks were to make true and complete lists of every male and female inhabitant in their jurisdictions and to deliver these to the Quarter Sessions before the first of April in each year. In 1824, claiming that this provision did not work well, the legislature made such enumerations one of the duties of the municipal property assessors.[8]

Under the 1824 Upper Canada Census Act (4 Geo. IV c.VII), the assessors were required to make accurate annual lists of all the inhabitants in their districts according to a specified form. The census involved a household enumeration, with the name of the household head alone recorded, and the enumeration schedule called for a return of the total population distinguished by sex in two age categories (above and below sixteen years of age). Unlike the clerks under the 1793 act, after 1824 the assessors were explicitly empowered to demand 'from every inhabitant householder or head of a family, a true and correct list of the number of persons composing such family, male and female, their respective ages, including therein persons employed by or resident with such householder or head of a family.' There was a 40s. fine for anyone refusing to answer. As well by 1824, municipal bodies were required by law to appoint assessors, and the clerk, on pain of a fine, was required to notify the Quarter Sessions of the appointment. Finally, the Clerk of the Peace was required to deliver an annual return of population to the governor and to report any negligent officials.[9]

In 1840, John Macaulay, Civil Secretary to Governor Arthur of Upper Canada, in an extensive report on Canadian social and political conditions, described the working of these arrangements and the development of the body of information collected by the assessors. He affirmed that 'the Census of Upper Canada is taken annually in each Township by the Assessor and returned to the Clerk of the Peace at the Quarter Sessions held next after the 1st day of March in each year. A General Abstract for the District is then prepared by that Officer and transmitted to the Governor by whom all the Returns of Population are annually laid before the Legislature.' In addition to the age and sex categories specified as part of the enumeration in the 1824 act, by 1840 the returns also included 'the several Christian denominations to which the Inhabitants belong & the number of Deaf & Dumb & Insane.'

The denominational count was a response to intense conflicts in the colony over the relative positions of the Church of England and other Protestant sects, and over competing claims to a share of the revenues derived from the sale and rental of the Clergy Reserves lands, which had been set aside for the support of 'the Established Church.' In the first decades of the nineteenth century, Anglican and Tory politicians at-

52  The Politics of Population

TABLE 2.1
Population of Upper Canada, 1824–1839

| 1824 | 149,301 | 1828 | 186,345 | 1832 | 260,992 | 1836 | 373,841 |
|------|---------|------|---------|------|---------|------|---------|
| 1825 | 156,886 | 1829 | 196,704 | 1833 | 296,870 | 1837 | 392,261 |
| 1826 | 164,703 | 1830 | 211,567 | 1834 | 320,735 | 1838 | 399,179 |
| 1827 | 175,128 | 1831 | 234,681 | 1835 | 346,165 | 1839 | 407,548 |

Source: John Macaulay's Report on Canada.

tempted to define and endow the Church of England as the 'Established Church.' Throughout the 1820s, members of other Protestant denominations suffered such civil disabilities as a legal prohibition on celebrating marriage. The High Church Tory party controlled the colony's General Board of Education, which was subsidized out of the public lands until it was abolished in 1833. Also, in a controversial attempt to secure an imperial charter for an Anglican University of King's College in the late 1820s, Bishop Strachan had produced a table of denominational membership purporting to show that the Church of England was the strongest denomination by far. Anglican pretensions were eventually defeated, but one enduring legacy was a continuing insistence that questions of religious allegiance be included in Canadian censuses – something dropped from English censuses as too controversial.[10]

Macaulay's report noted that the existing Upper Canadian census returns 'are doubtless imperfect & fail to state the full numbers under the respective classifications,' but he was quite prepared to use them as the basis for other calculations and to produce a tabluar return of population growth for the colony, year by year, since 1824.[11] While the municipal assessors were capable of producing annual returns of population, no provision existed in the western colony for the production of vital statistics. The failed attempt to establish the Church of England had removed the possibility of a single religious body acting as civil registrar.

### The Select Committee on Population Returns

The gravity with which reports of denominational membership were treated is evident in the case of those from Thurlow Township in the Victoria District, the object of an 1839 legislative Select Committee investigation. The mainly Tory MPPs were alarmed to discover that there appeared among the entries for religion in this township such things as 'Non-Professors and Honest Men,' 'God save the rest,' 'Honest Men,' 'Tremendious Lucky,' 'Do Good to all Men,' and 'Do as you would be done by.' Such entries appeared to the committee to be expressive of derision of the 'Christian Religion' and to be contemptuous of the authority of the legislature. The assessor responsible, David Read, was summoned to explain himself. Read admitted that he had entered some of the names in question, but only in the column intended for those professing no religion and only in place of far worse things suggested to him by some of those enumerated. People objected to being called to account for their religious allegiances, he claimed. Yet the committee noted that Read had not returned any religious denomination for himself, even though he professed to be a Methodist when questioned, and concluded as Macaulay did, that 'the Religious Census for the different Districts have been very imperfectly taken.'[12]

**Administrative Configuration of Population in Lower Canada**
In what had been Lower Canada, the situation concerning knowledge of population was the inverse of that in Upper Canada. In the lower province there were no representative local government bodies, nor was there any assessment of property in the countryside. Also, there were no locally elected municipal officials whom Parliament could instruct, either through legislation or administrative regulation, to conduct a regular enumeration. Special enumerations were made in 1825 and 1831 in order to determine the distribution of Parliamentary representation, but in each case a special enactment was needed to create the apparatus of enumeration. Indeed, when a dispute arose in 1836 over the competing claims of the counties of Montmorency and Drummond to Parliamentary seats, another special enactment was required to order a re-enumeration.[13]

Under the terms of the 1831 Lower Canada Census Act, which aimed at a simple head count, the governor appointed a census commissioner for each county and provided these appointees with enumeration schedules.[14] They were to cause the census to be taken within thirty days of their own appointment, between the first of June and the first of October, and they were authorized to enlist militia officers or church wardens to assist them. Commissioners who did not comply with the terms of the act were subject to a fine. Notice of the enumeration was to be given at the parish church door on two successive Sundays at least fifteen days before it was to be conducted. The commissioners or their appointees were empowered to visit every house and to require all persons, except those in actual service in the army or navy, to provide the information required by the enumeration schedules. A fine was specified for anyone over twenty-one not answering or answering falsely. A copy of the census return was to be deposited with the rector, curé, or minister of each parish, or with the senior officer of militia. Finally, the returns in triplicate were to be returned to the government by 1 November to be laid before the legislature, and if the returns showed that any county was not fairly represented, a new election was to be organized. The enumeration served few, if any, other administrative purposes beyond the distribution of county school monies.

The 1831 census reported 511,919 inhabitants in Lower Canada, although observers like John Macaulay thought it an underenumeration. Macaulay proposed that the Lower Canadian population had been closer to 520,000 in 1831 and that, assuming it had increased by about 40 per cent since that time, at the time of the Union of the Canadas, Lower Canada's population should have been about 728,000 in comparison to about 420,000 for Upper Canada (both figures exclusive of the aboriginal population).[15] In the absence of any highly developed projects of population government, such estimates were sufficient for most administrative purposes. It is worth underlining, nonetheless, that competing figures for the population of each section of the colony were offered by different observers, both at the time of the Union of 1840 and in subsequent years. There was no single authoritative representation of population.[16]

In the matter of vital statistics, in the eastern section a well-established system of civil registration was in place. In some places, parish records of vital events were continuous from the first period of European invasion. At the moment of the Union, priests and ministers of religion were required to make quarterly returns of vital events to district prothonotaries, who reported in turn to the government. Vital statistical returns for the eastern section were regularly published. These statistical resources provided the basis for some projects of social government: priests could use them in the regulation of marriages, for instance. However, they were not sufficient for some of the demands placed on them. As Governor Sydenham quickly learned through correspondence between his Civil Secretary and the district prothonotaries, no one knew how to use vital statistical resources to generate returns of current population and population distribution for Canada East.[17] Also, vital statistical returns were not organized in such a manner that they could be used to locate particular individuals – a recurring interest on the part of Colonial Office officials, and one that only the census of 1871 finally satisfied.[18]

**The 1841 Census Act in Principle and Practice**

The 1841 Census Act (4 & 5 Vic. c.XLII) called for a quinquennial household enumeration to be conducted by the municipal assessors. The act itself contained copies of the enumeration schedules. The schedules were to be distributed by the Provincial Secretary to district wardens and municipal mayors by the second Monday in January of each census year, beginning with 1842. Before 1 February in the same year, these officials were to distribute the schedules to the assessors, who on pain of a fine were to conduct the enumeration and deliver two sworn copies of their returns to the warden or mayor, who in turn was to return one copy to the governor to be presented to the legislature. For their efforts, the assessors were to be paid one-quarter of what they received for conducting the property assessment in the same year. The act contained no time limit for the assessors to deliver their enumeration reports. The enumeration schedules contained about 120 entries concerning numbers of residents and their occupations and religious affiliations, as well as agricultural and industrial production, rents, public institutions, and the number of 'coloured' people.

While the francophone press generally celebrated the idea of a census, the editor of *Le Canadien* predicted the act's failure as soon as it was promulgated. He claimed that because there had been no opposition to the act in the legislature, its provisions had not been scrutinized carefully. Particularly questionable was the clause requiring that municipal assessors receive one-quarter of the amount they were usually paid for assessment purposes to do the enumeration. In the only two cities in Canada East in which the office existed, assessors had acted gratuitously. The 1841 District Councils Act, which created local government bodies, was slow to come into effect in many parts of the province. Most rural municipalities had not appointed assessors, nor had they considered whether to pay them at all, and without them no enumeration was possible under the Census Act. 'This difficulty is really deplorable in the present case,' concluded the editor, 'where it is a matter of the execution of an enactment as useful as that for the census. The next census is supposed to provide the basis for the division of the £50,000 voted for the schools, and several of the demands of Lower Canada ought to be further supported by it, without mentioning the usefulness and the interest of the large amount of information it will procure.'[19]

Yet the failure of the 1842 census in Canada East was not simply due to a technical flaw in the act, as the editor of *Le Canadien* seemed to suggest.

The Census Act tied the fate of the enumeration to that of the larger liberal project of local representative self-government. Opposition to the District Councils Act of 1841 was general in Canada East, at least outside the recently settled English-speaking Eastern Townships. The councils became a focal point for opposition to the assimilationist design and economic imposition of the Union itself. They were seen as 'taxation machines' for extracting further resources from a peasant population already labouring under the dîme and seigneurial rents, and as menacing the hegemonic position of large landed property in the countryside. Opposition to and non-compliance with the District Councils Act deprived the government of the local administrative machinery necessary to execute a census in the eastern section.[20]

The municipal assessors in Canada West conducted a census in 1842 that revealed a rapidly growing number of inhabitants. Estimates in the francophone press claimed that over 500,000 people were returned in Canada West, without counting the 20,000 immigrants arriving during the year, in contrast to the 400,000 inhabitants assumed to be there at the moment of the Union. Except in the cities of Montreal and Quebec, and a few rural municipalities such as St-Enfant-Jésus de la Pointe-aux-Trembles, no enumeration was conducted in French Canada East. Cabinet refused a petition from one municipal councillor to enforce the law and refused the petitions of enumerators who claimed that they had done the work but had not been paid by their municipal councils. While Montreal was said to contain more than 40,000 inhabitants and to be growing rapidly, the 1842 census did not make it possible to formulate any general estimate of the number of residents of Canada East.[21] An immediate consequence was that J.-B. Meilleur, the Assistant Superintendent of Education, was unable to disburse much of the school money according to the terms of the School Act. Meilleur claimed that only about £9,300 of the £30,000 to which Canada East was entitled was distributed according to law, and he invoked his discretionary power to base the distribution of additional money on the population returns of 1831, supplemented by information from local elites.[22]

### The 1843 Census Act for Canada East

The Baldwin-Lafontaine government attempted to circumvent the barrier to an enumeration caused by opposition to representative self-government with a special Census Act for Canada East in 1843 (7 Vic. c.XXIV). As Governor Metcalfe explained matters to the Colonial Office, 'in consequence of its machinery depending upon the operation of the Municipal System ... which was not adopted throughout the greater part of Lower Canada,' only a few localities in Canada East had seen an enumeration under the 1841 act. The 1843 Census Act was 'passed to supply the omission, and to substitute an independent machinery adapted to the purpose' of enumerating the eastern section. He remarked as well that 'the Schedule is materially the same as that contained in the former Act, it being considered desirable to adopt the same form for both sections of the Province.'[23]

In point of fact, the government found itself compelled to revert to the clauses of the 1831 Lower Canada Census Act, which were only slightly modified for the 1843 act. The 1831 act had been designed expressly to deal with the question of the distribution of Parliamentary representation, but embodied the principle of direct central government appointment of local officers, against which Durham and Sydenham had so loudly railed. Nothing underlines more clearly the lack of progress at 'forcing government downwards' in the Canada East of the early 1840s than the inability of the administration to base this knowledge-producing project on the cooperative activity of the local government bodies.

The proposed enumeration schedules were discussed at length in the Legislative Council, and a committee appointed to consider them reported that in order 'to meet the views of Members of the Medical Faculty, who are desirous of ascertaining the number of deaths under five years of age in this Province, in order, if possible, to raise the standard of health during infancy,' it had 'adopted the division of age, as applied to the sexes, observed in Belgium.'[24] The census schedules adopted highly refined age categories, suggesting a Canadian link to L.-A.-J. Quetelet's state-of-the-art Belgian statistical enterprise – a link that has rightly intrigued J.-P. Beaud and J.-G. Prévost. Quetelet's *Sur l'homme et le développement de ses facultés* was published in Paris in 1835, and an English translation appeared in 1842. His age categories were discussed at great length, and vital statistics were one of his book's main topics. There was no copy of it in the Parliamentary library, but perhaps a Canadian doctor had seen it. More suggestive is the fact that Rawson W. Rawson, Sydenham's former secretary at the Board of Trade, honorary secretary of the London Statistical Society, and one of Quetelet's active correspondents, became the Canadian Civil Secretary in 1842. The occupants of this peculiar office – imperial appointees for most of the period – doubled as the governor's private secretary and as colonial government functionaries. They were intended to serve as the main conduits for colonial intelligence to the imperial government, commanding colonial documentary resources and vetting what was shipped to London. Rawson provided a direct link between Canadian and Belgian statistical practice, although the 1843 Census Act did not adopt the census-making innovations proposed by the London Statistical Society.[25]

Census making in Canada did not become tied to projects for investing social relations in medical forms, as it did under William Farr's direction in England. Other interests less conducive to systematic social observation would intervene. The working out of the struggles over 'responsible government,' which broke out soon after the passage of the new census act, politicized control over statistical knowledge production and prevented the pursuit of medical projects through the census. Still, discussions in the Legislative Council in 1843 suggest that a different trajectory of development was possible.[26]

The preamble to the 1843 Census Act repeated that the 1842 census of Canada East had failed and claimed there was a pressing need for statistical returns, without, however, saying anything about the source of this need. The act empowered the governor to name census commissioners in each colonial district to take an exact census of population on or before 1 May 1844. They were to be supplied by the Provincial Secretary with copies of the schedules reproduced in the act, and they were to swear to the accuracy of the returns they made. Census commissioners were empowered to enlist the aid of any officer of militia or churchwarden, or anyone else, in order to conduct the enumeration. They could visit all the houses in the county and demand of any person, except those in Her Majesty's army, whatever information was necessary to complete the forms. Any person over the age of twenty-one who refused to answer was liable to a fine of £2.10s.

The impending census was to be publicized by the commissioners' reading of an official announcement, contained in a schedule attached to the act, at the door of the parish church on two consecutive Sundays at least fifteen days before the enumeration. After it was read, the announcement was to be posted on the church door or in the most public place in the locality. The commissioners were required to report the results of their enumeration within fifty days of their own nomination. Certified copies of their reports would be distributed by the Provincial Secretary to the local curé, minister of religion, or municipal clerk or, if none of these persons existed, to the senior militia officer, who would preserve them and make them available for inspection by any person concerned. This provision, which departed from earlier treatments of census returns as state secrets, was meant to reassure reluctant informants. In addition, by 1 July 1844 at the latest, each commissioner was required to send signed copies in triplicate of the report for his district on the approved schedule to the governor, who would provide a copy to each branch of the legislature and a third to the government archive. Commissioners were to be paid five pence per enumerated house in towns and cities and ten pence in rural places, with their assistants, if any, to receive one-third of this sum. As municipal legislation for Canada East soon would do in an effort to force municipal councillors to perform their duties, the census act subjected any wilfully negligent commissioner to a fine of £25 and three months' imprisonment.[27]

**Executing the 1844 Census**

Only fragmentary sources have survived relating to the execution of the 1844, census. The first census commissioners were appointed early in February 1844 and there was wide support again in the francophone press for the proposed enumeration. *Le Canadien*, for instance, encouraged people to cooperate, stressed that those who refused to answer enumerators' questions would be fined, and underlined the importance of the census with respect to the distribution of school monies. Both *Le Canadien* and *La Minerve* reproduced the entire text of the census act.[28] As well, in late February and early March 1844 both papers published a lengthy dissection of the enumeration schedule in which it was explained how it should be completed. This piece, in the form of a letter apparently written by a census commissioner, served as the manual of instructions the government had neglected to provide.

The Montreal district enumeration, the commissioner's letter began, was to commence on the fifth of March, and the results had to be returned by the first of June. The enumeration was a complicated procedure, but people could avoid errors if they read the questions before the enumerators arrived. The author called on the press to print the schedules, and on the curés to work to overcome popular fear and prejudice concerning the census. He drew attention to a number of difficult or controversial columns in the enumeration schedule, and urged enumerators to follow a *de jure* enumeration principle. They should take particular care to avoid double-counting in the case of adult children, visitors, and children at school, and all minors should be returned to their parental residences unless they had been apprenticed out. The author pointed to the limited utility of the columns for reporting national origins, which were headed respectively 'British' and 'French': where should the others go, he wondered?

This correspondent anticipated the attacks that would be made on later census categories as instruments of English cultural domination. Two column headings on the 1843 schedule were imperfect translations into French from the English. 'Nombre total de personnes dans chaque famille' was an attempt to translate 'total number of persons in each household.' The sense of 'household,' the author remarked, would be better carried by 'maisonnée,' because it was intended that enumerators return servants living with their masters in this column. Also, the column that called for a return of enfranchised urban tenants did not make sense in Canada East, where different people were enfranchised for different electoral purposes. The author remarked that he intended to return everyone able to vote on *any* occasion in this column, but a better schedule would have distinguished parliamentary from municipal electors.

Before concluding with the note that he planned to modify his own schedules to include an account of the materials out of which enumerated houses were constructed (following a code he provided and that he claimed had been used by Jacques Viger in his 1825 enumeration of Montreal), the author also pointed to the inadequacy of the columns for recording 'coloured' men and women, and to the absence of a column for aboriginal people. As he put it, 'nor is any distinction made between full-blooded blacks and mulattoes – And as for the poor savages, the primitive children of the earth, we have great difficulty in knowing what to do with them. What corner shall we put them in? This is a prickly question. Shall we blacken their faces and line them up in the $39^{th}$ and $40^{th}$ columns, among the "people of colour"?'[29]

*Le Canadien* printed reports of opposition to the enumeration and complaints about the organization of the project as soon as it got underway, even as the editor continued to warn of the dangers of a small return when the distribution of school monies and subsidies for public works was at issue. 'People's repugnance at giving information,' stemming from 'a chimerical fear of taxation,' made it difficult for the enumerators to do their work, and in any case they had been provided with shoddy materials. The schedules were printed on such poor-quality paper that ink leaked through from the front to the printing on the back and it was impossible to make corrections.[30] In mid-April 1844, the editor of *Le Canadien* refused to print a letter from 'a farmer,' describing a rural meeting held against the census, because he claimed it contained scurrilous insinuations. However, he did print questions posed by this correspondent that hinted strongly at administrative improprieties such as a lack of advance warning of the enumeration, and at local opposition to the census, such as people being fined by justices of the peace for refusing to cooperate.[31]

Further reports of opposition and of wilful false reporting appeared in the press as the census returns were published. The subcommissioner for the parish of St-George-de-Kakouna claimed to show 'how little one ought to rely on the accuracy of the results obtained in light of the popular resistance [préventions populaires] that exists against censuses in general; resistance which for that matter, is not limited to the people of Lower Canada.' As this subcommissioner described his experience:

> In the month of April last, I was taking the census of the second concession of Kakouna when I entered the house of a farmer where there was only the wife, the husband being temporarily absent; there, I asked this woman how many sheep they had, and how many pounds of wool they had obtained in the previous year: Ten sheep and about six pounds of wool was her answer. As I had heard that her husband was a well-to-do farmer, I thought she was deceiving me, I said, madam, you must have more than that; she responded, oh, all right! sir, then put down around ten or fourteen pounds. Some time thereafter, I learned that this landowner had at least forty sheep and that he had got about fifty pounds of wool; I also learned that many people gave me false information and the only reason they answered was to avoid paying the fine.

Since this subcommissioner was running out of time, he reported what he was told, but with no confidence in its veracity.[32] In contrast, commissioner Gosselin from Bellechasse County claimed that he had had no difficulty in completing the enumeration. Encouraged by the curés, people had been quite willing to answer the census queries; Gosselin encountered no obstacles and fined no one. If the county's population showed only a slight increase from 1831, that was because its geographic area had been reduced.[33]

Finally, because no government official was charged especially with tracking census matters, no one was available to receive the commissioners' reports when they were delivered. The commissioners had been instructed to return their reports to Montreal between 23 May and 1 June. Those from the Montreal district, from Trois-Rivières, from Quebec, and from as far away as the Gaspé had come to the city but had been unable to find any office willing to receive their reports. It was claimed that the returns were left in the Montreal post office or taken away again by the commissioners, occasioning additional expense to the public purse.[34]

### Results of the 1844 Census

The first partial census returns began to appear in the press soon after the 1 June reporting deadline. *Le Canadien* first printed the report from Lotbinière County, where the population was returned as 13,764, compared to 9,191 in the 1831 census. The editor was quick to point out that if this rate of increase was extrapolated to the colony as a whole, the population in 1844 would be 766,625, in contrast to 511,919 in 1831. This figure showed a comfortable numerical superiority for the eastern over the western section.[35] Other returns dribbled in over the summer and fall of 1844, and in early December a comparative tabular return of population by county in 1831 and 1844 was published. This return, likely drawn from the official tabulations, again gave the 1831 population as 511,919 but now reported 678,590 for 1844.[36] Although the official return indicated a population increase of around 30 per cent in thirteen years, Canada West's population now seemed to be catching up. *La Minerve* claimed that the cholera of 1831–2 and the 'troubles' of 1837–8 had led to a population increase that was less than expected.[37]

### The Legislative Council Report

There is no surviving account of debate over the census in the Legislative Assembly – a peculiar situation that can perhaps be explained by the dearth of intellectual talent among the Tory members returned in the 1844 loyalty elections. However, the returns were the object of an investigation by a Special Committee of the Legislative Council, chaired by F.-P. Bruneau. Its March 1845 report contained a series of recommendations aimed at systematizing the returns to make them comparable with those for Canada West, which suggests an interest in actually using them for some purpose. The committee urged the clerk of the council's special committees to go over the commissioners' reports and produce a recapitulation of population by parish, township, county, and district. It proposed that a similar exercise be carried out on the Canada West census of 1842. The council clerk was instructed to find and correct errors in the returns and to 'submit such a Report ... as will place before the Province a statistical document that may be at all times serviceable.' The committee suggested that the original returns be bound and preserved.

The errors in the returns in need of correction were not specified, and the original returns themselves were destroyed in the 1849 Parliamentary fire. However, the committee's abstract showed that the enumeration results were not internally consistent. The total population was returned as 693,649, for instance, but adding up the age groups yielded a total of only 691,293. Nonetheless, the committee attempted some comparative statistical analysis, investigating, for example, the proportion of deaf and dumb residents in the colony relative to the proportion in the United States and some European countries. It seemed to be higher in the colony, although the report commented that there was systematic underreporting of these matters. The Special Committee called for the creation of a uniform census system for the two sections of the colony. Its procedures should be strictly followed, and before the commissioners were paid for their work, their reports should be examined carefully, not only to correct errors and omissions but also to ensure that the figures added up consistently. Given the expense, which in Canada East for 1844 amounted to about £4,800, such an insistence was considered justified. The report was accompanied by an abstract of population (the one already printed in the press), which was described by the committee as only approximately accurate, given that the clerk had yet to undertake the recommended corrections.[38]

The fruits of the Legislative Council clerk's efforts at correction were printed as an 1846 Parliamentary paper that contained both aggregate returns for the province as a whole, and returns for individual parishes and townships, with marginal comments. Including those reported to be temporarily absent, the province's inhabitants were now said to number 697,084. The marginal comments point to some of the anomalies in the manuscript returns. The most serious concerned Leinster County, where the clerk noted 'some error on the part of the Census Commissioners ... with respect to the quantity of land occupied and the quantity improved, as in most cases the quantity improved exceeds the quantity occupied. A similar discrepancy occurred in the Returns of the previous Census of this County.' Other commissioners had counted the aboriginal population as being of French origin; had returned no information about the religious affilations of substantial numbers of people; had been unable to report information about schoolhouses; and, finally, had described 'camps' as 'houses.'[39]

These sorts of reservations about the census returns, and the concern to systematize statistical information about Canada East and West, testify to a growing Parliamentary interest in configuring social relations as population for administrative purposes, even if such purposes were not often clearly specified. Which legislative councillor(s) were expressing this interest is unclear, and Rawson Rawson had already left the colony after a dispute with Governor Metcalfe. Under Metcalfe's 'irresponsible' administration, there was initially no Canadian government statistical office and no state servant or Parliamentarian whose energies were focused primarily on statistical questions. Still, the 1844 census results replaced those of 1831 for the purposes of administrative and other projects. However flawed from the point of view of a systematically executed set of invariant observations, the 1844 results became the official population of Canada East. They guided the distribution of school monies; and they served as resources in arguments about the placement of government offices.[40]

### The Abortive 1847 Census

The 1841 Census Act called for censuses to be executed in 1842 and 1847 and at five-year intervals thereafter. The 1843 Census Act was intended to make it possible to conduct the enumeration for Canada East that should have been conducted in 1842. Whether by design or accident, however, the 1843 act did not repeal the 1841 Census Act, so a census of population was to be conducted under the provisions of the latter in 1847. The government that passed the 1843 Act may have seen it as a way of getting the original census plan back on track, but there was no officer in the colonial administration charged explicitly with tracking these matters.

Moreover, none of the colonial governments had been successful in executing the Durham/Sydenham project of forcing liberal self-government downwards into Canada East through the creation of representative local bodies with effective powers of taxation. Repeated attempts had been made, and would continue to be made, to rejig the municipal and school acts into some workable form. These attempts were bound to fail until Parliament resolved the question of seigneurial tenure, which it was unable to do in the 1840s. Farmers and habitants paying tithes, church pew rents, *cens et rentes, lods et vents, la banalité*, and other feudal charges were not about to tax themselves for local improvements. In coalition with large landed proprietors and with politicians opposed to the Act of Union, they continued to block the effective operation of representative local institutions in many parts of the province until after 1854, when feudal obligations were commuted. Feudal property relations were perhaps less susceptible to statistical translation than those of free and common soccage because of the intermediate relations of social domination they contained, but more practically, changing tactical initiatives by the central government aimed at creating workable governmental structures met with very uneven success and resulted in repeated changes in local administrative organization. The configuration of social relations as population by means of an enumeration depended on the prior empirical administrative organization of those relations. Somehow, potential census informants had to be incorporated into administrative structures so that enumerators could locate them, make contact with them, and interrogate them successfully. To be categorized authoritatively as political subjects, residents of the colony had to be subjected to state administration; to this, feudal relations constituted a barrier.

Of particular importance to the projected census of 1847 was the belated recognition by Parliament that the 1841 District Councils Act was a failure in Canada East. The act was repealed in 1845. A new Municipal Act (8 Vic. cap.XL) removed the District Council structure, with its unpopular, centrally appointed officials, and allowed for the creation of elected parish, township, and municipal authorities, who would have broad powers of taxation as well as the power to elect their own mayors or wardens (a principle not accepted for Canada West until 1846). The act was temporary, however, and it worked no better than had its predecessor. More important, the 1845 Municipal Act abolished the authorities in Canada East who were responsible for conducting the census under the 1841 Census Act. While District Councils in Canada West were taking initial steps to prepare for the 1847 census, the official responsible for distributing enumeration materials, T.D. Harington, chief clerk in the Provincial Secretary's office, warned the Executive Council of the administrative impossibility of proceeding in Canada East. He stressed that census making was expensive and hardly worth doing for only half the colony. Incomparable information would result from such an enterprise because the 1843 Census Act had changed the enumeration schedule for Canada East but not for Canada West.

In any case, as far as Harington was concerned the 1841 census schedule was flawed. He claimed that 'the Schedule as it now stands in the Census Bill, is of such an unwieldy extent, and the questions so numerous, and at the same time, difficult to be answered – and when answered, in some instances, have proved useless for any statistics of the Province – that it would probably be advisable either to wait for an amended Act that could be carried out throughout the entire Province, or the Council might pass an Order, defining some method of procuring the statistical information, preparatory to a new Statute.'[41] The Executive Council moved in late January 1847 not to proceed with the 1847 census, but instead to prepare a new census bill. The Provincial Secretary sent a circular to the wardens of district councils in Canada West on 6 February instructing them to take no steps for an 1847 enumeration. The claims of the Home District Council for preparatory expenses were disallowed on the grounds that no council was empowered to act before the distribution of census forms by the Provincial Secretary's office. No contemporary discussion of the failure to take the 1847 census seems to have survived. Instead of proceeding with it, the Tory government laid the groundwork for a Canadian statistical office and placed census making under the direction of a loyal friend of the British connection.[42]

**The 1847 Census and Statistics Act**
A new Census and Statistics Act (10 & 11 Vic. cap.XIV) was accepted by Parliament in the summer of 1847. The act was drafted by the lame Tory ministry led by Henry Sherwood, a ministry so weak that it was defeated repeatedly on measures that were the least bit controversial, but that saw resignation as leading inevitably to the twin bugaboos of 'responsible government' and 'French domination.' Clearly doomed to defeat in winter elections, it could not have carried a census and statistics act to which there was any serious Parliamentary opposition.

Yet the 1847 Census and Statistics Act was innovative. It envisaged a dedicated Canadian statistical agency, the Board of Registration and Statistics, to oversee statistical matters generally, including the execution of the census. The board's three members, the Receiver General, the Inspector General, and the Provincial Secretary, represented the ministries most directly implicated in producing and managing the colonial official documentary system. The board was thus potentially an interdepartmental statistical commission, conceived well before such bodies existed in England or the United States. The act allowed the board to engage a secretary and to 'have the general supervision of the Statistics of the Province.'

The colonial documentary system itself was expanding rapidly and becoming increasingly complex. Administrative centralization under the Union, the creation of new state agencies, and the extension of novel information-producing practices caused a mass of documentary matter to accumulate at the centre of government. Internal administrative reforms sought to standardize reporting practices in various branches of the state system, albeit with uneven success. At the same time, members of Parliament were increasingly making demands on the government in the legislature, and on state agencies more generally, to be provided with factual information on a wide range of subjects. It was acceptable Parliamentary practice for any MPP to demand, and to have printed at public expense, whatever information he thought appropriate.

The weaknesses in the existing state structures of information production and management became increasingly obvious in the face of these rising demands. Meanwhile, the colonial Provincial Secretary was working to displace the imperial Civil Secretary as the colony's main information manager. Parliament's own printing costs were rising sharply. The production of the annual Blue Book – a return of colonial statistics, guide to the state service, and report on the activities of Parliament – was becoming difficult and burdensome. The kind and variety of information demanded by the imperial authorities increased in the 1840s, as did the volume of material generated by colonial state agencies. By 1846, T.D. Harington, the chief clerk in the Provincial Secretary's office charged with compiling the Blue Book, claimed that he had to spend at least three months of very long days to satisfy these demands. It was becoming physically impossible for him to do so, especially given the rising volume of other business in his own department.[43]

The creation of the Bureau of Registration and Statistics, then, was partly a much needed act of administrative rationalization and an initiative meant to overcome real administrative obstacles. It was also the government's response to the practical impossibility of using local representative bodies to execute the census, and to its inability to produce vital statistics for Canada West. Its form, however, was shaped by the concern of the Tory government to keep tight cabinet control over intelligence matters and by the weak central government's inability to undertake a serious administrative incursion. Moreover, the choice of the board's secretary was an act of political partisanship which ensured that Canadian statistical practice would continue to lag behind that of other countries.

**The Census and Vital Statistics under the 1847 Act**

The 1847 Census and Statistics Act required the Board of Registration and Statistics to deliver an annual report on statistical matters to the legislature – something it would rarely if ever do. The act also reorganized provisions for census making and established procedures for the production of vital statistics in Canada West. The census of the Canadas was now to be conducted under the direction of the board in February and March 1848 and 1850, and thereafter at five-year intervals. Yet the board remained entirely dependent on the cooperation of local government bodies, even while the act aimed to overcome the obstacles that had rendered the 1841 census law inoperative. From now on, the various municipal councils would divide the areas under their jurisdiction into enumeration districts and appoint census enumerators, whom they could pay at the rate they thought appropriate. So as not to be caught again inadvertently eliminating census officials, the government inserted a notwithstanding clause stipulating that the act was not to be interpreted as voiding the appointment of any persons now designated by law as enumerators.

The Board of Registration and Statistics would design the enumeration schedules and provide an adequate supply of them to local government bodies at least six weeks before the enumeration date. As in the earlier acts, enumerators were empowered to question heads of families or resident adults, but the act now explicitly extended their authority to include 'the owners or managers of all factories agents of companies and others.' Fines for refusing to answer were to be between 10s. and 50s., with costs, on conviction before two justices of the peace; if not paid promptly, these fines were to be levied by distress and sale or by imprisonment for seven days. A new clause promised half the fine to those who informed on people giving false returns.

Under the act, against the practice recommended both by L.-A.-J. Quetelet and the English General Register Office, the Board of Registration and Statistics had no involvement in the compilation of census data. Enumerators were to deliver their returns to the municipal clerk, who would examine them for defects and correct them as necessary. He was then to prepare an abstract in the form required by the board, and deliver three copies of it within a month of receiving returns from the enumerators. A copy of the abstract was to be submitted to Parliament, and the original enumeration schedules were to be kept by the municipality.[44]

Three clauses of the act attempted to organize the production of vital statistics for Canada West. They specified that anyone authorized by law to marry, bury, or baptize people in the western section was to keep a register of such events and to forward it to the municipal clerk quarterly. If there was no such authorized person within a reasonable distance, the head of any family in the relevant church or congregation was to notify the nearest municipal clerk. The clerks, in turn, were to report all this information to the Board of Registration and Statistics annually by 1 January. Finally, coroners were to report lists of inquests and jury findings, and municipal clerks were to forward lists of convictions before magistrates. Anyone refusing to comply with these regulations was guilty of a misdemeanour.[45]

On the whole, the act was declarative, and the government remained heavily dependent on local cooperation. There were few significant sanctions for local noncompliance, and local government officials controlled the enumeration and compilation processes. Administrative power had not yet developed to the point where the central authorities could invest social relations throughout the colony in statistical forms. No social group or set of state functionaries was in a position to observe and record events in a continuous manner. In this period of agitation over 'responsible government,' with a weak administration in office, incursions from the centre were strenuously resisted, although not always successfully. A serious attempt to extend central government control over census enumeration by creating new officials would have been opposed by the District Councils in Canada West, which were agitating for an extension of their own autonomy – for the right to elect their own wardens and clerks, for instance. The weakness of administrative infrastructures and the lack of effective sanctions meant that anyone charged with administering the Census and Statistics Act faced a challenging set of tasks. Moreover, the provisions for a Board of Registration and Statistics did not include any measures for creating a distinct office, archive, or permanent staff. Continuity was made possible by the appointment of a secretary to the board, but this functionary was to be one of the clerks in one of the ministers' departments, who would add the title 'Secretary of Registration and Statistics' to his existing duties.

**Secretaries**

In the middle decades of the nineteenth century, in both England and the colonies, some permanent secretaries and undersecretaries, and similar functionaries, were central figures in the extension of state powers and in the pursuit of social projects. As the domain of the social was delineated more clearly and made the object of governmental initiatives, ambitious secretaries and secretary-like figures found themselves well placed to innovate in policy matters and to establish substantial administrative empires. Obvious examples in the English case include Edwin Chadwick (with respect to the New Poor Law and sanitary reform), Sir James Kay-Shuttleworth (secretary to the Privy Council Committee on Education), and William Farr (of the General Register Office).[46]

Farr, the effective although not the nominal head of the General Register Office from 1839, transformed statistical practice in England

and on an international scale, even though his office had no legislative brief to conduct social inquiries and no mandate to make policy recommendations. He used his strategic relationship to new information-gathering practices under the Registration Act and his social networks to pursue many different statistically relevant projects. His annual report served him as a platform for intervening in debates over some of the leading policy questions of the day: how to deal with the cholera, for instance.

In the Canadas the secretary-like education superintendents, Egerton Ryerson and J.-B. Meilleur, used their offices to extend the reach of the state system markedly. Ryerson in particular exploited the statutory reporting obligations attached to his office to the full, using his annual report to trumpet the achievements of public schooling and to push for its extension, and undertaking to publish on his own account the monthly *Journal of Education for Upper Canada*, the delivery of which to every schoolteacher and every municipal government body in Canada West he eventually managed to convince the government to subsidize.[47]

The Secretary of Registration and Statistics occupied a position that was every bit as strategic. The statistics secretary had access to the colonial official documentary system as a whole. He was required to report annually to Parliament and thus had access to public opinion, yet he was not directly dependent on Parliament for his post. He was well positioned to innovate through his control of census-making instruments and the official interpretation of the census results, and through the production of an annual account of official statistics. These were just the kinds of powers that other secretaries enlisted in the pursuit of state-forming initiatives and policy innovations. It is reasonable to propose that as Secretary of Registration and Statistics, an activist intellectual could have given definite form and substance to the production of statistical information in the Canadas after 1848 in the pursuit of some project for 'improvement,' especially given the earlier concern for enlisting the census returns in an attack on infant mortality. But this is not how it happened in the Canadas.

### Walter Cavendish Crofton

The first appointment went to Walter Cavendish Crofton (c.1806–1871), a newly engaged clerk in William Cayley's Inspector General's office. Crofton served as Secretary of Registration and Statistics in Canada from 1847 to 1853, a period marked by the granting of Parliamentary responsibility to the colony, the Rebellion Losses struggles and the breakup of the Reform party, resurgent agrarian radicalism, the formation of a left-liberal coalition government, and, of course, the execution of the 1848, 1850, and 1852 censuses. At times, Crofton would command a substantial budget, for whose expenditure he was not called to account, but he made little of the strategic place he occupied in the developing state system. He never delivered an annual report to Parliament on statistical matters, and his implication in ultra-Tory political scheming was said to have caused him to neglect his other administrative duties.

As the first secretary of the first dedicated Canadian statistical agency, Crofton has some claim to be regarded as Canada's first official statistician, yet he has disappeared completely from Canadian historiography, the victim of the anachronistic attitudes to the history of statistics dominant until recently, but the victim also of his own incompetence. In his own time he was despised by Reformers and promoted by the more reactionary and less clever among the Tories. He was kept on the government payroll for five years by his patrons after he was ousted from the secretaryship in 1853, as one minister bounced him to another who tried to palm him off on a third; he would pass the last decade of his life as a clerk at Osgoode Hall in Toronto. John Langton, the Cambridge-educated head of the Audit Office, organized in 1855, has left a rare description of him. Taking charge of the office, Langton found that the Inspector General, William Cayley, had provided him with three clerks. Two he could work with but, as he wrote to his brother, he blamed 'Cayley for saddling me with' Walter Crofton, 'a black sheep who has been transferred from one department to another and found quite impracticable in all – utterly useless and worse than useless. Cayley knew this as well as I do,' Langton complained, 'and it was a mere excuse that they sent him to me with some books which he used to keep and which are now in my branch, because in fact, though he ought to have kept them, they never could trust him to do so.' A two months' acquaintance mellowed Langton only a little. Crofton was 'almost useless,' Langton wrote, but, 'I have got him at a job at present unconnected with financial business (for I cannot trust him with figures), more of a statistical character, which with other literary portions of the business he does pretty well, though a fearful nuisance from his constant interruptions to me in telling me what he has done or consulting me what he is to do.'[48] Langton, interestingly, was still making a distinction between numbers and statistical information. It is also intriguing that the person charged with one of the major exercises of numerical appropriation of society by agencies of the state could not be trusted with numbers.

Crofton was born about 1806, likely in Ireland, and claimed to have come to Canada around 1832 as a common schoolteacher. The first documentary evidence of his presence in the Canadas dates from mid-May 1835. He was appointed master of the Newcastle District Grammar School in Cobourg, Upper Canada, a position that paid the respectably modest salary of £90 a year to begin, rising to £100 in 1839. Crofton was described as 'formerly a scholar of Trinity College, Dublin,' although he left no traces there.[49] He left the grammar school in 1840, likely a victim of the heightened competition for students of higher education in Cobourg that resulted from the organization of the Methodists' Victoria College. For a brief time he edited the Cobourg *Star*, a paper opposed to the Union of the Canadas and described by John Macaulay as 'High Conservative, moderate circulation and influence'; he then began to write and publish pamphlets and occasional pieces, while spending at least some of his time importuning government officials at the new colonial capital of Kingston and serving briefly as Cobourg town school superintendent.[50]

While some of his newspaper work involved making descriptive inventories of settlement conditions and presented material abstracted from official census reports, Crofton neither engaged in serious analysis of existing statistics nor agitated for the investment of social relations in statistical forms. His two political pamphlets were strongly partisan attacks on Reform policy and Reform politicians, some of whom would later engineer his ouster from the state service, and it is more likely his partisanship than his talent or intelligence that recommended him for government service. Crofton's appointment politicized the office of official statistician; his incompetence and partisan activity while in office would prevent any systematic development of statistical inquiry.[51]

### The Educator and Would-Be Administrator

An exposition of Crofton's opinions on public education – the leading project for social government underway in this period – offers a clearer view of Crofton as social commentator and Tory ideologue. His bulky *Thoughts on Education in Three Letters* was an attempt to secure employment in the new educational bureaucracy of 1842. Amidst a smattering of grammar school Latin and much enthusiastic name dropping, Crofton revealed himself as opposed to most of the liberal educational innovations that would be adopted in the colony in the 1840s and 1850s. For instance, his plan for university education would have restored Anglican dominance by making both Queen's and Victoria colleges into theological schools of King's University in Toronto (an utterly unworkable suggestion), and he argued against the creation of normal schools for teacher training. With respect to the district grammar schools, while Crofton urged the teaching of practical subjects in addition to Latin and Greek, he also proposed that the institutions be restored to their earlier role as organs of class privilege. They should cease to offer financial aid to farmers' sons, who did 'not require such an education as that which the District schools profess to give,' and whose presence would force the respectable classes to 'place themselves on a level with paupers, and subject their children to insult.' In the 1830s, scholarships for poor grammar school students had been an important Upper Canadian Reform tactic in struggles against oligarchic control over secondary education.

In the field of elementary education, Crofton rejected the Irish education system, which the Buller Commission had recommended for the Canadas and which would be put in place, in Canada West especially, after 1844. 'Is it adviseable,' he asked rhetorically, 'to found a system of Common schools on the "National System" plan in which every one of the thousand sects, mormons, tunkers *et hoc genus omne*, is to have directing control'? Obviously not. The Bible must remain in the schools, and the schools must be under the control of the Church of England, the Presbyterians, and the Methodists, because these were the only recognized churches. If the Bible had been removed from the Irish schools it was because 'the dissenters forgetting the tenets of their fathers leagued themselves with the Irish Roman Catholics to force' it out. Anyway, nonsectarian instruction was all hypocrisy, because in Ireland Crofton had known personally 'one of the most noisy out-door advocates for the "Society for the diffusion of useful knowledge,"' a man who 'never would allow one of their publications to find a place in the study of his children all of whom were being educated by clergymen.'

Crofton's insistence on the use of the Bible in the schools of Canada East seems to have been a Tory fantasy. 'If we turn our attention to Lower Canada,' he rhapsodied, 'we find a large majority of the People Roman Catholic but happily free from much of the bigotry of European Catholicism and I do not think that generally speaking the Bible as a school Book would be objected to on the contrary from correspondence I have had with several gentlemen of that persuasion I am lead to believe that it is desired.' This after the new ultramontane bishop of Montreal had refused to countenance the use even of the supposedly non-sectarian Scripture Lessons of the Irish system in any school attended by Catholics.[52]

Crofton did not have a developed sense of public education as a way of administering social relations as population. Public education was arguably the leading contemporary colonial project for the 'conduct of conduct,' and a domain in which government policy sought to group together political subjects across their civil differences in an effort to refashion social solidarities. As a liberal political project, it defined the domain of rule in non-sectarian if still Christian terms. 'Our common Christianity,' as it was called, provided the substance of a civic religion. Public education was inextricably bound up with statistical thinking and state formation. Crofton wanted none of it, harkening instead back to a failed past where uniform religious allegiance grounded political subordination.

**Statistical Clerk and Blue Book Compiler**
It was most likely Crofton's partisan, high-Tory political opinions that earned him a position as 'statistical clerk' in William Cayley's Inspector General's department in the 'irresponsible Parliament,' where he started officially on 14 November 1846, six weeks before his position as Cobourg town school superintendent was eliminated under the provisions of the 1846 School Act. Two weeks later the chief clerk in the Provincial Secretary's department, T.D. Harington, wrote a lengthy memorandum to his minister complaining of his inability to produce the annual statistical Blue Book without extra pay and clerical assistance. Harington wanted to keep the work, but after considering his case, the Executive Council decided that 'as most of the necessary information can be conveniently furnished in the Inspector General's Department, it is recommended that one of the Clerks of that Office be charged with the performance of that duty, and be responsible to the Provincial Secretary for the proper discharge thereof.' The council meeting in question was attended by William Cayley, D.-B. Papineau, James Smith, William Morris, and William Henry Draper, the two last singled out for praise in Crofton's most recent pamphlet.[53] The compilation of the Blue Book was worth about £75 a year, and Crofton was also soon named to compile the register of bank notes issued under the Free Banking Act, and to sign those issued by the Bank of British North America, in addition to his clerical duties in the Inspector General's department. Under the tutelage of William Cayley, a man also known for his partisan Tory politics, the failed schoolmaster had become an important and highly paid government official, charged with the oversight of the colonial statistical apparatus.

## The Blue Book

Each of the three statistical officers discussed in this book began by trying to make something out of the Canada Blue Book. It gave its compiler the ear of the imperial government; also, it was the main colonial statistical compendium and an obvious vehicle for satisfying the statutory requirement for an annual statistical report. As I have shown elsewhere, Crofton began well as Blue Book compiler – if in fact he was not merely handing in his predecessor's work. The 1846 Blue Book, signed by Crofton and delivered to the Provincial Secretary on 6 May 1847, was markedly more extensive and detailed than the books that T.D. Harington had most recently produced. Crofton provided much of the requisite information, while suggesting that the next census would make a complete report possible. His first Blue Book may have convinced the Executive Council that Crofton was an appropriate candidate for statistical secretary, but it soon became apparent that he had neither the interest, nor the energy, nor the resources, to produce a consistently detailed Blue Book from year to year. Nor did he make any serious attempt to overcome the many weaknesses in the colonial statistical apparatus, which he claimed prevented him from providing complete returns. Governor Elgin would conclude that Crofton's involvement in political agitation, most likely including that spearheaded by William Cayley against Elgin's own colonial policy, led him to neglect his work.[54]

## The 1848 Census

Although the Census and Statistics Act was proclaimed in July 1847, it was early December before the Executive Council got around to considering a salary for the new Secretary of Registration and Statistics, settling on the sum of £75 after consultation with census commissioners in Canada West.[55] Crofton was not officially appointed until 12 January 1848, although preparations for the 1848 census, which the law required to be conducted in February and March, had been underway for some time. Crofton's detailed circular of instructions to census commissioners was dated 29 December 1847; by then the enumeration schedules had been prepared.

It is possible that the defeat of the Conservative ministry in the 1847–8 elections confused census administration, for the Reform government that took office on 10 March 1848 disallowed most of the recent appointments and salary increases that its predecessor had made. Crofton escaped these cuts; not only was his appointment of 12 January 1848 confirmed, but cabinet also accepted that his salary should be retroactive to 28 July 1847, the day after the proclamation of the Census and Statistics Act. Still, Crofton was placed on good behaviour by the resolution that the 'question which may arise as to the expediency of the duty' of statistical secretary 'being discharged by a Clerk in the Inspector General's Office, and the amount of further allowance, should remain open for consideration.'[56]

### The 1848 Census Schedules

Crofton reworked the schedules used in 1842 and expanded them to include 146 columns. He also prepared a circular of instructions, but otherwise he adopted none of the increasingly well-known international innovations in census making. The Canadian census remained stamped with its origins as an instrument for assessing men's property. There were now eight pages of forms to be completed, folded into a booklet containing space sufficient for reporting information on twenty-eight households. Only heads of households were named, and the first twelve entries concerned the household's location on the property rolls, the types of buildings it contained, and the head's trade or occupation.

The population count mixed *de jure* and *de facto* conceptions of people's locations; there were separate columns for the total number of people resident in the household at the moment the census was taken, the number of those absent who were 'members of the Family,' and the number of those present who were not. Social allegiance as kinship was still an operative principle. Sixty-three additional entries concerned agricultural and industrial production, and several columns were left blank for enumerators' remarks. A further twenty-six columns called for information about denominational religious affiliations and countries of origin, again for household heads only. Compilers, it was assumed, would extrapolate these characteristics from the household head to other household members. Only fifteen columns concerned matters of vital statistics, mainly in an attempt at an age profile of the population. The schedules treated men and women differently, however. Crofton abandoned the refined age categories used in 1844 in Canada East, and provided columns only for numbers of both sexes under 5 and between 5 and 14 years. Moreover, the additional age categories for males (by marital status) were 14 and not 18, 18 and not 21, 21 and not 30, 30 and not 40, 40 and not 60, and over 60 years of age. For women (by marital status), the categories were simply 14 and not 45, and over 45 years of age. This section of the schedules also required information about births, marriages, and deaths in the preceeding year. Finally, the schedules sought counts of those described as blind, lunatic or imbecile, deaf and dumb, coloured, male farm servants, and male and female domestic servants.[57]

**The Circular of Instructions**
For the 1842 and 1844 censuses, officials had been left to their own devices; for 1848, the Board of Registration and Statistics produced a circular of instructions for the use of commissioners and enumerators. However, it is not clear when or how efficiently it was distributed. Crofton was appointed secretary to the board officially only on 12 January 1848, and perhaps the circular, which bore his signature, was distributed after that date. The press got wind of it only late that month, with *La Minerve* printing it on 27 January 1848, although it did not appear in *Le Canadien* until 23 February.

The editor of *La Minerve* urged his readers to cooperate, encouraging them not to believe, as they had done in the past, 'that this census is being taken with a hostile objective in mind.' Rather, he hoped that people in the countryside would 'be convinced that it is in their own interests as well as in that of all Lower Canada that our population be known for what it is, so that we can know what proportion exists between ours and that of Upper Canada. It is not a matter of taxation or of recruitment for war or for anything of the sort,' and people would only hurt themselves if they gave false returns. 'In the last census, it happened, in a number of parishes, that the enumerators were unable to obtain accurate information; they were told that a family had five members, when the neighbour swore it had ten, and the same thing happened with possessions and property. What is the consequence of this?' asked the editor. 'It is that since particular localities appear to be of slight importance in the census, the government pays little attention to them. Make yourselves known for what you are; the advantage will be yours.'[58] Printing the circular to commissioners three days later, the editor of *La Minerve* returned to the charge: 'The necessity of an entirely accurate census will be especially felt, if attention is paid to electoral reform which is to be based on population. In a word, there may be far greater advantage in telling the real situation than there may be inconvenience.'[59]

Crofton made a similar plea to the assessors, who, he expected, would serve as enumerators. He urged them to explain to respondents that it was important for them to give complete information, as doing so was the only way that localities could hope to receive their 'just participation in the various Grants for Public improvements and Educational Purposes.' Enumerators were to reassure respondents that the exercise had nothing whatsoever to do with taxation. Rather, accurate returns of the 'great resources of the Country' would 'secure to the Province due consideration.' Crofton was confident that if this explanation was offered, 'little difficulty will be found in obtaining correct information, as each will see his own interest inseparably connected with the general welfare of the whole.' In case cooperation was not secured by these means, the enumerators were provided with a copy of the punitive clause of the Census Act and invited to move to prosecution.

While the enumeration schedules were detailed and Crofton explained how they were to be filled in, a very large role was left explicitly to the judgment and knowledge of the individual enumerators. Crofton concluded his instructions by inviting the enumerators to notice that although they were 'furnished with a form,' nonetheless 'all additional information will be most gladly received, and that any observations which you make yourself or others through you, shall receive the fullest and most attentive consideration.' Crofton declared that he was 'aware that many points of valuable information which could not be comprehended within the limits of a Schedule without fear of complexity or confusion' would be bound to occur to the enumerators. He stressed that the government relied on their 'local knowledge and judgment,' concluding that 'the Board of Registration confidently hope that no exertion will be spared on your part to render *your* return as complete and comprehensive as possible.'[60]

The invitation to enumerators to provide extra information underlines both the limited nature of the governmental project framing this census, and the inability of the central authority to engage in a prior configuration or investment of the object of investigation for the purpose of specifying clear observational protocols. The independent local observers were left largely to their own devices. The government did not command a sufficient knowledge of conditions in localities to know what to expect from the census inquiry. No major, clearly articulated project for generating knowledge about health, migration, settlement, or productive activity, or about the fate of any social policy initiative, was propelling the attempt to discipline entries on the census schedules. Making an inventory of resources so that the colony would appear in a favourable light, and distributing some government money among regions and municipalities, exhausted Crofton's political imagination and the administrative significance of the census. The inquiry attempted to centralize certain aspects of knowledge about population and thus was clearly a state-forming project. Yet it did not issue from any well-articulated attempt to problematize the 'conduct of conduct'; it was primitive accumulation of knowledge.

## The 1848 Census in Canada West

The execution of Crofton's census seems not to have posed a challenge to the assessors of Canada West. More information was to be collected in 1848 than in other years, but property was assessed regularly in the province and the assessors were experienced at the work. Because they typically had an entire township (i.e., one hundred square miles) to enumerate, the assessors cannot have conducted a strictly *de facto* enumeration. Also, they had two months in which to do the work (although this was a shorter period than that allowed their American counterparts, who had six). The lack of a specified census day, in combination with columns calling for numbers of those present and absent at the moment the census was made, was a potential source of inconsistent recording. Crofton specified no clear observational protocols in this regard.

The enumeration schedules repeatedly indicate that the assessors understood the project as being mainly about property. They used the 'remarks' sections on the schedules to comment on matters affecting their returns; here they noted things that were not as they expected them to be, circumstances that modified the quality of the information, and shortcomings of the categories of enumeration. The assessors pointed out the absence of columns for important crops, such as field peas and turnips. As Garret Doyle from Augusta Township in the Johnstown District put it, 'there is a good many had peas it is not mentioned,' and later, 'this man had peas he says he never measured his Land.' John Gray in South Gower Township simply returned the pea crop for each producer in the 'remarks' section.[61]

While occasionally noting the existence of such phenomena as an especially aged person, the assessors most frequently commented on variations in residence and property holding, both those variations that were likely to affect the quality of their returns and those that were simply unusual in their eyes. Thus, for example, John Elliott of Wolford Township regularly made an explanatory note when the household head's farm produce came from a lot other than the one on which he was resident. Other assessors indicated the existence of non-resident proprietors. Jacob Smith from Elizabethtown Township on the St Lawrence River noted that one of the household heads about whom he returned information actually lived 'on the American shore.' The municipal clerk, who compiled Smith's returns, counted this person as among the resident population nonetheless.[62]

Smith, a thorough enumerator with an original command of orthography, was particularly interested in the 'School Setchens,' as he called them, and their share in the provincial school grant, and also in variations in property holding. A sample of his comments on the enumeration schedules demonstrates the typical presupposition that the enumeration was mainly concerned with property relations. Smith wrote after various household entries: 'Lives on his fathers farm'; 'School Setchen 6 money £8 9s 9d'; 'holds this land By his mother'; 'this man has rented this farm last summer'; 'got this Farm with his wife last summer'; 'works on shares Has 1/2 of the grean'; 'works on shears has 2/3 of grean'; 'this faram is on Devided [undivided] untill the youngest son comes of age'; 'his mother holds the /deed?/ in Her own Hand'; 'has agreed for a please [place] but has got no writtings'; 'this land Belongs to his wife.'[63]

The returns show that assessors were willing and able to provide useful policy intelligence. For example, reports of such practices as sharecropping could have been quantified to inform debate about land-granting policy, had Walter Crofton thought beforehand to demand that enumerators observe such things systematically. The date of first settlement was certainly interesting for an assessor who wished to explain why he reported partial or no information about an individual's crops. For a census agency concerned with governing population, the systematic collection of information about dates of settlement could also have made it possible to evaluate the progress of colonization projects. Yet the Board of Registration and Statistics was not interested in collecting such information systematically. Other occasional items of intelligence, such as the existence of destitute families in the town of Prescott, were provided by the enumerators, but were taken up in no governmental project.[64] Against a functionalist account of social scientific development, one can see in the case of the 1848 census that the technology of knowledge production outpaced policy demands.

**The Returns**

By mid-May 1848, Crofton had sent out report forms to the district clerks, the men in Canada West responsible for compiling returns and producing abstracts of the information collected. The central authority did not have access to the completed enumeration schedules and had no means of regulating the compilation process. Crofton did not attempt any incursion in this domain, such as circulating a compilation template, so he had no guarantee that the observations would be consistent. A circular, dated 14 May 1848, shows that he sought a report of the numbers and the geographical distribution of heads of households from the clerks, who were also requested to produce an abstract of 'Persons engaged in Professions, Trade or Commerce, Agriculture, Laborers.' They seem to have cooperated, on the whole, although it is clear that they systematically excluded women from their compilations of the trades and occupations entries. Demonstrating once again the absence of a clear observational project, Crofton asked the municipal clerks for 'such remarks of general information as may have been returned to you by the various Assessors, and such also as may have come within your own personal observation.'[65] The replies to his circular provided Crofton with informational resources that he would work up into a report to the legislature. Yet, it is clear that the information on which he would draw was not produced through the systematic and coherent application of well thought out observational protocols to clearly defined objects of knowledge. What Crofton knew about the content of the census schedules in Canada West was what the municipal clerks considered it important that he know.

**The Failure of 1848 in Canada East**

While the 1848 census project was publicized by the press in Canada East and supported at least by the editor of *La Minerve*, organizational confusion and local resistance reigned again. Part of the problem stemmed from the consequences of yet another attempt on the part of the Conservative ministry to organize workable local government bodies in Canada East. The 1845 Municipal Act was due to expire at the end of 1847, but rather than renew its provisions, the ministry passed a new Municipal Act (9 & 10 Vic. c.VII), proclaimed on 28 July 1847, the day after the Census and Statistics Act. The new Municipal Act took effect less than a month after council elections had been held under the 1845 act. Another round of council elections was to be held on 1 January 1848 under the new act, which replaced the authorities of 1845 with a set of county councils, raised the property qualification for councillors substantially, and extended their powers of taxation. Besides disenfranchising poorer rural residents, in a further effort to overcome resistance to municipal government the new act gave government officers police powers to ensure that people could not cripple the councils by refusing to conduct elections.

Perhaps the new local government provisions of the 1847 Municipal Act were slow to come into effect; perhaps the Board of Registration and Statistics was slow in getting enumeration forms to the localities; perhaps both tendencies were at work. In any case, on 14 March 1848, the editor of *Le Canadien* wrote that while the corporation of Quebec had been sent the census forms, no instructions to enumerators had been received. The editor expected that the province's urban councils would cooperate in conducting the enumeration, but that it was extremely unlikely that rural municipal councils would act promptly in the matter. Political divisions over local government were so severe that members of local councils could not agree about even the most elementary questions, and the census enumeration required both good will and financial outlay. The editor argued that only the central government could hope to execute such a project.[66]

*La Minerve*, which had supported the announced census enthusiastically in January, concluded in May 1848 that it was simply not going to work because of the refusal of the local councils to act. The paper's editor claimed that many people erroneously believed that the government had the power to name enumerators and to proceed with the census, when in fact the Census and Statistics Act clearly vested this power in the local councils. If the councils had not fulfilled their responsibilities, it was to be regretted, but the government was dependent on them. The editor then pointed out that the act specified the months of February and March as the period of enumeration. Since the legally defined period was past, even if local councils were now to appoint enumerators, they would have no power to demand information, and those questioned would be under no obligation to respond. Given how difficult it had been in the past to make people give answers even when they were faced with legal penalties, how were the enumerators to enter people's houses and to question them now?[67]

In effect, the continuing inability of the central government to put workable organs of representative local government in place in the countryside once again blocked a census in Canada East. The failure of the enumeration project speaks to the limited capacity of agencies of the central government to lay hold of social relations in the eastern section. This weakness was largely one of administrative command and administrative infrastructure: to interrogate political subjects, one must first incorporate them in administrative structures of the kind that were absent in Canada East. Matters had not changed by the time Crofton attempted to conduct the 1850 census.

## The 1850 Census

On 26 October 1849, Walter Crofton addressed a close copy (with renumbered column headings) of the 1848 census circular to assessors in both parts of the colony, in preparation for the enumeration required under the law for the spring of 1850. He attached a list of fourteen questions for the assessors about topography, settlement conditions, land values, and agricultural crops. The circular was reprinted in *La Minerve* on 2 December, and the proposed census was discussed at length in the Montreal *Gazette* (reprinting the Toronto *Colonist*) on 13 February 1850. While the *Gazette's* piece outlined the provisions and requirements of the Census Act and stressed that the enumeration was not about taxation, the failure of the enumeration was again predicted for Canada East. Such a failure would be unfortunate because it would feed demands for political representation 'professing to be based on population, the foundation of which was merely the hypothetical calculation of connoisseurs.'[68]

A circular in French, dated 7 May 1850 and addressed by the board to municipal clerks in Canada East, enclosed report forms for an abstract of census information. In anticipation of an enumeration failure, the following notation was included: 'In case no census has been taken in your locality, have the goodness to return the forms.'[69] No evidence survives of an 1850 enumeration in Canada East, with the exception of population returns for the city of Montreal. The refusal of municipal councils to act was most likely responsible once again. *Le Canadien* commented well after the fact that the enumeration failed because 'our municipalities had no money and did not wish to tax the people to get any.'[70] In response to a question in Parliament in June 1851 calling for the 1850 census results for Canada East, the Inspector General responded that the census 'had not been taken, nor is the attempt likely to be made, as the attempt which had been made [in 1848] had proved a failure; and it was proposed to adopt further legislation on the subject.'[71] A further demand directed at Walter Crofton revealed that only the cities of Montreal and Quebec, and four counties in the Eastern Townships, had produced complete returns in 1848. Less complete returns had been received by the board from about thirty-five other localities, but together they gave a population for Canada East of about 312,000, less than half that indicated by the census of 1844.[72] In contrast, in Canada West the assessors returned an 1850 population of 813,485, almost double the figure returned for that section in 1840 and well above the 1844 population for Canada East.[73]

### The 1849 Report

The failure of census making in Canada East in 1848 did not prevent Walter Crofton from making returns of population. Even before the census was complete, he was claiming that Canada West's population was rapidly approaching that of Canada East. In his 1847 Blue Book, produced in the first quarter of 1848, he estimated the population sizes at about 800,000 East and 710,745 West.[74] In late September 1848 the governor, Lord Elgin, wrote with some pride to the Colonial Secretary, Lord Grey, about the growing population of Canada West, underlining the 'rapid progress of this interesting Colony, which derives mainly if not exclusively from Irish and British Immigration all additions to its population beyond natural increase.' Elgin's subtext was that the assimilationist policy urged by Durham and Sydenham was working, and he enclosed a copy of Crofton's tabulations of population growth in the colony since 1824. Using electoral divisions as his units of analysis and noting that, because some returns from the 1848 census had not been received, he had calculated the population by adding 12.5 per cent to the returns for 1841, Crofton was claiming that Canada West's population was now 714,964 – an estimate likely to be 'under the mark.' Grey's congratulatory reply shows that the Colonial Office was equating Canadian 'progress' with population increase.[75]

A modified version of this document of Crofton's was offered to Parliament in early February 1849 and caused alarm in the francophone press, where editors were watching the unfolding of an attempt by French-Canadian conservatives and liberals to secure representation by population. Crofton's document, which was reprinted in *La Minerve*, numbered the inhabitants of Canada West at 723,087, while estimating those in Canada East to be 768,334. The paper's editor drew the alarming conclusion that 'representation by population would be entirely to the advantage of Upper Canada and against that of Lower Canada! ... Since its population is growing so rapidly, that is certainly the reason that the Tories of Upper Canada are in favour of an immediate electoral reform on the basis of population.'[76]

The 1849 *Appendix to the Report of the Board of Registration and Statistics* was the first important document produced by Crofton's new agency and one of the first instances in which a Canadian state official attempted to read social conditions and developmental tendencies from the results of a census enumeration.[77] Its account of relative population growth in Canada East and West figured centrally in the Parliamentary representation debates of the same year, during which what was particularly germane politically was the decreasing sectional gap in population numbers. The census began to take on a new role here in the formation of a social imaginary, and claims began to be made that this novel technology of knowledge had the potential to reveal deep social meanings.

The bulk of Crofton's *Appendix* dealt with Canada West. He presented some fifteen printed pages of population returns from this section and then attempted to interpret them. His analysis varied between the inchoate and the nonsensical, and he sought to disguise design flaws in the census that were ultimately his responsibility. Crofton claimed that it was especially important to determine the proportion of men to women, 'for in all countries in which the increase arises from the ratio of Births to Deaths, we find the Females preponderate, whereas the contrary obtains in the United States and Canada where the chief increase is from Immigration.' In the same vein, he pointed to the importance of what is now called the age structure of the population, for 'this branch of Statistical information is looked upon, in all Countries, as of primary consequence; it indicates in a great degree the social character of a people, and with us it may form, after the lapse of a few periods, a satisfactory basis on which to rest a calculation as to the comparative increase by births within the Province and by immigration.'

The relative importance of immigration and natural increase was indeed at the heart of the colony's sectional, ethnic, and denominational struggles, because immigration was overwhelmingly from Britain, while the French-speaking inhabitants increased by the excess of births over deaths. But Crofton claimed that while the board's investigation of age structure closely followed 'the plan adopted both in England and the United States,' where 'the most minute particulars are entered into,' in Canada 'the means do not exist of following up the subject as connected with health and longevity.' He added that because there were no vital statistics for Canada West in the material he had received from municipal clerks, it was impossible to use the census returns to address the question. When he needed to do so, Crofton simply assumed that the birth and death rates were the same in the west as in Canada East: a birth for every twenty-one people; a death for every fifty-three.

Crofton was being disingenuous in these sections of his report. He did not reproduce or comment on the colony's immigration returns, which were detailed and extensive, even though it was clearly part his agency's mandate to command such information. A more competent and energetic official could also have examined systematically the prothonotaries' returns of vital statistics for Canada East.[78] Despite his claim to the contrary, the 1848 census did not replicate the English census's age categories. Crofton's confused schedules not only used gross age categories for women but also sought returns of deaths by sex but not age. The design of the census did not configure social relations in a manner that made it possible to address the important political question of the moment, and Crofton's oblique remarks in this part of the report were his only comment on his failure to fulfil the board's mandate of delivering an annual report of vital statistics. These reflections were typical Crofton: the ponderous pronouncement, empty of substance, amounting to an alibi for not doing what he was supposed to have done, followed by a promise of better information later.

**Religion, Work, and Agriculture**
In Crofton's opinion, the censuses of both religion and occupation had been poorly executed, the former especially because of the inclusion of the category 'No Creed or Denomination' and because of jealousies among religious sects. Crofton offered no critical reflection on the occupational returns. In contrast to English practice, he had not provided a catalogue of occupations for the enumerators, who thus used their own discretion and nomenclature. As well, compilers in their abstracts only counted occupations for men, despite finding side-by-side entries like 'farm labourer' for both men and women. Crofton simply reported that at least 80 per cent of the population was engaged in agriculture. He claimed that 'the average number of inhabitants to a house corresponding with that of each family, shews a population in a happy and prosperous condition, and is indicative of the advantages enjoyed by a rural settlement over a population confined in towns and cities.' Yet he followed this remark with the claim that the rising number of 'farm servants' showed the agricultural population in Canada West to be prospering. Even disregarding the fact that a single enumeration gave him no grounds for a comparative statement, these two observations were mutually contradictory; for if prosperity was obvious in the fact that there were few non-family members in rural households, the rising number of non-family members in the guise of servants could not, surely, be a sign of the same thing.

The failure of the enumeration in Canada East had led Crofton to distribute a circular to county registrars with questions about land and agricultural conditions. He produced an abstract of their responses in his report. He printed statistics of agriculture for Canada West, based on the census and on assessment returns, and compared crops in Canada and the United States (information for the latter probably taken from the 1840 U.S. census). Crofton quoted G.R. Porter's *Progress of the Nation* on the necessity of acquiring good statistics of agriculture for promoting national wealth – a fact that shows he had access to contemporary English statistical materials. Yet he did so merely to lament that in Canada, 'the least steps towards obtaining any statistical information, had hitherto been met with objections of all sorts, for there are never wanting persons who make it their study by misrepresentation to lead the public mind astray, and as soon as the idea of a Census is promulgated the cry of intended taxation is raised and the people deterred from giving true replies to the questions.' The failure of 1848, in other words, was not Crofton's responsibility, and in any case 'this difficulty is however rapidly abating, and in a few years a perfectly correct Census will be attainable.'[79]

Much of the material in the *Appendix* had little to do with the census of 1848; rather, it resembled things that should have been included in Crofton's 1848 Blue Book. For instance, after providing an abstract of revenues and expenditures for government departments, and before concluding that trade returns proved that the country 'had been over trading to a large amount,' Crofton launched into a long comment on jail and prison statistics. Part of this comment was an argument for an investment in statistical forms and parallel forms of practice in this domain: a system of classification and separate confinement, and the 'adoption of an uniform system of Gaol Registers' that would make uniform statistics possible. Crofton nonetheless presented a return of crimes by district and offence, intermingled with his own moralizing judgments. 'We must agree with Paley,' argued Crofton, 'when he asserts, that half the vices of low life arise from aversion to labour'; furthermore, everyone he had spoken with agreed with his own opinion that 'a serious error was committed when personal chastisement in the case of young offenders was abolished.' The census could have been employed to pursue a project for criminal statistics if Crofton had been seriously interested in doing so; he was not. In sum, the *Appendix* was characteristic of the least sophisticated mid-nineteenth-century statistical practice.

**The Representation Debates**

The *Appendix* might be dismissed as a demonstration of the weaknesses of the 1847 Census Act and of Crofton's incompetence had it not been injected into the rapidly intensifying political debates over representation, colonial governmental autonomy, and the future of French and

English in Canada. In the short term, Crofton managed not only to disguise his own conceptual bungling, but also to earn the praise of the Reform ministry for his glowing accounts of Canadian progress. The Inspector General, Francis Hincks, reproduced Crofton's statistical tables as evidence of Canada's flourishing condition in his boosterish pamphlet *Canada: Its Financial Position and Resources*. The pamphlet was meant to support Hincks's English mission to arrange matters concerning the colonial debt with Baring Brothers in the summer of 1849. He was anxious to calm investors' fears about the solvency and stability of the colonial government after the Rebellion Losses riot of April 1849 and the ensuing annexation crisis. Crofton's tables proved especially useful.[80]

Earlier, the January 1849 proposal of the Baldwin-Lafontaine government to reorganize electoral divisions in both provinces had provoked a heated debate over principles of representation, which implicated questions of population, census making, and the work of the Board of Registration and Statistics. The government aimed to redraw the electoral boundaries imposed by the Union and to increase the number of seats. Faced with increasing evidence of the rising population of the west, however, the Reform alliance opposed representation by population and sought to entrench further the principle of equal sectional representation contained in the Act of Union.

Opposition members from Canada East argued that reports of disproportionately rapid population growth in Canada West were a result of the faulty execution of the census and of misleading calculations proposed by the Board of Registration and Statistics. They used other methods to determine population size in support of their claim that Canada East's population was also growing rapidly. Coupled with all of this were criticisms of past census-making practice and demands for a new census that would demonstrate the underrepresentation of Canada East. Still incensed by the injustice contained in the overrepresentation of the west in the Act of Union, the opposition in Canada East agitated for representation by population. Clearly, census-making projects had acquired a heightened political importance.

The recently rehabilitated *patriote* leader, Louis-Joseph Papineau, was particularly vocal in the first round of the representation debate in January 1849, denouncing what he called Lord Sydenham's corrupt representation bill, with its high property qualification designed 'to keep out penniless agitators.' In the first phase of the debate, claims were made about Canada West's rising population, but no one yet called for a new census.[81] When debate resumed in March 1849, the eastern opposition members P.-J.-O. Chauveau, J. Laurin, and L.-J. Papineau sponsored motions on the unfairness of the Act of Union and the existing principle of representation, as well as a third motion which read: 'That in order to come to a more equitable apportionment of the representation of the people of this province in Parliament, it is expedient that there be taken a new census of the population of this province at the expense of the province, under the sanction of a law and under the immediate control of the executive.' Local government was not capable of producing a reliable enumeration of Canada East; the executive would have to organize it directly.

By this time, Crofton's report was in circulation. The opposition sought to discredit it, while government members drew on it for support.[82] In speaking to the motion for a new census, P.-J.-O. Chauveau insisted that all the Canada East censuses had been badly executed and had systematically underestimated the number of inhabitants. People in Canada East feared that the census was a preliminary to taxation and so minimized the amount of their crops, and did not report all their possessions nor all the members of their families. Municipal authorities had proved incapable of census making and so any successful census would have to be organized by the central government directly. Chauveau also criticized the presentation and tabulation of census returns in Crofton's report, claiming 'the tables we have are bad, we don't see in them the numbers of fathers of families, for instance,' and arguing that the presentation of the material should follow the improved methods adopted in other countries.

A protracted debate ensued, with lengthy discussions of whether the principle of representation by population actually existed in the United States and arguments over whether such a principle would be in the interest of Canada East. Speaking for the government, Louis-Hippolyte Lafontaine argued that by increasing the number of seats in each section the proposed representation bill both undid the damage done by Sydenham's attempt to disenfranchise the *canadiens* and offered Canada East the necessary protection of equal representation in face of the rising western population. Lafontaine remarked that Chauveau stated the existence of a larger population in Canada East without any statistics to support his position, while figures drawn from the 1844 census demonstrated such claims to be erroneous.[83]

**Crofton's Census Report Again**
Lafontaine's argument invoked Crofton's census report, which had begun with a brief summary account of the population of Canada East

from the earliest to the most recent records. In this part of his *Appendix*, Crofton claimed that the first census of Lower Canada had been taken in 1825, but that the redivision of districts and changes in parish boundaries made the comparison of its figures with others difficult. The first reliable census was that of 1831, those taken before that date being simply population estimates based on estimates of past increases. Crofton then compared the census totals of 1831 and 1844 to determine the rate of population increase and used an unexplained but 'well established rule of Statistics' to calculate the numbers of men, women, and children in Canada East in 1844. The ratio of men to women and children was supposed to demonstrate whether population increase resulted from an excess of births over deaths or from immigration. He next calculated the Canada East population in 1848 using the rate of annual increase from 1831 to 1844, returns of births and deaths, and reports of immigration. Deaths were subtracted from births, and Crofton assumed the death rate in Canada East to be the same as that in England. He then criticized other estimates of the population of Canada East for neglecting deaths from the cholera and emigration after the 'troubles' of 1837–8. He calculated the number of married and unmarried people in the colony, arguing that the large numbers of the latter pointed to 'a fearful increase in pauperism,' and concluded that the province was inhabited by 768,334 people. This was a considerable increase over the 697,084 reported in the 1844 census, but if Crofton's claims that Canada West now had a population of about 720,000 were correct, and if British immigration continued, representation by population was a principle soon to be against the interests of Canada East.

These were the calculations drawn on by Lafontaine in his response to Chauveau, and they were immediately attacked in detail by Louis-Joseph Papineau. People claimed that the 1844 census was accurate, Papineau said, but was there 'a single enlightened man in this country who might not know that this census was the most misleading, the most inaccurate of all the censuses that have been taken'? It had been conducted under the hated and dictatorial local governmental system imposed on Lower Canada by the odious and detestable Lord Sydenham. It was conducted after the imposition of a huge debt on the lower province and in the midst of fears about war occasioned by the Maine boundary dispute. The *canadiens* had good reason to be uneasy about the conduct of the government, and Papineau insisted that it was well known that their answers to census enumerators were 'in the highest degree misleading.'

Furthermore, according to Papineau, there was cause to doubt the 1844 returns on the basis of other evidence. He compared the numbers of communiants reported by the curés with population numbers given in the census and, claiming that two-thirds of the population communed, concluded that the census was particularly defective. Papineau also denounced Crofton's tables of vital statistics. The numbers of deaths returned included the many famine immigrants who arrived in their death throes, and Crofton had subtracted these deaths from the numbers of births. Papineau claimed that the result was a death rate more than half the birth rate – something seen nowhere else. If one took only the numbers of births as returned by prothonotaries, the population of Canada East would have risen by 100,000 since the last census and immigration would have contributed another 25,000. In fact, Papineau concluded, the population of Canada East was at least 150,000 greater than in the last census, which itself had given a low population return. Using even the figures given by those who 'wish their country ill,' one could see that population growth in Canada East was double the official claim. Papineau called for representation by population.[84]

A final day of debate on the representation bill was held on 29 March 1849, and it quickly degenerated, as did most debates during this period, into recriminations and accusations around the proposed Rebellion Losses Bill. The conservative opposition, led by Henry Sherwood, tried to have the representation bill tabled until another census was taken, and accompanied by the hisses of many francophone members, Papineau voted with them. He again claimed that a census was necessary because the population increase in Canada East since the last census was 150,000, not the 75,000 officially reported. The representation bill made second reading but could not command the two-thirds majority required for it to pass.[85]

The question of representation did not disappear, however, nor did the importance of taking a new census diminish, although the existing arrangements simply did not work. By the end of the 1840s, statistical knowledge of population had become both a subject of and a medium for political debate. Politicians like Papineau contested the official account of population, yet they also argued that a knowledge of population provided a basis for making political judgments. The contrast with political debate a decade earlier is marked. On 26 April 1849, however, the burning of Parliament in the Rebellion Losses riots pushed questions of census making and representation by population off the Parliamentary agenda.

Chapter 3

# Numbering Names

Distracted by the Rebellion Losses struggles, the movement for annexation to the United States, financial crisis, and the appearance of a left agrarian opposition that split its own ranks, the Baldwin-Lafontaine Reform government was unable to reorganize the unworkable census-making arrangements until the summer of 1851. Despite his increasingly evident incompetence and political partisanship, Walter Crofton managed to retain the post of Secretary of Registration and Statistics until 1853. So it was he who administered the first attempt the extend central government control over census making, which is the main topic of this chapter.

By the late 1840s, Canadian census administration was lagging seriously behind practice in England. In 1841, imperial practice was tied to the centralized administrative arrangements created by the new Poor Law and the Registration Act. Key dimensions of control over the production of knowledge of population were removed from the hands of local authorities and vested in the General Register Office.[1] Early in 1849, the imperial government urged the colonies to take a common census on a date close to that fixed for the 1851 English enumeration. Detailed instructions about how to administer a census, general regulations for compiling returns, and sample enumeration schedules were sent to British North America. Colonial administrators were urged to conduct censuses at regular intervals using clearly defined enumeration districts.

In fact, the colonists were urged to adopt the plan worked out by the London Statistical Society in consultation with L.-A.-J. Quetelet, a plan that Quetelet had followed in his censuses of Brussels and Belgium and that would later be held up as an international standard. The Colonial Office reproduced William Farr's original description of the plan in its communications with colonial governors. They were told that the best census design was of the *de facto* type in which people were to be recorded where they were found on a common census day, with particular care taken to avoid double-counting: 'Persons from home should be enumerated at the place in which they happen to be on the Census night; the words "(visitor,)" "(traveller,)" &C., being added in parentheses, after their names. If they are not out of the Colony, they should also be enumerated at home, with the word "absent" after their names. All persons marked "absent" should be omitted in the abstracts, otherwise the same person would be counted twice. This part of the census, relating to the "floating population", will require great care.' Correspondents were informed that the English practice was to leave the enumeration schedules in the hands of householders a few days before the enumeration and to have the enumerators fill in schedules only for the incapable or neglectful.

Particularly innovative for Canadian officials was the recommendation that colonies conduct the enumeration *by name* wherever possible. 'Without this, experience has proved that there can be no security for the accuracy of the returns. The Abstracts cannot otherwise be made satisfactorily and the Government will find enumeration by name useful for many purposes connected with the Police and defence of the respective Colonies.' William Farr was insisting again, as he had for the English census of 1841, that 'the names should be written at *length*' because 'an enumerator may sit at home and make *marks* and no examiner could detect his errors.'

In the English case, the shift from household to nominal enumeration came about as an administrative control measure. The political promise of identifying people by name might have been great, but the practice was aimed, modestly, at governing the conduct of enumerators. It was meant to control costs and to ensure that enumerators did in fact conduct a house-to-house canvass. The English census planners had conducted field trials, apparently to see how much work a competent enumerator could do in a day, with a view to estimating census expenses. It seems that here, fiscal and administrative discipline were propelling social scientific innovation – a matter of significance for an analysis of census making as a political technology of the 'governmentality.' Every-person identifiers extend dramatically the political potential of the results of census making, but they do not seem to have been introduced, in this case at least, because liberal political authorities were concerned with 'governing too much,' as some analysts have suggested.[2]

The English circular of instructions contained other recommendations meant to centralize authority over knowledge production. The enumerators were not to be allowed to make their own abstracts of returns, but were to send their schedules bound together to the central government, 'where the Abstracts should be made on a uniform plan under proper supervision.' Censuses should record the age and the race of the members of the population, matters described as 'sufficiently obvious' as to need no elaboration. The circular seemed to imply that the entries to be made for people's occupations would be guided by some sort of catalogue, one that would make it possible to execute a 'classification of the colonists: householders, proprietors, and masters, should be distinguished from lodgers, tenants, and workmen.' Date of settlement was also to be sought, as was information about physical condition: 'whether the person is labouring under any sickness – understanding thereby such severe sickness as incapacitates him from following his ordinary occupation – or any infirmity, such as blindness, deafness, idiocy, lameness, or the feebleness of old age.' The collection of this kind of information would make it possible to determine 'the sanitary state of different races and localities; as well as the relative proportions of the inefficient and efficient Population.' Both these matters were closely tied to William Farr's conception of the census as a medical survey.

Finally, the circular recommended that information about vital events be collected, but that questions about religion be excluded on the grounds that it was 'important not to crowd the Census with too many particulars.' This last remark was a disingenuous avoidance of the intense opposition to a census of religious denominations raging in England. If Walter Crofton saw this circular, it did not affect his 1850 census. Following all its provisions in 1850 would have required Parliament to pass a new census act to remove control over the enumeration from the municipal councils, but Crofton could certainly have altered the existing enumeration schedules. He did not do so.[3]

## Crofton and Crisis

The years 1849–51 were difficult for Walter Crofton, despite a promising beginning. In January 1849 he was mentioned favourably in a despatch to the imperial government for his careful compilation of statistical materials. On 25 April he was married in Montreal.[4] The next day, however, rioting followed the proclamation of the Rebellion Losses Act, and the Parliament buildings were burned by an angry mob. Street violence continued in Montreal and several other cities for some weeks, and opposition to the apparent domination of the colonial government by the 'French rebels,' in the context of a serious commercial crisis provoked by the repeal of the Navigation Acts and the coming of Free Trade, fuelled a movement for annexation to the United States. The legislature did not meet between 30 May 1849 and 14 May 1850, as the government attempted to reassure its London creditors that the crisis would not affect payments on the public debt and as it acted to purge the state system of voluntary signatories to the various Annexation Manifestos circulating in the colony. A resurgent agrarian radical movement split the government in late 1849, as elements of the Reform party's left wing defected toward a newly formed 'Clear Grit' faction.[5]

Walter Crofton took advantage of the political excitement in Montreal to neglect his work. He managed successfully to claim that the bulk of the 1849 *Report of the Board of Registration and Statistics* was destroyed in the Parliamentary fire, with only the appendix discussed above surviving. However, he neglected to produce the Blue Books for 1848, 1849, and 1850, and thereby exposed Lord Elgin to the dissatisfaction of the Colonial Secretary. Elgin managed to send off the 1849 Blue Book only in January 1851, but even then could not secure the 1848 volume. 'I believe the fact to be,' he wrote to the Colonial Secretary, 'that the Clerk who prepares them took advantage of the disturbances in 1849 to neglect his duty. He at first declared, when called to account, that the book had been sent in as usual and destroyed in the rows. But he has been driven from this position. He is, they say, of the ultra Tory faction, and probably was much interested in what was going on – I shall take precautions against such mishaps for the future.'[6]

Attempts to reconstruct a governmental alliance between Reformers and Clear Grits led to plans for a second government statistics agency, as we shall see in more detail in the following chapter. Cabinet discussion of the new agency was held in December 1851, and Crofton's days were clearly numbered when these plans would come to fruition.

**A New Census Act**

The political crisis and the breakup of the Reform ministry prevented a systematic consideration of census matters in 1850. The following year, the question again preoccupied Parliament. The government wished to approximate the English census date, but did not manage to secure passage of the necessary legislation in time to do so. After a lengthy debate, the 1851 Census Act (14 & 15 Vic. cap. XLIX) provided for enumerations in January 1852, in 1861, and at decennial intervals thereafter.

The Parliamentary debate focused on the impossibility of using local government bodies in Canada East for the execution of an enumeration. The municipal institutions were said to have been in 1848, and to remain in 1851, 'too immature' to execute a census. The 1847 Act had 'been found perfectly inoperative' in Canada East, and it was 'impossible ... to take any census' there using it.[7] Most MPPs now accepted that it was necessary for the central government to appoint census officers for Canada East directly. In June 1851, speaking for the last incarnation of the Baldwin-Lafontaine government, Inspector General Francis Hincks laid out a detailed census plan. The existing act was inoperable in Canada East, he claimed, because the local municipal officers refused to act, and its operation in Canada West could be improved. Hincks claimed that his alternative plan approximated practice in England and in the United States, where enumerations were conducted by 'officers appointed by Government.' The Canadian government planned to appoint a census superintendent for each county, who in turn would appoint the necessary enumerators and divide the counties into convenient enumeration districts. The superintendents would themselves be supervised by the Board of Registration, which would issue forms and instructions. Hincks thought it important to mention that there would be no less information sought than was the case under the 1847 Census Act. The American system of paying enumerators by the name would be adopted, although, since more information was being sought in Canada, the rate would be higher. As in England, the government would provide the necessary schedules.

Henry Smith and W.H. Merritt from Canada West spoke in opposition to the bill, protesting against the needless expense of another enumeration when that of 1848 had been so recently completed. Merritt, in addition, protested against what he saw as the creation of yet another government department in the guise of the Board of Registration. Francophone members from Canada East, however, insisted that a census of the east was necessary and that it could not be conducted there by local municipal officers. After some considerable discussion, the Assembly voted a series of resolutions in support of Hincks's plan.[8] The census plan was opposed in sections of the colony where agrarian radicalism was resurgent. The Lanark and Renfrew County Councils, for example, petitioned against the appointment of census commissioners by the government, arguing that counties should control their own officers. A successful attempt was made by members of the Clear Grit faction to amend the bill to ensure that information about religious affiliation, seen as important for the secularization of the Clergy Reserves, would continue to be included.[9] In the final round of debate, the opposition from Canada West again protested against the needless expense of re-enumerating the west and against the injustice of paying for an enumeration of Canada East out of general tax revenue. Hincks insisted that only the central government could successfully conduct a census in the east and that hence its expense should be borne from general revenues. The bill passed with a vote of thirty-seven to seven on 8 August 1851.[10]

**Ask a Silly Question, Get a Silly Answer**
For some francophone intellectuals, the proposal to conduct a census of both sections of the colony using uniform categories defined by the central government was politically menacing. The configuration of social relations as population seemed to be a dangerous form of political abstraction, perhaps one that would subordinate French Canadians to English cultural domination. The editor of *Le Canadien* was among those made uneasy. He claimed that Parliamentary debate over the census had taken place too quickly for a careful consideration of the question. At first he was in favour of a census law that would provide for quinquennial enumerations so that statistical series could be established quickly, even as he stressed that care was needed in census execution, and even as he expressed a lack of confidence in the past employees of the census board (Crofton was the only one).[11] Soon, however, he began to argue that funds for census execution should not be voted until 1855. In the meantime, a comparative investigation of census practice in other countries should be undertaken and attention should be directed to the careful selection of census officers, who should be intelligent, conscientious men 'knowledgeable of the language, customs and popular ideas' of the eastern section. Such men would differ from 'the officials sent into the countryside two years ago to get a census.' Protection against fraudulent returns was also required, as were guarantees of accuracy. This commentator argued that the proposal to pay enumerators by the name was a temptation to falsification and that it would be easier to check their work if they were paid per inhabited house.[12]

At the heart of the issue was the fact that the census would be used to make comparisons between the two sections of the colony, and the editor warned his readers that if care was not taken, Canada East would be the victim of new injustices. He argued against a common enumeration because the census was a sectional political project. 'It is not at all reasonable,' he maintained, 'to present the same framework of questions where everything is different, occupations, manners and customs, language and character, weights and measures, climate and products.' People in the western section would completely reject 'a long series of questions apt to be understood by a French Canadian; they should not then demand that we respond to theirs.'

A condition for a good census return, the editor continued, was the possibility of comparisons with past returns, but there had been no enumeration of the eastern section, except for the very defective efforts of 1831 and 1844. Care was particularly necessary because of the stupidities contained in the censuses of 1844 and 1848. The age categories used were incompatible and silly too; and the schedules mixed up different types of industry and asked ridiculous questions, such as that concerning the number of acres of rice, while not asking about immigration and emigration. In short, if great care were not taken, the government would find itself victim of the old adage '*à sotte question, sotte réponse.*'[13]

In the view of this influential commentator, central control over the enumeration would lead to uniform procedures for generating accounts of 'population' and production. But the quest for uniformity was an assimilationist initiative; totalization was domination – a theme that continues to echo through Canadian politics. Especially under the direction of the Board of Registration and Statistics (and, by implication, of the high Tory Crofton), a uniform enumeration would make a single Canadian population when in fact there were two. Clearly, sectional struggle in Canada had emerged early as a potential barrier to a uniform representation of social relations as population.

### The 1851 Census Act
'An Act to provide more effectually for taking the Periodical Census of the Province' (14 & 15 Vic. cap. XLIX) was proclaimed on 30 August 1851. It was too late to organize an enumeration for 1851, especially given that this was the beginning of the period of the peregrinating Parliament, and government offices were moving to the city of Quebec. The 1851 act created the legislative framework that guided the execution of the Canadian censuses of 1852 and 1861. It specified that an enumeration would take place under the direction of the Board of Registration and Statistics on the second Monday in January 1852 and 1861, and at decennial intervals thereafter. The board was to prepare forms and

instructions, and the enumeration schedules were to include the information specified by the 1841 Census Act, with such additional information as the board deemed to be 'of public interest and importance.' If it appeared that an enumeration could not be completed in any place in the month of January, the board could specify some other period.

Census commissioners were to be appointed by the government in each county and in each incorporated town with a population of more than 5,000. The commissioners were to appoint enumerators, using townships or parts of townships as units in rural Canada West, parishes, extraparochial places, or townships in rural Canada East, and wards in cities and towns. Penitentiaries, asylums, jails, hospitals, and houses of correction were to be separate enumeration districts. The commissioners were to instruct enumerators in the execution of the census and were to give public notice of the enumeration date and of the information respondents were to provide. The enumerators were to begin work on the second Monday in January and were to continue to work 'upon such number of days next after each such Monday as may be necessary,' although the act also specified that their certified returns were to be delivered to the commissioners by 15 February – half the time allowed under the 1847 act.

The clause of the act dealing with enumerators' duties reveals that the census was of a mixed *de facto* and *de jure* design, close to the English template. The enumerator was to visit every house in his district and 'diligently and faithfully [to] take an account in writing of the name, sex, age and occupation, of every living person who abode therein on the night of the Sunday next preceding' the enumeration date. The enumerator was to note which of these persons were 'transient passengers, having their permanent residence elsewhere,' and was also to record for every house information about 'every person usually a resident therein, but then casually absent, distinguishing such persons from others.' The commissioners were to examine carefully all the returns submitted to them and to correct or supplement them if necessary. The schedules were to be delivered to the Board of Registration and Statistics, which would produce such tables and abstracts as it thought appropriate. In this way the act centralized control over the working up of the census returns into an official account – a provision that Walter Crofton chose to ignore, but one that aimed to bring colonial practice into line with that in England.

In the cities and towns, the enumeration schedules were to be left at households by the enumerators during the week before the enumeration date. Occupants of houses or apartments were to complete and sign the schedules, on pain of a fine, and the schedules were to be collected by the enumerator on the second Monday in January. If the enumerator encountered an incomplete, erroneous, or defective schedule, he was to complete it himself. Completed schedules were to be delivered to the urban commissioner, who would pass them on to the board.

In both urban and rural areas, the act accorded the enumerators broad powers of inquiry, including 'free access to all Assessment Rolls and other documents containing statistical information.' Both enumerators and commissioners were subject to fines for contravening the act, and the Provincial Secretary was empowered to remove any census officer by notice in writing. Finally, the officers' pay was specified: commissioners were to receive a per diem allowance to a maximum of 12s.6d.; enumerators were to be paid according to the number of names recorded and how dispersed the population was. They were to have 10s. per hundred names in rural areas with the board having the power to increase this rate to 15s. where it judged the difficulty of the work justified extra pay, and to 20s. per hundred where there were less than 300 people in ten square miles. In urban areas, the rate was 10s. a hundred for the first 3,000 names and 10s. per 300 names thereafter. The Board of Registration and Statistics was to report the results and the cost of the census to Parliament within fifteen days of the start of the session following the enumeration.

The 1851 Census Act contained several provisions intended to prevent a repetition of past failures. It was now the central government that appointed and paid census officers, who were required to act. Also, the government could dismiss those officers at will. In these ways its dependence on local government bodies and officials was lessened. The parish was explicitly recognized as an enumeration district in Canada East, which severed the enumeration from past failed attempts at forcing representative government onto the eastern countryside. The government could alter the enumeration period if necessary. No clear time limit to the authority of the enumerators was specified, and if faced with doubtful testimony from respondents, they were empowered to consult the assessment rolls or other sources of information. For the first time, the enumeration was to be a nominal or every-person enterprise, with the 'normal places' of absent or transient residents noted. Such provisions could serve as control measures against fraudulent enumeration returns. Finally, the original enumeration schedules were to be the property of the central authority, which would carry out the official compilation of the results.

**The Census Plan in Conception**

With some variations, the Canadian census provisions approximated those in place in England. They still had to be translated into a practical enumeration plan, something Walter Crofton attempted to do under the supervision of Provincial Secretary A.-N. Morin. The enumeration was the most ambitious inquiry, and one of the most ambitious administrative projects of any sort, undertaken by a Canadian government to that time. It involved the assertion of new central governmental powers and required complicated logistical and infrastructural work.[14] The appointment of the census commissioners was key, for it was they who would manage the practical execution of the enumeration. Although commissioners were named by it, the central authority remained dependent on their cooperation, and they enjoyed an important degree of autonomy once appointed. There were forty-five commissioners in the western section and thirty-eight in the eastern, that is, one for each county and for each of the major colonial cities and towns (Hamilton, Toronto, Kingston, London, Bytown [Ottawa], Montreal, and Quebec). The appointments of these eighty-three commissioners were to be gazetted, after which they were to be contacted in their official capacity by the Board of Registration and Statistics.

There was no attempt to assemble or train the census commissioners. Crofton planned to send each commissioner a package of documents containing his official commission and sample schedules and forms. A table would be included in each package describing the component parts of the commissioner's jurisdiction and stating the population such parts contained at the last census. The commissioners were to examine the tables, ensure their accuracy, and use them to divide their jurisdictions into discrete and contiguous census districts of a size that could be thoroughly canvassed within fourteen days, making certain that no area was omitted. Having done this, commissioners were then to appoint a sufficient number of competent census enumerators and, using the population at the last census and their own local knowledge, were to estimate the current population in each district. They were then to notify the Board of Registration and Statistics of the names of their enumerators and the location of the enumeration districts, preferably by providing a map. The commissioners were also to order the number of personal and agricultural census schedules (or slips in the cities), beyond those sent as samples, that they expected to need to conduct the enumeration, along with sufficient copies of instructions to enumerators and copies of the form of oath that enumerators were to submit with their completed schedules.

The clear scientific and administrative limits of the power of the central authority stand out in these arrangements. The Board of Registration and Statistics, even though it was chaired by the colony's most strategically placed ministers, did not even command a comprehensive list of local government units below the level of the county. It did not possess the elementary geographical knowledge of its own administrative domain that would have enabled it to define its own enumeration units. From the outset, it depended heavily on the commissioners' 'local knowledge.' Census making was administrative exploration in a strong sense of the term.

Crofton planned to provide the commissioners with handbills announcing the enumeration, but he did not manage to do so, and the commissioners were not given time enough to meet with enumerators to discuss the schedules before the census day. During the enumeration period they were expected to travel to consult enumerators and to deal with problems that might arise. The Board of Registration and Statistics was to design and organize the printing and distribution of all the relevant census documentation.

The plan called for the enumerators to be responsible and competent men with literary skills and good moral character. They were to begin the canvass on 12 January 1852, inquiring about conditions on the previous night. They could spend as much as fourteen days on the work, although their inquiries in principle were always to have reference to conditions on the night of 11–12 January. They were to visit every house and establishment in their enumeration districts. If the plan worked, they would meet informants who were expecting them and who would be familiar with and willing to respond to the questions posed. Rural enumerators would complete the schedules on the spot and would deliver them no later than two weeks after their start date to the census commissioner, along with a signed copy of an oath attesting to their accuracy. In the cities, householders would have received their census slips some days before 12 January and would have completed them in anticipation of the arrival of the enumerator. If faced with a blank slip, the urban enumerator would inquire for the necessary information and complete the slip himself. If everything went according to plan, the commissioners would have the completed schedules in hand by 27 January 1852.

The commissioners would then inspect the completed schedules, ensuring that they were complete and accurate; if necessary, they would seek such additional information as was required to make them so. Here, however, Crofton abdicated the control over the compilation process that had been accorded to him by the Census Act. The commissioners were made responsible for the initial compilation of the census columns and were instructed to prepare an abstract for the Board of Registration and Statistics. The manuscript schedules were to be bound locally and returned with the abstract to the board in Quebec. At the same time, the census commissioners would send the board a certified account of their own expenses, along with a request for enumerators' pay based on the numbers of names recorded on the personal schedules. No extra pay was to be had for the agricultural schedule. These accounts would be examined by the board, and payment would then be issued by the Receiver General. Finally, the board would hire a number of census clerks to compile the returns in preparation for Crofton's report to Parliament. Under this elegant and seemingly simple plan, a thorough and uniform enumeration of Canada was to be conducted in a period of about three months.

**Appointments of Commissioners**
Crofton's plan involved 'action at a distance' in a strong sense of the term. There was little or no direct personal contact between central government officers and local officials; their relations were largely textually mediated. The 1852 enumeration reveals the extent to which the effectiveness of textual mediation depends on prior infrastructural work aimed at establishing how texts are to be interpreted and deployed.

Crofton's plan unfolded differently in the two sections of the colony, and parts of it proved unworkable, especially the proposal to give advance publicity of the enumeration.[15] The plan was set in motion in most of Canada East about a month before it began in Canada West, and its execution was not uniform across the two sections. In the board's dealings with commissioners in the west and on the frontiers of Canada East, there was early evidence of administrative bungling.[16]

The Canada East census commissions were gazetted on 8 November 1851, but some commissioners had already been consulted informally by a member of the government about their willingness to act.[17] The packages of census material were mailed to eastern officers, the majority of whom were state servants, on 11 and 12 November in virtually all cases. The commissioners for Quebec city and Quebec county, as well as the commissioner for Gaspé (who happened to be in Quebec and got his commission by hand), all had their sample materials during the second week of November. Thus, although there were exceptions, the first tier of Crofton's census organization was in place in Canada East six weeks before census day.[18]

Matters were quite different in Canada West, where most nominations were gazetted only on 20 December. Indeed, the final seven western appointments (for the counties of Ontario, Peel, Wellington, Brant, Victoria, Grey, and Elgin, where municipal boundaries had recently changed), along with a substitution for Prescott-Russell, were made officially only on 3 January 1852. State servants were a minority among the western commissioners; businessmen and lawyers predominated.[19] It is true that some men in the west had either solicited an appointment or had learned well in advance through their patronage networks that they would be named. Some had been contacted by Crofton before the official announcement of their appointments and may have had census materials before they received their commissions. John Kirby, for one, had received a letter about the Hamilton city census dated 11 December. Yet even these attempts to give western commissioners preparation time were often confused. The Kent County commissioner Alexander Knapp had been sent a package of census materials on 17 December 1851, but it visited Chatham, Canada East before arriving at Knapp's post office in Chatham, Canada West, on 8 January 1852, three days before the enumeration was to begin.

Knapp's case was by no means exceptional. Many western commissioners learned that they had been appointed by reading the official *Gazette* or by receiving the census materials in the mail some short time before census day. 'I have got no Commission from the Governor,' wrote Ezra Annes of Whitby to Crofton, in response to the arrival of a package of census schedules on 24 December 1851, 'nor had I any Knowledge of the appointment until I received the papers from you.' Annes's package had actually been addressed to someone named Ezra Amos, although Annes assumed it was meant to be his. The address had been torn off the package containing the official appointment of Andrew McCord as Toronto city commissioner. McCord, who had seen the appointment gazetted, found it in the post office on 1 January 1852 by opening a likely-looking bundle.

In Prescott and Russell County, a dispute delayed matters until well after the initial appointment date, when the government replaced its first appointee, the Clerk of the Peace, Donald McDonald of L'Orignal, with Charles Waters of Vankleek Hill. The government did not even have a correct address for Waters, and after finally receiving notice of his appointment as commissioner on 3 January 1852, Waters had difficulty making a 'very condescending' McDonald surrender the census materials.[20] Waters was still better placed than Thomas Heffernan of Wellington County, who claimed to have learned of his appointment as commissioner by the arrival of a package of forms and documents on the census day, 12 January 1852. Heffernan observed to the board that he would require some extra time to execute his duties, and in fact he finished the division of his county into enumeration districts on 28 January, after the census plan called for enumerators to have finished their work. These instances show that one of the elementary preconditions for the organization of a common enumeration period – rapid, well-directed communications with known individuals in localities – remained beyond the capacity of the colonial state system, at least away from the centre of government. Moreover, if the measure of a scientific census is its foundation on the coincident observation of common objects by trained observers, differences in the preparedness of commissioners and in the time allowed for them to organize the enumeration are an obvious source of incoherence.

**Defining Enumeration Districts**
Commissioners in the east were able to consider the arrangements for the census before its execution and to seek direction from the Board of Registration and Statistics about issues that arose. Two immediate concerns related to the board's inventory of parishes and extraparochial places and the clause in the Census Act that seemed to imply that each parish was to be assigned to a separate enumerator. The administrative capacity of the state system was so little developed, and the resources commanded by its different branches so little coordinated, that the census agency did not command a reliable inventory of the names or locations of religious and civil administrative units. Local government acts for Canada East had failed to put in place a uniform administrative grid. Local variation in the determination of enumeration districts, and hence in the extent and intensity of enumerators' work, was an inevitable consequence of the fact that the central authority did not command a knowledge of the existing administrative infrastructure. No robust, generally replicable demarcation of enumeration districts was possible, and incoherence in enumeration practice was structured into the census plan by the underdeveloped character of the state system – a further demonstration that population depends on state power.

At least ten eastern commissioners offered corrections to the board's inventory of places, although many were minor.[21] In some cases, however, the relationship between parishes and extraparochial places made the parish seem an unlikely choice as an enumeration district. In the counties of Huntingdon, Nicolet, and Verchères, at least, parish boundaries crossed those of counties, requiring commissioners, who were appointed for counties, to determine the points where the two intersected. Edmund Cox, the Drummond County commissioner, wrote that the table of places for his county was riddled with errors and omissions. For instance, 'the Parish of St. Norbert of Arthabaska is stated to include part of the Township of Chester. The Parish of St. Guillaume does not extend over the whole Township of Upton – two portions being considered extraparochial – a settlement distinct and unconnected by nearly 20 miles, with St. Guillaume having within it a Protestant Church or chapel and a Gore or augmentation on the north side of the River St. Francis and entirely bounded by the Signories of Pierville & St. Francis.' Cox added that there was 'also a Gore of Wendover similiarly [*sic*] situated to the Gore or augmentation of Upton and nearly adjoining to it.' As for 'the Gore of Stanfold,' which had been included in Crofton's list, Cox had never heard of it, had 'inquired after it but ha[d] not yet received a reply.' He also mentioned that Crofton had omitted to include the township of South Ham 'added to the County by Proclamation.' A uniform configuration of social relations as population demanded the positing of a uniform relationship between bodies and spaces. While parochial organization often did provide workable, bounded units, it also gave rise to fragmentary or splintered extraparochial places, which in the census plan had to be set aside as separate enumeration districts. Cox's solution for Drummond was to query 'whether this County should not rather be taken in its several Townships, than by Parishes' – something he did.[22] In contrast, in the newly settled Stanstead County, Marcus Child, the commissioner, reported, 'this county being a good deal cut up by Lakes and Rivers, I have made them boundaries to my Enumeration districts whenever I could well do so.'

To many eastern commissioners, the choice of the parish as enumeration district made perfect sense. L.A. Olivier for Berthier County chose parochial divisions as districts 'because they are the best known, and in following them, the Enumerators can run no risk of mistake in the limits of their respective Districts.' Louis Archambault took a similar line, telling Crofton that while he couldn't provide an exact description of the parish boundaries in Leinster because he hadn't been able to find a copy of the canonical decrees that established them, his enumerators were longtime parish residents and knew the limits of their districts perfectly well. Given its inability to define local units, the board was invited, but also constrained, to have confidence in the local knowledge of individual enumerators.

Yet the choice of the parish as district was often more complex than these examples suggest. Many commissioners did not wish to have a single enumerator for each parish. For some, this was because the pay for the enumeration would be so low as to make it difficult to find people willing to act. Others echoed Nazaire Larue of Montmorenci, who argued that naming so many enumerators would force him to choose 'mediocrities.' In either case, the enumerators would not be residents, and thus the problem of identifying the limits of their districts reappeared. Careful commissioners attempted to locate parish boundaries formally so that non-resident enumerators could find them. John Heath of Rimouski, for instance, visited the localities omitted from Crofton's table in order to determine their physical limits, and François Vézina travelled throughout the county of Quebec, consulting the curés and seeking from them the names of inhabitants on the boundaries of parishes. Yet such efforts yielded enumeration districts whose description was like those offered by Louis Grenier of Lotbinière: 'No.6 – Part of St. Croix from Platon to Ans. Ouellet's residence' and 'No.7– Part of St. Croix, except that part from Platon to Ans. Ouellet's residence.' There was a real possibility both of overlapping and of discontinuous enumeration districts when their definition depended on transient features in localities about which the central authority could know nothing.[23]

The confusion on the part of Crofton's office about territorial subdivisions caused delay in counties such as frontier Ottawa. Here the commissioner, André Larue, acknowledged the receipt of Crofton's table of places on 22 November and pointed to the omission from it of the Parish of St-André-Avellin. Larue thought the omission must be a mistake and proposed to 'name no enumerators until I receive from you instructions to that effect.' He heard nothing in reply, and on 10 December he wrote to Crofton for the fourth time to warn him that some of his enumerators lived 140 miles away and would be hard to reach on census day. Increasingly anxious about hearing nothing from the board, Larue then contacted the Montreal county commissioner, sent his son Narcisse to the city of Quebec to consult with the Quebec commissioner, and finally called on the local lumber magnate, John Egan, who wrote a sharp letter to A.-N. Morin on 26 December complaining that Larue had written to the board weeks earlier and had received no reply. Finally, on 29 December, Larue got a package of schedules and forms, although most of them were in French and of no use to his anglophone enumerators. A second package was mailed to him on 7 January 1852, and Larue had to travel through the county to furnish many of the enumerators, although he apparently never received an answer to the question of parochial boundaries.[24] On the whole, the board's ignorance of the subdivisions of counties, the patchwork quality of religious and secular administrative units in Canada East, and Crofton's own administrative inertia – magnified, one suspects, by his petty tyrannical character – all combined to produce confusion and delay.

The problems posed by the absence of municipal organization did not arise in Canada West, although changing county boundaries produced some confusion. Most commissioners simply divided their counties into some multiple or subdivision of township units. Yet there was no uniformity in such divisions, and the districts varied from a few concessions – that is, less than fifty square miles – in the populous townships, to four whole townships or four hundred square miles on the frontiers of settlement. In many instances, the districts were chosen on the basis of what commissioners could get enumerators to agree to do on short notice.

Urban enumeration districts were based on the ward system. A final issue that concerned commissioners was the enumeration of the aboriginal population. No Parliamentary debate took place with respect to enumerating aboriginals, but the board wished to include them in the census totals. The Portneuf commissioner defined parts of L'Ancienne-Lorette and St-Ambroise as separate districts, and the Grey commissioner also made the 'Indian territory' one of his districts. The Drummond commissioner wished to know how to designate the 'Native Indians' in the township of Durham, who were proprietors of land, although he does not seem to have had a separate district for them. More challenging was the question of the village of St-Regis on the American frontier in Beauharnois County.

L.-H. Masson wrote twice to the board about this matter, although no replies seem to have survived. On 19 November 1851, Masson wondered if he was in fact obliged to enumerate the 'village of the savages' and, if so, how he was to go about it. Again, on 6 December, he wrote, 'with respect to these Savages, I have to say again, that half the population of Saint Regis are *american Savages* resident in Canada – for religious reasons only – I would like to know if I must do the Census of them – I'm afraid of meeting opposition for they are very attached to their Government.' Masson's concerns were partly shared by Alexander Knapp of

Kent county, who wrote that 'there is in my County an Indian village and settlement of parts of certain tribes of the aborigines of this country am I to proceed to Enumerate them as I would the negro population are they not returned in some other way – if I have to Enumerate them I shall be obliged to Employ an interpretor [sic].'

The board insisted that aboriginal settlements be enumerated, but this insistence does not seem to have stemmed from a reflection on aboriginal citizenship, in the sense of the political rights and duties of such people. Most politicians and intellectuals were convinced of the inevitability of aboriginal assimilation – or extinction, but counting them in the interim would increase the number reported as the colonial population, something in which the board was interested – while perhaps satisfying imperial government demands for information about the magnitude of its treaty obligations.

**Appointing Enumerators**

In all, 1,073 enumerators were paid by the Board of Registration and Statistics for their work on the 1852 census (all of them men, with the exception of Florence McCarthy and Delorma Phillips in Leeds County), although more than this number were involved.[25] It was difficult for the commissioners to find people willing to do the work, and many who agreed were incompetent. The low rate of pay was said to discourage qualified men, and enumerators complained about the lack of additional payment for taking the agricultural census. In Canada West especially, commissioners had little time to enlist enumerators and had to travel personally through their districts to find them. The manner in which the census plan was executed made the selection of enumerators a matter of chance and happenstance.

Some commissioners managed to draw on established networks to locate quickly people they thought competent. Thomas Eyre for Northumberland County received his notice of appointment only on 8 January 1852, but immediately contacted the township councillors and through them claimed to find 'persons who really feel an interest in the Work.' Charles Robinson for Brant County enlisted 'persons who had previously done the duty of enumerating or assessing.' In rear Lanark County, on the Île d'Orléans, and in many other places, commissioners had to create large districts in order to attract potential enumerators. On the other hand, several commissioners claimed, with Alexander Knapp of Kent County, that it was 'impossible in some circumstances to get competent Persons to act as Enumerators.' The Renfrew County commissioner,

John Paris, got his instructions, without the list of places, on 26 December 1851, and had three enumerators each doing two whole townships. As he later put it, 'in some Townships there was no selection but to take the man that would accept of it.' Especially confused were the appointments in Wellington County, where Thomas Heffernan learned of his commission on census day. Heffernan hired someone to help him find enumerators by going through the back townships, but the experience was not a happy one. 'I agreed to give him 12/6cy per day,' wrote Heffernan, but 'he disobeyed all my instructions and delivered the papers to his own confederates none of them fit for the office on hearing this I started off in pursuit of him did not overtake him untill all the harm was done.' By 'harm' Heffernan meant that the enumeration had already started and he had to take back the schedules, many of which were ruined. Here, some of the enumeration was done twice.

**Furnishing Forms**

The initial print run for census schedules and instructions seems to have been for only 12,200 in English and 6,800 in French, enough to enumerate 610,000 anglophones and 340,000 francophones, or less than half the estimated population, even if there were no wasted or damaged schedules.[26] Crofton adopted the practice, common in other jurisdictions, of making an initial distribution of materials and then waiting for commissioners to order more. The practice aimed at economy in the use of schedules and at the prevention of inflated returns.

The commissioners, in contrast, wanted enough census materials so as not to run out in the middle of the enumeration, to be able to replace damaged and dirty schedules, and to make corrections where necessary. Several contacted Crofton to seek a double supply because they had heard that 'it is very unusual for the sheet on which information is taken in each house to be usable without being copied over.' Crofton was warned by Louis Olivier that if he wanted to get legible census schedules he had better furnish twice the number required, 'for in the deep cold of January, it will be difficult for the Enumerator, who will be almost continually out of doors, and who will spend only a short time in each house, to write cleanly.' However, the Board of Registration and Statistics often did not manage to deliver enough schedules even to cover its own estimates of local population, quite apart from any allowance for waste. For Olivier's Berthier County, whose population Crofton estimated at 32,986, the commissioner received 172 agricultural and 588 personal schedules – only enough to enumerate about 30,000 people. Olivier was requesting more on 5 January 1852. L.-H. Masson's estimate of the population of Beauharnois at 35,304 produced a more generous shipment of 760 personal and 190 agricultural schedules, enough to enumerate 38,000 people – an allowance of less than 10 per cent for waste and spoilage. Masson's enumerators were asking for more sheets before the enumeration began.

Other commissioners in the east followed Crofton's instructions to estimate the current populations of their counties and to order additional forms in advance of the census day, but in most cases this proved to be a waste of their time, for the board failed to respond to their orders either at all or at all efficiently, and when it did manage to respond the materials sent were sometimes defective. John Heath for Rimouski complained that the agricultural schedules he had received were flawed by 'the most important blank or column being so small that it is thought and considered impossible to write within the two lines the names of each proprietor.'[27] Other eastern commissioners were frustrated by receiving fewer schedules than they ordered, by receiving an inappropriate mix of personal and agricultural schedules, or by receiving schedules in English when their enumerators and county residents were French.[28]

Even in Canada East, where his timelines were more relaxed, Crofton could not execute his own plan. In Canada West the board had no time to ask for population estimates from county commissioners: it simply sent them a shipment of schedules and forms with their notices of appointment. In almost all cases the western commissioners were undersupplied. In the counties of Essex, Frontenac, Kent, Lanark, Norfolk, Prince Edward, and Welland, the commissioners seem to have received no agricultural schedules before census day; while the Lennox commissioner was oversupplied. The Grey commissioner pointed out that three township enumerators had no census schedules until 19 January 1852, that is, 'until 7 days after their labours have commenced.' Whether Crofton was encouraged or dismayed by the additional remark that 'the result however will not be affected by the delay' is unknown.

In many cases the board effectively abdicated its control over the production of census materials and with it the assurance that objects of observation would be defined uniformly. Many western commissioners either arranged for the printing of census schedules locally (in Haldimand, for example) or instructed their enumerators to manufacture their own (as in Middlesex, Perth, and Peterborough). William Elliot, the Lambton commissioner, proposed to use schedules left over in his possession from the 1850 census.[29] Yet even these expedients proved unworkable in some counties, and the suggestion is strong in the fragmentary surviving correspondence that the relations between Crofton's office and the Hincksite Reformers among the commissioners were marred by wilful incompetence or petty vindictiveness on the part of the former. Crofton was likely aware that the government, led by Francis Hincks, was organizing a new statistics agency, and he seems to have been attempting to undermine the work of Hincks's allies. Bureaucratic politics seems to have taken precedence over social scientific observation.

At least this suggestion allows one to make sense of the comedy of errors in which Alexander Knapp for Kent found himself caught up. Knapp telegraphed the board immediately on receiving his commission on 8 January 1852, asking to be provided with information on a number of points he did not understand and to be sent a shipment of agricultural schedules, of which he had received none. There was no response. On 14 January he wrote to Francis Hincks complaining that the board had not replied to him and, among other things, stating that he needed agricultural schedules. Hincks, or someone in his office, contacted Crofton, who responded to Hincks on 24 January, in a letter forwarded to Knapp in Chatham, where it arrived on 4 February.[30] In the interim, Knapp had received an ample supply of agricultural schedules. Now he wrote to Crofton asking for more personal schedules. Crofton's office proceeded to bury Knapp in agricultural census schedules, responding to this first request for more personal schedules, and then to a second, and then to a third, with more agricultural schedules. At the end of Feburary 1852, Knapp finally borrowed a few extra personal schedules from his counterpart in London and got some suitable paper to manufacture more. Interests other than the dispassionate pursuit of social observation seem to have reigned in the Bureau of Registration and Statistics.

There were repeated complaints in the urban press of households not receiving enumeration slips before the census day. The Montreal commissioner, John Jordan, found himself faced with a Mr Dinning, who advertised in the newspaper that he would provide households neglected by Jordan with the necessary forms. The *Gazette* denounced the enumeration as 'another specimen of the bungling, which has marked the career of the present administration.' Similar charges of maldistribution of the census slips were made in the city of Quebec, where the conservative *Journal de Québec* denounced the census commissioner as a 'rouge' appointee, whose work was an instance of 'the worst kind of socialism.'[31]

## The 1852 Enumeration Schedules

The enumeration schedules for 1852 had been simplified, in comparison with those for 1848, although they were physically larger. There were two schedules: a personal/industrial and an agricultural schedule. Each contained fifty rows and was split into two pages of columns that could be folded into book form.

The personal schedule contained forty-one columns and sought to identify people by name, occupation, birthplace (country of origin), religion, age, sex, marital status, and religious affiliation. Those normally residing outside the enumeration district were to be indicated, as were household members who were absent. Enumerators were also to identify any 'persons of colour – negroes' ('personnes de couleur, ou nègres') and 'Indians.' In place of the 'relation to head of household' category contained in the English censuses, which was intended to give a sense of social stratification, the Canadian schedules called for enumerators to identify resident members and nonmembers of the household or family by sex. Columns provided space to identify the deaf, dumb, blind, and 'lunatics or idiots' by sex, as well as those who were attending school. Vital statistics were sought in columns seeking to identify those born in 1851 by sex, as well as those who died in 1851 by age, sex, and cause of death. Enumerators were to identify building types; and in a very wide column they were to enter information concerning industrial establishments: mills, factories, and so on, with the amount of capital investment, the motive force employed, the product, and the number of employees. A final column on the first schedule invited the enumerator to make general observations.

Crofton had not incorporated any textual device on this first schedule to make it possible to reconstruct or verify the work done by the enumerators. The board had no means to check that enumerators had gone systematically from house to house in the countryside, nor in the cities unless they cared to record street addresses.

The agricultural schedule, of which the enumerators particularly complained, contained fifty-six columns. Enumerators were to identify occupants of land by name and location. The size of their farms and areas under cultivation, under crop, in pasture, in gardens or orchards, and in wood or uncultivated were to be given. Next came the area devoted to, and the past year's yield of, particular crops: wheat, barley, rye, peas, oats, buckwheat, corn, potatoes, turnips, forage crops, carrots, mangelwurzel, beans, hops, hay, linen, and tobacco. Then, after recording the past year's production of wool, the enumerator was provided with three blank columns in which to identify other crops, before giving the past year's production of maple sugar and cider. Cloth production was next, with columns for fulled cloth, linen and flannel. This was followed by columns for an inventory of livestock: bulls, oxen, and steers; milk cows, calves, and heifers; horses; sheep; and pigs. The farm's production of butter, cheese, beef, and lard was called for, as was a record of prepared or dried fish. A final column was available for observations. Crofton had learned not to ask for the colony's production of rice, although he had not included columns for poultry and poultry products – an important omission according to some observers.[32]

Metrological uniformity was not established in Canada until the 1870s. Contrasting systems of weights and measures existed in Canada West and Canada East and within different areas of Canada East itself. The absence of uniform standards is an indication of the administrative weakness of the colonial state, and it hampered attempts to centralize knowledge of population and social relations in 1852 and again in 1861. Whether as a response to eastern sectional concerns about cultural imperialism, or simply as a result of translation practices, the English-language and French-language agricultural schedules employed different measures. Acres and arpents for land, bushels and minots for dry measure, and hundredweights (Cwt) and quintals for beef and lard (although the enumerator could choose barrels) were specified. Also, the enumerator could choose to report hay in bundles or tons, but no measure was provided for reporting turnips, carrots, mangel-wurzel, or fish.[33]

The schedules or 'slips' meant to be filled in by urban householders contained forty-three columns for personal information and for information about industrial establishments. This schedule folded in two, but the columns to be completed ran over three of four faces. It ended with a space for the householder's signature on the left, and a notice and stern warning about the obligations of people under the Census Act, signed by Walter Crofton, on the right.

**Enumerators' Instructions**
For the 1852 census, the board provided more detailed instructions for enumerators than it had done in 1848. Enumerators were to begin by ensuring that they knew the limits of their districts and by writing a description of district boundaries and distinguishing features on their first schedules. They were to ensure that they understood all the col-

umns in the schedules and to seek advice from their commissioners when necessary. Instructions as to the manner of completing many of the columns in the schedules followed.[34]

The first column, 'Names of Inmates,' was to include the name of every person who had spent the night of 11 January in the house, including 'strangers' and 'members of the family.' However, it was also to include the names of those who usually resided in the house but were temporarily absent. In the occupations column, the enumerator was to record something for each person; the instructions made no distinction with respect to sex or age except to insist that a son working for a parent be listed as a labourer if the parent was a farmer, and as of the same 'trade or calling' if the parent was engaged in a trade. There was no instruction about multiple occupations, nor was there an occupational catalogue. The instructions concerning place of birth – a source of confusion – read in part, 'you will here note that those born of Canadian Parents are to be marked with an F.'

**Constructing Normally Resident Population**

Crofton's attempt to configure social relations involved a mixed *de facto/ de jure* conception of space that was confusing for enumerators. Every person was to be named, but enumerators also faced the challenging task of connecting people to places and to 'families' without clear criteria for doing so. Having named everyone in column one, in column five, headed 'Residence if Outside of Limits,' enumerators were to name the usual residence, if possible, of a person who merely 'chanced to stay in a house on the night of the 11$^{th}$ of January.' If it were not possible to specify the usual residence of such transients, they were to enter 'UNKNOWN.' In columns seven and eight they were to distinguish those named by sex.

In columns twelve and thirteen, headed 'Residents: Members,' enumerators were to indicate, by sex, 'those who are actually members of the family' who stayed in the house on the relevant night. No definition of 'actually members' was given. In columns fourteen and fifteen, headed 'Residents: Not Members' by sex, enumerators were to identify 'those who stopped in the house on that night, but who are not members of the family, such as travellers, lodgers, clerks, servants, &c..' Then, in columns sixteen and seventeen, 'Members Absent' by sex, they were to indicate 'those being members of the family or usual FIXED residents, who may perchance have been absent on the night of the 11$^{th}$ of January.'

Crofton informed the enumerator that, with this way of designing the

116   The Politics of Population

schedules, 'you can easily check your returns: thus if columns 7 & 8 [sex] and the columns 12, 13, 14, 15, 16 & 17 agree each with the number of names on the sheet, you are correct, thus if the sheet gives 50 names: column 7 being 31 and column 8, 19 – 50.' He provided an example:

| Col. | 12, 14M. | | |
|---|---|---|---|
| | 13, 10F. | Members of the family | 24. |
| | 14, 10M. | | |
| | 15, 7F. | Not members | 17. |
| | 16, 6M. | | |
| | 17, 3F. | Members absent | 9. |
| | | | 50. |

While these instructions may have made it possible for the moderately literate enumerator to have column totals that added up to fifty, they did not establish reliable protocols for distinguishing the 'normal' from the 'transient' population. The 'not members' and the 'residence if outside of limits' categories were not mutually exclusive. Furthermore, no definition of 'absence' was provided. Enumerators were forced to depend on the expectations of informants about who was absent from the household and who had left it permanently. The design of the schedules ensured that some names would appear in more than one place. This was the case because some people would be listed both where they happened to be on the census day and in a place they were entitled to be. Rigorous compilation practices would be required to remove such repetitions.[35]

To column 9, 'Married or Single,' enumerators were to add 'Wr' for widowers and 'W' for widows, although the instructions did not tell them what to put for married or single people. Columns 10 and 11, 'Coloured Persons – Negroes' and 'Indians, if any' were explained as 'You will apprehend by the term "coloured persons," is meant negroes.' This instruction was likely directed at urban enumerators, for the relevant column on the urban slips was headed simply 'Coloured Persons.'

Having completed their inventory of persons, enumerators were to record observations about houses, shops, public buildings, and churches by size and denomination on a second sheet. They were to identify factories by kind and motive power, and note the number of 'hands' usually employed and the capital invested. From whom were they to get such information? What if the enterprise was not attached to a household? Crofton provided no guidance. He did not provide a common numbering system for rows on the first and second pages of the personal schedule, which made it difficult for enumerators to follow their entries from one sheet to the next without laying out the cumbersome schedules end to end. Enumerators were to complete the first schedule by making any general observations they wished to share about their districts, and Crofton hoped that the 'form now adopted will not only save enumerators much trouble, but also render mistakes or inaccuracies easily to be avoided.'

Having completed the personal census schedule, the enumerators would be ready to move on to the agricultural schedule, which was intended 'only for the occupiers of land.' Crofton thought most of the columns to be self-evident. Three columns had been left blank so that enumerators could enter any crop not listed, and they were encouraged to 'pay particular attention' to the crop returns. Here again enumerators had to ensure the correspondence of several column totals. The total amount of land held was to agree with the total land 'cleared' and the total 'wild.' The total land 'cleared' was to correspond with the total 'under crop,' 'under pasture,' and 'under gardens or orchards.' Crofton again gave an example and informed the enumerators that 'the several columns of this return are to be added up previous to their being delivered to the Census Commissioner.' Finally, Crofton instructed the enumerators to return the hay crop in the 'usual method of the Country, whether by bundles or tons,' although they were not instructed to indicate which measure they employed. No comments or instructions dealt with other metrological issues: 'the usual method of the Country' was to apply to other measures. Enumerators were told that their districts had to be enumerated within fourteen days. Crofton stressed that if they compared these schedules with those for past censuses, they would see that the board had attempted to 'lighten as much as possible the labours of the enumerators.' In the cities, householders were to complete the enumeration schedules themselves. The schedules were as complex as those used in the countryside, but urban householders received no instructions of any sort.

**Questions**
There was no field trial for the 1852 census schedules. At best, Crofton was able to communicate with commissioners before the enumeration

began to explain issues of procedure and interpretation. Some questions were quite straightforward. Commissioners asked repeatedly if the enumerators were in fact to be paid for all names or only for the names of heads of households, and if they were to be paid extra for the agricultural schedules. One commissioner wondered how to return schoolhouses that served as places of worship on Sundays, given that there were separate columns for churches and public buildings; another wondered whether schoolhouses under the control of school commissioners in rented buildings were in fact public buildings. The Leinster County commissioner wondered where on the schedules the enumerators were to enter their descriptions of their districts. He had told them to put these on a separate sheet, but asked for Crofton's opinion. The Kamouraska County commissioner sent Crofton a sample finished schedule for comment, although no comments survive.

The commissioners for Montreal, Hamilton, and Quebec were sceptical of the plan to distribute slips for householders to complete before enumeration day. Joseph LeFebvre was categorical on this subject shortly before his death: 'I believe it to be completely useless to leave at the house the *Blanks* meant to be filled in by the residents in the working class neighbourhoods [Fauxbourgs (*sic*)] ... the majority not knowing how to write will not bother to answer the questions which appear on the *Blanks* and this procedure will do nothing but cause delay.' Crofton responded to LeFebvre that the government was determined to proceed, and LeFebvre agreed to follow the plan, although he was right.[36]

**Weak Abstractions**
More serious questions concerned the method of reporting agricultural activity. Crofton provided no definition of an agricultural holding. Thus, for instance, the St-Maurice County commissioner wondered if the small bits of ground around houses in unincorporated villages were to be reported as agricultural holdings, while the Rouville commissioner wondered if small holders [occupants d'emplacements] or only farmers were to be enumerated. The Toronto city commissioner pointed out that there were farms within the city limits, for the enumeration of which he would need agricultural schedules.

A conceptual difficulty surrounded the reporting of the holdings of proprietors of geographically separate parcels of land. Crofton's guiding conception of the 'normal distribution of the population' assumed that land was attached to households, not to proprietors. He did not mobilize an abstract conception of property. How, then, to report property at a distance from the household, especially when some holdings were outside the enumeration district? Crofton was asked this question from both sections of the colony. The Champlain County commissioner had the luxury of inquiring before the enumeration began. He pointed out that his enumerators could either change one of the columns to note holdings outside the district, or they could report only holdings in their districts. He sought a ruling. Louis Grenier for Lotbinière County inquired as to whether 'the Enumerators should enter, in the 1$^{st}$ Column of the Agricultural Census, the name of a man who cultivates several farms, situated in different concessions, as many times as this man owns farms, or should they not rather enter his name once and put in the 4$^{th}$ Column the total *arpents* including all the lands that he owns or cultivates.'

Matthew Howard for Leeds County had to decide what to do about the matter himself because the enumeration date loomed at the moment of his appointment. He explained that he needed more agricultural schedules 'in consequence of a difficulty occurring in columns 2 & 3 of the agricultural sheets in giving the description of two or more lots or parts of lots on the same line in some cases is impracticable, and the only alternative in giving the full description in such cases is to occupy a line for each description, where one person occupies a number of lots or parts of lots.' Howard was 'aware that this will destroy the arrangement of the number of occupants to be inserted on each Sheet but I cannot devise any other method to surmount the difficulty and give a full description.' The difficulty seems again to have stemmed from Crofton's notion of one farm, one owner. No reply to any of these communications survives. I think it improbable that Crofton used correspondence with commissioners and enumerators in the field to attempt to put consistent observational protocols in place. Rather, the communications reveal that the complexity of colonial social relations could be captured only by a level of abstraction and by representational devices not present in Crofton's census grid – or, indeed, in any of the social analysis he authored.

**Multiplying Canadians**

The census's encouragement of overenumeration – that is, the multiple recording of names – was not raised explicitly by commissioners, although some queried Crofton as to whom to count and how to do so. In addition to his questions about proprietors of multiple farms, Louis Grenier for Lotbinière wondered about 'the names of the *members of the family absent* mentioned in the 16$^{th}$ & 17$^{th}$ Columns of the Personal

Census, are they to be written in the 1st Column, or should the Enumerators simply place a dash in one or other of these Columns for each member of the family who will have been found absent from the house on the night of 11th January, without writing at all the name of the person absent?' Henri Caron for Kamouraska asked who was to enumerate colleges, whether students were to be recorded in their families as temporarily absent, and whether any information was to be entered for those born and deceased in 1851. These were key sites for double-counting.

In suggestions for future improvements, Aemelius Irving for Waterloo wrote that it would be 'desirable to have a Column headed for the names of the deceased, their ages and causes of death, instead of at present included in the General list of names.' The enumerators, he claimed, had 'almost invariably misunderstood the Columns' dealing with births and deaths, 'notwithstanding the full instructions as furnished by yourself and my own assistance.' Earlier, Louis Grenier had asked, 'Should the births and deaths be entered in the columns assigned to them without attending to any of the earlier or later columns?' And it seemed clear to Nazaire LaRue for Montmorenci that the names of those who died should not be included in the list of the living.[37] Of course, the name of a dead person included on the schedule with full particulars was worth $.02 to an enumerator, and most made such entries.

Given the ethnic and sectional conflicts of the time, the design flaw most immediately obvious to commissioners in Crofton's 1852 census concerned 'place of birth.' The relevant column was intended to make it possible to estimate the strength of the anglophone and francophone populations. Enumerators were instructed to write 'F' in this column to indicate 'those born of Canadian parents,' but a problem of interpretation arose. For francophones in Canada East at least, 'Canadien' meant quite transparently francophone, and hence 'F' meant 'Français.' But in English translation, 'Canadien' became 'Canadian' and could easily be understood to mean children born in the Canadas, in which case 'F' was senseless. The confusion likely stemmed from Crofton's own high Tory, high church conceptions, whereby the French were Canadians and the English were British, with the role of the census being to show the dominance of the latter over the former.

Charles Robinson, the Brant County commissioner, raised the issue first in a letter to Crofton of 3 January 1852. 'Inform me by return of post,' he wrote, 'if by the Term "Those born of Canadien Parent – to be described. F" is meant French Canadian as some people are of the opinion that is its meaning.'[38] The board issued a new circular of instructions (of which no copy survives) for this column, likely dated 16 January 1852, explaining that the first instruction had aimed at children of French-speaking parentage, and asking commissioners to correct the returns. The enumeration was already well underway before this second circular reached many commissioners, and then some (including Edmund Cox for Drummond) couldn't figure out what was wanted of them. Aemelius Irving for Waterloo replied to the circular on 6 February with the remark that it would cause him delay and that the confusion could easily have been avoided if Crofton had simply indicated at the outset that it was 'those born of French Canadian parents' that he was seeking to identify.

**Commissioners and the Missing Protocols**
In the absence of clear protocols for the completion of many of the census columns, commissioners exercised their own judgment, and party politics reappeared in this matter as well. Several attempted to remedy weaknesses in Crofton's census design by specifying their own protocols. Such practices systematized observations at the county level to some extent, but of course introduced variations among counties. One particularly active commissioner was the Oxford County Hincksite Reformer Thomas S. Shenston, with whom Crofton had a number of sharp exchanges.[39] Shenston was critical of Crofton's work from the outset, complaining on 27 December 1851 that he could not say if the 600 personal and 155 agricultural schedules he got, 'badly done up and with only one sheet of paper,' were enough, because no statement of the townships for which he was responsible was included. When Shenston announced that his enumerators were to include the Baptist preacher and school inspector W.H. Landon and the Rev. W.C. Beardsell, Crofton attempted to have his enumeration plan and his appointments of clergymen disallowed by the Provincial Secretary, A.-N. Morin. It was Landon who had had Lord Elgin as a houseguest during Elgin's 1849 tour of Canada West, and Crofton and his patron William Cayley were said to be scheming against Elgin's colonial policy. Morin refused to disallow the appointments, pointing out that 'there does not appear to be any thing in the Census Act to prevent the appointment of Cleryman [*sic*] as Enumerators.'

It is not clear whether Shenston got wind of Crofton's attempt to undermine him, but his next communication was far from friendly. He wrote on 8 February 1852 to acknowledge the arrival of the circular concerning returns of origins, but pointed out that 'in accordance with my *first* instruction I divided the County into such Enumeration districts "*that the enumerators may be able to make a perfect Census thereof in at most 14 days*". Consequently the sheets are all in and I am unable to require the Enumerators to "*rectify the same*" "before signing the *certificate*."' In any case, Shenston stressed, 'the *certificates* sent are "*oaths*" and the *statute* require[s] "*declarations*" – three very different documents.' Shenston continued that his enumerators had carefully followed their original instructions with respect to the 'place of birth' column but could not give the information with respect to children of francophone parentage. Still, with 'fit assistance,' Shenston was 'working almost night and day' to make a list of persons born in Canada whose parentage wasn't given, which he would send to the various enumerators so that they could collect the necessary information. 'They would of Course expect to receive extra pay' for this labour. Shenston concluded that 'no exertion of mine will be wonten [*sic*] to make the return as perfect as possible but I must be allowed to say that your "Instruction" [*sic*] are any *thing but plain or complete.*'[40]

In the last week of February 1852, Shenston sent Crofton his population abstracts and explained the protocols he had urged on his enumerators. In the absence of any official instructions, Shenston had the enumerators report trades only for those over fourteen years of age and had them attribute to children the religious affiliations of their parents. 'S' was used to indicate a single person in the marital status column. Shenston noted that 'with reference to the "*Agricultural Census*," Column No1,' he had 'instructed the Enumerators to disregard the "Instructions" issued by you + viz: – "in this (Column) you will observe that only the *occupiers of land are to be inserted*", for had these instruction[s] have been followed a great many horses, cows, hogs, & houses would have been omitted.' Moreover, Shenston added, 'with reference to Column No.8, I requested the Enumerators to give the acres occupied as orchards *in addition* to that "*under cultivation*" for in almost every instance the ground – occupied as a[n] orchard is under some kind of crop.' The procedural autonomy enjoyed by commissioners, necessary given the lack of resources and expertise on the part of the central authority and the lack of administrative infrastructure, resulted in the adoption of a variety of observational and reporting protocols for the 1852 census. Commissioners changed the census design better to seize social relations in their localities, perhaps thereby ensuring uniformity within county returns, but also destroying uniformity across them. Further variety was introduced in the work of enumeration.

## The Enumerators at Work

Despite the nominal census day of 12 January 1852, the work of enumeration began at different times in different parts of the colony, and enumerators found themselves faced with districts that varied markedly in physical area, topography, and transportation infrastructure. Many of them lacked adequate supplies of enumeration materials. Some were able to meet with their commissioners and to discuss the enumeration schedules at some length. In some counties, commissioners contacted their enumerators in the field. In others, enumerators were left more or less completely to their own devices. Some enumerators were assigned small districts with which they were well acquainted and whose residents cooperated freely. Others had to cover hundreds of square miles of unknown territory and encountered opposition and resistance. Some enumerators travelled in pairs. Peter Winter, the Gaspé commissioner, 'considered it prudent to send two persons together, as a means of imposing more respect for their Office and thereby to obviate difficulties which I anticipated in obtaining information.' Two of his enumerators were apparently sent by hired schooner in late December to winter on the Magdalen Islands.

Contrasting settlement patterns in parishes, seigneuries, and townships shaped the work of enumeration. The Drummond commissioner Edmund Cox thought 10s. per hundred names would not be enough for enumerators having to deal with the townships, where one found 'the farms dotted about to suit the convenience of the farmer, with no attention to concession lines – the houses generally standing considerably back from the main roads.' This contrasted with 'settlements in places occupied by French Canadians – where each concession line answers for two ranges of lots,' and where the enumerator had simply to travel concession roads to find all the houses.[41]

Enumerators complained of the distances they were compelled to travel. One in Orford township, Sherbrooke County, went more than thirty miles to enumerate a single family. The *notaire* Meunier-Lapierre claimed that in his district, the parish of Ste-Brigide-de-Monnoir, County Rouville, 'about two-thirds of the land is uninhabited – the roads in the different Concessions, numbering about 14 and two Gores almost impassable. Which caused much difficulty and Road to cover for the Census officer in this locality, who was obliged to cover Sixty arpens of dangerous roads ... swamps and lakes before being able to find a few of the households.'

Enumerators appealed for the maximum allowance of 40s. per hundred names when the population in their districts was sparse or widely dispersed. In much of Saguenay County, European settlement had begun only in the late 1830s and winter travel remained particularly arduous. One of the enumerators here appealed to the commissioner to be allowed to do the enumeration in March. Several of the others demanded extra pay, with John McLaren's case ending up before the Executive Council after Crofton reduced his claim for £62.5.1/2, for taking 2,335 names at 40s. per hundred, to £39.18.8. The council awarded McLaren the full amount.[42] Isidore Morin's petition for extra pay was supported by the Saguenay commissioner, Charles Huot, after Crofton reduced his claim for £19.8.9 to £9.14.4. Morin had been assigned six enormous enumeration districts on both sides of the Saguenay River, from present-day Anse-St-Jean to the lumber camps north of Chicoutimi, but managed to collect only 972 names. He had been 'forced to cover parts of these census districts on foot on very rough roads, sometimes through the bush, given the great distances separating inhabited houses in this part of the Saguenay, which took him three times as long to complete his duties.'[43]

The weather was often foul. It slowed the enumeration, further exacerbating administrative difficulties. Interrogations regarding the night of 11 January involved increasingly distant memory work. January was a peculiar choice as census month. Given the official references to the 1852 enumeration as the '1851 census,' it was likely intended to allow the government to claim that it had responded to imperial demands for a common, empire-wide census. January was also seen as the month during which rural people would be 'at home' and at leisure to respond to census queries. As well, travel by road was often easier in the winter than in other seasons. Thus, D.G. Sloane, commissioner for Sherbrooke, waited until the winter roads were open in December before travelling to name enumerators.

Even so, many commissioners reported that the enumerators' work was slowed by inclement weather, and in frontier counties such as Huron and Bruce in the Canada West snow belt, 'the entire absence of roads' made enumeration 'not only a very difficult but a very dangerous duty.'[44] In at least eight counties, commissioners reported that snow retarded the initial enumeration; and many enumerators, like those in Rimouski, travelled on snowshoes. Marcus Child for Stanstead commented on 22 January 1852 that 'the census of this Co is progressing as well as I could expect – under most adverse weather and almost no roads at all – Our's being almost entirely a farming county and lying high it is very much exposed to deep and drifting snows – There is now between three and four feet of snow on the ground.' 'I desire to call your attention to the labour that has been required to complete the enumeration of the above named District at the Sason required,' wrote Levi Adams, the enumerator for part of Edwardsburgh Township in Grenville County, to his commissioner. The enumeration was made difficult 'Owing to the Enclmancy of the Weather and the Stormes of Snow I had to encounter during the time I was performing the afore mentioned work and the extra time required by the inhabitants not being notified and Concequently not prepared to answer the necessary questions required by Law.'[45]

In many parts of the colony, the late arrival of the schedules affected the returns. The enumerator of Orford Township in Kent County noted, for instance, 'Column No 5 ["Residence, if out of limits"] is left blank reason why, the Blanks came so late that it was impossible to come at it at all.'[46] Elsewhere, enumerators inadequately supplied with schedules manufactured their own by ruling paper, or used schedules produced by their commissioners. As commissioners had predicted, even printed schedules were often rendered illegible by the physical conditions under which the enumeration was being conducted. Both circumstances caused enumerators or commissioners to copy initially recorded information onto official printed schedules.

The schedules were difficult for moderately literate men to complete coherently. The commissioner Aemilius Irving argued that for the next enumeration, the schedules should be printed in such a way as to have all the columns dealing with personal information on one sheet. 'Having to turn the Sheet and follow out a number as at present arranged,' he commented, 'requires a great deal of skill and aptitude, more than the class of Persons to whom the remuneration of an Enumerator can tempt into the employment generally possess.' John Star, the enumerator for Buckingham and Portland townships in Ottawa County and, as the Crown Lands agent, a reasonably literate man, acknowledged the presence of 'a discrepancy between the sum totals and the aggregate Colums 12.13.14.15.16. & 17' of his personal schedules. 'This descrepancy amounts to ten persons less in these Colums than the sum totals. It is very difficult,' he pointed out, 'to get all those Colums to agree. But I am certain that it is correct in other respects.' Star had acted out of a sense of public responsibility, but after the enumeration was 'tired of the work for the persons appointed to take the Census in [Buckingham] Township refused and it would have been undone had I not performed it. I had also to take the Census of Portland the person appointed there having also refused.' Star earned £13.1.1 for his trouble.[47]

Part of the problem for the enumerators was that Crofton had not specified clearly and completely the objects to be observed. George G. Brown for Warwick Township in Lambton County pointed out that his agricultural 'colums do not agree as laid down in the instructions as many People do not crop all their cleared land. for instance – 30 acres cleared – 12 ½ under crops. The remainder may be a summer fallow.' In fact, Brown's columns were corrected by someone and the totals made to agree. Also, the agricultural schedules allowed enumerators to choose between different measures of products without requiring them to specify their choices.[48]

Seasonal considerations affected the quality of the returns in two other ways. Many enumerators reported that they could not get reliable accounts of field crops because most producers had not threshed out their harvests. Threshing in turn was retarded by the seasonal employment of men in lumbering. As Crofton's translation clerk summarized the comments of the enumerator for St-Isidore parish in Dorchester County, 'the produce given was much inferior to what he really was – caused by the absence of most the husbands who are employed in the woods & the greatest quantity of the grains being not trashed yet.' In parts of Nicolet and Verchères, enumerators made similar remarks, suggesting that the census would be better taken in March or May or July.

It is possible, of course, that claims that the threshing had not been completed were a device adopted by reluctant informants, although the surviving correspondence has little to say directly about resistance to the enumeration. Elijah Ketcheson for Hastings County reported that his enumerators 'complain of having to go several times to one house very often to get the necessary information and they say the agricultural part is far the most troublesome.' The severe weather combined with 'ignorance and jealousy' of the people slowed the Leeds County enumeration, and in Grenville Township of Deux-Montagnes, 'the enumerator had great difficulties in obtaining informations.' In St-Henry of Dorchester, the enumerator claimed in 'most cases the quantity of produce was not half given & also the number of animals,' a view echoed in Ste-Mélanie-de-Daillebout in Berthier, where the enumerator was said to remark, 'the agricultural produce given is much less than he was really as for the pork he is sure it is a quarter less than it should be.'[49]

Seasonal labour patterns led to the multiple recording of names. The Crown Lands agent, John Star, described at length the lumber camps and mills in his district, pointing out that there were about 420 men working in the woods. For about 170 of them, seasonal workers from outside the county, Star 'could not ascertain their age or religion correctly or whether they were married or single therefore it is not stated in the Rolls. But where my own personal knowledge of those persons gave me an opportunity of knowing their Birthplace and religion I stated it – Those of French Canadian origin I designated Catholics.' Star suggested that these workers 'may with propriety be said to be residents of this place as being young men without fixed habitations, they have been employed here the greater part of them a number of years. They are almost all young single men.' Given the census design, such men could easily have been returned as 'temporarily absent' from another household. Indeed, farmer-teamsters may have worked for more than one lumber camp, creating further occasions for multiple recording. Other enumerators besides Star recorded seasonal workers as permanent residents. For example, the members of a household on the Quebec waterfront who declared themselves to be seasonal workers were recorded as part of the permanent population, as were 138 students attending the Collège de Ste-Anne-de-la-Pocatière in Kamouraska County.[50]

Very few enumerators reported that potential informants refused outright to answer queries. Resistance generally took the form of wilful distortion – something more difficult to identify and attack. The inquiry seems also to have been satirized by some respondents – the clerk of a carriage factory in Hamilton, Canada West, for instance, who listed the names of eighteen men as present on the premises on the night of 11 January 1852, adding 'the aforegoing are the names of the Men who sleep on the premises in comfortable apartments. Reading room, &c. &c.'[51] A rare instance of direct resistance was reported by Amable Nazaire Blouin, enumerator for St-Valier in Bellechasse, who encountered an aboriginal hunting party. He claimed that 'twenty savages men and women of the Huron Tribe are living temporarily at St. Valier to hunt moose – their residence is at Lorette They peremptorily refused to answer the enumerator's questions.'[52] Elsewhere, enumerators either could not or did not trouble to get complete information about aboriginals. The Plympton Township enumerator in Lambton County listed an aboriginal household as 'Old John,' 'Mary,' 'Young John,' 'Eliza,' '2nd Daughter,' and '3rd Daughter.' These people were also described as non-residents but were included in the population totals.[53]

Finally, entries on enumeration schedules varied in keeping with enumerators' senses of efficiency and propriety. At times, entries were shaped by local conflicts over people's self-presentation. The Bellechasse commissioner provided a reading guide to Jean Baptiste Gagné's returns, noting that he used 'mm' and 'nm' to indicate married and single people respectively; that one of his sheets had fifty-one columns and to make sense of them one had to 'follow the hand-written figures without attending to the printed ones'; and, finally, that Gagné returned Genieve Thibaut as a 'widow' because she had 'a natural daughter.'[54] Indeed, one observable consequence of the shift to a nominal enumeration was an attention on the part of enumerators to individuals they perceived to be morally 'out of place.' Thus, Narcisse Mégritte of the parish of St-Remi in Huntingdon thought it worth noting on one of his sheets 'that the children Number 25, 26, 27 and 28 are natural children of whose names I am ignorant.'[55] Mégritte probably knew who had been baptized in his parish. James Shipley, who enumerated Chatham town in Canada West, noted after one entry, 'Father left this Boy in this town about 6 mos. Ago he is left without any friends.'[56] Milo McCargar, the Grenville commissioner, who enumerated a district himself, wondered what to do about Daniel Browne, 'who has given his Profession M.D., and another professional person in this locality has given me notice that he will take proceedings against me if I do not fine Mr. Browne.' [57] Similarly, the enumerator for St-Jean in the city of Quebec annotated Marguerite Kirkham's claim that she was the keeper of a boarding house: 'House of Ilfame [sic] – the Inmates are all Prostitutes.' Her neighbour Luce Rochon's occupational claim met the same fate.[58]

**Urban Enumerators**
Relatively few of the original enumeration slips for incorporated cities and towns survive, with the exception of those for Hamilton, Canada West, about which so much has been written.[59] Still, the surviving urban census field is particularly rich and instructive, given the interpretations of the column headings made by hundreds of self-enumerators. In the absence of any written explanations, the urban self-enumeration reveals that social scientific instruments had penetrated only slightly into popular culture. The colony's urban residents, even the literate ones, were not accustomed to filling in lengthy forms or questionnaires, and some of them seem to have been puzzled by the census schedules. They treated the spaces in the schedules in a variety of ways; some paid little attention to the columns and column headings, while others were exaggeratedly scrupulous in respecting them. A respondent in St-Jean in Quebec, for instance, ignored the columns when it came time to report on his

children, scrawling '5 enfants 3 filsle 2 garson' across the schedule. A Montreal respondent, who seems not to have understood that numbers or other signs entered in the columns would suffice, wrote his answers in the columns but had to break words up into three or four letters to fit them in vertically.[60] Respondents had not mastered the technology of knowledge in use.

In the French-language urban schedules, the 'race' column was headed simply 'Personnes de couleur,' in contrast to 'Personnes de couleur – nègres,' which is what appeared in the rural schedules. Urban householders read this column in a variety of ways. In Quebec, Narcisse Croteau thought he was being asked his hair colour and so wrote 'brown' in the column, while his neighbour, F. L'etourneau, wrote 'blond.' Other respondents entered 'white' or 'white people,' and these entries tended to be made for rows of houses, suggesting some discussion of the schedules. In the column headed 'Married or single,' Mich. Moisan wrote 'yes.' The Toronto commissioner noted that many people understood the column asking for the number of families per building to be asking for the number of people per family.[61]

Such variation made the work of abstraction difficult, but variation was lessened by the fact that most urban respondents did not fill in the schedules themselves. Enumerators in all urban areas were compelled to complete and correct householders' returns for those many who were unable or unwilling to do so. Victor Regnaud, the enumerator for part of St-Laurent ward in Montreal, has left a rare account of the work involved. 'I take pleasure,' he wrote, 'in doing Justice to the good will of almost all the inhabitants of this neighbourhood who made a point of giving me an answer to all the questions I addressed to them. A very small number of the Schedules were ready when I arrived at the houses to collect them; also I had to lose considerable time in filling them in myself, or correcting them.' In fact, Regnaud had more difficulty with those whose schedules were incorrectly filled in because his corrections 'touched the pride of those Individuals who claimed to have well and duly completed them.'[62]

On 14 March 1852, a committee of the Executive Council decided to award extra pay to the Quebec city enumerators, 'allowing, for the whole population, at the rate of 10% per hundred, inconsequence of the enumerators being compelled, in a great majority of cases, to fill up the schedules which the Law required the Occupants to fill. The attempt to enforce this, besides proving ineffectual, would have created difficulties in other respects, and the Committee have the less difficulty in recommending the allowance, as the course adopted appears to have resulted in obtaining an efficient Census.'[63] As the Quebec commissioner had anticipated, many urban householders had been unable or unwilling to give the kind of account of themselves sought by the Board of Registration and Statistics.

### Commissioners Make the Returns 'Clean' and 'Uniform'

Crofton's circular of 16 January 1852 instructed commissioners to prepare abstracts of their returns before binding the manuscript schedules and shipping them to the board. Commissioners were also 'to rectify' the returns of places of birth so that 'F' in this column referred to francophones; to remove 'errors' in the returns; and to ensure that they were as complete and correct as possible. In the course of this activity, commissioners often reworked the materials provided by enumerators, or caused the latter to seek additional information, in order to make the returns complete and uniform.

One immediate task faced by many commissioners was to have the enumeration results copied onto clean, printed schedules. Few homemade and hand-ruled schedules survive as part of the current 'manuscript' census field for 1852 (or 1861). It is clear that many enumerators used such schedules and that others copied material from dirty printed schedules onto clean ones. It is impossible to determine how closely homemade schedules replicated the columns of the printed ones. The Frontenac County commissioner reported that he had instructed his enumerators to 'head and rule sheets similar to those furnished' by Crofton, but just how similar they were is unclear.[64]

Sometimes the copying was done in the presence of the commissioner, as in Peterborough County. In Middlesex County, where the commissioner found that 'some of the Enumerators are not the best' and that several of them 'used other paper to complete their returns,' the enumerators were simply told 'to copy these, so as to present a uniform return.' Elsewhere, well after the enumeration period, commissioners were seeking extra supplies of schedules in order to correct and recopy materials submitted by enumerators. Edmund Cox ordered additional supplies on 6 February because 'the Census is completed but filled in on papers not furnished to [the enumerators].' Cox apparently had himself to go and enumerate four households in Acton Township missed by the enumerators. William McDonald for Victoria ordered extra schedules on 27 February so that he could correct erroneous returns, and John Heath for Rimouski returned some schedules with errors to the enumerators for correction during the first week of March.

It is thus clear that the uniformly clean and regular character of many of the existing 'manuscript' 1852 returns, which has given some researchers confidence in the 'accuracy' of the enumeration, is in many cases at least the result of local and unregulated editorial work done after its completion. Editorial and recording conventions, which aimed explicitly at 'uniformity' in the returns, but which are inaccessible to scrutiny, intervened in many cases between household enumeration and official reporting. The commissioners were often quite diligent in their attempts to ensure that the schedules were free of errors and that the picture presented of their districts was clear and coherent. That being said, many of them regarded the agricultural returns with scepticism, maintaining that farmers underestimated yields and livestock for fear of taxation, and noting that the schedules did not report on such local products as ashes, pine logs, poultry and eggs, hides, and, in maritime regions, fish and seal oil.[65] Several of them attempted to remedy these defects in their own discursive accounts.

Barthélémy Pouliot for Bellechasse was particularly diligent in attempting to complete the returns of vital events. He sent a circular letter to the clergy asking for a summary of births, marriages, and deaths from the parish registers and also sought an account of the priests' incomes from both the tithe and fees. He contemplated legal action against recalcitrant priests, although Crofton warned him that his power to demand information did not extend this far.[66] Several commissioners consulted Crofton about how to finish the enumerators' schedules. The religious returns were especially problematic because of tensions resulting from informants' claims to affiliation, the absence of an inventory of denominations, and the prejudices of enumerators. Dennis Moynahan for Essex County sought the board's advice about one of his enumerators, a Mr King of Gosfield Township, who refused to attribute a religious affiliation to children under the age of ten. King claimed that people in his district chose their own denomination on reaching 'the age of discretion.' Households were frequently composed of members of a variety of denominations, but 'children under ten years of age, were not possessed of sufficient reason to choose for themselves.' Moynahan had told all his enumerators to list children as the same denomination as their parents, but King refused to change his schedules. Crofton advised Moynahan not to change the original entries, but to add a note explaining the absence of denominations and then to give a summary 'so many families Ch: of Eng; with – children.' It was difficult for commissioners to abstract the enumerators' returns of denominational affiliation, in the absence of an enumeration catalogue to begin with (Aemilius Irving for Waterloo

County urged the creation of one for the next enumeration), but the children of Gosford acquired an affiliation through Moynahan's post-enumeration work.[67]

Some commissioners, like Thomas Shenston for Oxford County, remedied what they considered defective reporting protocols by providing enumerators with their own instructions. Shenston used these protocols in producing his census abstracts. Other commissioners either acted similarly or pointed out what they considered inaccuracies in the returns. While Shenston had caused the enumerators to record 'orchards' in both the 'orchard' and the 'land under crop' categories (thereby multiplying the amount of cultivated land in his county), Aemilius Irving pointed out that by using Crofton's land categories in his abstract he would produce 'discrepancies.' Such 'discrepancies' were increased by confusion on the part of enumerators about the recording of fallow land, although Irving did not identify how he had addressed them.

Edmund Cox also corrected what he considered to be illegitimate reporting in the agricultural schedules for Upton Township. He noted, 'from the number of occupiers of land in this Township is deducted 175 Names holding 12,611 Acres as they are non-residents. The quantity of land opposite their Names being taken up by their parents or themselves with the ultimate purpose of settlement but which may not be made for several years: the settlers in Upton generally coming from the adjoining [divisions?].'[68] As the central government attempted to locate people through census practice, those enumerated attempted to use the census to lay claim to locations.

Finally, Crofton's instruction to generate an abstract of census returns by adding up the various census columns before forwarding the schedules to the board seemed confusing, useless, and in any case impossible to the remarkably literal-minded Montmorenci commissioner Nazaire Larue. His confusion is instructive:

> I don't think it can be necessary, or even possible to add up Columns 2.3.6.9, for in column 2 [Profession etc] are to be found different conditions – in column 3 – different places of birth – as for column 6 [age at next birthday] – I don't see what the use could be of such a total – as for column 30 the age and cause of death is called for? and their names I don't see where to put them. – I forgot the 9$^{th}$ column, the married being mixed in with the unmarried, one cannot add them together either, without making a Separate summary for each condition or trade, for each birth place &c – As for the column 31 [types of construction] its the same thing – 32

[number of stories] ditto— As for the Census of Agriculture, I do not see either that it would be useful to add up columns 2-3 [concession and lot].'

Larue could not easily distinguish those areas within the domain of social scientific knowledge where new entities could be created by aggregation from those areas where this was not possible. After the cognitive-political transformations worked by official statistics, through which practical equivalences have been established among certain classes of objects and conditions, his lack of perceptiveness seems quaint. On the one hand, of course, he was obviously correct: adding up lot numbers or people's ages would yield a number that did not signify (lot 600 when there were only 22 in a township; age 8,000, which even Methuselah did not reach). On the other hand, he had not learned a lesson most contemporary citizens have: adding up abstractly equivalent entities creates new orders of existence; adding up abstractly equivalent bodies makes a population.

The first census abstracts reached the Board of Registration and Statistics on 14 February 1852, and most commissioners had completed the abstracts of their districts by early March. They shipped the schedules to Quebec, along with their own reports on the conduct of the enumeration and on conditions in their jurisdictions, and submitted their accounts, at times arguing for extra pay for particular enumerators. (Most census enumerators did not see their pay until at least six months after the enumeration day.) It was from the commissioners that initial publication of census results came. The official compilation of the census returns went forward after commissioners' and enumerators' results had begun to appear in the press. This work was carried out in the midst of a politically charged reorganization of the colonial statistical apparatus, which is the focus of the following chapter.

# Chapter 4

# Calculating Canada in the 1850s

Walter Crofton's hold on the position of government statistician was increasingly tenuous even as his preparations for the 1852 enumeration were underway. His neglect of the Blue Book and his high Tory politics had alienated the governor. The Reform government led by Francis Hincks organized a second statistical agency. As the compilation of census returns began, Crofton was forced to share space with the new agency and, worse, found his work placed under the supervision of Malcolm Cameron, one of the very Reformers whom Crofton had attacked in print in the previous decade. Crofton's performance was criticized in Parliament. In the spring of 1853 he lost his secretaryship to William Hutton (1801–61), a cousin of Francis Hincks, and with it control over the final compilation and publication of census results.[1]

The publication of the official census returns provoked a major political crisis in the colony, forcing francophone intellectuals to refashion their conceptions of ethnic-religious destiny. The results fuelled sectional rivalries in the 1850s, as an insurgent, fundamentalist Catholic church contested the extension of the secular powers of the developing colonial state system and as Liberals agitated for representation by population. The production of statistical knowledge acquired a heightened importance as colonization and settlement schemes figured more heavily in colonial finance and as a new government statistics office promised to investigate an array of colonial conditions. Still, useful statistical intelligence proved to be quite elusive, outside the intensely administered domains of the school and jail. The census scheduled for 1861 came to be anticipated as the means for grasping many dimensions of colonial social relations that seemed otherwise to be inaccessible.

Although tables giving returns of population by origin and religious affiliation, and returns of farm sizes and yields, were presented to Parliament in October 1852,[2] the two official reports of the Board of Registration and Statistics on the 1852 census were delivered only in August of 1853 and 1854 respectively. The curious situation was that constructions of the nature and meaning of population had social and political consequences well before the official compilation of census returns was complete. The fashioning of official representations out of the piles of census schedules delivered to the board took place in the face of competing representations in the press and other media. The law would have permitted Crofton to instruct commissioners to ship their returns directly to the board and to reveal nothing about them. Such was the English practice, which the Canadians had been urged to adopt. Instead, the Canadian commissioners made up the regional returns and published their own reports as soon as they were forwarded to the board. Before the official census compilation was fairly underway, the commissioners' census results had been widely publicized.

There was occasional local controversy about the quality of commissioners' reports, but generally a booster ish spirit prevailed in the press and no one suggested that the commissioners' returns might be inflated. Yet despite some correspondence with the Board of Registration and Statistics about whom to count, commissioners seem to have reported the number of names on the enumeration schedules as the populations of their districts. The Queteletian practice of carefully separating transient from permanently settled inhabitants, again urged on the Canadians, was ignored. Newspaper editors trumpeted the rate of population growth in various counties as the returns came in, emphasizing that it far outstripped that of the United States. Speculation was rife about the relative population balance between the two sections of the colony.[3]

The commissioners' census reports contained both literary and numerical statistics and are of considerable interest for social historians. Newspaper readers were exposed to descriptive accounts of topographical, geological, social, cultural, and economic conditions in various counties, as well as to discussions about the progress of the enumeration itself. Commissioners described 'how things were' in their counties in terms of economic infrastructure, agricultural production, education, crime, and state institutions. They outlined 'what needed to be done' to improve things and how improvements should be undertaken. Readers could learn about the useful effects of agricultural societies, the disastrous forestry practice of clear-cutting, and the menace faced by youth through the foul trade in immoral publications across the American frontier into rural Canada East. The reports provided occasions for government appointees to exercise leadership and gave definition to component parts of the colonial territory. Yet they were also haphazard, directed by no coherent governmental project, and prone to the idiosyncratic interests of the commissioners themselves. They provided no overview of 'the nation,' and they did not configure social relations throughout the colonial territory as 'population.'

**The Political Scale**

The commissioners' reports addressed the contentious issue of sectional population totals and propelled debate about political representation before the Board of Registration and Statistics could act. Even before the official compilation was presented to Parliament, Thomas Shenston had given the western results in his *Oxford Gazeteer*,[4] and such early reports created intense interest in the official return. On 7 July 1852, the editor of *Le Canadien* denounced his 'annexationist and republican counterparts in Montreal' who were claiming, 'on who knows what authority,' that the census results showed a net superiority for Canada East of 200,000 people. The editor announced that the official results were about to be published and that they would show, sadly, only 15,000 in favour of the east.[5] He returned to the charge two days later, urging his readers to resist the 'senseless and suicidal polemic' being made in support of representation by population. A table was given now showing a western population of 940,903 and an eastern population of only 904,782.

The editor of *La Minerve* similarly denounced claims made by the liberal *rouge* party of eastern population superiority and reprinted a table from the Toronto *Leader* presenting the returns as 946,425 west and 912,545 east, with a second table from the *Globe* giving the western total as 950,530. The same day, 21 July 1852, *Le Canadien* gave the *Globe* table in full and reported that Canada West's population had grown by 69 per cent from 1844 to 1852, from 560,000 to 950,530, and Canada East's by 31 per cent in the same period, from 690,772 to 904,782, although both 1852 figures contained estimates from some places.[6] The official confirmation that the western section had outstripped the eastern came in a mid-October report from the Board of Registration and Statistics. The official totals were now 952,004 west and 890,261 east, facts of population accepted as such by most commentators in the east and institutionalized in subsequent legislation, commentary, and social research.[7]

## Scrambling for Identity

These facts of population had a dramatic impact on Canadian political debate and on the collective representations fashioned by anglophone and francophone intellectuals. They provoked a crisis of hegemony that fuelled new conceptions of cultural worth, ethnic-cultural and ethnic-religious destinies, agricultural development and innovation, immigration, popular education and, of course, the system of political representation. Residents of the western section could now pride themselves on the 'go ahead' character of their society, and xenophobic intellectuals found ammunition for attacks on francophone legal institutions, national character, and religious beliefs.

The demand for representation by population was dropped immediately by most of its political supporters in the east, although it would reappear. The demand had been a key element in left-liberal visions of a secular, democratic Canada East, tied to agrarian radicalism. The cultural crisis provoked by the census results and the discrediting of the demand by French-Canadian liberals for representation by population made it easier for conservatives and religious fundamentalists to assert leadership over the destiny of francophones. Conceptions of French cultural superiority, often closely tied to struggles by an oppressed majority against the political dominance of an English minority, had now to be refashioned. Calls for democratic representation smelled of cultural treason.

In the 1850s, a generation of francophone intellectuals and state servants, men who had come of age in the insurrectionary period and who had contested anglophone political dominance in the 1840s, embarked on a wide-ranging project for the solidification of a *canadien* identity. Important among them were Joseph-Charles Taché, who would organize the census of 1871, and Pierre-Joseph-Olivier Chauveau, later Chief Superintendent of Education East and first premier of the Province of Quebec. Both these men were heavily involved in projects for the creation of a *canadien* social imaginary in history, literature, and culture. Their attempts at cultural politics encouraged alternative readings of the census facts.

Both men took up and extended a cultural mythology already appearing in the press in the summer of 1852 about the remarkably prolific character of the French population in North America.[8] In a lengthy note appended to his early novel *Charles Guérin*, Chauveau claimed that in 1755 the population of New France, Acadia, and Louisiana together was about 80,000, with at most 60,000 in New France. The British Conquest of 1759 provoked a massive outmigration. The cholera of 1832 killed off thousands, and thousands more fled the 'troubles' of 1837. Agricultural misery drove many more French Canadians out of the colony in the 1840s – as many as 20,000 a year. Despite these facts, the census of 1852 gave the French population of the Canadas as 695,949.

This population was the result of natural increase, not of the 'artificial stimulus' of immigration. The census returns listed only 1,366 people as born in France or Belgium, even though since 1829, 735,305 immigrants had landed at Quebec and Montreal. Moreover, the French population of Louisiana was about 160,000, and the northeastern United States contained, conservatively, another 100,000, and about 40,000 more were in eastern British North America. 'From all of this one may conclude with complete confidence,' Chauveau observed, 'that the descendants of the 80,000 French presently compose one million people.' This population had doubled in each period of about twenty-four years, more rapidly than the political economists claimed was the maximum possible for any population! Chauveau drew the lesson that

> the fact of the extraordinary growth of our population, the numerous social reforms which have been introduced among us in recent years, the development of the colonization of the wilderness by men of our race, our slow but sure progress in commerce, industry, and literature, the nationalist reaction which has taken place since the *Union*, despite the *Union* and rather because of the *Union*, the progressive entry of a large number of our fellow countrymen into functions of government, ought to prevent despair today on the part of those who did not despair in the worst days of our history.[9]

The meaning of the census was clear: French Canadians should remain true to their religion and culture while making political union with Canada West into a stimulus for improvement.

Joseph-Charles Taché made the same argument repeatedly, especially in the pages of *Le Courrier du Canada*, the ultramontane newspaper he edited at the invitation of Bishop Bourget of Montreal in the later 1850s. 'The French race is the one which increases the most by the natural route of the excess of births over deaths,' he stated on one occasion, stressing 'the vital force of this element whose growth, in itself, is truly a phenomenon.' Two things were evident to Taché from his analysis of the 1852 census returns: first, 'the Catholic element will always be one of the most powerful elements everywhere in these beautiful provinces; the second is that the French race is established here in such a way as never to be dislodged.' Taché, like Chauveau and others, saw the Union of the Canadas as a source of progress for French Canadians. He claimed that the 'separate but harmonious' existence of the 'nations' promoted the material and intellectual development of both, and that in fact it was the French population that was 'the civilizing element *par excellence* in this America still so little civilized, despite its pretensions.'[10]

In counterpoint to this argument, some Protestant anglophone intellectuals claimed that the census demonstrated the cultural, moral, religious, and economic superiority of the British over the French. According to this analysis, religious superstition and archaic legal institutions in Canada East kept the mass of the French-Canadian population in poverty and ignorant thraldom to a scheming priesthood. Representation by population, so that Canada West could claim the leadership role it merited, and the strict separation of church and state, were urgently demanded. MPPs squared off along these lines repeatedly in the 1850s.[11]

Yet successive coalition governments in the 1850s and 1860s opposed representation by population. The opposition parties could not muster the two-thirds majority necessary to change the representation provisions in the Act of Union. Most members for Canada East were not about to relinquish the increased political weight they had acquired through the principle of equal sectoral representation, and party divisions were such that no government could do without a substantial block of supporters from the eastern section. Parliament did accept Morin's 1853 Representation Act (16 Vic. c.CLXII), which increased the number of seats from each section to sixty-five from forty-two. However, as John Garner has shown, the act did nothing to apportion representation to population within the two sections. In 1861, for instance, the 80,000 people in Grey-Bruce elected the same number of representatives as did 4,100 in Brockville and 4,500 in Niagara.[12]

### Reorganization of the Statistical Apparatus

The compilation of census returns and perhaps the execution of the 1852 census itself were affected by the Reform government's reorganization of the statistical apparatus. Plans for a new statistics agency were underway in the fall of 1851, and Crofton likely heard of them from his Tory patrons. His snippy and obstructionist communications with the Hincksite Reformers among the census commissioners may well have resulted from the threat to his position. It may also explain his distribution of a detailed questionnaire about agricultural conditions to commissioners and other observers in late 1851 and early 1852.[13] The questionnaire replicated parts of the agricultural census, with supplementary questions about wages of labour and agricultural societies. Some respondents found it peculiar that they were required to question farmers again about matters that had been on the census and thought it would be difficult to secure cooperation. Similar questionnaires were distributed from 1853 by the new statistics agency, the Bureau of Agriculture.[14]

This bureau was a by-product of Francis Hincks's efforts to form a new ministry in the summer and fall of 1851 and of his financial policy. Hincks courted members of the dissident Reform Clear Grit faction who had broken with the government in 1849 over its failure to pursue what they saw as the substance of political reform. When the Hincks-Morin ministry, formed initially in October 1851, met Parliament in August 1852, it included two of the faction's leading members: John Rolph as Commissioner of Crown Lands, and Malcolm Cameron as President of the Committees of Council and Minister of Agriculture.[15]

Cameron, a successful timber and land dealer, and lumber manufacturer, and the Assistant Commissioner of Crown Lands in the second Baldwin-Lafontaine ministry, had broken with the moderate wing of the Reform Party in December 1849. While no annexationist, he had allied himself with the Clear Grit faction, supporting Caleb Hopkins in the election of 1850 against the ministerial candidate and participating in the Toronto Anti-Clergy Reserves agitation. He seconded the Clear Grit call for cheap government, with a cabinet of no more than six ministers, and for the abolition of what was denounced as the useless and expensive office of President of the Executive Council, the cabinet business manager. Cameron's acceptance of this very office in the Hincks-Morin government was a matter of controversy. The creation of a Bureau of Agriculture, with the President of Council as Minister of Agriculture, was seen at the time as the condition demanded by Cameron for accepting office, and was roundly denounced by ministerial opponents, from George Brown to John A. Macdonald, as a political job – a view repeated by most historians. This view has meant that the bureau's history has yet to be investigated seriously.[16]

Dismissing the bureau as an organ whose interest is exhausted once its partisan origins are revealed is not an adequate treatment. For Francis Hincks, the architect of the colonial financial policy, an agency to create and diffuse knowledge of agricultural conditions, to encourage innovation, and to promote colonization and settlement had an importance well beyond the slender opportunities it created for the distribution of patronage. As Michael Piva has shown, Hincks's attempt to deal with the public debt and to encourage investment centred on capitalizing the Crown Lands. The success of a policy aimed at borrowing against public land depended heavily on revenue from the sale and rental of this land to new colonists: such people would have to be attracted to the colony, directed toward the appropriate settlement areas, instructed in agricultural practice, and exposed to technical innovations. Attracting colonists also meant making Canada look like a more appealing destination than its competitors, Ohio and Australia particularly; and in the 1850s numerical arguments sustained claims about the relative promise of different destinations. The task was the more daunting since the imposition of a heavy immigrant head tax in the wake of the Irish famine immigration had redirected part of the Canadian immigration stream to the United States. The Bureau of Agriculture would use statistical production as an adjunct to the colonization effort. The census results of 1852 were interpreted in part in light of their promise for this political-economic project, and the bureau's control over the enumeration of 1861 would tie that census as well to the interest in advertising the colony's resources. The leading, but not the sole, project of government guiding the imaginary of population came to be an advertising project in which disciplined social observation did not necessarily play a leading role.[17]

Furthermore, although the creation of the bureau was a condition for Malcolm Cameron's entry into the governing coalition, it was continuous with his own political projects, for he had actively promoted the extension and bureaucratization of the state system in the 1840s. In an extensive report to the legislature on the management of the customs in 1843, he had urged that the competitive, market-driven, and venal system be replaced by rational bureaucratic management.[18] Even his most notable championing of the 'Scotch democracy' characteristic of his native Lanark county – the abortive School Act of 1849 – involved plans for collecting and centralizing knowledge in standard forms, and for diffusing 'improvement' from a central authority.[19] As his systematic promotion of the cause of temperance and his efforts to enact a version of the Maine Temperance Law for Canada show, Cameron found it entirely legitimate for the capacities of state to be used in moral regulation.[20] Finally, for all his sporadic flirtations with populist democracy, Cameron, like other members of the faction, would vote against several key Clear Grit planks in order to keep the Hincks-Morin coalition in office.

The projects pursued by the Bureau of Agriculture were entirely consistent both with those that had engaged Cameron in the past and with those of the 'agricultural interest' that the bureau would speak for, encourage, and help to define. The creation of the bureau not only shifted control over the colonial statistical apparatus into Reform hands but also shaped Canadian statistical practice in the longer term by tying it to concerns with agricultural development. A focus on vital statistics and public health, or crime and insanity, for instance, could have produced quite a different statistical apparatus and practice.

The Hincks-Morin ministry met Parliament in August 1852 and announced its project for an agricultural bureau 'for obtaining correct statistical information respecting the productions of the country, and for diffusing knowledge which may be serviceable both to those engaged in Agriculture and to persons proposing to become settlers.'[21] Hincks justified the new bureau on the grounds of popular demand for a specialized Minister of Agriculture, and because 'the Ministers comprising the Board of Statistics were so occupied with the duties of other departments, that they were unable to devote the necessary attention to that important subject.'[22] The Minister of Agriculture would now supervise Registration and Statistics.

Even though the project was announced publicly only in late August, and legislation passed only in mid-November 1852, the Bureau of Agriculture was launched in the midst of the census compilation. Indeed, the scheme had been floated in an Executive Council memorandum of 15 December 1851, and Cameron received formal cabinet permission to hire personnel and purchase supplies on 10 May 1852.[23] The bureau's first clerk, W.R. Wright, received a quarter's salary on 30 June 1852, and a messenger was also hired, while an account was opened with the Postmaster General on 2 July. William Hutton, future secretary to the bureau, claimed that the management of the office had been offered to him as early as 3 October.[24]

Cameron had worked to enlist the support of the existing agricultural associations before presenting his bill. He wrote to P.E. Leclaire, president of the Lower Canada Agricultural Society, seeking approval of the clauses in the 1851 Agricultural Societies Act (14 & 15 Vic. c.CXXVII), which had created a Board of Agriculture for Upper Canada, and announcing the establishment of his own office. Here the bureau was said to be intended to act 'to condense and arrange for practical use all the Statistics of Agriculture, to attend to the Agrcl. interest ... and to aid by every possible means its full development.' A subtext was the necessity for the creation of a parallel Board of Agriculture for Lower Canada, and

Cameron claimed that he wanted 'such an organization of the Agricultural Societies of Canada as will enable me to correspond with one central Association in each section of the Province which shall be in instant communication with every part of that section and prepared and authorized to make such recommendations to this Office as may seem best on behalf of the Agricl. interest.'[25] Cameron through this project was seeking administrative control over a new network of central-local relations for statistical production; he had also presented his proposal to a public meeting in Toronto's St Lawrence Hall, with the president of the Upper Canada Board of Agriculture in the chair, well before the meeting of Parliament. As the man in question, Tory MPP T.C. Street, later observed in the Assembly, the board supported the project in principle, although it objected to specific clauses in the bill.

**Dangerous to Liberty**
While several MPPs protested the fact of the bureau's existence before any bill to create it had been submitted, the idea of a special government agriculture office received broad, non-partisan support. True, W.H. Merritt and George Brown warned that an agricultural bureaucracy would destroy farmers' self-initiative, but most MPPs agreed that a governmental instrument was needed to promote improved agricultural practice, immigration, and settlement, even if they differed over the means to this end. The draft bill had included a clause making the Minister of Agriculture president *ex officio* of the Boards of Agriculture, and permitting cabinet to name the boards' vice presidents. The Board of Agriculture for Upper Canada strongly opposed the clause as one that destroyed its independence from the government, and it was withdrawn before second reading.

The bill's centralized information-gathering clauses had a rougher ride. They replaced the Inspector General as chair of Registration and Statistics with the Minister of Agriculture and gave the latter management of the census and of the preparation of statistical returns. Patents of invention, formerly directed to the Provincial Secretary, now came also to the Minister of Agriculture. Moreover, all public institutions and public officers in the colony were required to respond promptly and diligently to requests for information from the bureau. So far so good. However, officers of bodies that failed to respond to the minister's demands for information would be dismissed by an order-in-council and new officers would be named to them by cabinet. 'Was there ever anything so monstrous?' demanded Harmanus Smith of Frontenac. 'An attack on the liberty of the subject!' exclaimed J.-E. Turcotte, and Joseph Cauchon went further, warning that 'if it became law,' the bill 'would be a powerful engine of tyranny and oppression in the hands of the government.'[26] The clause was modified to substitute a fine for the power of cabinet to dissolve public bodies, but debate continued over the purposes to be served by official information-gathering.

Supporters of the bill argued that farmers and agricultural societies wanted an authoritative government office to which to appeal for information about agricultural improvement and about the progress of agriculture more generally, although several members did not consider this to be a matter of 'statistics' and saw no reason for connecting an agricultural information bureau with a statistical office (or, more likely, with *the* statistics office – a political rather than an epistemological objection). Walter Crofton's name figured in the debate, and his days were clearly numbered if Statistics joined Agriculture. Such a fate for him caused William Lyon Mackenzie little alarm: as far as he was concerned, Crofton did little work, was tardy in delivering his Blue Book, and needed the Inspector General to 'call in upon him and stir him up.' In contrast, the Tory Edmund Murney, who opposed the bill, argued that no new government statistical department was needed, and 'if Mr. Crofton's office required to be made more efficient, another clerk might be added to it.' Some other members supported the principle of a bureau of agriculture but argued that it should be (in W.H. Boulton's words) 'unconnected with statistics' (i.e., the Bureau of Registration and Statistics).[27]

Malcolm Cameron's defence of the bill stressed the publicity dimension of the bureau's statistical capacities. He claimed that 'the importance of conjoining the office of President of the Board of Statistics with the office of Minister of Agriculture became apparent, from the fact that the supply of labour in this country is so unequal to the demand, in consequence of the emigration from it of the young men, that it has become necessary to spread statistical information through the countries of Europe, for the purpose of inducing immigration.' The necessity for action was clear, for 'if some measure of this kind is not adopted, it will soon be impossible for the small farmers to hire labour, from the rapid increase in the rate of wages.' The amended bill passed the House by a vote of 28 to 9.[28]

No other Canadian law contained an information-gathering provision resembling that contained in the Bureau of Agriculture Act. Under the Census Act, people could be fined for wilfully refusing to answer census queries, and various statutes contained reporting provisions with fines for non-compliance. But such penalties were directed toward specific and narrow inquiries. The Bureau of Agriculture Act imposed a fine for refusal to answer any queries 'relating to the Agricultural interests, or the Statistics of this Province' posed by either the minister or his authorized deputy, yet it did not define either 'interests' or 'statistics.' How useful these powers proved to be in practice is, of course, another matter. More practically, the passage of the act extended the central government's knowledge-generating capacity, and Cameron's position as minister meant this capacity was in Clear Grit hands. The compilation of the 1852 census results was still underway.

**William Hutton, Secretary**
Walter Crofton lost the secretaryship of Registration and Statistics to William Hutton officially on 1 April 1853. Hutton was the youngest son of an Irish cleric and had been apprenticed out to a farmer after a grammar school education. Married, with three children and a fourth on the way, he came to the Canadas in the early 1830s, with borrowed money to buy a farm. He first visited the Peterborough area, where he was shocked by the whisky-drinking immorality of the settlers; soon after, he bought a large farm near Belleville in Hastings County, Canada West, sent for his wife and children, and set about applying rational English methods of land cultivation.

Hutton's practices included mixed farming, regular manuring, and crop rotation. Through the toil of all family members as well as some hired help (including fugitive slaves), Hutton's household was quickly rich in kind. It remained poor in cash. He cast about for money-making activities to supplement the farm income: he taught school, acted as district warden and then council clerk, and served as Superintendent of Schools under the School Acts of 1843 and 1846. When none of these activities earned him enough to pay off his debts, he approached his cousin, Francis Hincks, for government employment. His son, Joseph, had already secured a well-paid government position with Hincks's help, and there was talk of Hutton's daughter Mary going to live in the Hincks household. In the later 1840s, Hincks found Hutton work as an inspector of agencies and arbitrator for the Board of Works.

Hutton was a moderate Reformer in party politics and a Unitarian in religion, a unilingual anglophone but no francophobe. Not an active proselytist, he regarded Catholicism as pompous superstition and intellectual subordination; but he was also convinced that liberal freedom would lead to Catholic conversion.[29] John Ross, the Belleville Reform leader, thought Hutton's political commitments in the 1840s too lukewarm to merit an important government position. Matters improved for Hutton in the early 1850s when he became connected to Ross by marriage.

Hutton was especially eager to get the position of secretary to the Bureau of Agriculture. He had been writing pamphlets and essays on agricultural improvement, two of which attracted considerable attention at a strategic moment. His 'Agriculture and its Advantages as a Pursuit' won a gold medal at the 1851 Exhibition of the Canada West Provincial Agricultural Association, and in June 1852 his 'Report on the State of Agriculture in the County of Hastings' won the essay prize sponsored by the Upper Canada Board of Agriculture. Both were published in the *Canadian Agriculturalist*, the first in January 1852. Clearly and cleverly written, the essay on agriculture as a pursuit summarized the reigning wisdom on agricultural improvement. Farmers had the power to govern the incredible capacities of nature if they would proceed rationally. This meant they should employ a crop rotation, use animal and green manure, plough dry and deep, sow thick, give shelter to and produce winter fodder for their animals, and not waste their money on tile drainage. As a pursuit, farming was more secure than commerce or manufacturing and surrounded with fewer anxieties. Farmers' way of life gave them a spirit of independence, but they could profit from practical education, the moreso as they had the effective management of local government. Their pursuit was society's most healthful and had the added advantage of giving them ample opportunity to contemplate God's glories in Nature.

Hutton's other prize essay was a statistical work of much the same kind as those produced in the 1840s by Walter Crofton. It contained a descriptive inventory of the County of Hastings and reproduced numerical information about productive activities drawn from the assessors' returns, the 1848 census, and, perhaps, the Belleville Collector of Customs. The work differed from others in the genre in one important particular: Hutton, the scientific farmer, provided a cost comparison for the production of wheat and potatoes, arguing that for wheat 'the farmer has not even laborers' wages,' while potatoes were 'the most profitable of all crops.' He had no remedy for the potato disease, but he used statistical calculation to adjudicate between possible courses of conduct. His second essay also proposed a way of measuring rural economic development. He wrote that 'nothing shows the prosperity of a county more than the increase of the number of pleasure carriages,' anticipating one of the items of information collected in his 1861 census. Although the examples are minor, they highlight a change from Crofton's work, in which descriptive statistics did not figure in a social calculus.[30]

William Hutton was not a stupid man, but his intellectual interests were comparatively narrow. He was what was known as a 'good practical farmer' and hence a reasonable candidate to head an agricultural information office. However, he had no mathematical education and no connection to the increasingly well-developed international statistical networks. His first appointment at the seat of government was as a clerk in the check office of the customs branch of Hincks's Inspector General's department, where he spent his time comparing and compiling navigation returns. The work began officially on 21 August 1852, and may have been a test to see what Hutton could do with figures.[31] Exactly how he came to be seen as Crofton's replacement is unclear, especially since he wanted to head Agriculture, not Registration and Statistics. He had clashed at least indirectly with Cameron in the struggles over the 1849 School Act, so perhaps Hincks could not place him in Agriculture while Cameron presided over it. Still, while in Registration and Statistics Hutton wrote the official census reports without having had any involvement in the planning or execution of the enumeration. The compilation process was largely complete before Hutton took over as secretary, and in any case conclusions about the enumeration had already been widely published by census commissioners. Hutton claimed to have found errors in material Crofton had published months earlier.[32]

**Compiling the 1852 Census Schedules**
The work of census compilation went forward in the time left to the recently hired statistical clerks after Parliamentary demands for other returns had been satisfied and after 'furnishing information to the various Railway Companies.' Demands from the latter, 'although in many cases calling for Statistical Tables extremely voluminous, and requiring considerable research and calculation,' were 'promptly attended to, although interfering materially with the ordinary work of the Office.'[33] Several government ministers were members of the board of the Grand Trunk Rail Road.

It is unlikely that the census compilation was systematically planned, or that the compilers were closely supervised, or that their work was consistently checked. Compilers were paid out of the board's contingent funds, and no compilation item appeared in the Parliamentary estimates. Crofton himself described the compilation work as day labour:

148  The Politics of Population

'the clerks are employed solely for the completion of the Census – are paid by the day – and have been increased or decreased in number, from time to time, as circumstances appeared to require.' Pay lists for November and December 1852 indicate eleven clerks at work in the board: three earning £15 a month and 5s. per extra half-day; the others £11.5s. a month and 3s.6d. extra. Many extra half-days were worked, yet the compiled schedules suggest that the clerical contingent included more people than were on these lists.[34]

Perhaps Crofton supervised the compilers himself, before his ouster on 31 March 1853, but he had a number of concurrent occupations. He audited the commissioners' accounts, disallowing claims for the agricultural census and reducing or rejecting claims for higher than the minimum rate of pay. There were eighty-three commissioners' reports, and the audit was done during the compilation of population totals.[35] Crofton produced the 1851 colonial Blue Book and delivered it to A.-N. Morin on 10 November 1852 and, for some other project he seems not to have completed, set one of the clerks to translating French-language enumerators' comments into English and assembling them in a separate volume.[36]

In pursuit of a further project of his own, Crofton carried off census materials (along with all the Blue Book forms) when he was removed from Registration and Statistics and returned to the Inspector General's office. After the return of his patron, William Cayley, as Inspector General in the Morin-McNab ministry, Crofton managed to extract £40 from the Executive Council for producing census tables and a map, 'it being understood that these Tables and the accompanying Map are to become the property of the Government, and that they should be deposited in the Office of the Agriculture Department.'[37] It seems unlikely that Crofton was closely checking compilers' work; no one else seems to have done so, and the removal of census materials may have affected Hutton's ability to report the results.

**Hutton's Account of the Compilation Process**

Only the most fragmentary documentary information about the work of compilation survives. Hutton's published report revealed that the compilation clerks were left to interpret a great many ambiguous and confusing entries on the schedules, but made no mention of any system governing their interpretations. His description of the enumeration process itself was misleading. He made no mention of difficulties with census design and logistics and derived no lessons from 1852 that led to improvements in census-making practices for 1861. Existing problems were entirely the personal fault of enumerators, commissioners, and informants. Hutton claimed that the census was executed carefully in Canada East but that in the west, 'many of the Enumerators proved themselves wholly unfit for the duties assigned to them; and the negligence and ignorance displayed in the work of them has added materially to the labours of the Office.' Matters were exacerbated by the resistance of census informants, who believed that the enumeration was about taxation and who refused to answer enumerators at all or at all truthfully. 'The only remedy for this,' Hutton commented, 'is to be found in the increasing intelligence and education of the community.' Finally, some commissioners omitted to include all the information required in their abstracts, while others produced erroneous abstracts that had to be verified. Hutton impressed on his readers that his office had had 1,722,000 columns to compile and 21,390 urban enumeration slips to sort.[38]

According to Hutton, the compilation began with the columns of origins and religious affiliations. These were indeed the first results released, but beginning here shows that no effort was made to separate the 'normally resident' from the 'temporarily absent,' the 'transient,' and the 'deceased' sections of the population. The published population totals were based on counts of names on the schedules, and many names appeared more than once.[39] Hutton also made the manifestly false claim that 'the trade or occupation of every individual was then extracted from each sheet, and classified as to Counties and Townships.' In fact, the compilers did not count women's occupations and applied various decisional rules to exclude returns for boys below a certain age. Status entries in this column such as 'wife,' 'daughter,' and 'scholar' were also disregarded.[40]

According to Hutton, the compilers moved on from here to the columns concerned with age, births, deaths, school attendance, and the incapacitated, and with family data. Here they attempted to determine the number of families, apparently by using the number of married couples as a proxy.[41] An average compiler was said to be able to do about 2,500 names a day, so 'the analyzation of this part alone would occupy two Clerks over 700 days.' The compilation process then moved to number and condition of houses, public buildings, and places of worship (by sect), and lastly, shops, stores, mills, and manufactories. The manufacturing column provided difficulties for compilers because the schedules did not distinguish clearly among categories of establishments, nor among capital investment, rent, and market value. 'Some Enumerators have given one characteristic of value and some another,' Hutton remarked, and 'in many cases a sum of money has been set down ... and it was left to the mere surmise of the Clerk abstracting whether such sum was rent, outlay, or net profit.' There is no record of any compilation grid that would have made such surmises consistent.[42]

The agricultural compilation demanded an effort that was 'immense, owing to the gross negligence of some of the Enumerators. In many cases the figures were almost illegible – in few cases were the castings [i.e., column totals] correct.' The compilers were apparently obliged to make the column totals add up, although the rules they applied in doing so were not indicated by Hutton. However, among the improvements he suggested for the next enumeration was 'to designate the particular weight of the Beef, Pork, and Fish.' Such a designation was called for because the absence of measures meant 'the returns have been made in such a manner as to leave every thing to the judgment of the Clerk, whether they denote Barrels, Hundred weight or Pounds.'[43] Measurement issues did not prevent Hutton from reporting totals of agricultural produce, but he left no description of how land and dry measures in Canada East and West, different during the enumeration, came to be reported as identical in the official account, except to say that there had been a conversion.[44]

There were three other areas in which the compilation of returns was left to the judgment of the clerks: causes of death; trades, occupations, and professions; and religious affiliation of places of worship. Hutton mentioned in passing that there were enormous sectional variations in the reporting of causes of death, but offered no explanation. Moreover, the 'fact that so many diseases are called by different names in different localities, amongst the uneducated classes' made it necessary for the compilers to 'compress the materials supplied by the Enumerators, in order to place in the clearest light ... the material to be given to the public.' No account of how this was done was given.[45] Again, there were about ninety named affiliations in the religion column on the enumeration schedules. Compilers somehow condensed these to thirteen religious categories in Canada West and ten in Canada East, even though there was no 'other denominations' entry in the Canada East compilation. One can only speculate as to how the 616 'pagans,' 59 'heathens,' 4 'infidels,' 1 'free thinker,' 87 'free-thinkers,' and 18 'Ebenezer Socialists' were assigned one of the official affiliations.[46]

Finally, Hutton cautioned that the occupational returns were published despite his hesitations about them. At least, he claimed, they contained 'as few absurdities' as those of other countries and would 'serve to point out where improvements may be made' for the next enumeration. After pointing to suspicious peculiarities in the returns, such as the absence of edge-tool makers from Canada West outside Toronto (where there were seven), Hutton noted that the compilers had excluded anyone holding less than ten acres from the occupation 'farmer' because such small holders were 'most of them probably persons following other avocations than farming, and returned accordingly.'[47]

The surviving evidence about the process of census making should give pause to researchers tempted to use aggregate 1852 census returns as quantitative evidence in debate. Inconsistent and idiosyncratic observational techniques applied to suspicious informants' stories about social relations and practices (themselves little susceptible to quantification), and the repeated reworking of observations by individuals applying their own judgments after the fact, make the translation of observed social relations into numerical form particularly problematic in this instance. Unless researchers can work with subprovincial units where the surviving schedules have not been 'corrected' and where enumeration protocols can be reconstructed, quantitative information generated from this enumeration must be highly suspect.

**Governing Population**
Still, the aggregate census returns had real social consequences. They were reported as social facts and used in contemporary political debate. They were seen as signposts by intellectuals and politicians interested in shaping the contemporary social imaginary. They came to serve as administrative instruments. Hutton's reports on the 1852 census worked up the returns into an official description of Canada. The census became 'made science.'

His remark 'Canada may hold her head up proudly' encapsulates one of the discursive formations in which his reports to Parliament placed the census returns. As an inventory of wealth and a statement of colonial population growth, the returns served as indices of colonial progress and improvement. Working them up gave identity and material form to the colonial political body, now personified as 'Canada' – an object that emerged out of the aggregation of discrete entities.[48] Through his selective comparisons of this statistical artifact with similar artifacts created in other countries, colonies, and American states, Hutton worked assiduously to fashion pride in 'Canada.' One thrust of such images was to push home the claim that some of Canada's component parts, especially population and agricultural output, were growing more quickly than those of other countries, especially the United States. Such rapid growth was a good thing, and 'Canadians' could look forward to more of it. Potential immigrants would find a fertile field for their labours in the Canadian colonies.

Yet the comparison of statistical artifacts also gave rise to proposals for more direct governmental projects – projects for the 'conduct of conduct.' In his first report, Hutton concentrated particularly on agricultural 'improvement.' A lengthy comparison of agricultural practices and output between the two Canadian colonies and the state of Ohio (a favorite destination for immigrants) led to seven recommendations for change in the agriculture of the former. As Hutton framed them, 'Canada should attend to the improvement of the breed of Milch Cows ... make more Cheese ... grow more Clover and Grass Seed ... keep more sheep ... grow more Indian Corn ... have fewer acres under wheat,' and, finally, 'Canada might grow more Tobacco.'

These proposals stemmed from a simple comparison of the reported production of the two places and involved no further analysis of the census returns. Instead, the discussion of the agricultural schedules provided a venue for Hutton the farmer, agricultural essayist, and candidate for agricultural secretary to promote government intervention in support of scientific agriculture. Thus, it seemed initially that Canada should grow more clover and grass seed because Ohio did and the climate in Canada was just as suitable. Yet Hutton used the occasion to promote one of the leading tenets of agricultural improvement: that green manure was a basic agricultural input and that grain crop yields were directly proportional to the amount ploughed under or consumed by livestock. Growing green manure also encouraged good moral character. 'The farmer should not be under the necessity of purchasing clover seed – the very purchase makes him sparing' and thus led him into improper agricultural practice, encouraging him to rob rather than replenish his land.[49]

According to Hutton, changing the conduct of individual farmers in simple matters of agricultural practice would have dramatic consequences for the development of 'British America.' British America was physically larger than the United States, containing 'nearly a ninth part of the whole terrestial surface of the Globe.' Much of this land mass appeared to be sterile, 'but it should be recollected that as the Country becomes cleared up, the climate improves.' Such had been the case in Europe, where before the generalization of agriculture, the Rhine froze regularly and savage beasts roamed freely. The spread of scientific agriculture in new settlements would mean climactic change in British North America similar to that in Europe, 'with this difference, that the improving climate will keep pace with the vastly accelerated movements, and more rapidly increasing numbers of New World Settlers.'

What was needed was the means to attract immigrants and to instruct farmers in practices of scientific agriculture. In this regard, Hutton wrote, 'the formation of a Bureau of Agriculture is an important feature in the history of Canada, and the most important results may be expected from its labours.' The Canadian farmer had no rival in industry and perseverance; he needed only to be provided the correct information that he was incapable of acquiring unaided, and 'it has been found that the issue of Pamphlets, emanating from a Government Department, possessing as it does so much greater facilities for the collection and distribution of knowledge, has been of incalculable value to the community.' 'Talented and practical men' needed to be set to the production of clear and concise agricultural treatises, the distribution of which had 'already created a vital change in the operations of the industrious and hard-working farmer.'[50] Agricultural improvement and the related immigration and colonization movements were the main governmental projects propelled by the census from within the state system and they constituted a state-forming project. Under Hutton's later initiative, the colonial statistical apparatus would be more closely tied to agricultural improvement and colonization. Yet Hutton was also faced with the necessity of interpreting the rest of the census returns – something he attempted in his second report of August 1854.

The second report was more firmly situated on the discursive terrain of the 'population thinking' characterized by Michel Foucault as the 'governmentality.' It sought significance from the selective aggregation and disaggregation of the returns and from their comparison with returns from different administrative units. Thus, at times 'Canada' was contrasted with 'Ireland,' 'Great Britain,' and the 'United States'; at times Canada East and Canada West were contrasted with each other; and at times, Hutton broke the returns down by county and town. The laws of motion said to be evident in large aggregations were juxtaposed to identify problematic subcategories, and at times Hutton identified single individuals. The analysis contained totalizing and individualizing moments.

Hutton compared Canadian fertility rates with those of Great Britain, and the Canadian age structure with that of the United States. Canadian families were larger than those of Great Britain, and there were far fewer childless couples, both responses to the expense of labour in Canada, according to Hutton. There was a higher ratio of men to women in Canada West, which showed Canada East to be 'more influenced by the ordinary laws of population than the Upper Province' (i.e., most immigrants were in the west). Hutton claimed that only half the Indian population had been counted but simply gave the number of 'blacks' as a fact. The name and place of residence of all enumerated individuals one hundred years of age and over was given, and the greater number of them in Canada West was cited as proof of its healthfulness.

Only two projects calling for direct government emerged out of Hutton's second report, both for the management of problematic categories of population. Hutton disaggregated the returns of those in the 'deaf and dumb' and 'blind' categories to the township and parish level, gave an exposition of supposed causes of their members' condition, and discussed the management of such categories in other jurisdictions. Perhaps nothing called 'for legislative interference as some provision for the education and comfort of these unfortunate individuals,' wrote Hutton of the deaf and dumb, and this interference meant the creation of special institutions. Government had a similar obligation toward those reported as 'blind,' who could be managed more efficiently if they were concentrated in urban institutions. Hutton regretted that the census schedules contained a single category for 'Lunatics and Idiots,' for these were quite different phenomena. The returns made it difficult to engage in comparative analysis, but Hutton supposed that 'one half of those denominated Lunatics in the Census of Canada are Idiots,' which made the proportion similar to that in the United States. Still, 'it is the opinion of many that fully two-thirds of those in Canada denominated Lunatics are Idiots,' but the census did not enable one to judge. Members of this category too were located by county, township, and parish.

Besides calling for the education of the blind, deaf, and dumb, Hutton repeated what he claimed was the agreed upon view: deafness, dumbness, idiocy, and lunacy were caused by improper conduct in the form of intermarriage and incest. As he put it, 'it is an understood fact that families who intermarry too often *die out*, but the misery that preceeds this dying out has been too little regarded, especially when the evil arises from a disregard of natural laws.'[51] Hutton's analysis went no further. The paucity of projects in his report for governing the 'social' speaks as much to the truncated conception of this domain in the census itself as to the narrowness of Hutton's own understanding of the pressing problems of the day. Hutton offered no serious critique of the existing census categories and proposed no changes that would have made it possible to use the census to gain leverage over a domain of conduct beyond that of agriculture and colonization.[52]

**Improvements for 1861**
Walter Crofton had invited census commissioners to make suggestions for improvements for a subsequent enumeration. Many did so, and some of them invited their enumerators to do likewise. Commissioners suggested ways to make the schedules easier for enumerators to complete and proposed that certain columns be modified in order to better capture agricultural production. Among the enumerators, J.B. Commeault, for St-David-de-Yamaska, called for the addition of a column for 'lentils,' of which his parish had produced 1,500 minots in 1851 – far more than it produced of some crops, such as rye, that had been included on the schedules. Commeault also suggested that a better method of taking the census would be for the enumerator to announce that he would be available at a central point for a certain period and for householders to travel to him to make their returns.[53]

Hutton picked up on some difficulties caused by reporting practices, yet the often dramatic differences in the returns for Canada East and West and between administrative sub-units did not lead him to reflect critically on enumeration practices. Thus, while he discounted the possibility that the markedly higher death rate in Canada East could be the result of enumeration error, for 'the Census was taken with care in the Lower Province, perhaps with greater care than that of the Upper Province,' he did not draw the conclusion that enumeration error produced the lower rate in Canada West. Nor did he consider the possible consequences on vital statistics of sectional differences in systems of civil registration. Similarly, Hutton made no comment about the fact that Montreal returned more than six times the number of deaf and dumb persons and five times the number of blind persons than did Toronto, and he made no effort to explain why out of 936 towns, townships, parishes, and villages, there were 329 in which no lunatics or idiots were reported.

Hutton did propose some minor modifications. 'Indians' should be enumerated by sex; returns of death should be made by occupation (in keeping with English practice); and idiots and lunatics should be enumerated separately. Hutton thought that the addition of a column for reporting wheeled vehicles, especially pleasure carriages, would give a measure of rural prosperity. Finally, in an addendum to his first report, Hutton urged that the English practice of having a very large number of enumerators be adopted for 1861. That way, not only would each enumerator 'have a knowledge of his own locality,' but if those chosen were schoolteachers, 'their *character*' would be 'at stake in the correctness of the additions and abstracts' and 'the writing and figures' would be 'clear and distinct.'[54]

Hutton engaged in no systematic reflection on the consequences of the census design for the configuration of its object 'population,' nor did he make any proposals for basic organizational change. He made no suggestions for ways of producing consistent social observations, despite his reports of how much had been left to the judgment of compilers in 1852. His suggestion that the number of enumerators be increased shows that he remained committed to a *de facto* enumeration, if he thought about different census models at all. The confused and haphazard 1852 approach to replicating the Queteletian-inspired practice recommended by the Colonial Office would be applied again for the 1861 enumeration. Still, Hutton did attempt to extend and integrate the operations of the colonial statistical apparatus.

**Statistics in the Wake of the Census**
In the colonial state system the position of Minister of Agriculture was an adjunct to that of President of the Committees of the Executive Council until 1862, when the two offices were separated. For the first decade of its existence, the Bureau of Agriculture was, in consequence, particularly susceptible to the vagaries of colonial politics. Nominally, seven men served as minister between November 1852 and March 1862 (although the 'double-shuffle' of 1858 produced three different ministers in five days), with the longest tenure that of William Hutton's patron John Ross (August 1858–March 1862). In the two years after Agriculture was separated from the Council presidency, there were four more ministers. It was often the case that the nominal minister was not the active member of cabinet in relation to the bureau. In consequence, until the accession of T.D. McGee as minister in 1864, the bureau was not the site of a sustained and systematically executed political project. This is not to say that the bureau did not figure in political projects, but simply that those in which it did figure were not pursued systematically.

Malcolm Cameron's ambitious plans for the Bureau of Agriculture to become a central statistical agency and motor of agricultural improvement were short-lived. While he quickly launched projects for investigating agricultural conditions, encouraging technical innovation, and promoting immigration, he failed to name a secretary to coordinate the bureau's efforts, nor did he develop a long-term agenda for it.[55] In August 1853 he was succeeded by his Clear Grit colleague John Rolph, and Rolph in turn was replaced by the conservative Sir Allan MacNab in the Morin-MacNab ministry that took office in September 1854. Each of these men was at the same time president of the Board of Registration and Statistics.

After displacing Walter Crofton as Secretary of Registration and Statistics, William Hutton worked mainly on the official census reports, both of which he projected, but failed, to complete by October 1853. As a reward for delivering his first report in August, Hutton was sent on a paid lecture tour of Ireland, so he was out of the country from early November 1853 until late February 1854.[56] The compilation work was probably finished before he left Canada, for Frances Hutton announced to her daughter that the clerks were about to be dismissed from the statistics office, and she expected that when his reports were finished, William's position would be 'almost a sinecure, except during the meetings of Parliament or until another census is taken.'[57] Despite having his salary increased from £150 as clerk in the Inspector General's office to £250 as Secretary of Registration and Statistics and then to £312.10s., Hutton was finding the cost of living too high in Quebec to be able to have his family with him. He was attempting to sell his immigration lectures to an English publisher while casting about for some other means either to retire to his farm or to raise his standard of living in the colonial capital.

Having submitted his second report on the census for Rolph's approval in mid-June 1854, Hutton complained of his financial difficulties and suggested that he should take over the compilation of the Blue Book. Rolph agreed, and Hutton hoped soon to add to his own income the £75 paid annually to Crofton for this work.[58] The Board of Registration and Statistics and the Bureau of Agriculture were still housed together, and although Hutton had no official connection to the latter, he considered himself to be 'the head of the whole office' and was incensed when the two Agriculture clerks had their salaries raised to the same level as his own, given that they were 'both uneducated illiterate & worthless men in the office.'[59] His plan to take over the compilation of the Blue Book was scuttled by the resignation of the Hincks-Morin ministry in September 1854 and by the replacement of John Rolph as minister by the conservative Sir A.N. MacNab.

### Statistical Wheat

Still, Hutton saw the coming into office of MacNab in a hopeful light. 'I think he will put the Agricultural bureau on a different footing,' Hutton wrote to his daughter Anna, 'nothing has been done by it yet.' His own position seemed secure: 'I cannot be *reduced* either in position or salary & may be advanced.'[60] Whether on his own account or under MacNab's direction, Hutton presented an ambitious plan for the reorganization of the colonial statistical apparatus to the Executive Council early in 1855.

The plan had been foreshadowed in an August 1854 retrospective report on the agriculture department signed by Malcolm Cameron. While it had an agrarian radical tone, parts of the report were probably Hutton's work, since Cameron knew nothing about agriculture and the report contained many of Hutton's favourite remarks about scientific farming. The report presented agricultural improvement as a matter of 'national importance,' and as an object of government to be pursued by 'wise legislation.' The point was pushed home by a statistical demonstration of the economic consequences of a small improvement in wheat yields. The census showed that the colony produced 16,155,946 bushels of wheat which, if valued at 5s. a bushel, were worth £4,038,986. An increased yield of only one bushel per acre would produce an additional 1,136,311 bushels or £284,078, which if capitalized would represent £4,734,633.

'Our Government,' the report commented, 'regarding labor as the source of wealth, has adopted a policy in reference to the subject under review as wise as it is enlightened. We now possess a system almost as complete in its naked arrangements, without reference to action in any of its divisions, as the theorist can devise. It is only desirable to discover, if possible, the proper adjustment of the parts to the whole, and the amount of tension each part is capable of sustaining without hazard to the movements of the machine.' The 'proper adjustment' in question consisted of placing all resources for the comparative investigation and improvement of agricultural conditions under the direction of the Minister of Agriculture. Moreover, while Cameron's report could claim that 'facts are chiefly to be valued' in the pursuit of improvement, the successful conduct of agriculture extended beyond statistical demonstration to the moral instruction of farmers. Rational agriculture did not just mean more manure and mangel wurzel, because if 'the farmer does not possess large intelligence and a taste for fine animal forms,' for instance, he would have neither the foresight required to improve his stock nor the aesthetic sense to appreciate improved stock should he see it.[61]

## Amalgamation of Agriculture and Registration and Statistics

In a lengthy memorandum discussed in the Executive Council on 20 February 1855, Hutton observed that neither the Board of Registration and Statistics nor the Bureau of Agriculture had carried out the duties required of them by law. The board had dealt only with the census, entirely neglecting that part of its mandate which called for the delivery of an annual statistical report. The agricultural statistics gathered by the bureau were of no practical use because they were never compiled, compared with similar statistics from other jurisdictions, or published. Hutton proposed that the two offices be merged under the supervision of the Minister of Agriculture and under the immediate direction of a permanent secretary. The mandate of the new Bureau of Agriculture, Registration and Statistics would be broadened, and the duties of its secretary clearly specified. Annually, the new agency would present Parliament with 'a Statistical Report of the Agricultural, Manufacturing, Commercial, Sanitary, Criminal, and Educational progress of the Country, in Tabular forms, giving the value of assessed and unassessed property of all kinds to be ascertained from the Municipalities.' It would take over the Blue Book and would control the annual returns of vital statistics, which the 1847 Census Act had required doctors, coroners, clergymen, and others to report to the Provincial Secretary's office. It would compile returns on mining and fishing, and diffuse information on these subjects. It would control the granting and registration of patents of inventions. In addition, Hutton proposed that the new agency should correspond with the two colonial Boards of Agriculture and with local agricultural societies, both to gather statistical information and to diffuse 'useful knowledge' on matters of agricultural improvement. It would encourage the Boards of Agriculture to publish annual volumes of their transactions, and, finally, it would maintain a stud and herd book. Hutton made a number of suggestions about personnel and salaries.

In short, under Hutton's plan, a dedicated Canadian statistical office would draw on the extensive information-gathering powers contained in the Census and the Bureau of Agriculture Acts, both to provide detailed information to policymakers about colonial conditions and to press for 'improvement,' especially in domain of agriculture. The plan received cabinet approval, and Hutton was to head a staff of five. His salary was increased to £400, and three of the clerks involved in compiling the 1852 census returns joined him.[62] The bureau's contingencies fund was used to hire additional clerical assistance after the useless Donald McLeod was paid to stay home in the summer of 1855.

Soon after it was announced, the entire project was loudly criticized in a Parliamentary debate over public salaries. An increasingly curmudgeonly William Lyon Mackenzie was particularly voluble, going through the proposed salaries and denouncing them all, and especially the fact that Hutton – someone he claimed had been 'imported into this country' by Francis Hincks – was to get $1,600 a year 'while this country was so poor that the farmers had to be supplied with seed grain.' Hincks, out of office but still an MPP, came to Hutton's defence as a person whom everyone knew to be 'highly competent.'[63] The new arrangements were set in motion.

**The Bureau of Everything**
Hutton's memorandum to the Executive Council captured only a portion of the activities into which the Bureau of Agriculture and Statistics found itself drawn. In this period of rapid growth in the state system, these activities seemed to acquire a momentum of their own. They mutiplied from 1855 until the preparations for the 1861 census were fairly underway, despite attempts at government retrenchment after the 1857 economic crisis. Even with its modest staff at the seat of government – a staff which by the time the peripatetic Parliament headed for Quebec in 1860 had grown only by the addition of A.J. Cambie to do the work of the pensioned off McLeod – the bureau seemed to be everywhere.[64]

The bureau became increasingly involved in promoting immigration, although this became part of its mandate officially only in 1862. It organized or oversaw the production of pamphlets and settlement maps and arranged for their distribution in Europe by emigration agents. It attempted to estimate the demand for labour in various parts of Canada West by circulating questionnaires to municipal clerks and publishing the results. After 1856, the Chief Emigrant Agent reported through the Minister of Agriculture and the bureau became involved more or less directly in arrangements for receiving immigrants at points of entry and for their forwarding to interior destinations. In an attempt to coordinate arrangements for immigrant passage, Hutton began a detailed correspondence with the London agents of the Grand Trunk Rail Road.[65]

Much of Hutton's day-to-day activity came to be caught up with the supervision of an ill-fated scheme for constructing colonization roads and distributing fifty-acre settlement grants in Canada West. Similar projects in Canada East were under the supervision of Crown Lands.

The western project was launched when the proceeds of sales of Crown and Clergy reserves and School Lands were earmarked for local improvement and colonization funds. In the Parliamentary estimates between 1852 and 1860, $375,000 was set aside for this purpose, most of it after 1856. In part through the influence of J.A. Macdonald, MPP for Kingston, who feared that the opening of the west would lead to a shift in the centre of political gravity, many of the colonization roads were surveyed in the east and the east-centre of Canada West.[66] Hutton was quite enthusiastic about these largely ill-conceived projects, which had many settlers scratching away at hardscrabble bush lots that refused to yield a living once the timber had been cut. One road promised to open up the hinterland to the north of Hutton's own farm in Hastings County, and there is evidence that he, his nephews, and his minister were engaged in land speculation. The colonization roads consumed much of the bureau's time, with Hutton involved in detailed correspondence with road superintendents and contractors about individual survey lines and bridges.[67]

The bureau also supervised the two sectional Boards of Agriculture, which in turn oversaw the operations of local agricultural societies. Disputes about the distribution of the Parliamentary grant (based in part on population distribution) and about the legitimacy of certain societies were referred to the bureau. The pursuit of agricultural improvement involved the bureau in the publication of tracts on scientific farming; the encouragement of imports of seed grain and improved breeds of farm animals; investigations of the culture and processing of particular crops (flax especially); and the promotion of various forms of agricultural education. The bureau sought remedies for the crop losses due to the wheat midge and generally attempted to monitor annual agricultural production, which was the core of the colonial economy. The bureau was involved in organizing and publicizing the annual Provincial Exhibitions and also organized and supervised the colonial entries in permanent and temporary exhibitions in Europe and the United States.

After 1857 the Bureau of Agriculture also coordinated and financed the activities of the two sectional Boards of Arts and Manufactures, agencies intended to perform the same functions for Canadian industry that the Boards of Agriculture did for agriculture. The Boards of Arts and Manufactures funded Mechanics' Institutes and attempted to diffuse 'useful knowledge' about industrial pursuits while fostering technical innovation and providing venues for capitalists and middle-class intellectuals to exercise leadership over the growing class of artisans.[68]

Closely related to its functions as the agency for encouraging agricultural and industrial innovation was the bureau's role as patent office. Applicants for patents of invention submitted plans and a working model of their inventions to the bureau. The bureau maintained a museum of models that grew so rapidly during William Hutton's tenure that no attempt was made to move it to Quebec with the government offices in 1860. Complicated negotiations also led to the acquisition, at some expense, of a complete set of the English government's huge illustrated volumes of patented inventions. In 1857 the bureau was proposing to produce its own illustrated volume covering the 820-odd colonial inventions patented since 1824 and to print 1,000 copies for distribution to libraries and Mechanics' Institutes. The registration of copyright and of patterns and designs was also added to the bureau's mandate.[69]

**Not Statistically Speaking**

The multiplication of the bureau's administrative activities and the heavy demands of the colonization projects left Hutton and his staff little time for statistical investigation. There appears to have been no one more adept at statistical matters than Hutton himself, and the bureau proved incapable of producing the annual statistical report that he had promised the Executive Council in 1855. Hutton tried in a variety of ways and on a number of occasions to generate the required information. He discovered that the necessary administrative infrastructure did not exist. Often, social relations had not been invested in forms that made it possible to appropriate them as statistics, and while Hutton lamented this state of affairs, he proved unable to change it. The bureau's inability to generate statistical information heightened the importance of the 1861 census as an administrative instrument. The same inability drew Hutton into exercises of statistical estimation that created exaggerated expectations for the enumeration. Inflated expectations were shaped by the bureau's implication in projects for increasing immigration and for raising agricultural and industrial production, as well as by Hutton's inability or unwillingness to recognize the effects on both projects of the crop failures and depression of 1857–8.

Hutton treated the Blue Book project as the occasion to attempt an exhaustive statistical inventory of Canadian conditions under the headings he proposed to the Executive Council in 1855. He began the work in earnest late in the fall of 1855, but was initially slowed down by Walter Crofton's refusal to hand over the Blue Book forms and circulars in his possession and by confusion on the part of his own minister about who was to do the compilation. Hutton was obliged to communicate repeatedly with Crofton, with Crofton's superior in the Inspector General's department, and with the Minister of Agriculture in order to extract materials from Crofton and in order to compell him to meet for a discussion of past practice.[70] Hutton managed to deliver a large and quite detailed Blue Book that drew together the growing mass of statistical returns generated by agencies of central and local government. His book gives a good overview of the statistical capacities of the colonial state at this moment; it also points to the lacunae that drew Hutton into exercises of statistical estimation and that shaped expectations for the 1861 census.

He had proposed to the Executive Council that his bureau would be able to produce tables of 'Agricultural, Manufacturing, Commercial, Sanitary, Criminal, and Educational' as well as municipal statistics. Yet Hutton had no statistics for manufacturing and could produce no criminal statistics for the eastern section. His repeated circulars distributed to men involved in the mining industry and in fishing produced no useful quantitative information. He complained that the township agricultural societies, meant to funnel statistical returns to the bureau through the sectional Boards of Agriculture, were not providing the required information, despite their Parliamentary subsidy. Other domains of investigation proved equally problematic, and Hutton quickly concluded that the distribution of circulars to local observers was an ineffective method of generating statistical information. As he wrote to one correspondent, 'the true method' of getting statistical information was 'to take a Census every five years as they do in the State of New York & employ really respectable responsible people to take it and pay them well.'[71]

**Assessment Returns**
Hutton had told the Council that his office would produce an annual report on property values. In the 1855 Blue Book he provided a return of assessment statistics from the reports of municipal clerks; later, however, he wrote to one correspondent that his tables were 'erroneous & no reliable inferences can be drawn from them *as a whole*. Some of the Counties may have made correct returns but the returns of a great many are *evidently* absurd.'[72]

Criticism of these returns is particularly significant because earlier they had been the main source of claims about population size and distribution in Canada West. The censuses of 1842, 1848, and 1850 had been household enumerations conducted by the municipal assessors;

Hutton maintained that the assessment returns made after 1853 did not provide a reliable basis on which to make population estimates. He explained to the Attorney General for the western section, John A. Macdonald, that the assessment rolls contained a great many duplicate names and that different categories of people were returned in the urban and rural rolls. 'In all cases,' he noted, 'there are 20 pr cent more names on the asst: Rolls of Cities & Towns than of Counties in proportion to the population. The Landlords & Tenants are in many cases both put on one for the Property & the other for Income &c&c The Farmers are their own Landlords.' On the London assessment rolls, Hutton found 5,018 names. However, 'upon writing to the City Clerk for an explanation of this,' he was told there 'were about 1000 names on the list which were repetitious.' As far as Hutton was concerned, the assessment returns could not serve as a device for estimating population reliably.[73]

**Vital Statistics**

In the domain of 'sanitary' or vital statistics, the best information the bureau could command concerned immigration. The 1855 Blue Book contained a detailed table of immigrant arrivals at Grosse Île and Quebec since 1829 and also presented information about the declared occupations of male arrivals. This was information collected under the administration of the imperial Passenger Act. However, the bureau could say nothing about immigration and emigration at border points other than the main point of entry. Nor could it say anything about the subsequent movements of arrivals at Quebec. Immigration was often treated as a component part of population growth in Canadian debate, but on the basis of no solid evidence.

Hutton also discovered that he could generate no useful information about births, marriages, and deaths in Canada West, and he seems to have been mystified by returns of such information by the prothonotaries of Canada East.[74] In his proposals to the Executive Council, Hutton had made it sound as if the failure of the Board of Registration and Statistics to report on vital statistics was a simple matter of neglect. The 1847 Census Act required officials to make the relevant returns; hence, the board's failure to compile them, even in the face of imperial demands for regular reporting, was another instance of the laziness and incompetence of Walter Crofton.[75] Hutton soon learned that the matter was more complex.

Demands for an effective system of civil registration were common in the anglophone press of the period. An editorial in the *Canada Free Press*, for instance, urged the adoption in Canada of a system like that in place in England as a 'safeguard to property and the rights of the community.' A modest reform to the marriage laws in 1857 (20 Vic. c.LXVI), which contained some registration provisions, caused the editor of the *Montreal Witness* to warn that unless a better system were put in place, 'great difficulties will, doubtless, be experienced many years hence in establishing legal points concerning inheritance, &c.'[76] The Catholic church's control over registration in Canada East was an issue in sectional debates, and the privileged position of the Churches of England and Scotland in Canada West was criticized as iniquitous in a country with no state church.

Hutton's interest lay in vital statistics as indicators of population growth, and he intended to collect them by sending a circular to those responsible for reporting under the 1847 act, especially the clergy and the municipal clerks, to whom the former were to have made returns. Yet here, too, the infrastructures necessary for reporting were lacking and standard social practices susceptible to statistical appropriation were absent. It proved difficult even to locate potential clerical correspondents, and the municipal clerks, who themselves advertised the demand for returns, received little in the way of information. Hutton had to appeal to the clerical establishment and to popular almanacs and guide books even to find the names of clergymen. When the legislature called for a return of births, marriages, and deaths in May 1856, Hutton was unable to provide it. He claimed that many clergymen refused to acknowledge the government's right to the information, that many had kept no records, and that in any case, many people were born and buried without the presence of a minister of religion or doctor. The prothonotaries for Canada East, Hutton remarked, sent returns to the Provincial Secretary, but he, Hutton, could not judge of their exactitude. Hutton concluded that 'any attempt to procure correct Returns' under the registration clauses of the Census Act was bound to 'be fruitless.' Moreover, the returns could not serve as a basis for estimating population increase.[77]

The case of vital statistics nicely illustrates that statistical appropriation depends on a prior investment of social relations in forms. Until vital events were inserted in regular administrative systems, until common practices of birthing, marrying, and dying held sway, and until a regular interest in reporting was created, vital events would remain beyond the capture of official statistics.[78] Hutton told F.B. Hough, the superintendent of the New York state census, that he was aware of the weakness of the existing registration system, noting that 'the General census appears to me to be the only correct means of ascertaining births & deaths & if taken every five years it would answer every purpose. There is always a column for Births within the year & also for the number of children of one year old & two years old & so on – which is almost equivalent to a return of the Births every year – except as far as emigrants are concerned – and the deaths which have occur[r]ed amongst children of those ages.' He concluded that 'these are very strong reasons why the Census should be taken every five years.'[79]

**Multipliers**

In the spring of 1856 the Liberal opposition was agitating for a quinquennial census. A May 1856 motion from George Brown calling for a January 1857 census was amended by G. Jackson to specify that such an enumeration would be followed by a change in the basis of representation. Brown and some of his supporters were inflammatory in Parliament in their remarks about the sectional domination of Canada East over Canada West under the current arrangements, and insisted that a census was urgently needed to demonstrate that the population of the west was growing. Brown claimed that the western population was now 300,000 greater than that of the east and that a census would lead either to representation by population or to the dissolution of the Union of the Canadas.

The government opposed the expense of a new enumeration and argued that decennial enumerations were the common practice in other countries. Besides, an enumeration would be unreliable in the existing context of sectional conflict. 'Such an excitement' had been raised by the representation debate, claimed John A. Macdonald, that 'there would be such a struggle between the two Provinces that the returns would be falsified.' The government strongly opposed the argument for representation by population made by G. Jackson of Grey County: 'if the Union is to be maintained in its usefulness and integrity, boundary lines and sectional legislation must become extinct. Canadians should feel that they were one people.' The dynamics of party politics once again prevented the emergence of a uniform Canadian population, for the party in power depended on sectional alliances and the members from the east supported the preservation of ethnic-political distinctions.[80]

The political explosiveness of census making was certainly clear to Hutton. In a letter of February 1857 to Sir C.P. Roney, the London director of the Grand Trunk Rail Road, Hutton was 'quite of the opinion that ten years is quite too long to be without a *general* Census, but hitherto the excitement has been so great with regard to the disparity of Population in Upper & Lower Canada & also with regard to *Creeds*, that it would perhaps be scarcely safe to order a Census till the excitement passes somewhat off.' Political excitement meant 'the *truth* would not be arrived at, the desire to excel might also extend to the returns of produce &c.' Still, Hutton claimed, 'Canada has made more progress in the last year than in two years' and 'five years more *of these times* will make a wonderful change in the Census.'[81]

Faced with demands both political and administrative for detailed population returns, prevented from using assessment returns, vital statistics, circulars, or questionnaires, and unable to conduct a new enumeration, Hutton invented another method for making up the Canadian population: he applied multipliers to returns of numbers of schoolchildren. He did this in the same boosterish spirit that characterized his other statistical work. These estimates were taken up by the press, published widely, and debated. They established a set of expectations for the census of 1861.

Hutton explained his method first in a letter reproduced in the 1855 Blue Book. He took the return of school-age children (i.e., those between the ages of five and sixteen) for Canada West and multiplied it by 4 for county returns and by 4.25 for returns from towns and cities. He compared the totals obtained in this way with the total obtained by calculating the average annual population increase as 6.66 per cent, about what it had been for Canada West between 1842 and 1852. As he put it, 'the Population calculated upon either basis comes within a fraction of the other and with perhaps two or three exceptions may be relied upon as correct. The School Population of Cities and Towns does not constitute so large a proportion of the Population as that of Counties, there being more boarders, lodgers, and single persons than in the Country and therefore the School Population therein requires to be multiplied by 4 1/4 to approximate to the total Population.'[82] Hutton did not reflect deeply on this matter. He did not consider the possibility that the totals generated by his two methods corresponded because they were equally arbitrary. They yielded the population totals he needed. Using his method of calculation, the population of Canada West would surpass 1,700,000 in 1861.

The Superintendent of Education East did not make a return of school-age residents for 1855. Hutton had contacted P.-J.-O. Chauveau about the matter in June 1856, confessing that he was 'at a loss to know how to arrive at a proper basis for ascertaining the population' of the eastern section in the absence of a return of schoolchildren and of municipal assessment returns. Hutton claimed that for Canada West he had an excellent method, under which 'for the Cities & Towns I multiplied the School Population by 4 1/2 & in Counties & Villages by 4 & from assessment rolls & a Census of the People actually taken I find my calculations correct.' However, all he knew to do for Canada East was to assume that the rate of increase between 1852 and 1857 was the same as it had been between 1844 and 1852 – doubling every thirteen years, in contrast to every ten years for Canada West.[83] Hutton's multiplier had changed from the one he reportedly used in May 1856, and his earlier hesitations about the assessment rolls seem to have vanished. Under these calculations, Canada East's population would be over 1,400,000 in 1862. Hutton in other communications repeated this method of calculating population and the resulting totals, which he sent in an official communication to the imperial Board of Trade. In a letter to the notorious (but now rehabilitated) radical Robert Gourlay that accompanied his census reports, he concluded, 'to find the increase of Population add one tenth *per annum* in U.C. & 1/17th in L.C.'[84]

Hutton's estimates were institutionalized in an increasingly self-referential knowledge system. Having attempted to learn the number of school-age children from Chauveau in 1856 as a means for calculating population totals for Canada East, in 1857 he instructed Chauveau how to use Hutton's own estimates of population totals to calculate the number of school-age children! Hutton wrote that 'in *Cities & Towns* in Upper Canada,' to determine the total population, 'the school population requires to be multiplied by 4 1/4, in the Counties by 4 – as there are always more single persons mechanics servants &c in Town than in the Country.' For Chaveau to determine the 'school population in *Cities & Towns*' in Lower Canada, he should 'divide the *whole population* by 4 & deduct 1/17th & in Counties you simply divide by 4 – or in all Lower Canada divide the whole population by 4 and deduct 1/29.' Or, as Hutton laid it out for him,

```
Total population up to Janr 1857    4 / 1.152.708
                                        288.177
                        Deduct 1/29       9.937
      Total school population            278.240
```

'I think you will find these calculations very nearly correct,' Hutton concluded, informing Chauveau that he had sent them to the ministry to aid in the preparation of a new bill for locating courthouses and jails.[85]

At times, Hutton backed away from calculating population by assuming constant annual growth rates for the two sections of the colony, and his forward estimates of population varied. In 1857 he wrote to the MPP H.W. McCann that the 'Population & Produce &c &c have encreased one half in the Upper Province. By adding one half except in places like Huron & Bruce, which have more than doubled, you will come near the truth.' In a report to the legislature in September 1859 he was more conservative, giving the population in the eastern section on 1 January 1859 as 1.165 million and in the west as 1.436 million. This difference amounted to the 300,000 claimed by the Brownite liberals.[86]

A lengthy description of his methods for calculating population totals, which yielded yet another set of figures, appeared in the Hamilton *Spectator* in late 1859. It was immediately translated by the *Journal de Québec* and reprinted by several other papers, including the *Courrier du Canada* and *La Minerve*. This article stimulated a considerable amount of debate and also shaped expectations for the 1861 census. Hutton stated that the sectional populations were nearly balanced. Now he claimed that the population aged five to sixteen was slightly over one-quarter of the total population returned in 1852. Taking the returns of school-age children from the 1857 annual reports of the Chief Superintendents of Education, multiplying their numbers by 4 and 1/8th, and adding 7 per cent for natural increase and immigration, would give 1,340,930 for the west and 1,270,500 for the east in 1858. To estimate the population in successive years, one should multiply these totals by 1.07 for each year, meaning the 1861 census could be expected to uncover a population of 1,641,605 west and 1,556,416 east, for a total of 3,198,021.

Hutton admitted that these were approximations, but he claimed that they were not more than 10,000 off the true figures. He had checked his figures not only against the voters' list, but also against the 1856 militia returns. The latter gave the number of men aged eighteen to forty on the active list and aged forty to sixty on the reserve list. They needed to be corrected somewhat; but adding them together, doubling the result to count the female population, and multiplying the number of men by four gave a population in 1856 of 1,246,858 west and 1,102,160 east – very close to the other estimates.[87]

Hutton did have one hesitation about these calculations. In December 1859 he contacted both Superintendents of Education with respect to their returns of the school-age population. He had seen newspaper reports for Canada East apparently drawn from Chauveau's annual return and wondered if they could be correct, for the totals were much lower than he had expected. He again explained his method of estimating population and wondered whether Chauveau's returns had not excluded some children, perhaps those from the Magdalen Islands. At the same time, he contacted the Superintendent of Education West, Egerton Ryerson, and explained his method of estimation again, adding, 'I have no doubt the Coming Census will prove that my calculations are near the mark.'[88]

Much was thus expected of the 1861 census. Other attempts at configuring social relations as population and at appropriating knowledge about social activity either did not work or were stopgaps until such time as a census enumeration was made properly. The official statistics agency had been unable to fulfil its mandate to produce statistical information because many of its inquiries were blocked and because the necessary investigative resources and instruments did not exist. At the same time, the Bureau of Agriculture had a direct interest in a large return of population numbers, for such a return would both vindicate its efforts in the field of immigration and colonization and bear out the estimates it had been providing for the press and the government. Furthermore, political debate in the colony had become caught up in a variety of ways with issues relating to the balance of numbers between the two sections, the degree of agricultural development and economic prosperity, and the relative strength of ethnic groups and religious denominations.

The census would address all these questions. Yet under William Hutton's regime in the 1850s, the possibilities and limitations of census making as a knowledge-producing and knowledge-centralizing instrument had not been subjected to serious critical analysis. As the next two chapters show, the 1861 enumeration proved to be a fiasco on a larger scale than that of 1852.

Chapter 5

# Setting up the Sectarian Census

The looming 1861 census heightened cultural anxieties and intensified sectional, ethnic, religious, and linguistic rivalries. The conservative majority of francophone politicians and intellectuals feared the census would show that the rapid growth rates of the western section and outmigration from the eastern section had continued in the 1850s. This anxiety was sharpened by the vociferous demands of the anglophone liberal press, echoed less loudly by its francophone liberal counterpart, for representation by population. Particularly vitriolic and chauvinistic was George Brown's Toronto *Globe*. Brown, the western Liberal leader, had been manoeuvred out of office after only three days in 1858 in the so-called 'double-shuffle.' In alliance with the eastern *rouge* party, his administration would have attempted to pursue representation by population. Political manoeuvring kept a conservative coalition in power but did nothing to defuse mounting conflict around what many saw as undue Catholic influence over social policy in Canada West.[1]

Throughout 1860, the *Globe* hammered away at the injustice of what Brown called the 'French domination' sustained by the Macdonald-Cartier ministry and imperial colonial policy. Under the arrangements that gave each section an equal number of seats, unpopular legislation affecting the west could be carried by a government alliance based on an eastern majority. By all measures, Brown insisted, Canada West was superior to Canada East, and its subordination to a priest-ridden, ignorant francophone minority was deeply unjust. According to Brown, the west contributed three times as much as the east to the colonial revenue. Protestants outnumbered Catholics in the whole country by 928,804 to 914,275 and, faced with the increasing numerical superiority of the west, desperate eastern politicians saw francophone immigration as their only hope. They stacked a Parliamentary immigration committee and went so far as to encourage settlement by the Swiss soldiers who had defended the Vatican, 'cut throats of the Pope' as Brown called them.[2]

As the census approached, Brown announced that it would 'have the effect of hastening the solution' to the leading political question of the day; it would 'settle the question' of representation by population and lead to the dissolution of the Union by demonstrating the overwhelming superiority of Canada West in population and resources. 'French Canadians and even ... some Western dogfaces, hope that Upper Canada will not have a large preponderance in population over Lower Canada. They hope in vain.' Brown scoffed at claims that the sharply falling number of immigrants arriving in Quebec and a large outmigration from Canada West after the recent depression would reduce the western advantage. 'Frauds in the Lower Canada census returns might lessen the preponderance' of the west, Brown insisted, 'but they could not abolish it altogether without detection and exposure.'[3]

*Le Canadien*, like other ministerial papers in the east, regularly contested Brown's claims about sectional superiority. When Brown wrote that Canada West contained 400,000 more people than Canada East in 1860, and thus was entitled to 27 more MPPs, *Le Canadien* responded that the populations could reliably be estimated at 1.55 million west and 1.45 million east and thus Canada West could claim at best 67 of 130 seats.[4] *La Minerve* discounted Brown's claims that Protestants outnumbered Catholics in the colony by citing the 1852 census returns, which gave the numbers as 914,561 Catholics and 880,149 Protestants of all denominations, and 'these facts are certain since they are based on data included in the framework of the last census.' Brown's claim of Protestant superiority was a result of his inflating their numbers by including those returned as Jews, Mormons, Universalists, and others.[5]

*La Minerve*, too, in the first of a series of boosterish pieces in anticipation of the 1861 census, drew on Hutton's calculations from the Hamilton *Spectator* to suggest that sectional population differences were only a few thousand. The enemies of the eastern section, the editor claimed, were constantly basing 'their demands on statistics extracted from the census by means of erroneous calculations based on exaggerated figures.' Because of the unfortunate tendency of French Canadians to give false returns for fear of taxation and conscription, the last two censuses had understated the true population and wealth of the east; people in the west, on the contrary, were prone to exaggeration. 'Far from diminishing his riches, the Upper Canadian never misses an occasion of increasing them; we do not even know if, faced with agents of the authorities, he would not go so far as to increase the number of his children.' The census, according to *La Minerve*, was a tool in the hands of those interested in representation by population, and this measure was nothing other than a continuation of the hated Durhamite plan to destroy the French-Canadian 'race.' People in the east played into the hands of their political enemies by hiding the facts of wealth and population: they should respond in detail to enumerators. There was another reason for francophones to respond truthfully: 'the well known spirit of certain fanatical sects to accuse Catholicism incessantly of blocking the material progress of nations ... Considered from this point of view, a census acquires a whole other importance; for it will shut the mouths of imposters and calumniators who, like Brown, make their disciples believe that Lower Canada is nothing but a horrible desert.'[6]

Several eastern newspapers were taking a similar line in mid-1860 while stressing the importance, both political and administrative, of the forthcoming census. *Le Courrier du Canada*, for example, argued that the census was 'a sort of inventory of the forces and resources of the country, the measure of progress accomplished, the indication of the path that one must follow and the ground that remains to be covered.' It was a particularly important event, given the strong sectional antagonisms which existed and which, in the editor's opinion, should not be increased, although his pen did nothing to diminish them. There was no doubt that the census would have 'an immediate and energetic effect' on sectional feeling. But even without raising 'burning political questions,' such as representation by population, there would be 'permanent causes of irritation' through the 'daily application of facts, if the census is not what it should be.' The facts created by the census determined the distribution of school money, and the editor charged that the west got $20,000 more annually than it ought because of inflated population returns. Again, money for general public improvements was distributed according to the supposed contribution of each section to the public treasury, and the western section was doing extremely well – too well – under this arrangement. If the west 'sins in the evaluation of its riches, of its commercial operations, etc., you can be sure that it is neither by too little reserve nor by excessive modesty.' The editor then repeated the claim that overly timid eastern census respondents, afraid of taxation and conscription, underestimated the size of their families and the degree of their wealth. These fears were groundless, and a rural education campaign was wanted to convince people to report accurately: 'if ...

it is wrong to exaggerate, it is at least as little sensible and patriotic to remain below the reality' of wealth and population.[7]

On the eve of the enumeration, many eastern newspapers again called for efforts to ensure that respondents would answer the enumerators truthfully and completely. *La Minerve* denounced the sectarian press in the west, which was constantly denigrating the accomplishments of the east: 'The next census provides us with a favorable occasion to shut the mouths of these shameless critics.' The editor urged all enlightened people to discuss publicly the importance of the census and called on the clergy to remind people of their sacred duty to answer truthfully to authority. Statistics drawn from the census were a measure of the progress of different parts of the world, and those places which could demonstrate the greatest growth in population and resources were the ones which attracted immigrants.[8]

The census manager, William Hutton, was himself attempting to publicize the forthcoming census in this period. Hutton urged the president of the western Board of Arts and Manufactures, William Edwards, to advertise the forthcoming enumeration in the first issue of the board's transactions, commenting that 'a good article calling particular attention to the census would do much good.' He wrote to another newspaper editor urging attention to the census, noting, 'with regard to an Editorial on the Census, I will send you my "Instructions to Enumerators" when printed & shall be obliged by your notice of them.'[9]

Brown's *Globe* did not protest against the government's attempts to ensure cooperation in the enumeration, but it mounted a virulent attack on a sermon preached by the ultramontane Bishop Bourget of Montreal on 30 December 1860 that was later embodied in a pastoral letter and a circular from Msgr Larocque of St-Hyacinthe. The sermon, reprinted in the eastern press, both conservative and liberal, urged cooperation with census enumerators and stressed that resistance to civil authority was resistance to divine authority. Msgr Larocque urged the priests in his diocese to remind their flocks that a good census was the only defence they had against the 'homicidal measure' of representation by population.[10]

In an editorial titled 'A Large Census Wanted in Lower Canada,' the *Globe* warned its readers that in the east, 'the Press, the Priests and the Bishops, are all at work, impressing on the *habitans* that their political salvation depends on their returning to the Census Commissioners as large figures as possible.' Such activity was in contrast to the silence of the western press on the question of the census, but then, the *Globe* continued, it would be insulting to citizens in the west to suggest that they might do otherwise than respond truthfully to the enumerators. Not so in the east. There 'for some months the French newspapers have been most assiduously inculcating upon the people ... the frightful hazard they will run of political absorption by another race, and the loss of their own nationality if they make low returns.' The eastern press could have only one objective: 'Mr. Cartier's scribes ... take the course which is most likely to secure an exaggerated return of the numerical strength of the population.' They were aided in this by the clergy, especially the Bishop of St-Hyacinthe, whose message was 'dinned into the ears of an ignorant populace.'[11]

*La Minerve* thought this editorial sufficiently insulting to print it in its entirety in translation, with phrases like the last italicized, and wondered how the liberal eastern *rouge* party could possibly continue to claim Brown as an ally, since even their organ, *Le Pays*, had reprinted the bishop's call for cooperation. The *Courrier du Canada* also reprinted Brown's editorial in translation, while the editor of *Le Canadien* denounced the 'savage and blind fanaticism' of the *Globe*, describing each of Brown's charges as a vile lie.[12]

Yet the suggestion that the census was a sectional and sectarian political tool was widely accepted. It filtered down into the regional presses both east and west. Even the obscure Perth County *Weekly Argus* would later claim that errors in the enumeration process locally were the result of the fact that the census was to be taken 'negatively' in the west and 'positively' in the east because 'the Ministry and the Lower Canada allies' wanted it to be so.[13] In the east, similarly, trivial administrative problems took on a broader political significance. In March 1861, for instance, *La Minerve* printed an letter from the parish of St-Anicet, where there had been one French and two British enumerators at work, which reported that 'the French [census] sheets were on very bad paper and were few in number; the English ones were much more numerous, easy to get and on very nice paper' – clear evidence of 'contempt which escaped no one.'[14] We shall see that the francophone intellectuals who gained control over census making before 1871 set about undoing the damage the past censuses were perceived to have done to French Canada.

### Setting up the Census

Despite rising rhetoric and anxieties, little was done concretely by the Canadian ministry to prepare for the 1861 Census until the early months of 1860, and then the impetus came primarily from the imperial government. It is true that William Hutton carried on a modest correspondence with census officers in other jurisdictions after the reorganization of Agriculture and Statistics in 1855. He was particularly impressed with the work of F.B. Hough, the superintendent for New York State, with whom he exchanged census materials and discussed enumeration practices. Hutton admired the 'graphic declinations' in Hough's census report, 'quite a new feature in our dry details,' and encouraged him to publicize his work in Canada.[15] Hutton also exchanged materials with the Secretary of the State of Maine, and with officers in the imperial Board of Trade, and sought detailed information about statistical matters from the Registrar General in Ireland. He had studied the reports on the 1851 English census, and as the preparations for 1861 began, he twice sought information about the 1860 American census, including copies of the enumeration schedules, while inviting the Americans' reactions to his own plans.[16]

In 1857, petitions from clergy about the denominational categories used in the 1852 census were referred to Hutton for a response, and he invited suggestions for improvements. Perhaps as a result, a schedule in the revised Census and Statistics Act in the Consolidated Statutes of 1859 contained a catalogue of religious denominations. Finally, in 1859, in his reply to a demand to indicate the accommodation necessary for his office on the return of Parliament to Quebec, Hutton mentioned the necessity of office space for census clerks.[17] Apart from these activities, Hutton seems to have done nothing before imperial despatches announced the approach of the fourth International Statistical Congress in London.

The Statistical Congress, a brainchild of the remarkable Belgian statistical pioneer, L.-A.-J. Quetelet, had met biennially since 1853. By 1860 it was the showpiece of the international statistical movement, attracting leading intellectuals and statesmen of the highest rank from throughout Europe and America. The Congress was a rare venue for discussion, for debate, and for the articulation of projects aimed at global coordination in such matters as the monetary standard, weights and measures, climactic observation, social sanitation, and, certainly not least, census making. Earlier congresses had produced an agreed upon template for census organization.

For 1851 the imperial government had attempted to secure a common, empirewide census date and to have colonial administrations follow the General Register Office's enumeration procedures. A second attempt at coordination was made for 1861, originating, on this occasion, from South Australia, where the governor had communicated with his fellow administrators in 1859, urging a common Australian census. His correspondence had been copied to the Colonial Secretary with the suggestion that all colonies be urged to make a common enumeration in 1861; forwarded to the English Registrar General; and then copied, with his comments and with sample English enumeration schedules and enumerators' instructions, to other colonial governors, including governor Head in Canada. Colonial officials were sent a copy of the resolutions of the 1857 Statistical Congress on the conduct of censuses. It was suggested that they might wish to name delegates to the next Statistical Congress. A second despatch soon followed, again stressing the desirability of establishing a system of uniform international statistics and inviting the nomination of a Canadian delegate to the 1860 London Congress.[18]

The 1857 Congress resolutions specified both how enumerations should be conducted and the minimum kinds of information they should gather. Following Quetelet's Belgian model once again, enumerations should adopt the *de facto* principle, although special circumstances might make it interesting to discover the *de jure* population. Censuses should record names and should be conducted decennially, preferably in the month of December, by specially engaged agents. There should be one enumeration schedule per household or family, and the completion of schedules should be supervised by the enumerator or filled in by him directly according to information provided. This information was to include for each person: name, age, birthplace, language spoken, religion, marital status, occupation, and residency status in the district (regular, temporary, or transient). The number of children at school and the size of living spaces were to be recorded. Those with various kinds of infirmities ('maladies et infirmités apparentes': deaf, blind, dumb, lunatic, and idiot) were to be counted. Finally, the congress urged jurisdictions to produce census abstracts according to a standard form. There was no recommendation concerning an inventory of agricultural or industrial production, but the list of standard information was a minimum.

In response to the imperial census circular, the Canadian Board of Registration and Statistics met on 28 February 1860, and instructed William Hutton to prepare a memorandum outlining necessary changes to the 1852 enumeration schedules. Hutton responded within a week, and although his memorandum has not survived, annotations on the despatched copy of English enumerators' instructions suggest that one concern was to define districts that could be enumerated in a day, as the *de facto* model supposed. Yet six weeks passed before a Bureau of Agriculture clerk was detached for census preliminaries, and it was 4 May before Hutton directed a preliminary inquiry about census account keeping to the Auditor General. Here he noted that 'no steps can well be taken for printing the Circulars &c until after the European Congress of all Nations meets in July next – when valuable suggestions will be submitted by the Reg. Genl. &c..' On 2 June, Hutton wrote to a number of Protestant clergymen inviting their suggestions for categories for the denominational returns. The same week, he sought the reaction of Richard Nettle from the Saguenay region to the categories he proposed to use for acquiring returns of fresh fish.[19]

Only on 19 June 1860 did the Executive Council nominate A.T. Galt, the Minister of Finance, as its delegate to the conference, scheduled for the week of 16 July. Council decided that Galt should 'submit copies of the Census taken in January 1852, and also the improvements contemplated in the Columns of the approaching Census of 12th January 1861 (recently reported on by the Secretary of the Department) for the purpose of comparison, and if need be for amelioration.'[20] Hutton immediately sent Galt sample census materials and sought permission to accompany him to London. Hutton pointed out that he would be able to provide information on the 1852 census, and would himself be able 'to glean much information which would be useful to me in taking this coming Census in Jany 1861 & in reporting thereon.' The congress would also furnish an opportunity for Hutton to attend to pressing family matters in Dublin.[21]

Galt, however, preferred to invite the educator, explorer, and statistician Henry Yule Hind. The Canadian delegation also provided credentials for the African colonization activist Dr Martin Delany. Perhaps one of the Canadians did attend the census section of the congress, although the only traces of them in the congress proceedings are of Galt in the section on statistical measures, which dealt with weights, measures, and banking statistics, and of Delany in the section on medical statistics. The delegation made a dismal showing. It was one of the few not to have a statistical paper in the published congress proceedings. Galt and Hind seem to have waited about in London for some time after the close of the congress, while Hind arranged for the August printing of another edition of his *British North America*, a 219-page statistical compendium containing six maps. Perhaps he circulated versions of the manuscript at the congress. Galt had earlier published *Canada from 1849 to 1859* (London: 1860), and was preoccupied with securing English support for his tariff and banking reforms. There is no surviving discussion of the proposed Canadian census in the Congress proceedings.[22]

Hutton's absence was doubly unfortunate. The delegates in the census section debated many aspects of census making – especially the framing of census categories – and Hutton could have profited from these exchanges. As well, having to await Galt's return and his report on the proceedings of the conference before finalizing his plans for the census of 1861 forced Hutton into very narrow timelines that effectively prevented a trial enumeration, had he thought to make one.[23] A Colonial Office despatch of mid-August finally announced the English census date, urged colonial authorities to attempt to approximate it (an earlier Canadian date was already fixed), and again stressed that the information defined as desirable at the Statistical Congress was that which should be gathered in colonial censuses.[24]

**Devising and Printing Census Forms**
As the Canadian press debated the prospects of the census, William Hutton was awaiting the official report of the Statistical Congress. It was not until 10 October 1860 that he sought 120 copies of the Census Act from the Queen's Printer for the use of census commissioners. In a memorandum to the Board of Registration and Statistics of the same date, Hutton drew attention to the necessity of acquiring several tons of paper for the printing of census schedules, forms, and instructions. Samples of the material were 'to be submitted to the Board early next week for their Examination & approval,' and Hutton sought instructions about letting the printing to tender. While the call for tenders was made between 16 and 20 October, it was 24 October before Hutton submitted copies of his instructions to enumerators and commissioners for the board's approval, and the last day of October before tenders were officially awarded.

While Hutton's deputy was sending copies of enumerators' instructions in some form to selected MPPs early in November, the printing of census materials lagged.[25] Printing contracts were a prime source of political patronage, and they were distributed widely. Communications between several of the presses in Canada West and Hutton's office in Quebec were slow. For example, manuscript copies of some census schedules were sent to the Toronto *Leader* and the Hamilton *Spectator* on 10 November, with a request for a speedy return of the proofs. The printed proofs left Hamilton for Quebec on 24 November, and then another ten to fourteen days passed before the corrected proofs were returned to the printers. After their return, Hutton sought to make additional changes.[26] Responsibility for the translation of at least some manuscript material from English into French was left to Augustin Côté of the *Journal de Québec*, which suggests that Hutton's office did not contain an effectively bilingual census clerk. When Côté encountered difficulties in the task of rendering the names of, to him, arcane Protestant religious sects, Hutton was again compelled to contact the clergy for guidance, and this led to a further delay in the printing process.[27]

Twice as many schedules were printed in English as in French: enough to enumerate about two million people in English, but only enough in French to enumerate one million. Hutton's published calculations anticipated a total colonial population of close to three million; clearly, then, he had made no provision for waste or spoilage in the use of schedules. The large number of copies of instructions to enumerators, and of enumerators' oaths, shows that Hutton was anticipating that there would be many small enumeration districts.

Political influence over the distribution of printing contracts and the attempt to use the Board of Registration and Statistics in Quebec as the clearinghouse for all census forms and schedules created serious logistical problems. All the English-language instructions to enumerators and commissioners, along with the enumerators' oaths, were printed in Quebec and had then to be shipped to commissioners in Canada West. Some of the French personal schedules were printed in Toronto and then shipped back to Quebec. All of the English urban schedules were printed at the Quebec *Chronicle*, but most of the rural English census schedules were printed in Hamilton and Toronto. Some, perhaps all, of the first press runs were shipped to the board in Quebec for redistribution. One western census commissioner was told at the offices of the Toronto *Leader* on 27 December 1860 that all census material had been shipped to Quebec.[28]

The organization of printing presented Hutton with problems of coordination, given the slowness of overland communication away from the railway net and given the lethargy of the Executive Council, on which his own lack of administrative autonomy forced him to depend to appoint census commissioners. It was the last week in November before the Council decided on the appointments; only then was Hutton able to contact commissioners and send them copies of the Census Act and their instructions. The official appointments were made about two weeks later than they had been in 1852, although Hutton managed to avoid most of the worst stupidities that surrounded Crofton's appointments.[29] By the end of November, however, the season for water navigation was closed, and enumeration materials could not reach such remote areas as Sault Ste. Marie and Pembroke in Canada West, and the Magdalen Islands in

TABLE 5.1
Distribution of Job Printing for the 1861 Census

| Press | Printing job | Language |
| --- | --- | --- |
| *Journal de Québec* | 50 instructions to commissioners | French |
| | 2,500 instructions to enumerators | French |
| | 2,500 declarations of enumerators | French |
| | 10,000 small personal sheets | French |
| | 10,000 large personal sheets | French |
| | 3,000 large agricultural sheets | French |
| *Chronicle* (Quebec) | 20,000 small personal sheets | English |
| *Mercury* (Quebec) | 3,500 instructions to enumerators | English |
| | 3,500 declarations of enumerators | English |
| | 70 instructions to commissioners | English |
| *Leader* (Toronto) | 10,000 large personal sheets | English |
| | 8,000 large agricultural sheets | English |
| | 8,400 large personal sheets | French |
| *Spectator* (Hamilton) | 26,000 personal sheets | English |

Source: NAC RG17, vol. 2418, 31 October 1861.

Canada East, before the enumeration date. In the case of the latter, Hutton concluded that it would be May of 1861 before the islands could be enumerated; he suggested to the prospective census commissioner that 'notices ... might be sent to the People to take notes as to their Population, Cattle &c, on the 14th January so that they might answer the Questions as up to that time & not later.'[30] An important gap was anticipated in some areas between the nominal and the actual census day.

**Appointing Census Officers**
As with the awarding of printing contracts, commissioners' appointments were patronage matters, and although some who had acted in 1852 managed to claim that the office rightly belonged to them again in 1861, cabinet used the Board of Registration and Statistics to invite loyal MPPs to nominate candidates.[31] Commissioners were to appoint their own enumerators. The board also appointed census clerks, although several of Hutton's suggestions for appointments were followed.

Applications from potential census clerks had begun to arrive at the bureau as early as April 1860, and Hutton made his first appointments at the end of July, although it was specified that the work and the excellent pay ($2 per day including Sundays) were not to start until 1 November. Hutton chose two men he had known well from Belleville, Canada West, to direct the work: Thomas McNider as chief compiler, and S.S. Finden, the former collector of customs, as McNider's assistant. By mid-November 1860, seven census clerks had been hired, and as the work of compilation began in 1861, their numbers swelled.[32] The first group of census clerks was hired immediately after census contingency funds were authorized in the first week of November; matters moved much less quickly with respect to census commissioners.

One cause of delay was the issue of which units to use for the commissions. Hutton and the government faced a difficult choice between electoral divisions and municipal units. The glaring electoral frauds of the 1850s, during which in some ridings more people voted than the total population enumerated in 1852, had made voter registration a leading plank in the opposition party platform. Enumerating by electoral district might deflect the demand. On the other hand, reporting census results by ridings rather than by municipal units had the potential to affect the political fortunes of MPPs, whose electors might use evidence of local 'improvement' produced by the census to evaluate their performance. This issue was still undecided as late as the third week of November. Hutton's difficulty was exacerbated by the fact that many new counties, townships, and towns had been established since the census of 1852. His office did not command a current list of municipal units – an elementary infrastructural condition for the centralization of census knowledge. He feared that 'recent changes in the Counties ... might embarrass' commissioners appointed for Canada East, either because they would find it confusing to administer the census or because changed boundaries would lead to declining population totals for old counties. Finally, in the last week of November, the board settled on counties and cities and towns as units.[33]

**Commissioners and Their Instructions**

Commissioners in Canada West were notified unofficially of their appointments on 25 November, and officially toward the end of December. On the former date they were sent copies of the Census Act, of their official instructions, and of the instructions to enumerators, along with the promise that 'more copies of the Instructions & the census sheets' would be sent 'in a few days.' Although Hutton claimed that these instructions were being mailed so that commissioners would 'be in readiness to select ... Enumerators with due regard to their required qualifications,' and to 'divide the Census sheets in conformity with the instructions herewith forwarded,' many commissioners did not have time to do so.[34]

Hutton managed to improve on Walter Crofton's dealings with the commissioners by offering procedural guidance in a circular of 'Instructions to Census Commissioners.' They were told to begin by dividing their jurisdictions into enumeration districts, taking care to specify the boundaries clearly and to ensure that there was no overlap and that nothing was missed. Districts were to be numbered sequentially – an improvement over 1852 – so that the recapitulation of results would proceed smoothly. Towns, cities, and incorporated villages were to be separated from rural enumeration districts and were to be subdivided as necessary. A list was to be made of public institutions, and these were to be enumerated by their superintendents, guards, governors, or principals.

Hutton reproduced material from the English General Register Office about the choice of enumerators. These men were to be intelligent and active, able to read well and write clearly, temperate, regular, and respectable in their conduct, and governed by sentiments of good will. They should also be thoroughly acquainted with their enumeration districts, disposed to carry out their duties faithfully and efficiently, and willing to offer their assistance whenever possible to the residents of their districts. Commissioners were told they could remove unsatisfactory enumerators and conduct a second enumeration of any place they felt had been poorly served. They were to scrutinize the enumerators' reports, making sure they had followed the instructions and that they had written clearly and made legible figures that would be easy to add up. The commissioners were to ensure that the enumerators' column totals were internally consistent.

Hutton told the commissioners to notify the board of the boundaries of districts and of the names of enumerators; then, 'in November or December,' the board would provide them with sufficient census schedules to conduct the enumeration. They were to acknowledge receipt of these in writing and to impose a similar obligation on their enumerators, among whom the sheets would be divided. To enable commissioners outside urban areas to define enumeration districts, Hutton planned to provide each with a skeleton map of his district, and enumerators, 'if competent,' were to provide sketch maps of the areas they had actually enumerated. Commissioners were to publicize the forthcoming census by posting handbills in conspicuous places. Supplementary instructions offered to at least some commissioners informed them to deliver copies of schedules personally to enumerators and to meet with them to explain how the schedules were to be completed. They were again expected to travel throughout their districts during the enumeration in order to supervise enumerators' activities. Finally, the commissioners were reminded that upon their efforts would depend 'the reality of the representation not only of the population, but of the material resources and the social condition' of their districts, and they were urged to fulfil their own duties faithfully.[35]

**'How did this happen?'**
Providing commissioners with the appropriate mix of census documents in a timely fashion proved once again to be beyond the capacity of the Board of Registration and Statistics. The sectional differences of 1852 reappeared, with commissioners in the counties close to Quebec and Montreal generally better and earlier supplied than those farther away. Many of the latter were forced to appoint enumerators at the last moment and were unable to discuss census schedules in detail with them or to explain their duties clearly. Enumerators waited past the census day for schedules to arrive or took the information on hand-ruled sheets or scrap paper. Things were not necessarily easier for those commissioners who were closer to the centre of supply. They tended to get their forms and schedules in time to study them and to meet with enumerators, but such investigations revealed serious inconsistencies in the census instructions, an important typographical error, and missing columns. Once again the board was compelled to issue supplementary instructions after the enumeration was underway. The board had only a rudimentary system in place for receiving, checking, packing, and shipping census materials – one that used scribbled notations on commissioners' letters as the main control device. The recently engaged office staff consisted of men whose first qualification was their political connections. Hutton himself was distracted by the slow and miserable death of one of his daughters at home, even as his own health was failing. He was repeatedly bemused by logistical problems, pencilling comments such as 'How did this happen?' across commissioners' letters of complaint.[36]

**The Limits of the Urban**
Confusion reigned even in the census office as to the requirements of the enumeration plan. Hutton and his staff did not share a common understanding of a clause in the Census and Statistics Act of 1859 that

had extended the practices of self-enumeration to 'Cities and incorporated Towns' and that also allowed such practices to be adopted in 'such other localities as the Board of Registration and Statistics [shall] think proper.' On reading the Census Act sent them by Hutton's office, commissioners in Canada West reasonably concluded that all incorporated towns would undergo self-enumeration. There was a general expectation that villages would be treated similarly, and at least one commissioner expected that in the rural districts, the enumeration schedules would be left for householders to complete.[37] While Hutton had planned for a self-enumeration only in the seven cities where it had been held in 1852, his staff, likely in his absence, shipped self-enumeration schedules to some commissioners, who intended to distribute them in county towns. Other commissioners thought they could not follow the census plan because they had not received urban enumeration schedules. The confusion meant that some urban areas were enumerated twice, and that some enumerators and commissioners transcribed householders' returns onto rural personal schedules.

Thomas White for Peterborough County excused himself for not following what he understood to be the procedures: 'I have not been able to cause that portion of the Instructions to Enumerators, *in Towns*, requiring them to leave schedules at the different houses during the week previous to the taking of the Census, to be complied with, owing to the non receipt by me, of the blank schedules.'[38] On the other hand, N.S. Appleby, the commissioner for Hutton's home county of Hastings, requested and received self-enumeration schedules for the county town. He acknowledged the receipt of a shipment of 800 personal and 130 agricultural schedules on 5 January 1861 and promptly ordered more. 'Before I can get all the Enumerators at work,' he inquired, 'will there be any schedules sent for the Enumerators for the Town of Belleville'? A week later he received a second shipment of 100 personal and 30 agricultural schedules, as well as '200 slips 40 of which I immediately distributed to the Enumerators for the Town of Belleville.' Hutton was taken aback when he saw Appleby's letter, pencilling in the margin, 'What does he mean by Slips.'[39]

John Beatty, professor of natural science at Victoria College and again the commissioner for Northumberland County, complained twice that he could not follow his instructions concerning the urban enumeration because he had 'no supply of the "*schedules*" to be left by the Enumerators at each house before Saturday night, in the Town [of Cobourg].' 'Can you tell me why none of the slips required for Towns have been sent?' he telegraphed to the board on 7 January 1861. Five days later he received an urgent telegram from Hutton, informing him that no self-enumeration was to be conducted outside the main cities. Nonetheless, there, waiting for Beatty that very morning in the post office, was a package of urban enumeration schedules. A second telegram on the morning of the census day instructed him to return them at once. 'I could not account for the contradiction apparent between the slips arriving and your telling me to return them,' wrote Beatty, 'but in the face of the fact, that the enumerators for the Town were clamarus for the slips, – that they were in hand and really required them to obtain any thing like satisfactory returns from manufacturers and business men – I entrusted them to the Enumerators.' For this reason, he informed Hutton in response to another telegram sent him on census day, 'it is out of my power now, to obey the injunction received this morning, to return them.'[40] Hutton had to get Beatty, Appleby, and perhaps some other commissioners to replace the urban schedules sent them by mistake and had also to offer an explanation of the confusion around self-enumeration in his report to the Minister of Agriculture.[41] Of course, such re-enumerations further weakened the principle of a *de facto* procedure by distancing social observations in some areas from the common observation period.

**Supplying the Countryside**
Logistical problems extended beyond the confusion around urban self-enumeration. In many parts of the colony, time constraints and supply problems led to variations in enumeration practices and periods. Commissioners paid to advertise the census in the local press, only then to receive the official handbills and the intelligence that the board would not cover their advertising costs. Circulars informing them to modify certain census columns arrived either before the commissioners had seen the schedules themselves or after the schedules had been mailed on to enumerators. John Beatty's enumerators had been at work for a week before he received detailed instructions as to how entries should be made in the manufacturing columns.[42]

Often, the commissioners had insufficient time to discuss the schedules with their enumerators. For instance, William Gunn of Bruce County received the bulk of his blank census forms in Kincardine on the evening of 12 January 1861. He reported that he 'lost no time in dispatching messengers to the north and north East portions of the County, and blasted off through the South and South East portions' himself. He noted that 'the weather was at the time the most severe we had all winter.'[43] Other commissioners, such as John Jarvis of Perth County, found that they had more time and enumerators than schedules. Jarvis enlisted his enumerators by mail in early December and ordered a supply of schedules, but received only a part of what he needed. On 10 January 1861, he telegraphed in desperation to Hutton: 'Sent for four hundred (400) personal sheets & agricultural to match only received one hundred & thirty (130) The population is forty thousand (40,000) why not send me the required quantity – several enumerators have resigned.' The following day: 'Have you sent me any more sheets fifteen enumerators are waiting.' In fact, not until the afternoon of the census day, 14 January, was Jarvis able to distribute his census schedules, and since 'many of the Enumerators were so annoyed at having to call so often for their sheets [that] they would not take the office,' he was obliged to enumerate several districts himself. As they were elsewhere, Jarvis's enumerators were already demanding extra pay for the troublesome agricultural census.[44]

Some commissioners, especially those close to the census offices in Quebec, were equipped with the necessary forms and instructions as much as two weeks before the census day. Once again it was relatively easy for many commissioners in Canada East to receive extra census materials and instructions, and given the compact nature of settlement in the old parishes, many could communicate easily with their enumerators. Thus Solyme Bertrand, the commissioner for Rouville County, acknowledged receipt of his unofficial appointment and of a number of agricultural census sheets on 9 December 1860. He immediately set about finding his enumerators, choosing the county's seven parishes as his districts, and announcing that he would 'prepare the notices which are to be read and posted at the church doors in the different parishes and in the most frequented places.' Bertrand received 500 personal census sheets on 20 December, all that he thought he would need, and took the time to examine the sheets, perhaps discussing them with his enumerators as well. On 31 December he wrote to the Board of Registration and Statistics, posing detailed questions about sections of the personal and agricultural forms.[45]

The *notaire* P. Labelle, commissioner for Laval County, acknowledged his official appointment on 2 January 1861, as well as the receipt of a bundle containing 232 personal census sheets (220 in French), fifteen copies of enumerators' instructions and certificates, and eleven official census notices. He needed a few extra personal sheets, enough copies of the instructions and certificates for each of his twenty-one enumerators, and, especially, the agricultural census sheets, of which he had received none. Two days later, he wrote complaining that he had received two agricultural sheets, but they were in English. He asked the board to do him 'the service of sending me only Blanks in French. The number, if you please, that I asked you for and that as quickly as possible. For the Enumerators to acquit themselves of their obligations with satisfaction, it is appropriate that they study the blanks some days before the period fixed for the said Census.'[46] These commissioners and several others in the east were provided with materials before census day, were able to discuss them with enumerators, and were able to use well-defined parish boundaries to delineate enumeration districts. If the schedules had only made sense, they would have been able to proceed efficiently to the enumeration.

**Out of School**

Differences in municipal organization between the parishes and townships of Canada East and the municipal divisions of Canada West again affected the enumeration. As a rule, in the compactly settled, established francophone parishes in Canada East, commissioners defined far fewer districts and employed far fewer enumerators than did their counterparts in the townships of the east and in the counties of Canada West. In the eastern Chambly County, for instance, ten enumeration districts were enumerated by seven enumerators, while in Kamouraska there were eighteen enumeration districts, two of them convents enumerated by a religious superior. Yet Leeds County in Canada West was divided into twenty-five districts outside the county town. Norfolk County had twenty-seven enumerators, and Middlesex County fifty-three. There were fifty-seven enumeration districts in Carleton County and ninety-three in Huron. The eastern parish enumerators typically were notaries, with an occasional doctor or merchant pressed into service. The western enumerators were farmers, with an occasional school teacher or merchant also at work. Class-cultural and local administrative differences combined with logistical conditions to produce diverse enumeration practices.

Hutton attempted to base the 1861 enumeration on the units of the school system. He was a former school inspector, and the administration of public schools provided the most clearly organized connections between localities and the central government. He planned to use schoolteachers as enumerators. They were literate in principle and had at least some experience with practices of observation and reporting. Had this,

his most serious attempt at innovation, succeeded, greater consistency and exhaustiveness in observational practices across enumeration districts might well have resulted. He might also have been able to approximate the requirements of the *de facto* census design for a rapid enumeration by observers well acquainted with the residents of their districts.

In his second report on the 1852 census, Hutton had pointed favourably to the English practice of having extremely small enumeration districts that were well known to enumerators and easy to enumerate in a day. Later in the decade he corresponded with both colonial Superintendents of Education just enough to assure himself that school sections were sufficiently well defined to serve as enumeration districts and to enlist an expression of support from the superintendents for the use of them. In May 1860 he mentioned to P.-J.-O. Chauveau, Superintendent East, 'it is especially desired that the Enumeration Districts be very small so that one Enumerator will be able to take the whole district in four or five days.' He even agreed to Chauveau's suggestion that completed enumeration schedules be vetted by the local *curé* before being returned to the board. Hutton repeated his proposal about school sections in a letter to the American census superintendent in June 1860, in which he revealed that 'we contemplate giving each Enumerator one School Section having about 60 or 70 families & consequently we shall have several thousand Enumerators & a Comr. for each Electoral Division containing about 23.000 souls (represented by one Member of Parliament).' Such a plan, Hutton hoped, would 'expedite the work so that it can all be done by the Enumerators within 2 or 3 weeks.' The inclusion of 6,000 copies of the enumerators' instructions in the census printing order indicates that the plan for school districts survived the Statistical Congress.[47] Yet there is no indication of a serious effort to prepare the education offices, the school inspectors and superintendents, the county boards of education, or the teachers themselves for participation in the 1861 census. The plan proved unworkable.

In the official instructions, commissioners were allowed some latitude in defining districts, especially in rural areas. They were told to divide their jurisdictions into enumeration districts sufficiently small to be covered by a rural enumerator in at most six days.[48] School sections were suggested as enumeration districts, although commissioners were first to ensure that the districts selected would include all areas under their supervision. For towns and cities, Hutton's instructions initially held to the proposition that each enumerator should have at most 70 to 100 families; but it immediately became apparent that the pay for such small districts would make it difficult to attract enumerators. On 29 November, Hutton wrote to the urban census commissioners in Canada West to announce that 'each Enumerator in Cities may have the Census of *200* families to take (say 1200 Individuals or thereabouts).' A similar letter reached county commissioners. In practice, many enumerators returned more than 1,500 names.[49]

With a few exceptions, commissioners did not attempt to adopt school sections as enumeration districts. The Huron County commissioner, John Leary, a former Irish 'Head Constabule' who boasted of his experience as an Irish census commissioner for 1851, pointed out that 'School Sections as suggested in my instructions could not be made Enumeration districts as they are often changed and very much divided.' William Gunn, the Bruce County commissioner and a school inspector, had also 'thought of taking the School Sections as Enumeration Districts, but the number, some 150, is so great, and the area, generally so small, that ... the instructions of the Department could not be carried out.' Thomas White Jr. from Peterborough County noted: 'In one Township alone, Monaghan, I have fixed the School sections as Districts, and appointed the Teachers Enumerators. They happened in this Township to be well qualified for the task; although it would not be safe to make this class of appointments the rule throughout the County.'[50]

As John Beatty for Northumberland pointed out, if enumeration districts were to be restricted to the number of families contained in a school district, 'the Chief difficulty here is to get reliable, capable men to act for so small a remuneration as such districts would pay.'[51] Indeed, at $.02 per name, enumerators would have earned about $5 for taking the census of 70 families. Even after Hutton allowed the commissioners to expand the enumeration districts, the fees offered were considered low. The eloquent A. Macdonald Lockhart of Haldimand County argued that fees should at least be doubled because '2 dollars per hundred would induce no man of talent to leave a warm fireside, to toil through dub & mire, & wind & rain & sleet & snow, to receive abuse from every Tom, Dick, & Harry upon whom he might have to call.'[52]

Beatty's mention of difficulties in finding 'capable men' in school sections should probably be taken literally: Hutton's design to use teachers as enumerators did not take into account that women were rapidly entering the occupation. At the time Beatty was writing, slightly over 30 per cent of teachers were women. No women seem to have been hired as enumerators for 1861.[53] Francophone commissioners in the eastern section of the colony seem simply to have ignored the suggestion that school sections be adopted.

**No Maps**

Hutton's confidence that the administrative units of the school system would serve to define enumeration districts may help explain his failure to undertake a mapping operation. He promised to deliver county-level skeleton maps to commissioners, but none has survived in their papers, and it is not clear that the board managed to provide many. For instance, John Jarvis complained of not receiving maps, a concern echoed by William Holmes for Kent County, who pointed out in December 1860 that 'the *map* promised in the Instructions to commissioners has not yet come to hand.' Holmes thought having it 'would be a very geat convenience in this County' because of 'the recent changes of the boundery between Kent and Lambton' and also because there had been 'new surveys in the Township of Orford which are not shown in any Map here.' As we shall see below, the Orford census would prove particularly difficult for Holmes.[54]

The plan to use the school system to define districts meant that Hutton did not attempt to extend any new administrative infrastructures into localities. The census was an occasion for intensifying the administrative capacity of the state system; but Hutton had not the time, and likely not the resources or the clout or the imagination, to do otherwise than attempt to piggyback the census onto the existing administrative organization. As he had received a general assurance from the education superintendents that the school sections were sufficiently well defined to serve as local census units, he did not attempt to map enumeration districts independently; thus, the failure of the plan to use the school districts left Hutton, like Crofton before him, entirely reliant on the administrative energies and local geographical knowledge of the commissioners and enumerators.

Projects to map the colonial territory, still very much in their infancy before the 1852 census, were much more advanced before the 1861 census, and Hutton was well placed to know exactly what cartographic resources were available. In the 1850s his bureau repeatedly arranged for the production of maps to be included in immigration pamphlets – both maps of the colony as a whole and smaller-scale maps of colonization roads. Hutton's office had used the work of the Geological Survey to indicate mineral deposits on settlement maps, and the colonization effort had established regular connections between the bureau and the Department of Crown Lands. By 1858, Crown Lands was displaying two colonial maps: one of them was sixty-nine feet long by thirteen wide on a scale of two miles to the inch; the other was on a scale of twelve miles to the inch and measured twelve feet by five. The maps covered all the territory from the Labrador coast to west of Lake Superior and showed all lots of land in the surveyed townships in both sections of the colony, and in the seigneuries in Canada East, and the location of cities, towns, and villages. They also showed railways, highways, and some other roads, as well as some topographical features. The maps testify to a major state-forming project underway in the 1850s, and at least in principle it would have been possible for Hutton to specify enumeration districts 'on the ground' to a degree well beyond what was possible in 1852.[55] He did not do so.

At best, Hutton's imaginary of social bodies in time and space tied people to educational spaces. With more extensive and diligent preparation, the administrative framework of the public school system might have served to freeze mobile bodies for observational purposes, although the mixed *de facto/de jure* design tended to confuse the matter of people's 'true' locations somewhat. More important, neither Hutton nor his political masters sought to use the census to configure social relations in keeping with a general project for governing population that contained a transcendental vision of bodies, spaces, and time. While it was important in terms of political debate, and especially for the issue of sectional strength, and while it was necessary for the resolution of a number of administrative questions, the 1861 census was driven by no larger governmental ambition conducive to rigorous investigation.

**Whom to Count?**
The nomadic aboriginal population presented particular difficulties for a configuration of social relations that tied people to a single 'normal' place. Even where Indians were settled on reservations, some commissioners wondered if it was worth the trouble to enumerate them. W.W. Holmes of Lambton County pointed out that neither of the reservations on Walpole and St. Anne islands was in his county for municipal purposes, although they seemed to be so from a geographical point of view, and asked if he should bother with them. Alexander Vidal of Sarnia in Kent County wondered, 'Is the "Indian Reservation" adjoining this Town to be included in the County for Census purposes?' adding, 'There are, I believe, none but Indians residing upon it, except the Missionary and his family.' Vidal did proceed with what he considered the 'very troublesome and difficult work' of enumerating them.[56] Enumerators complained that aboriginal informants refused to acknowledge their queries, and the enumeration practices were often applied to them partially.[57]

While it was not clear to some commissioners that Indians formed part of the Canadian population, the Board of Registration and Statistics insisted they did. The question at hand was not one of aboriginal citizenship. The legal basis for a political regime centred on rights-bearing citizens was little developed at the time, and neither Hutton nor his government ministers were interested in extending it. Like most other state servants, Hutton likely believed that the aboriginal population was bound to disappear. Attempts to count aboriginal peoples were mainly about creating a complete inventory of colonial resources, as Hutton's correspondence with Richard Carney, sheriff and census commissioner on the northwestern frontier, suggests. Carney was urged to 'endeavour from every source' to 'ascertain their number and also the Value of the Furs sold by them, distinguishing the different Furs.' Hutton also sought to discover 'the Venison sold by them.' Such items of information would give a more complete account of the colony's flourishing natural wealth for advertising purposes.

Yet the logic of enumerators canvassing fixed districts did not apply to the aboriginal population in the northwest, for reasons relating to the material conditions of Indian life and the absence of developed administrative infrastructures. Carney sent census schedules and detailed instructions to the Chief Factor of the Hudson's Bay Company and the Collector of Customs at Sault Ste. Marie inviting them to get such information as they could. 'Should there be any Indians resident about your Post or within a short distance,' wrote Carney to the factor, 'enter their names, their Wives and Children, as you would other Men their Wives and Children, only marking them "*Ind*" in the proper column, and give the probable number of Indians within your District.'

The Hudson's Bay Company was prepared to cooperate, but Carney was informed that the company's annual accounts were completed only in June and so he would have to wait for information about the fur trade. He suggested to the Board of Registration and Statistics that conditions of travel made it impossible to take a census of the Indian population in the winter and urged a delay. 'As the Red Men of the Forest are fast passing away,' he wrote, 'it would be a satisfaction to the present generation to know their correct Statistics and to posterity to note their gradual decline. – This can be done by defering the Indian Census till summer. – By that time the Indians with their families will be all out on the large Lakes and at the Hudson's Bay Company's Posts, and by sending persons to visit the different Posts and Lakes, the name and Statistics of every Indian can be as accurately taken as the whites are taken in the settled parts of the Country.' Three men with a canoe could do the work,

Carney suggested. His suggestion was not taken up, and the census of the northwestern aboriginal population was based primarily on the estimates and personal knowledge of traders and factors.[58]

Some commissioners also wondered if people falling into the census's 'race' category were part of the population. Charles Waters wrote to the board with this query: 'I believe there are no "Coloured Persons, mulattoes or Indians["] in this County – but should there be such are their Sex, ages, widowers or widows, married or Single. &c Enquiries and Entries throughout be made from the Entering of their names &c the same as the White residents? It would be difficult in most cases – to ascertain their Names Religion birth Place – ages or any thing Else.'[59] Hutton wanted to have everyone counted.

**'Farmers are generally awkward'**
Outside the francophone parishes in the east and the lakefront counties in the west, many commissioners scrambled to find men willing to do the work, and ended up defining enumeration districts according to whom they could hire. 'I spent three or four nights running round in Rainham & Walpole looking for Enumerators,' complained A. Macdonald Lockhart, 'and then had to go upon my hands and knees to parties to take the office; and many a one in the County only accepted from love to me.' Lockhart thought the Census Act should be amended 'so as to make it compulsory upon parties whom the commissioner might see fit to appoint as Enumerators to accept the office or pay a fine.'[60] In Carleton County on the Ottawa River, Francis Clemow, the commissioner and road agent, finished delivering schedules to the fifty-seven enumeration districts on the census day: 'It was no easy matter ... to find competent men to undertake the duties of enumerators.' Clemow thought he would have had less trouble if he had been allowed to use whole townships as districts; as it was, he hoped the small districts would mean the work would be done well.[61]

On 4 January 1861, Hugh McDougall, the commissioner for Russell County on the western side of the Ottawa River, wrote that he was having 'great difficulty in obtaining competent persons to act as Enumerators.' Several likely candidates were away on business, and others found the pay too low. 'I have almost failed in getting enumerators in some Townships owing to this fact,' McDougall continued, and 'in some districts I have not as yet succeded in getting any to act. In such an emergency what am I to do?' McDougall wrote to the board again on 23 January, pointing out that he had been compelled 'in some instances to make the districts very uneven owing to the fact that most of the Townships are settled in parcels here & there & not easily accessible.' Sarcastically, McDougall reassured the board that even though, in two districts, he had 'not found any competent persons who would undertake the work for the remuneration ... no difficulty will arise' because he had not had 'as yet one *single* sheet for these Districts & not sufficient in many others.' McDougall eventually received a supply of census schedules, but early in February, he revealed that he had 'found it necessary to unite enumeration districts 2 & 3 of Russell into one, as the enumerator appointed for Dis no 3 proved incapable & wished to be relieved from his duties.'[62]

Charles Waters, again commissioner for Prescott County, and now seventy-four years of age, was 'as Particular as the state of the Country would warrant in selecting fit and proper persons to take the census.' It had been no easy matter to find them. Waters had been forced to travel around the county in a hired sleigh, which cost him £7.10, and 'at the risk of my life' he went out in a blizzard to supply the enumerators with schedules on the eve of census day. 'I had my Face Frozen,' he noted. Waters had used the township assessment rolls to define districts of nearly equal extent and was grateful that his instructions had been changed to allow him to have an enumerator for every thousand or so inhabitants. 'Otherwise,' he commented, 'I would have found greater difficulty not only in dividing the several townships in to Enumeration Districts but also in Selecting a greater number of Efficient Enumerators in the several Localities. for Merchants if otherwise qualified nor their Clerks if qualified could be induced to neglect their business to perform the duties of Enumerators – and farmers are generally awkward and in many respects not qualified to make Efficient Enumerators.' In the end, Waters's enumerators were mainly township collectors, clerks, and assessors, with a law student for L'Orignal village – men who 'would not willingly have devoted their services only for a desire to assist me in Carrying out my Instructions.'[63]

Elsewhere in the west and in the townships of the east, commissioners reported hiring whom they could get; having to replace those who proved incompetent and thus to start parts of the enumeration over again; and finding that their enumerators subcontracted the work.[64] John Barker for Lincoln county claimed that 'some of the most competant persons whom I had selected in the Municipalities refused on their seeing the Blanks and I had to take almost who I could get. in Consequence I have had all of [the schedules] to corect & some to coppy over again but although they are not quite as handsome as I could have wished I hope they will prove to be Corect.'[65]

With a staff selected by patronage criteria and confused about the details of the plan it was to execute, with commissioners chosen for their political loyalties and undersupplied with necessary materials, with enumerators whose qualifications were dubious and who were in it for the money, with districts of incomparable size, and with a census supervisor who was ill and distracted, the stage was set in 1861 for another census fiasco, as the following chapter shows.

Chapter 6

# The 'Reality of the Representation'

William Hutton had learned little from the enumeration of 1852. His 1861 census grid attempted to configure social relations in much the same way as that which had earlier proved incoherent.[1] He cannot have examined the board's own records carefully, for he neglected to alter the 'place of birth' column, which had been unworkable in 1852. He was forced to issue a supplementary instruction to commissioners in the field so that they would distinguish anglophones from francophones.[2]

In four areas, Hutton did seek to extend and reshape the intelligence generated by the census. *First*, given the absence of civil registration in Canada West, the enumeration was to generate information about vital events. A new column was introduced headed 'Married during the year,' and two others, headed 'Widows' and 'Widowers,' supplemented the 'Married or not Married' column. Births and deaths were now separated by sex, and a column headed 'Age and cause of death' was added. *Second*, Hutton sought information about literacy by adding a column for men and women over twenty years of age not knowing how to read or write. With the existing columns concerning school attendance, this addition might have yielded information about the comparative progress of public education, the colony's most extensive governmental project and a subject of sectional conflict.

*Third*, Hutton attempted to specify more clearly the contours of the agricultural economy by distinguishing farm from non-farm agricultural production. New columns sought a count of and value for horses, cattle, sheep, pigs, and pleasure carriages and other conveyances 'belonging to residents of towns and not farmers.' A tenth column in this section sought a report of land area attached to nonfarm households. However, Hutton provided no criterion for the urban/rural divide.[3] *Fourth*, the schedules now attempted to define more clearly the developing industrial economy; twelve columns were included querying the nature of each enterprise, the materials employed by kind, quantity, and value, the motive force employed, the number of employees by sex and their average pay, and the quantity, kind, and value of the product.

The agricultural schedules closely replicated those employed in 1852, but with a number of additions and some specifications. Hutton sought a return of the value of farm machinery and of pleasure carriages (the latter were his measure of prosperity). Three columns addressed the production of fish, and four the production of iron and copper ore. A new column asked for a return of the value of the product of orchards or gardens. Tobacco had been dropped from the schedules. As in 1852, no attempt was made to produce a return of poultry and poultry products. Nor did Hutton address the metrological issues arising from sectional differences in measurement systems: French-language schedules again called for returns in arpents and minots, English for acres and bushels: these were not equivalents. Hutton's only metrological initiative was to specify the measures to be used for reporting carrots, mangel-wurzel, beef, and pork.

**Making Sense of the Census Schedules**

The 1861 census applied normalizing judgment to bodies in space and time in order to produce its account of 'population,' again invoking a mix of *de facto* and *de jure* principles of enumeration.[4] In the Canadas, everyone reportedly having slept in a given locale on the night of 13–14 January 1861 was to be enumerated in that place. Those not normally resident were to be indicated; however, so too were those who had not actually slept in the place in question on census night but whose 'normal residence' it was. Such people were to be described as 'temporarily absent.' The census schedules would thus be reporting both where people 'actually were' on census day and what informants considered to be their regular places. It was again intended that during the compilation process, those who were not in their 'normal residences' would be identified and reassigned to them. Reports of the 'actual' placement of bodies on census day would be used to assign people to a *single normal* place. It proved confusing, however, to have more than one account of the placement of individuals on a given census schedule, and the criteria adopted to guide the assignment of people to their normal places were not rigorously specified, nor were they even clearly conceived.

In an attempt to facilitate the execution of the census plan, Hutton provided more detailed instructions to commissioners and enumerators than did his predecessor. However, if the officials in Quebec believed their forms and instructions to be simple and lucid, correspondence from the field must have disabused them quickly. The official instructions demanded that enumerators do things that were logically impossible. Commissioners were told to ensure that enumerators obeyed. If the enumerators refused, the commissioners were to do the impossible things themselves. Most complied. An important typographical error confused matters further, and several of the instructions were significantly vague. At least three and perhaps five times, the Board of Registration and Statistics was forced to change the schedules while enumerators were at work. The inadequate preparation time allowed to enumerators, the absence of field trials for the schedules, the internally contradictory instructions issued, and ultimately the incoherence of the census design itself made it impossible to generate consistent social observations. Enumerators adopted a wide variety of observational protocols. Census commissioners attempted to systematize and coordinate the observations of enumerators, but again in ways not anticipated by the board, and often after the enumeration was complete.

**The Personal Census**
Confusion reigned especially in the areas where the possibilities for consistent interpretations were greatest: enumerating human bodies in given locales. With the partial exceptions of the aboriginal and 'coloured' populations, there were no status differences in the colony that led to conflicts over whose bodies were worth counting. There were no slaves, whose bodies in other jurisdictions were worth only part of a 'free' body. The convention that a child's body was the equal of an adult body, and that a woman's equalled a man's, was generally accepted for enumeration purposes. Enumerators, who were paid by the name, had an immediate individual interest in naming as many bodies as they possibly could. Collectively, they were encouraged by the census design to record many names more than once.

Of course, the census could not be executed by counting 'bodies in general,' the abstract bodies that make up 'population.' Population is produced by establishing relations of equivalence among empirically diverse human bodies; and access to information about the latter – the raw material of population – demands that social relations be modelled in some way that can practically guide inquiry.[5] The 1861 schedules modelled the world in which William Hutton and other gentlemen proprietors lived, and attempted to capture aspects of the class divisions and forms of mobility characteristic of this world. They presupposed a social organization consisting of independent commodity-producing households in which would be found male heads, wives and children, and various servants, farm labourers, and casual visitors. Male heads were to be the census informants. The proprietor's family would be returned to the household site, wherever the members happened to be on census day, as would the resident farm labourers. Short-term employees would be reassigned to their households of origin if these could be determined, or allowed to float if they could not. Casual visitors would be sent home. The single normal place people were to occupy was that of a household member, and as we have seen, households were to be contained in school districts.[6]

Hutton had given some thought to the dangers of multiple recording under this design. For instance, he was well aware that seasonal lumber workers might be counted twice. In supplementary instructions to the Algoma District census commissioner, he wrote, 'with regard to Shanty Men you will "take" all you can find in your District distinguishing if possible those Shanty Men who have permanent homes, and who are merely temporarily in the Bush, [from those] who have no regular homes. The Former will probably be entered elsewhere as absentees. The others would be no where noted unless by you or your Enumerator.'[7] Yet Hutton had not appreciated the confusion that would arise from attempting to indicate on the same enumeration schedule both where people were and where they were supposed to be. He did not specify any protocols whereby enumerators could determine what constituted a 'temporary absence': enumerators were allowed to make their own unregulated choices about who was in his or her normal place. Those who were normally in more than one place were either assigned to a single place or recorded more than once on the enumeration schedules. Because the duration of a 'temporary absence' was nowhere discussed or examined, people who resided away from their families but who were not transients could easily be returned twice. No practical means existed for eliminating multiple names in the compilation process. Such multiple counting could be uncovered, if at all, only by linking particular individuals returned as 'non resident' to their 'normal' residences – an extremely complex task, given that people were mobile across enumeration districts. This task proved to be of no interest to compilers.

The census design thus ensured that a great many names appeared more than once on the census schedules. To take one example, young schoolteachers were often returned in their parents' households as absentees, and again as resident non-family members in the schoolhouse or in the place they boarded while teaching. English-speaking commissioners pointed out that the requirement for enumerating institutions such as schools and jails produced double-listing. John Beatty warned the board that 'every name entered on the Census roll of the Cobourg, Colborne and Brighton Grammar Schools, will be found on the sheets for these places, or the districts immediately contiguous.'[8] No protocols were specified for dealing with people in hotels, inns, or taverns. Francophone commissioners and parish enumerators were somewhat less prone to multiplying names because they tended to adopt a more explicitly *de jure* enumeration principle. Still, such places as the hotels in Longueuil enumerated by Jacques Olivier Labranche contained clerks and travelling salesmen, who could easily have been reported elsewhere as absentees. Teachers, like eighteen-year-old Vitaline Paradis, who appeared with her parents in District 15, and again in the household where she boarded in District 17 of Kamouraska County, were returned more than once in the east as well as in the west, and all the boarders at the Chambly convent were returned as residents there and as absentees in their own households.[9]

**Impossible Demands**

The enumerators' instructions ensured that the systematic separation of casual visitors and strangers from regular members of households would be difficult or impossible. Enumerators were instructed to list on their schedules the names of *everyone* who had slept in a given house on the night of 13–14 January 1861, 'as well strangers as members of the family; and also those members of the family who are temporarily absent, but whose usual residence it is.' People out of place were to be indicated in two ways. A column (number 6) headed 'Residence, if out of limits' was reserved for listing the normal residences of 'strangers,' and this column was the principal means of identifying transients. Two subsequent columns (numbers 18 and 19), headed 'Members of the family absent,' distinguished by sex, were to identify usual residents who were temporarily absent. The schedules also contained two columns (8 and 9) jointly headed 'Sex.' For these columns, the enumerators' instructions simply said, 'need no explanation.'

In fact, detailed explanation at just this point was necessary to make it possible to reassign people to their single 'normal place.' The practical issue for commissioners and enumerators was the amount of information to be provided about transients, visitors, absentees, and people in public institutions. Below this lay the conceptual-political issue of just which single normal place each enumerated individual was to occupy. Consistency in applying the enumeration grid depended on enumerators disregarding the instruction that told them to enter information for every individual. If they had entered nothing for transients on the schedules except their names and usual places of residence, compilers would then have been able to identify transients with relative ease and to separate them from the 'normally resident' population. Yet for the underpaid enumerators a complete entry was worth 2¢, and so most followed their instructions.

Those who entered information in the 'Sex' column for transients found themselves faced with the impossible demand that the total number of people, listed on each census sheet and identified by sex, correspond to the total number of people on the census sheet after strangers and casual visitors had been removed. As the official instructions to enumerators read:

> Nos. 14, 15, 16 and 17. – These four columns should include all the residents in the house, whether members of family, Clerks, Servants, or Apprentices – but not casual travellers or visitors, as they are noted in the 5$^{th}$ [*sic*] column. Nos. 18 and 19. – In these columns note the members of the family temporarily absent. These six columns from 14 to 19, both included, should, when added up, agree with columns 8 and 9 [sex] together. – You are requested to take care that they do agree.[10]

Note that '5$^{th}$' ('Religion') was a typographical error for '6$^{th}$' ('Residence if out'), which Hutton was forced to correct in correspondence with commissioners – in many cases, after the enumerators were in the field.[11]

Any enumerator who identified transients by sex would find a larger number in the sex column than in the household columns. Yet he was told these two numbers had to agree. Enumerators responded in a variety of ways. Some disregarded the instruction to provide complete information for everyone and entered nothing for transients except their names and their usual place of residence. Although it was not universal there, such a response was common in the francophone parishes of Canada East, where commissioners had at least the time and perhaps also the good sense to notice that the enumeration would be incoherent if this practice was not adopted.[12] Others treated transients as if they were normal residents, providing full information for them. In between these extremes was a large number of variations that resulted in the partial completion of schedules. As well, many enumerators dealt with the demand for matching column totals in both parts of the census by not doing any addition at all. It fell to commissioners to do this work, yet their instructions also insisted that they take care 'that the columns from 14 to 19, inclusive, once totalled, correspond with the columns 8 and 9 together; if not the error must be corrected.'[13]

The board had been warned of an incoherence in its design before census day by the Rouville commissioner, Solyme Bertrand, although he did not quite grasp the problem. He thought that the enumeration should be conducted according to a strict *de facto* principle. If one adopted this strategy, then nothing should be recorded about absentees anywhere. Bertrand wrote to the board on 31 December 1860 noting, 'now, in the personal Census, it says in the instructions that the columns 14 to 19 must contain the same quantity of persons as those contained in columns 8 and 9.' He wished to know 'if we are to mention the names of the persons absent from the family,' and warned that if enumerators did report 'the absent members and the strangers, we will find more than in columns 8 and 9.' Since the census was 'a matter of taking in each house the names of the persons who slept [there] on the night of the 13$^{th}$ to the 14$^{th}$,' he concluded that 'the absences cannot be mentioned, given that they will be taken in another locality.' Bertrand thought that the simplest way to proceed was to indicate in the margins on the schedules the number of people who were absent, without naming them or reporting anything else about them. No evidence of a response to him exists.[14]

David White of Woodstock, pressed for time, attempted to protect himself from errors by publishing a supplementary instruction telling enumerators to make a rough draft of the returns so that they could make the census columns agree before submitting them. As he put it, 'the Commissioner would suggest that as certain columns are required to agree with certain other columns, these entries should first be made in pencil, or proved on waste paper, before making the entries on the Sheet.'[15] Other commissioners attempted to force the enumerators either to correct errors in their entries, or (if they refused) to pay their salaries to someone who would make the corrections. Regarding one characteristic of the completed schedules, however, the commissioners were agreed: as William Gunn grumbled, 'not one sett in ten is added up and some that are had better been left alone – Some in adding up columns 8 & 9 leave out strangers, persons not members of Family, and members of family absent, instead of making these two columns united foot up 50 – they may be 47. 46. or any number.'[16] John Leary observed of his enumerators' sheets, 'with very few exceptions they were all wrong and scarcely any of them made up at bottom, and mostly all incorrectly totted up, I done the best I could with them.'[17]

**Please Multiply the Names**
A query similar to Solyme Bertrand's was repeated four months later by Alexander Vidal. Looking over the completed schedules, Vidal found 'that the instructions given have been differently understood by the different enumerators in some respects.' He had 'many corrections to make to reduce them to uniformity,' and so wondered:

> Inquiry No.1 – Should casual visitors have any mark or letters in any of the columns except 1 and 6 – in most cases I find all particulars entered in the intervening columns and marks in columns 8 or 9
> No.2 By this plan columns 14 to 19 inclusive do not agree with 8 and 9, shall I make them agree by erasing the marks in 8 or 9 in visitors lines[?]

Pencilled responses, likely in Hutton's hand, were made on Vidal's letter. The response to the first question read, 'I think all Col 1 – 8 or 9 & in 16 or 17'; to the second, 'from 14 to 19 inclusive must contain as many as 8 & 9 together & 8 & 9 must agree with No. 1.' These instructions made it possible to make column totals correspond. They also told the commissioner to count transients and absentees as part of the resident population, ensuring they would be counted twice.

Perhaps a more formal reply was made to Vidal after the matter received further consideration, for his official report adopted a different method of compilation. He corrected the schedules so that there were entries for strangers only in columns 1 and 6, and he dealt with the tendency of his enumerators to count the dead among the living by excluding all information about them from all but columns 1 and 29 and 30 (deaths). This made columns 8 and 9 represent 'the *actual population* of the district.' As we shall see, this was not the practice followed by the board's compilers, and most enumerators included the dead in the population totals to make their columns agree.[18]

**Requires No Comment**
Columns in the census schedules whose meaning seemed transparent to officials at Registration and Statistics proved not to be so for enumera-

tors. The instruction 'requires no comment' attached to such columns was often interpreted as an injunction to leave them blank. Perhaps enumerators thought they would be filled in by someone else. Hutton's attempt to use the census to generate vital statistics was undermined for this reason. The fourth census column, 'Married during the year,' was provided to gather a return of the marriages that had taken place during 1860. However, the instruction to enumerators concerning this column simply read 'Requires no comment,' and the vast majority of enumerators interpreted this to mean that the column could be ignored. Some interpreted the heading to mean they should enter the year during which couples had been married, while a few interpreted the column as Hutton had intended.[19] The instructions for the columns dealing with births similarly read 'require no comment.' Thus, many enumerators returned the names of people whose age at their next birthday was one year, but made no mark for them in the births column.[20] Combined with the tendency for enumerators to count the dead among the living, the lack of instruction concerning returns of vital events ensured that the census would be useless as a source of vital statistics. In addition, the literacy columns – the subject of a later debate among social historians – were also described as 'require no comment.' These columns were headed 'Persons over 20 years of age not knowing how to read or write'; here, 'or' could easily be interpreted to mean 'and.' The vast majority of enumerators left these columns blank, leading some historians to claim that popular literacy rates were well over 90 per cent for those enumerated, while the matter may be primarily one of recording conventions.[21]

## Catalogues

The fruit of Hutton's earlier communications with the clergy was the inclusion of a truncated catalogue of religious denominations in the instructions to enumerators. The census was meant to tie everyone to a religious identity. The various sects of Presbyterians and Methodists were to be indicated in specified ways, but 'no sects other than these two require special distinguishing marks.' Hutton had omitted the Primitive Methodists from his list and was forced to issue a supplementary instruction indicating that they were to be identified by the letter 'P' in the religion column. His instructions seem to have had little impact on enumeration practices, for enumerators substituted their own descriptions for those in the official list. James B. Powell in Leeds County allowed his own views to serve as religious catalogue and commentary, preferring 'Papist' for Roman Catholics. He also described the notable Colonel E. Buell's occupation as 'Prophet,' gave his religion as 'true faith of Christ,' and said his son Lazrus was 'born by the spirit.' Nicholas Willoughby in the same county described religions as 'Babtist,' 'Not Babtised,' 'free thinkers,' and 'No religion.' George P. Wight added a note to his schedules in order to avoid confusion on the part of his commissioner, showing at the same time that he had not had or at least not followed Hutton's supplementary instructions about Primitive Methodists. 'Not[e],' Wight alerted his commissioner, 'in colum No 5 P signififes that the persons belong to no Church but they wish to be understood that they are Protestants not only on this sheet but on all sheets where the letter P are found in colum No5 .' Wight described other denominations as 'Baptise,' and 'Tucker.'[22] Urban self-enumerators were provided with no catalogue of denominations at all and chose their own self-descriptions – a potentially rich source for social historians. One cloth worker in Toronto's St Andrew's ward gave his religion as 'Fear God and honour the Queen.'[23] Compilers faced a challenging task with such returns.

Not even a truncated catalogue of occupations or trades was provided. The instructions to enumerators said clearly that they were to 'enter the Trade, Profession, or calling, of each person' named on the census form, and continued, 'Where a Son works for the benefit of his Father – if the Father be a Farmer, enter the Son or Sons as Labourers – if a mechanic or Tradesman, enter the Son as the same, unless he follows a different trade.' Literal-minded enumerators in Canada West, noting that something had to be entered for each person in this column and that no age limitations were specified for occupations, filled the column with the most diverse material. As William Gunn remarked, 'under the head of Profession trade or occupation, the term "wife" "son," "daughter," "sister," "nephew," "grandmother" &c is given. In many cases the information is too profuse and superfluous.' John Beatty added, 'some Enumerators in entering "Laborers" have included all the male children of a farmer for instance down to the age of one year.'[24] Sectional differences were also evident, with francophone notary-enumerators tending to follow the standards of the *Coutume de Paris*, under which women had no occupation apart from that of their husbands or fathers. For many women in Canada East, the occupations column was a catalogue of their civil disabilities.

Enumerators applied diverse methods of interpretation to most other personal census columns. In the absence of consistently defined observational protocols, individual enumerators were often left to invent their own marks and symbols for recording the accounts that informants offered them. The 1861 census remained very much an instance of 'literary' statistics, precisely because the central authority had not extended its administrative power to the point of being able to minimize the observational discretion exercised by enumerators in the field. On the other hand, helpful enumerators wrote explanatory remarks that are often of interest to modern-day investigators because they indicate the sense that enumerators made of the inquiry, and because they reveal the enumerators' cultural lexicons and literary abilities. Consider the explanation offered by Nicholas Willoughby to his commissioner:

> In all cases the word DO or Ditto means the Same as for instance where the parence are Church of England the Children are Markeddt Do or Ditto Meaning the Same &c &c farmers Sons are Marked Laboureres from the oldest to the youngest alhough not old Enough to Labour Sons of tradesmen are Marked the same trade unless at a Different trade those Marked not Babtised are to be taken to have No Religion as that was their way of Expressing that they did not profess any Religion Married Ladies are Distinguished from from others by being termed Matrons or Mothers the younger Marked Spinsters there being onley one Collum for Married and Single the Letter M. M. means Married the Blanks are all Single or unmarried.

If the commissioner would follow his explanation, Willoughby was sure that 'in Counting them up there will be less Liability for Mistake.'[25]

### The Agricultural Census

Confusion also reigned in the agricultural census in the area in which the possibilities for uniformity of interpretation were highest: the acreage devoted to different uses. Columns 4 through 9 inclusive concerned 'Number of Acres of Land' and were headed as follows:

4. Total held by each Person or Family
5. Under Cultivation
6. Under Crops in 1860
7. Under Pasture in 1860
8. Under Orchards or Gardens
9. Under Wood or Wild

The initial instructions to enumerators read, 'You will take care ... that columns 5, 6, 7, 8 and 9, when added, correspond with column 4.' This was, of course, nonsensical, because adding the total amount of land under cultivation to those areas of land cultivated in different ways and those left wild would yield an acreage larger than that held by each person or family. Once again, the Rouville commissioner, Solyme Bertrand, noticed the problem and wrote to ask, 'What should be placed in Column 5 in the agricultural Census. Columns 6, 7 & 8 composing the part of the property that is under cultivation and Column 9 the part that is in woodland[.] Columns 6.7.8&9 together compose the number of acres occupied by the owner of the lot.' Bertrand suggested that 'it would be better not to put anything in column 5, for I think it is useless.'[26] This time Hutton himself had noticed the inconsistency, and on 28 December 1860 he instructed the commissioners to modify the instructions to enumerators to read, 'Columns 5 and 9, when added, correspond with column 4, and Columns 6,7&8 should agree with 5.'

Some commissioners received Hutton's corrections before the census date and modified the enumerators' instructions. Thomas White, Jr., received them so close to the census day that he was 'compelled to send special messengers with the papers to the more remote parts of the County.' Other commissioners, such as Simon Johnston, got the corrections after their enumerators were in the field and couldn't make sense of them in any case. Many enumerators attempted to take the agricultural census in keeping with their original instructions.[27] Yet even the corrected instructions led to confusion. Once again, Hutton had not profited from the experience of 1852, which had demonstrated that the land categories were not mutually exclusive. 'Some difference has occurred with reference to the true meaning of the column "under cultivation" in the Agricultural Census,' noted Thomas White, Jr., when his first returns came in. 'Some of the Enumerators have assumed it to mean all the land which has passed under the plow – all except the "wood & wild"; while others have taken it as referring to those portions of the farm which are neither "under crop", in "pasture", in "orchards & gardens", nor in "wood and wild" – such, for instance as summer fallows, new clearances &c, – all those portions of the farm which are in a state of preparation for crop.' The confusion with respect to fallows and meadows was so great in David White's district that he published a special instruction to enumerators in the field, suggesting that they make returns for such acreage in the final 'remarks' column. Enumerators were confused, as they had been in 1852, with respect to orchards that were also under crop. Also, at times they interpreted returns of crop yields in diverse ways.[28]

Other lacunae existed in the design of the agricultural census. Yields of flax and hemp were to be returned, but not the area of land planted in either crop. Milch cows were to be counted, and returns of butter and cheese were to be made, but not of milk. As in 1852, no provision was made for returns of eggs or poultry, despite the economic importance of both, especially to farm women. There was no space for reporting potash, an important source of farm income. More significant for later debate was the fact that some commissioners and enumerators were not sure whether the information to be given about yields was to concern the total product or simply the marketable surplus. The aptly named Increase Bullock, for instance, pointed out that 'the headings of the Agricultural Sheets do not seem calculated to include Stock sold off the farms during the year which amounts to a large item in the wealth of the country parts.' Bullock told his enumerators that the information 'should be supplied by including all Buy Sold in column "Beef in Bbls" and into columns at end in place of "Remarks" for sheep & horses,' and requested of Hutton 'if this is not proper you will please inform me – I suppose it to be the wish of the Government to have all the Products of the Farms returned of whatever nature for the year 1860 as well what is in hand as that sold and consumed.' However, enumerators elsewhere reported recording only the surplus.[29]

The Vaudreuil County commissioner, J.O. Bastien, pointed out that the livestock columns seemed to have been mixed up in the printing process. Enumerators were invited to return numbers of oxen, steers, milk cows, and horses over three years of age; then they encountered a column headed 'value of same'; then they were to return numbers of colts or fillies, sheep, and pigs before completing the column 'total value of all live Stock.' Bastien asked whether 'value of same' should not have been omitted or at least placed differently. No response to him survives.[30]

Because they had a financial interest in filling as many sheets as they could, and because rumours circulated early that payment for names on the agricultural schedules would be made, Hutton's attempt to distinguish farm from nonfarm production failed. On their agricultural sheets, census makers routinely enumerated people who had extremely small amounts of land, or occasionally no land at all.[31] Others included plots as large as 5 acres on their personal sheets. Proprietors of multiple farms were enumerated in a variety of ways, some with their land aggregated in a single row, some with a separate entry for each of their lots, and some with lands attributed to other members of their families. Joint tenants might be enumerated as one proprietor or as two. Farmers who were renting land were occasionally returned as 'tenants,' with no information provided by the enumerator. The attempt to assign one 'normal place' to each agricultural producer, combined with the limitation of reporting to the enumeration district, led to practical difficulties for enumerators in the field. In Grenville County, one enumerator made this note:

> By the present mode of taking the Agricultural Census, much of the cultivated land and other property must obviously and necessarily be omitted, since the enumerators are only required to take what they find in their own particular District, though it must frequently happen and has happened, that parties owning land and being in one District own also a valuable farm or other lands in an adjoining District ... It would have been well to have taken all lands, no matter where located, if held in possession by the owner or occupant, with their products, if the owner or occupier derived all the benefit therefrom and not leased – or let on shares.[32]

The same sort of difficulty presented itself with respect to the census of industry. To take one example, Thomas Boyd, the enumerator for district 2, Kitley Township, Leeds County, listed full information for a forty-three-year-old mill owner named Chauncey Bellamy on a personal census sheet, including a description of his saw and grist mill. Bellamy was included as resident in the McCarthy farm household and described as married, but there was no return for his wife or family in Boyd's district. In neighbouring Yonge Township, the enumerator for District 3, Geo. P. Wight, provided full particulars for Bellamy again in the personal census, this time as a head of household, and described also his wife and children. Bellamy's occupation was given here as 'milling,' but instead of describing the enterprise in the industrial columns, Wight noted 'carrying on business in the adjoining Township.' Bellamy appeared a third time on Thomas Boyd's agricultural schedule as the proprietor of lot 27 on the 7th concession of Kitley Township.[33]

Attaching property to households while containing households in the administrative unit of the enumeration district was both practically and conceptually inadequate as a technique for statistically appropriating property relations and production. The difficulty would have been lessened if Hutton, as census manager, had been able to mobilize a more abstract notion of property – one that detached it from individuals in single locales. Of course, many aspects of social relations had not yet been invested by the kinds of standardized practices that facilitate their appropriation as statistical knowledge. Not all forms of social relations and practices are equally susceptible to statistical translation. For example, 'enough butter for their own use' was a quantity not easily represented statistically, at least without further conceptual work (e.g., constructing average household size and average individual consumption). The intermingling of commodity and subsistence forms of agricultural production and the partial penetration of uniform measurement conventions into social practice likely encouraged the survival in the census of particularistic or 'representational' measurement units such as the household bound to land.[34]

The wide interpretive discretion allowed to enumerators shaped the work of the commissioners and the compilers, who were constrained to work up the raw material produced in the field into standardized returns. The materials they had to work with were affected by the conditions under which the enumeration took place – both the technical-physical conditions of the work and the intersubjective conditions prevailing in the field encounters between enumerators and potential informants. A limited but revealing body of evidence about such matters survives in the census correspondence and on the census schedules.

**'I wont Knock the Senses out of myself'**

As a labour process, the 1861 enumeration went forward under difficult environmental and other material conditions. Despite the experience of 1852, the board attempted a winter enumeration; yet most enumerators were given nothing with which to protect their cumbersome bundles of census sheets, and nothing on or with which to write. Their official instructions made mention of a 'book' in which they were to present a sketch map of their district, but the board provided no such books. Few commissioners seem to have followed David White's initiative in producing 'stout pasteboard folios' for the use of enumerators.[35]

Many enumerators were set to work with insufficient numbers of census schedules, and thus made their own rough sheets and transcribed information onto printed forms when these became available – or let commissioners do this work. Schedules for part of District 1 of Artemesia Township in Grey County are among the few handmade ones that have survived. Here the enumerator managed to cram many more rows onto each sheet of paper than the original schedules contained. He changed the order of presentation of columns from one sheet to the next and found it difficult to follow his own rows; thus, he returned one-year-old

Robert Kennedy as an illiterate person over twenty years of age. Other runs of census returns include agricultural sheets transformed into personal census sheets, and vice versa. In such cases enumerators replicated only those columns they considered important.[36]

As a rule, January is not a clement month in central Canada. In January 1861 the colony was swept by a series of bitter winter storms. Travel was difficult or impossible. Ink froze, thawed, dribbled across the schedules, and blotted. Enumerators risked freezing themselves. In Perth County, 'the snows at the time the census was taken was so drifted that the side roads & lanes were completely blocked up and in several instances the Enumerators were nearly frozen to death.'[37] In Lanark, the pollyannaish commissioner commented, 'the Enumerators have had an unusually unpleasant job this time owing to the severe and protracted Snow Storms ... wading up to their necks in snow where no beast could make any headway ... There is this much to be said in favor of the storms it had the effect of keeping people in door thus giving the Enumerators an opportunity of finding the Heads of families at home and eliciting thereby satisfactory replies to their enquiries.'[38]

James McLeod, the enumerator from Kinloss in Bruce County, had to make his own blank census schedules by hand, travel thirty-two miles to deliver them to the commissioner when completed, and then pay fifty cents to a magistrate to administer the oath to him. 'I would further say,' wrote McLeod, 'in regard of the different lines of Roads that had not been traveled during the winter in this [district] ... & the Several snowstorms that I suffer much fatigue.' McLeod's fellow enumerator from Greenock finished enumerating his district 'after two weeks travel through what is called the Greenock swamp, reluctantly having often to retrace my own footsteps upon very partially beaten tracks and making many rounds in order to get to a House. I have been so much bothered at times that I would willingly cast the census to the winds.' An enumerator named William Burwash reported that much of the land held in his district was in the possession of absentees and was uninhabited. He had 'frequently travelled on snow shoes from four to six miles between the houses.' Even so, Burwash had better luck than John Young of Leeds County, who could not force his horse through the snowdrifts. On one of his schedules Young wrote in exasperation: 'Elizabethtown Jay. 24 1861 traveled half mile on the 11 Con. the Snow is up to the mares back must return I wont Knock the Senses out of my self and the mare for all the census in the Township into your Stable Nancy.' In a neighbouring district the enumerator wrote after the entries for two households, 'these people the snow was so deep I could not get to the house but got the best Information I could.'[39]

The difficulties of travel, in Bruce County at least, were such that enumerators crossed each other's enumeration districts and at times redivided the districts assigned them. William Bull of Amabel, who had to break trail into every house he enumerated, reported: 'It appears that I was only appointed for Albemarle, but Mr Gould [sic] told me I had better take down the few families who were living in the north of Amabel, as it would have taken Mr Burwash two or three days to come up, there being no road whatever.'[40] William Hutton himself pointed to the 'heavy snow storms, and very severe cold, which have, in many cases, retarded the enumerators' when explaining to the legislature in April 1861 why the census returns were still outstanding: 'On the 10$^{th}$, 11$^{th}$, and 12$^{th}$ of January – the days for leaving the schedules at the houses – the thermometer ranged from 20° to 36° below zero, and the enumerators could not work; and, in the country, the snow has been so deep in both Provinces as seriously to interrupt travel.'[41]

These conditions slowed the conduct of the enumeration, made some enumerators less than thorough, and meant that encounters between enumerators and informants often involved distant memory work. W.W. Holmes, the Kent County commissioner, discovered that an 'enumerator neglected to visit three or four whole concessions' in Orford Township, and instead 'took such information as he could get from people in the neighbourhood.' Since it was 'probable that a hundred names are left off – and others improperly inserted,' Holmes named a second enumerator to do the work. When it still wasn't done by the last week in April, he appointed yet a third.[42] In what seems to be a similar case, a priest from the parish of Ste-Agathe, Lotbinière County, complained to the Provincial Secretary that the enumerator had refused to canvass all his parish. Despite the priest's efforts to cooperate, to the point of showing the enumerator the parish limits, he 'positively refused to take the *Eight ranges of the Township of Nelson, Two of Leeds* and *a part of a place called Armagh.*' The priest was incensed for '*fully one third of my parish is left out.*'[43]

Commissioners claimed that the schedules which resulted from the adverse environmental conditions of the period were often so dirty and smudged as to be illegible. As Louis Isaaë Dézil of Joliette County explained to his commissioner, 'despite the best of intentions, and the care I took to keep my census sheets clean, it was impossible for me to achieve this goal.' The schedules were printed on 'very Common and very bad' paper, there was often no table on which Dézil could write, and then there was 'the bad weather we had during all of the days' he was 'forced to Walk' around his district. Dézil's commissioner complained to the board of 'a great many difficulties in obtaining correct information' because of dirty and illegible schedules. [44]

Dézil's was a common experience. Henry Pollock's 'first page Sheet met with Blots by ink,' because when he 'went out first to take the Census it came on a Storm and my sheets and my self were abused.' And William Cassidy submitted schedules that were 'not very neat nor clean being almost impossible to keep them tidy for in many places I had to spread them out on the floors and get upon my knees and perhaps kept there for nearly one hour.'[45] Commissioners complained of having to have portions of the census taken again, or to return sheets to enumerators. 'Prosper Archambault, one of my Enumerators, not having sent me a satisfactory report,' wrote the *notaire* P. Labelle, 'his census being deficient above all, under the heading of cleanliness I had to make him do it over again entirely.'[46] It would be useful to learn if Archambault and the others whose schedules were said to be illegible returned to question informants again, or if they worked from memory, although we should also be somewhat skeptical of the commissioners' accounts of the enumerators' work, given the example of the Grenville County commissioner who cheated his enumerators out of their pay in order to use the government census money to pay his own debts. This commissioner, when called to account, attempted to claim that the enumerators had not done their work adequately and that he had paid them what they were worth.[47]

**Ignorance or Resistance?**
Despite the seductive appeal to some later analysts of the objective, printed figures contained in census reports, the census was oral history based on memory work. Enumerators were to question heads of households, and they generally assumed that these would be men, despite the injunction to return the holdings of women landowners on the agricultural schedules. Enumerators often went out of their way to find male informants, making second visits to houses to obtain information if only women were present the first time; and when forced to report women's opinions, they expressed reservations about their worth. Many enumerators listed the eldest son of a widowed householder as the household head. The facts produced by the enumeration came from men telling things to other men about the conditions of themselves and of women

and children. The enumerator Samuel Young expressed a common opinion about women informants. 'The amount of crop raised I think is pretty corect,' he commented for one household on his agricultural schedule, 'but the acres that produced the crop cannot be depened upon as I had to get my information a good deal from the woman which some times was not corect.' Young added that 'if there was more pay for the work perhaps a better conclusion would be arived at,' suggesting that a higher rate would have made him willing to return to speak to the male household head.[48]

Even male informants, if they could be found, were often reluctant. 'At the rate of two dollars [per hundred names] the Enumerators in the most favored localities would not make one dollar per day,' John Jarvis wrote, 'as it took them over half an hour at each house and often they had to go to the Barn or woods to see the occupant, and the stubbornness with which information was given retarded them very much.' Both James Wight and Joseph Bouchard from Chateauguay sought extra pay for 'having to return in many instances to get information, Heads of the Families not being at home and could not get the information required.'[49]

What some observers saw as stubbornness or resistance, others claimed was ignorance; and some saw ignorance as an individual moral failing. The Board of Registration and Statistics and the commissioners assumed that heads of households would possess the information sought from them and would be willing and able to share it. This was not always the case. Not all farmers kept accounts and records, and for semi-subsistence producers, market measures of produce consumed on the farm may not have been available. Enumerators did not themselves measure farm output or acreage devoted to particular uses, and the interests of informants could easily shape reporting, especially when queries were made as to the value of machinery and products. There was no system of civil registration in place in Canada West, nor were there any administrative infrastructures that tied eligibility for social participation to proof of age or civil status (except perhaps for elementary school attendance). Enumerators reported that some people did not know how to answer them.

'Enumerators does not get sufficient remuneration for the vast amount of labour bestowed on these sheets,' one census maker from Deleware Township in Middlesex County groused. 'The price paid may do for the personal census but for the agricultural it is next to no compensation.' This enumerator complained of 'often not finding the man or head of the family at home, and very many of them when comeatable, did not know how to answer my questions with regard to acres of different crops, value of stock &c &c so that the task of the Enumerator was tedious with many.' Such people were ignorant, according to this commentator, because of their poverty and poor moral character. 'I have seen sallow complexions discontent and circumstances not the most afluent, to much Buck wheat bread and pork grease does not agree with or constitute good living ... people who make the above articles of food their chief Bread and meat are neither healthy nor intelligent.' But Abdiel G. Cradmore from an adjoining district claimed that forces of a more technical nature prevented him from getting thorough responses to the agricultural queries: 'The Wheat Crop being all thrashed is a very corect return, the other Grain a good deal only partly thrashed and is gauged as correctly as possible – The Butter in consequence of so much being consumed in the Family could only be ilgauged, but all the other part of the Census is very correct.'[50] James Cassidy, who complained of getting his schedules dirty while kneeling over them on log cabin floors, tells us that his time was spent 'trying to get direct Answers giving them time to reckon, How old is Jane[?] "Well she was 2 years the christmas after I came in the Bush and took the land up in 1854 and I came in here the winter twelve months following so reckon that up["]. Many such cases as this occurred and many more interesting so that Job's patience would be put to the test.'[51] Cassidy's remarks suggest that in the absence of an effective system of civil registration, some people did not know the year of their birth or the ages of their children – a further example of census knowledge depending on administrative infrastructure.

Some potential informants refused or were not given the opportunity to speak at all. Edward D. Buchner, postmaster-enumerator for District 2 of Middleton Township in Norfolk County, noted, after listing the names of a large number of lumbermen, 'a part of those names are transient persons engaged in Lumbering and not seeing the persons themselves was obliged to go to the foreman for information consequently the ages and religion and residence of some of them are only supposition of the foreman the same thing occurs on some of the other sheets.' Thomas White, Jr., consulted Hutton about a communication 'from the Enumerator appointed for the Township of Galway, in reference to the refusal of the shanty men to give there names. What had better be done? To attempt to bring any of them up would involve a pretty serious risk unless supported by a posse of constables. My own impression is that the true plan would be to obtain the names, if possible, from the employers; but the ages, religion &c would still remain unknown.'[52] Charles Waters stated that merchants refused to answer enumerators' queries about their investments, regarding such questions as 'too inquisitorial.' The fear of taxation lingered in other parts of the colony. As William McKie put it, 'it was impossible to get the people generaly to give a fair statement the amount of Clearing or what their stock was worth a majority of them being afraid it had something to do with Taxation.' The Huron County commissioner, John Leary, invoked the power of the law to have two people fined for refusing to answer enumerators.[53]

It fell to the commissioners to work up the idiosyncratic reports drawn from field encounters into uniformly coherent entries on printed schedules, which was the next step in fashioning what Hutton called 'the reality of the representation.'

**Reducing the Schedules to Uniformity**
Commissioners were to deliver clean, legible, and coherent enumeration schedules to the Board of Registration and Statistics, along with an abstract of the population of their districts. They could extend the time of the enumeration if they needed to seek additional information, but they were to correct erroneous census schedules before submitting them. To meet these obligations, commissioners reworked the information fashioned by enumerators, using their own protocols of interpretation. In other words, editorial practices intervened between the 1861 census schedules produced in the field encounters and those submitted to and preserved as 'manuscript' schedules by the Board of Registration and Statistics.

All commissioners corrected and copied original submissions from enumerators. The material produced in the field was often dirty, illegible, incomplete, or erroneous, and was often submitted on homemade enumeration schedules. As Increase Bullock put it on 2 March 1861, 'some of the agricultural sheets are so worn and blotted & require so much correcting that I shall have to copy them.' Still at it two months later, he noted that 'the agricultural part has been very tedious.'[54] David Morrow attempted to save time by meeting the enumerators in each township to go over their schedules. 'The Bayham sheets I found on the appointed day as nearly perfect as Possible except the mater of addition,' he wrote, but 'the Dorchester sheets not so good particularly the agricultural which have all to be written over again and forwarded to me.' Morrow did the work of addition himself, later reporting that for a month he had 'been from morning until 11 & sometimes to 12 at night busy adding, stitching & Pasting Diagrams to each Set' of returns.[55]

James Kintrea billed the board for the cost of an assistant 'to aid me in arranging looking over and correcting the Several Sheets and adding up the several Columns of the Agricultural Sheets.' He had tried to force the enumerators to do it, but most of them refused, 'being of opinion that their duties were confined to simply taking the Census and entering the figures required in the several Columns.' Kintrea discovered 'errors' in the schedules whose correction was a complicated and time-consuming process. S.B. Fairbanks of Ontario County ordered thirty extra personal schedules on 2 February 1861 because some of those submitted had to be copied and corrected. It took him six weeks' work to be able to send them to the board 'properly completed.' N.S. Appleby of Hastings County discovered that the enumerators had used their own paper and entered information in the wrong columns. In 'examining the returns of the Census Enumerators,' Appleby found 'the most of them have omitted to give the information required in the Instructions respecting Churches and School houses, I have written to them to send it to me at once so that I can place it upon their sheets before sending them down.' It was mid-April before he shipped the schedules to the board, having had to do some of the copying and correction himself. Jacob Hespeler complained that 'to check the Enumerators returns & making up calculations &tra has been a great deal more Labour' than he had anticipated and 'in almost every instance the returns had to be refered back frequently twice & three times for some mistake or another.'[56]

Commissioners' attempts to 'reduce the schedules to uniformity' led to demands for re-enumerations and to conflict with enumerators. The Laval commissioner Pierre Labelle wrote to the board in late February to ask 'if in the case where some of my enumerators refuse to correct the errors which have occured in completing their Census blanks, or to do the recapitulation of their District, I can force them to do it, or appoint in their place a competent person who would be entitled to their salary.' Labelle ordered eighteen extra personal schedules because 'one of my enumerators has to begin his whole census over again.' He then discovered that there were other cases, and wrote to the board again: 'Some of my enumerators, not having satisfied my wishes with respect to writing, and seeing myself, in consequence, forced to begin three Census Districts over again, I would be much obliged if it were possible for you again to send me fifty personal blanks and a dozen agricultural sheets.'[57] If Labelle found he had to re-enumerate 2,500 people, John Leary, the puffed-up former Irish Chief Constable, likely enumerated a large part of his county twice. Leary divided Huron into ninety-three tiny districts in keeping with Hutton's original plan, but then had great difficulty finding enumerators. He claimed to have 'done the best I could' with the erroneous returns he received. Later he revealed that there had been a heavy turnover among his enumerators. His accounts contained the names of people not initially reported as census makers, 'as many of these gave it up some stated sickness to be the Cause, others incompetency and one of them died Consequently I was obliged to appoint others.' Leary had ordered 1,120 personal schedules before the enumeration began – so many that Hutton pencilled in the margin of one of his requests, 'How many has he had?' Parts of the Huron enumeration were probably done twice by different enumerators.[58]

**Changes**
Commissioners' 'corrections' changed the returns substantially. William Gunn, faced with schedules embodying a variety of observational practices, 'considered that my best plan was to go over them carefully myself, and rectify them, and in any case of a meterial nature, apply for information. It is a tedious business, but on fully considering the whole matter, it is the cheapest way in which the work can be done.' Gunn ensured that each full, corrected schedule contained the names of fifty people, and he removed status indicators from the 'occupations' column. He changed the information reported for crop yields in District 4 of Aderslie Township, where the enumerator had returned average yields per acre, in order to give total yields. James McDougall of Middlesex County, who assured the board that in his jurisdiction 'the work has been faithfully and correctly performed,' submitted bundles of agricultural schedules that had been heavily corrected and recorrected and whose column totals, even so, did not correspond. The material for West Williams Township was in especially poor condition, heavily scored and scarcely legible. In one district of the township the enumerator returned 939 bushels as the yield from 497 acres of spring wheat; in this instance the commissioner noted, 'Spring wheat is evidently a mistake I have allowed the average of the enumerator of the Township.' In an adjoining district, McDougall added an acreage total for a person described by the enumerator as a 'Tenant.'[59]

Double-counting was one of the 'errors' commissioners faced, given the confusion over how enumerators were to deal with transients and absentees. John Beatty found 'in checking the returns of Enumerators that, where visitors have been returned, they have almost without exception (so far as examined) carried the Sex into the columns for Sexes, and of course in addition these two columns make the exact number of 50. Then this of course requires them, as they have done, to dispose of the Visitors under the head of "Not Members" so as to make 14 to 19 agree with 8 & 9.' As did other commissioners, Beatty sought advice: 'Must I correct this throughout, which of course must be done by striking out all visitors from columns for Sexes, that is from 8 & 9, and also from 16 & 17, and then columns 8&9 with the addition of visitors, under column 6, will make 50?' The matter did not seem to Beatty likely to 'make any great difference in the return as the number of Visitors is small,' but he was willing to make the correction if the board required him to do so. He thought the practice of the enumerators was a result of the 'defective' instructions issued by the board, which 'did not plainly state that entries of visitors were in no case to be carried beyond column 6.'

Beatty made no attempt to produce an abstract of capital investment because he found that 'the Enumerators have taken such diverse views on these points, notwithstanding I instructed them in accordance with strictures from you, that I have deemed it best not to meddle with these particulars at all.' He was not so reluctant about the returns of occupations, however. Complaining that 'some Enumerators in entering "Laborers" have included all the male children of a farmer for instance down to the age of one year,' Beatty informed the board that he had 'in all observed cases omitted counting any under the age of Sixteen years, as a laborer, as I think to enumerate boys under that age would give a very false presentation of the labour power of the County. Where I have found Males as well as females entered as "Servants" I have enumerated the former as "laborers" putting down the females as "Servants."' This editorial convention excluded women from agricultural field labour.[60]

On the northwestern frontier, the sheriff-commissioner Richard Carney conducted much of the enumeration himself by post, without meeting or providing census schedules for his enumerator, a Hudson's Bay Company factor. He was unable to provide any information concerning the capital investment of fur traders, because they believed his inquiries were a prelude to taxation 'and there has been so much deception practised towards them, that their doubts cannot be removed entirely.' In the absence of the schedules, the enumerator was 'compelled to condense and insert the Names as headed' on sheets of paper. 'It fell to me,' Carney noted, 'to carry out into the Columns and add up. I have filled in Omissions according to my knowledge and judgement to make the Sheets complete as possible, to do so was compelled to seek information from various sources.'[61]

The explicit discussion on the part of commissioners of their corrections and modifications, and the marks of corrections and additions on many surviving census schedules, point to the ways in which post-enumeration observers transformed the materials recorded by enumerators. The interpretive chain connecting observation and reporting was considerably stretched by the conditions of the field encounter between enumerators and informants. Environmental conditions moved the field encounter away from the nominal census day and thus transformed what was supposed to be a report of current conditions into memory work. Enumerators and their informants often did not share a common understanding of what was being sought and for what purpose, while some informants did not command the relevant information. Enumerators were forced to rework their field observations before these were acceptable to commissioners; the interpretive chain was then stretched further by re-enumerations, and further still by the editing, amplification, and reinterpretation carried out by the commissioners. The explicit discussion provided by commissioners of their editorial work may aid researchers interested in using the surviving schedules to reconstruct the observational protocols in use at the regional and local levels. Perhaps ironically, it is the more carefully executed enumeration in many francophone parishes that should especially give researchers pause. In these cases, no discussion on the part of commissioners or enumerators survives, so it is generally not possible to detect subsequent alterations to the enumerators' observations. For example, in the parishes of St-Aubert-du-Portjoli and de L'Islet in L'Islet County, many of the surviving schedules bear not a single blot, smear, pen stutter, deviation, or correction, despite complaints about snowdrifts, cheap paper, and runny pens. The 'manuscript' census is a handsome exercise in penmanship, probably conducted in the notary's office.[62]

It was the commissioners' reports of the census returns that were first made public.

### 'The remarkable fecundity of our race'

The official population totals for the census were made public in October 1861, but the first of the board's two volumes of tabulated results appeared only in August 1863. Once again, the board controlled neither the initial compilation nor the publication of results. Reports from enumerators and commissioners began to appear in the press as soon as local enumerations were complete. As early as 2 February 1861, *La Minerve* was printing preliminary returns for towns in Canada West and offering to publish any commissioners' reports it received. Many commissioners responded, and by 14 February the returns for Montreal city were in print. In Canada West, the Stratford *Weekly Beacon*, like other western newspapers, was printing local returns by the second week in February, although the *Argus* was still urging people missed to make themselves known to enumerators on 18 February. County returns appeared with increasing frequency from mid-February onwards, the majority of them by late March 1861. Enumerators' reports were also printed, and William Hutton himself was giddy in correspondence about the success of the census in demonstrating a growing population. He informed one of the colony's English emigration agents in late March that 'the increase will be very large viz from 1.850.000 to 2.850.000 or somewhere near that figure (in 9 years). Our Exports are enormous & exchange consequently very low. The bal[an]ce of Trade is not much against us. Our last crop was a splendid one in U.C.'[63] The population claim was within 10 per cent of the most enthusiastic estimate Hutton had made in the late 1850s.

Early reports figured in local rivalries and led to charges that results were being padded; however, newspaper editors do not seem to have questioned the coherence of the census design or the interpretive practices that were producing the population numbers. Some commissioners did not hesitate even to make public the details collected about named individuals. For example, John Jarvis sent a list with the names of local businessmen and the amount of their capital investments to the local Stratford newspaper, which promptly published it.[64] More important, as soon as the first results became available, the conservative eastern press began arguing that the census would put an end to western demands for representation by population. The *Courrier du Canada* proclaimed that population growth in the west and in the city of Toronto was slowing, while Quebec's growth had accelerated: 'Everyone knows that Mr. Brown's hobbyhorse is representation by population; the census may well put an end to it. So, farewell to all that [Donc adieu veau, vache, cochon, couvée]!'[65]

Sectional population totals had appeared by early May 1861. While the figures would vary over the next several months, the conservative press in Canada East declared, with considerable relief, that the census results marked the end of the dominance of Canada West. According to *La Minerve*, early returns gave a total population of about 2.7 million, with a difference of only 170,000 in favour of the west. The west now had a weaker case for demanding an increase in the number of its representatives than the east had had at the moment of the Union. Moreover, the period of population growth for the west was clearly finished, 'while that of Lower Canada is only beginning.' This claim was supported in an article from the Toronto *Leader* which noted that most of the good land in Canada West had already been settled, with what remained no better than that in the Saguenay and Gaspé, where there was five times as much of it. The *Leader* concluded that future immigration would be directed toward Canada East, where new colonization roads would make settlement easy and attract new settlers at the end of the American War. By 1871, the *Leader* concluded, the east would undoubtedly equal and even surpass the west in population. In this, the editor of *La Minerve* concurred.[66]

The *Globe* was attacked for fabricating the returns. According to *La Minerve*, George Brown was showing the commissioners how to inflate the Canada West numbers by grouping together figures from small towns and villages for comparison with the 1852 figures and then adding these same figures again into the population totals for counties.[67] *La Minerve* also castigated the *rouge* paper *Le Pays* for its stance on representation by population. The former cited 1852 figures in its piece, but the twist it give to 'representation by population' underlines the importance that was being attached to the census's attribution to people of a national origin and a religious identity. *La Minerve* argued that Catholics and French Canadians were heavily underrepresented in the existing Parliament. Among the MPPs were 51 Catholics and 79 Protestants of various denominations, and 43 French Canadians and 87 members of other origins. According to 1852 population figures, there was one representative for each 17,932 Catholics, but one for each 11,743 Protestants; one for each 16,216 French Canadians but one for each 14,171 of other origins. *Le Pays* had preached representation by population but had made no demands to redress this scandalous underrepresentation of its own countrymen.[68]

Press debate was not hindered by the fact that the cited population totals were continually changing. On 6 May, *Le Courrier du Canada* gave the sectional totals as 1,369,733 west and 1,103,911 east, a difference of only 265,822, and thus was 'persuaded that Upper Canadians must be extremely downcast at the slender excess of Upper Canada's population over that of Lower Canada.' Six weeks later, *La Minerve* gave the figures as 1,394,013 west and 1,092,519 east, but again repeated that immigration to the east would soon smooth out the difference. In mid-October the figures were given as 1,335,223 west and 1,203,666 east, while in mid-

December they were claimed to be 1,394,222 west and 1,103,611 east. Later still, the official totals would be given as 1,396,091 west and 1,111,566 east. Newspaper editors were able to find the essential meanings of these numbers without being overly concerned by their variability.[69] Interestingly, there was no press comment on the fact that the population total of about 2.5 million was considerably below the estimates Hutton had been making, some of which had proposed a figure over 3 million.

The francophone press celebrated the fact that French Canadians were well over one-third of the total population and had increased their share from 35 to 38 per cent. 'The English and Canadian papers which speak continually of drowning our nationality should be convinced by these figures that the operation won't be as easy as they thought at the outset,' crowed *Le Courrier du Canada*. More complete census tables led the editor of *Le Canadien* into a more extended reflection. The tables of origins showed that the native-born French-Canadian population had grown by 3 per cent as a share of the total since the last census, 'a new proof of the remarkable and much remarked fecundity of our race.' This relative growth took place even though 'in the course of the last ten years thousands of our compatriots emigrated to the United States, who, if they had remained, would have shown our reproductive force in an even more favorable light.' The lesson was clear: 'Our race owes this advantage to its moral and religious virtue: may it never be lost!' The pronatalist and nationalist analysis invented to contest the relative decline of the French-Canadian population in 1852 served equally in 1861 to promote the idea of its relative increase. Moreover, *Le Canadien* argued, with much of the rest of the eastern press, a systematic pursuit of colonization projects would allow this remarkably fecund population to express all its natural powers in the period leading up to the next census.[70]

The official census tables made it possible for newspaper editors, and other interested observers, to aggregate and disaggregate elements of population in support of such projects. These uses of census data point to the development of the 'governmentality' in public debate, in that census returns were being invoked to support a variety of projects for the 'conduct of conduct.' For example, *Le Canadien* separated those counties in Canada East composed only of townships (i.e., the more recently settled) and claimed that their population had more than doubled – something that augured well for colonization projects. Other editors reflected on the meaning of returns in other categories – for instance, that because more people in Canada West reported themselves as professing no religion, the people of Canada East were more moral; and that the greater number of centenarians showed the east to have a healthier climate. There was a tendency in the contemporary press to naturalize the concept 'population,' even as editors began debating the legitimacy of some of the practices involved in identifying its elements. Remember, finally, that in 1861 as in 1852, the Board of Registration and Statistics was compiling the census schedules in a climate in which the government did not control the publication of results and in which results published by commissioners and enumerators had already entered debate.

**Compilation, or 'Rabbit Alias B. Abbott'**
In the winter of 1861, in cramped quarters in a Quebec house, fourteen census clerks under the supervision of the two chief compilers, Thomas McNider and S.S. Finden, awaited the arrival of the enumeration schedules. Those for Toronto, Ottawa, and London arrived first, and the clerks were let loose on them. At the height of the compilation process, twenty-one men were working in the census office; during the month of July 1861, two of them worked standing up for lack of space to place a chair. There was so much work to do that the compilation of the industrial columns was farmed out to the Department of Finance.[71]

The compilers were young men: some were not out of their teens, and several were in their early twenties. Except for E. Byrne, none of the clerks and neither of the chief compilers had previously done any census work. As they worked at the compilation, they were also used as a labour pool, to be shifted about in response to the press of business elsewhere in Agriculture and Statistics. For example, in the first months of 1862, illness incapacitated many of the immigration inspectors, and George Willoughby was employed to inspect the sanitary conditions on ships arriving in the Quebec harbour. Though he was required to board vessels at dawn and late at night, Willoughby continued to show up regularly for his $2 day in the census office.[72]

The census offices were in disarray. Between census day and the dismissal of the compilation clerks in July 1863, five different men served as Minister of Agriculture. The census offices were physically separate from the rest of Agriculture and Statistics and largely exempt from supervision other than what was exercised by the chief compilers. Perhaps the latter were sharp and energetic men, although 'Pa Finden' (S.S. Finden) was described, soon after the compilation was finished, as 'a ruin, sick and completely unfit for work.' William Hutton watched the initial progress of the compilation closely, putting the best face possible on the aggregate returns as they fell well below his early estimates. Yet Hutton's other obligations continued, and he was especially occupied with the proposal by the Parliamentary Emigration Committee to give his office complete control over immigration and colonization. He was suddenly and completely incapacitated in mid-May 1861, and died in July. At the onset of Hutton's illness, the chief clerk, Evelyn Campbell, took over as acting secretary, but Hutton was unable to brief him in any systematic way. One correspondent heard that Hutton was 'seriously if not dangerously ill, & so much so as to be unable to read your letters or even hear them read. His Medical Man insists upon the most perfect quiet.' No permanent replacement was appointed for Hutton until August 1864.[73]

Scrambling as he must have done to master the various files included in the department's growing mandate, it is improbable that Evelyn Campbell exercised any practical supervision over the compilation process. The burden of work so affected his own health that he was granted a month's leave of absence in November 1861. The minister, N.F. Belleau, concerned that his department had no permanent secretary, then detached the most promising of the census clerks, Henry May, to replace Campbell. May immediately discovered that at least one of the senior clerks in the bureau had taken advantage of Campbell's illness to stay home. It was May, kept on as assistant secretary after Campbell's return, who reported on the progress of the census to the ministers, who prepared the circulars for collecting information about the demand for immigrant labour in the colony, also issued instructions to the growing corps of foreign emigrant agents, and who wrote the 1861 *Report of the Minister of Agriculture*. Despite a raise in pay to $3.50 per diem in September 1862 and a mandate to occupy himself 'in the preparation of the higher classes of Statistics connected with the Census,' May continued to be paid as a casual employee out of the census contingencies. On 6 February 1863, though a likely candidate for secretary, May resigned 'to battle with the world in a mercantile life,' rather than 'accept the comparative ease of a Government situation.'[74]

One can imagine the tedium involved in compiling 50,000 census schedules by hand. Administrative discipline would have been required for it to be conducted systematically. As it happened, the compilers worked through the columns in turn, sometimes in teams of two. To relieve the tedium of the work, they used the schedules as sketch pads, drawing pictures of crowned female heads and goats smoking cigars, tracing out their names in various styles, and composing lines of doggerel. They also left bits of juvenelia behind for the amusement of the compilers coming after, clearly assured that their supervisors would not be inspecting the manuscript schedules. Edward Abbott was a favourite target of the other compilers; one can read in the 'Idiots' column, 'Woolley Rabbit alias Ned Abbott,' and elsewhere, 'Rabbit alias B. Abbott,' 'Willow Willow Willow under Abbott,' and so on. The beginning of one compiler's run was marked: 'Hi Randy Dandy Oh'! Some of these inscriptions covered the original entries on the schedules.[75]

The sectional distribution of population, and the relative numbers of francophones and anglophones and of Protestants and Catholics, were the census results most eagerly awaited by the press and by politicians. The board was being pressured to produce these returns quickly. Thus, a careful post-enumeration separation of *de facto* and *de jure* elements of population was simply not carried out: the compilers counted everyone listed on the census schedules. The method of compilation made it inevitable that they would do so, for they controlled the accuracy of their count by ensuring that the number of listed names corresponded to the numbers in the columns for sex and in the columns for family members, non-family members, and absentees. Only if transients, dead people, and those absent were counted as part of the 'normal' population could such columns correspond. Those compilers later set to work on other columns were compelled to match the first set of totals. Where enumerators had not reported the ages of transients or others, the compilers of the age column could not make their count correspond to the first count. 'Ages not taken!' they wrote in exasperation on some schedules. The published census report of population by age had an 'Ages not given' column (4,673 for Canada West).[76]

Compilers read the materials in front of them selectively, and altered schedules to make entries intelligible to their reading practices. If commissioners' original compilations of population totals excluded the deceased, transients, and others, these were crossed out and replaced with new population totals. The figure '1' in some columns became '0' to make column totals correspond. Occupations for adult men were entered, on schedules where these were missing, in a hand other than that of the enumerator. In the town of Simcoe, Canada West, one of the enumerators entered the names of two merchants on a single line; one of these was later scratched out and added to the bottom of the schedule in a different hand. The Board of Registration and Statistics received an intriguing letter from William Dickinson, the Grenville County commissioner who stiffed his enumerators, concerning an anomaly discovered in the Oxford Township manufacturing returns. 'Mr Jno Dickinson,' wrote the commissioner, 'who was Enumerator tells me he cannot account for the error unless he thinks in Enumerating Mr Meikles property at Burritts Rappids he has put down 100 Bbls Saltet fish when he should have written 100,000 saw logs.' The offending schedule was evidently in the hands of the board during this exchange. The surviving 'manuscript' personal and agricultural census schedules for Oxford Township both contain returns for Mr Meikles, yet there is now no mention of any 'fish,' 'Saltet' or plain.[77]

**Selective Counting and Attributions**

The compilers dealt selectively with the returns made by enumerators. Their compilation of the 'race' columns was suspect even to contemporaries. P.-J.-O. Chauveau commented on the pamphlet returns circulated late in 1861, 'There are in the table by origins some evident mistakes, for instance the number of colored people given for the whole Province of L.C. seems to be so small that I believe I see every day more *darkies* in Montreal than is given for the whole. The number of Indians is also very small – It must be much higher – and an allowance ought to be made for Indians out of the reach of census officers.' We do not know what decisional rules the compilers used to produce the count of 11,223 people of colour for Canada West that appears in the official census report. They seem often simply to have been negligent in totalling entries in the race column. Michael Wayne's meticulous recompilation of the surviving schedules identified 17,053 in the west. However, Wayne also shows that using another set of rules, Joseph-Charles Taché's recapitulation of Canadian population in connection with the 1871 census reported 13,566 people in this category. Alternative methods for configuring the object 'population' affected what William Hutton called 'the reality of the representation' of the census.[78]

The column headed 'Profession, Trade or Occupation' allowed compilers wide scope for invention, and their practices could furnish material for a separate study. Enumerators were instructed to make an entry for everyone in this column, and as a result many described infants as having occupations. At the same time, the market for wage labour was not characterized by regular occupational specialization, and cultural conventions regarding the legitimacy of women's employment were diverse. I attempt only a sketch of what compilers made of what enumerators recorded. Enumerators often mixed status and occupational indicators and used their own nomenclature. Multiple occupations were entered for some men, and single occupations for other men who had more than one. Odulphe Ouellet enumerated the occupation of one resident of Ste-Anne-de-la-Pocatière as 'lawyer,' but on his second page described a flour mill operated by this person that had ground 25,960 minots of grain worth $17,000 in 1860.[79] There were wide variations from one district to the next and between the two colonial sections in the extent to which occupational data were entered for women. Many though not all enumerators in Canada East recognized only teacher, nun, and servant or day labourer as women's occupations. Some in Canada West called all women of working age 'seamstress' or 'spinster,' and we have seen John Beatty rechristening women field labourers as 'servants.' What constituted a working age varied. Women entered as agricultural proprietors on the agricultural schedules might not be returned as having an occupation on the personal schedules, and to deal with widowed proprietors, enumerators such as James Kendrick of Bastard Township resorted to such tergiversations as 'widow farming' or 'living with son.'[80]

Compilers were placed to make occupational attributions. Judging by the check marks they left on the schedules as control devices, which occupations they counted and for whom they counted an occupation followed no plan. For instance, when faced with the entry 'Labourer' for farmers' sons in Canada West districts, some compilers checked off all the names for those over eighteen years of age, while some checked off the names of seventeen- or sixteen-year-olds as well. Generally speaking, women were not counted as agricultural labourers, even in the many cases in Canada East where the occupational entry read clearly 'journalière' [day labourer]; on the other hand, they were counted when returned as 'servante.' Like the commissioner John Beatty, compilers seem not to have considered field labour women's work.

Compilers consistently checked off double-occupations for men when these were reported. They also overrode enumerators' accounts of local domestic organization. In Longueuil parish in Chambly County, the notary-enumerator, P.E. Hurteau, placed a number of widowed women on the personal schedules as heads of their households. Sixty-year-old Archange Pagé, for instance, was listed as household head and her occupation was described as 'cultivante' (farming). The compiler placed a check, not beside her occupation, but beside her son's name, for whom no occupation was listed. A similar practice was followed in the same district by the compiler for Sophie Mongeau, Josephte Oren, and Julienne Vendendaigne; but where another widowed woman was described as 'cultivateur' (farmer), her occupation was checked off.[81] The

230   The Politics of Population

same kind of inconsistent fabrication of 'population' took place with respect to other parts of the enumeration process. Even in the part farmed out to Arthur Harvey in the Department of Finance, similar practices reigned. Thus, Harvey claimed that the counties of Ontario and Northumberland in Canada West were the only parts of the colony containing 'Melodeon Factories.' Yet the enumerator for the village of Gananoque in Canada West had returned a household of melodian makers.[82]

It is safe to say that by the end of the compilation process, the information reported in the field encounters between enumerators and informants had been subjected to repeated reinterpretation. The 'reality of the representation' became what was made of these multiple interpretations.

## The Census of the Canadas, 1860–61

Requests from other governments for copies of the Canadian census results began to arrive while the compilation process was underway. Despite attempts to push the census compilers, it was August 1863 before the first census report appeared from the Quebec press of S.B. Foote. Foote's tender had been the highest, but his *Chronicle* was a friend to the ministry. The second report appeared a year later, and Foote managed to convince the government to take the 1,500 extra copies he had printed on speculation. The Department of Finance had attempted to force matters by letting a contract of its own for the manufacturing returns.[83] The two-volume *Census of the Canadas, 1860–61*, consisted of tables of returns from the various census columns, aggregated for township and parish and county, and for Canada East and West. Eveyln Campbell delivered no commentary on or analysis of the returns, but the government was using them in administrative decision-making even before the appearance of the official reports. These 'facts' about population had social consequences. Claims to entitlements in the indemnity fund created after seigneurial tenure was abolished in 1854 were being adjudicated on the basis of census returns. They were being taken up in other projects and again injected into political debate.[84]

## Brazen Falsifications

The publication of the census tables and volumes produced a further round of criticism from francophone intellectuals concerning the official representation of French Canadians in the population totals and their distribution in the country. At issue immediately were the practices of enumeration and compilation as they related to 'origins.' This was followed by debates over sectional, ethnic, and sectarian religious strength, and over morality and 'progress,' and hence over the census itself as a political initiative. In general terms, the debate points to some of the ways in which the census enabled observers with different interests to enlist their own reconfigurations and retotalizations of the elements of 'population' in political projects. However inconsistent and incoherent its knowledge-producing practices, official social science was defining a terrain on which political conflicts were increasingly being resituated. After francophones gained control over Canadian census making, the domain of knowledge was structured more rigorously and the configuration of the population's 'origins' became a central preoccupation.

As we have seen, the matter of origins was problematic from the outset; William Hutton had omitted to instruct enumerators clearly to distinguish French Canadians on their schedules, and had then issued a supplementary instruction as the enumeration was underway. The conservative press in the east was suspicious about the board's intentions; after all, francophones and Catholics held none of the responsible positions in Registration and Statistics. *La Minerve* greeted the news that the Montreal commissioner had been instructed to compile an abstract of origins for his report to the board by commenting that all commissioners should be similarly instructed. The schedules themselves were defective and misleading, and the paper warned that the board was not competent to compile this part of the schedules, 'given the absence of French-Canadians in its midst.'[85] Yet the Montreal commissioner's abstract was criticized by the Irish Catholic *True Witness*, which claimed that the number of people of Irish origin in Montreal had been seriously underestimated. The number given, 14,469, included only those actually born in Ireland, while their children born in Canada were returned as English. According to this paper, these children were of Irish origin, so the true number of Irish in the city must be 28,700. The subtext was that the *Witness*'s Irish Catholic audience was flourishing; another implication was that national allegiances were not first distinctively Canadian.[86]

The board's first compilations of origins were mixed up and defective, according to P.-J.-O. Chauveau. Tables sent to him for Stanstead and Wolfe counties in June 1861 seemed to contain transposed figures, with 8,000 French Canadians and about 200 anglophones reported in the former. Chauveau was also critical of the pamphlet edition of population by origins released later in 1861. The debate over ethnic-religious representation in the Canadian population soon spilled over into the press and periodical literature in England and France, especially through the intervention of the French historian and statistician François-Edmé Rameau de St-Père. Rameau corresponded regularly with several French-Canadian intellectuals, including Chauveau, who may have provided him with a copy of the board's origins pamphlet. In the 1850s, Rameau had toured British North America, documenting the existence and size of French parishes in both the Canadas. His *La France aux Colonies* (1859) was an important resource for those concerned with demonstrating the prolific character of the 'race.' Rameau had been in Canada while the 1861 census was being compiled, and in March 1862 his criticisms of the returns of origins were widely reprinted in the conservative eastern newspapers.[87]

Rameau claimed that French Canadians were seriously under-represented in the tables of origins for Canada West. Matters were reasonably fair in the border counties of Prescott and Russell, where their numbers had doubled since 1852; the mischief began with Ottawa city. There it was common knowledge that the population was evenly distributed between French and English, yet the census gave a large English majority. Worse, Rameau knew that in Carleton County there were more French in a single parish than the census gave for the whole; the same was true for Renfrew. However, the worst robbery had been committed in the western regions, where Rameau had himself earlier enumerated the inhabitants of the French-Canadian parishes. These were growing rapidly, yet the census gave figures that were 'shamelessly falsified.' A comparison of the 1852 and 1861 returns of origins made it appear that French Canadians had declined in Essex from 5,424 to 3,706, while Rameau knew they had increased to at least 8,000. In Kent, a small increase from 1,100 to 1,603 was given, even though the number had doubled; and the 18 returned for Lambton should be at least 100.

At issue were compilation practices whereby clerks counted only those born in Canada East as French Canadian. Rameau had proof of these practices 'in the very conversations I had in the office where these statistics were manipulated in Quebec.' 'If the same veracity presided over all the census operations in Upper Canada,' he told his readers, 'you risk nothing in demanding that it be begun again.' The editor of *Le Canadien* demanded that the Board of Registration and Statistics call on the enumerators to explain the contrast between the 1852 and 1861 returns, although nothing seems to have been done.[88]

Later analyses by Rameau invoked census returns to support claims about the superiority of the French over the English in Canada – claims that were enlisted in the promotion of the colonization project in Canada

East, and that bolstered the alliance of conservative politicians and ultramontane Catholic clergy in the making of a cultural imaginary for francophones. The official census figures showed that 'in the rural townships, with few exceptions, the English race gives way really or relatively, faced with French Canadian expansion.' The effete English were doing better in the cities, where they had government employment and immigration to bolster their numbers. Nonetheless, it could not be contested that 'on the same pitch and all other things being equal, the French Canadian knows better than the English how to make his way and establish himself solidly in the country, that little by little he carries all before him and that sooner or later his turn will come like that which belongs to every nationality.'[89]

Rameau's work helped fuel the pronatalist ethnic-national project that defined the historical trajectory and cultural worth of French Canadians in terms of agricultural colonization and human fecundity. This project has markedly affected the political and cultural life of Canada over the last century-and-a-half. Even though census making subjected all residents to the authority of a colonial state, sectional divisions and cultural politics ensured that social allegiance would be lodged elsewhere. The 'population of Canada' operated as a touchstone for differentiating ethnic-religious groups, rather than for producing a uniformly aggregated social body. More concretely, Rameau's work also helped sustain the widely held view among francophone intellectuals that the 1861 census was an instrument of cultural domination, conducted by an anglophone organ of state interested in belittling French Canada. Control over census making became a political ambition of these intellectuals – one soon to be satisfied.

**Boiled Numbers**

The 1861 census returns were taken up and treated as significant for political debate and for some administrative practices; yet it was increasingly apparent to a growing number of intellectuals and state servants that the existing arrangements did not produce the kind of knowledge that made it possible to gain effective leverage over social relations. There was a growing number of projects of government to which 'population,' as made up by the census, did not lend itself.

An attempt to consider census-making practice in a Parliamentary committee came to nothing when the session ended before the committee could sit. Still, influential opinion on the census can be drawn from a critical paper read in 1864 to the Literary and Historical Society of

Quebec, a leading venue for intellectuals, scientists, politicians, and state servants, by John Langton, the Cambridge-educated head of the Canadian Audit Office. Langton informed his audience that he had himself attempted to use the recent census reports as the basis for a paper on vital statistics, but had been convinced that many of the figures published were 'manifestly wrong.' Errors in vital statistics, he suggested, were due partly to misreporting by informants and, perhaps, partly to some carelessness on the part of enumerators. But as far as Langton was concerned, the main sources of error were to be found in the work of compilation, 'a kind of work, which, unless a perfect system of checking be established, is always liable to produce errors.' In the case of the recent census, however, 'there was no uniform system, under the inspection of a responsible head, and it is rumoured, I know not with what truth, that when the details did not correspond with the totals, from which they were distributed, the correspondence was arbitrarily forced, or, as the expression goes, the figures were cooked.' Langton concluded his paper with a call for a system of compulsory civil registration and for a reorganization of the colony's statistical activities. He did not have long to wait for a response to the second of these demands.[90]

# Chapter 7

# Facts, Figures, and Fundamentalism

Despite the revolving cabinets and shifting governmental priorities of the period preceding the Confederation of 1867, the pursuit of statistical and other administrative projects was systematized in Agriculture and Statistics after 1864, when Thomas D'Arcy McGee became Minister of Agriculture. The bureau acquired departmental status under a permanent deputy minister. Fundamentalist Catholic and francophone intellectuals came to direct the statistical apparatus and organized the new Canadian dominion's first scientific census of population. At the same time, the political stakes in census making were altered dramatically by the British North America Act's resolution of the issue of political representation.

By the late 1850s, as we have seen in an earlier chapter, the debates around representation by population had become particularly intense. The existing Canadian arrangements, under which each colonial section had the same number of seats in the Assembly, created a climate of sectional and partisan political manoeuvring that blocked the capacity of government to deal with many other pressing issues, such as the intercolonial railway, tariff and the public debt, and northwestern expansion. Quite apart from any other consideration, repeated changes in ministries after 1858 made any policy continuity difficult. Then, rather to the surprise of many observers and of the participants themselves, in the summer of 1864 the lines of political division were dramatically redrawn when Reformers from Canada West joined with most Conservatives from Canada East to form a coalition in favour of a federation of the British North American colonies. Although the details remained to be worked out, under the plan for federation, representation to the new state's lower house was to be made on the basis of population as determined by the census. Francophone conservatives had long been the staunch opponents of representation by population, perceiving it as religious and national suicide; yet now they scrambled to argue that the same principle in a federal state would be benign. Each province would control its own internal affairs, and the institution of an appointed upper house with fixed representation would counterbalance the potential dangers of representation by population as applied to the lower house. As it was passed in 1867, clause 51 of the BNA Act (30 Vic. c.III) enshrined representation by population for the House of Commons, with alterations to be made periodically, in keeping with the results of the census. The initial allocation of seats was to be based on 1861 census returns – a fact that increased political interest in that census's configuration of population.[1]

**The Department of Agriculture and Statistics**
Change in the principle of representation was accompanied by change in the organization of the Canadian statistical agency. Such change had been demanded repeatedly since William Hutton's death in July 1861 had left Agriculture and Statistics without a permanent secretary. François Evanturel, the agriculture minister from May 1862 to May 1863, claimed that the bureau's 'organization and internal discipline had been left in a condition so little efficient that the public had begun to doubt the importance of keeping it up.' The activities of the Board of Registration and Statistics had effectively ceased. Even though 'the great value of a systematic collection of facts in figures – or statistics – in the administration of the affairs of the State, for the furtherance of political science, and for the general information of the country' was universally recognized, 'in the collection and analysis of statistical information' Canada now stood 'far behind most other civilized countries.' The production of such material was urgently required and could not be left in private hands. It ought to be produced by 'the State,' according to Evanturel, 'since the machinery of executive business enables a Government readily to collect statistical facts, and, it has, moreover, the right to demand information – a right which is denied to private individuals.'

Evanturel urged cabinet to make the board an entity separate from the rest of the bureau, dedicated solely to 'the pursuance of statistical investigation.' He appointed Henry May to be in charge of this activity in the meantime, and set him to work making abstracts 'of all the statistical information to be found scattered throughout the official records of the country.' The fruit of his work would be 'the ground-work of a complete

"Hand-Book", so to speak, of the statistical history of the country.' However, May resigned soon after Evanturel's report was written, and nothing was done.[2]

The call for an effective statistical agency of state was repeated by Evanturel's successor, Luc Letellier, who insisted that no minister alone could hope to master all parts of the bureau's mandate. While not recommending a new statistics board, Letellier stressed that 'the surest remedy for the defects' of the bureau was 'the appointment of a permanent deputy-head, perfectly well-qualified in respect of the acquirements [sic] more particularly connected with the objects' of its mandate. This person should 'possess ideas of governing and systematizing service, which may ensure the prudent management of the office' despite changes in its political head. Again, no change occurred.[3]

It was T.D. McGee, newly pushed into the arms of the conservative Macdonald-Cartier government by the Catholic hierarchy's refusal to contemplate the Irish school system for Canada East, who finally transformed the bureau and board into a full-fledged department. McGee's peculiar mix of intellectual capacity, sympathy for ultramontane versions of Catholicism (including their anti-industrial, pro-agricultural thrust), and advocacy of a strong, administratively efficient, publicist state and of civic harmony, was conducive to the formation of new kinds of francohibernian political alliances in Canada, especially in the summer of 1864 as the new coalition government pushed the project of British North American federation. Under McGee's direction, the statistical powers of state were refashioned and Agriculture and Statistics ceased to be an anglophone organ. The sycophantic drivel of the Tory Crofton and the haphazard boosterism of the gentleman farmer Hutton were replaced in census making by a systematically planned and meticulously executed (albeit controversial) exercise in political specification.[4]

After Confederation, the Department of Agriculture and Statistics would engage in an array of state-forming projects. These aimed mainly to centralize knowledge and standardize practices on a national scale. That being said, reform of the statistical apparatus was not simply a by-product of plans for a federal system of government. Well before the confederation debates, McGee had laid out a plan for revamping Canada's statistical apparatus in his 1863 'Report on Government Departments,' which was the first attempt since Durham's 1839 *Report on the Affairs of British North America* to assess the capacities of the colonial state system as a whole and to analyse its strengths and weaknesses in terms of rational bureaucratic management. McGee proposed an overhauling of the mandates of existing bodies and of the processes by which state workers were recruited. However, his recommendations were very unevenly implemented.

The report contained a sharp critique of the 'inefficiency of the Statistical board & Bureau as at presently worked.' While the colony might not require 'those elaborate Statistical returns which characterize the official publications of old established States,' the existing arrangements caused needless expense and were 'a source of humiliation to every advocate of judicious progress.' As McGee put it, 'figures and tables of vital importance to the proper understanding of our annual progress ... which ought to be within everyone's reach, must now be laboriously compiled by interprizing inquirers, each for himself, or dispensed with.' McGee claimed that while 'every civilized Country has given great attention to this subject,' in Canada, 'whether from some inherent defect in the present Constitution of the Board of Statistics, [or] from the absence of a properly qualified Secretary to that Board to classify, collate, digest, tabulate, and index, such returns as are made, the large annual outlay on reports, is, in a great degree thrown away.' McGee aimed to model the Canadian statistics office on the Dutch Statistical Commission, which had so impressed delegates to the 1860 Statistical Congress. The Dutch office was attached to the Interior Ministry and possessed very broad powers to command statistical information directly from all governmental and non-governmental bodies and to engage in social research. Its Canadian counterpart, according to McGee, should be composed of 'seven branches, including the chief subjects of our internal economy and Social Science, which classify naturally together': agriculture, registration and statistics, patents, arts and manufactures, immigration and colonization, fisheries, and mining.[5]

On its face, this recommendation was quite modest: it would tighten the department's hold on immigration and add fisheries and mines to its existing mandate. It was the appointment of a deputy minister and the engagement by him of new functionaries that proved to be most significant. Although McGee's appointee would attempt, with very modest success, to establish a Canadian interdepartmental statistical commission, statistical practice became quite different under his direction.

**Joseph-Charles Taché, Deputy Minister**
McGee's choice as deputy minister was the fundamentalist Catholic doctor, administrator, and scientific and literary intellectual Joseph-Charles Taché (1820–1894). Taché laid out an ambitious statistical project

and quickly enlisted his friends and former schoolmates Stanislas Drapeau and the abbé Cyprien Tanguay, as well as an Englishman with statistical experience, W.H. Johnson, to carry it out. Unlike his predecessors Crofton and Hutton, Taché was interested in a grand project of social reform that contained a transcendental vision of human subjects moving through history and tied to territory. His project made the census into something other than an advertising mechanism. Past biographical treatments have made it difficult to estimate Taché's work as census maker. They have either seen his statistical work as a diversion from his literary career, or severed it from that career and from his religious-national politics. Taché's biography is particularly relevant because statistical practice had yet to be 'black-boxed.' Standardized procedures, indifferent to the personae of those following them, were still in the making.[6]

Joseph-Charles Taché came from one of the colony's leading political families. After his father's death when he was five, Joseph-Charles became the ward of his uncle, the seigneur Jean-Baptiste Taché of Kamouraska, a member of the Lower Canada Special Council, and then of the Legislative Council until his death in 1849. Another uncle was Sir Étienne-Pascal Taché, government minister and coalition leader in the 1850s and early 1860s. Joseph-Charles's younger brother, Alexandre-Antonin, became in his early twenties the co-adjuteur to the bishop of St-Boniface, with right of succession. He succeeded to that office in 1853 and became a leading figure in national politics. He helped inspire in Joseph-Charles a deep commitment to ultramontane Catholicism.

As befitted his social standing, Taché was educated first at the Petit Séminaire de Québec, an institution where the abbé Jean Holmes offered instruction in mathematics. He left in 1840 without completing the course to study medicine in Quebec, where he was one of the organizers of the St-Jean-Baptiste Society. It was likely during this period that Taché circulated the prospectus for a 'Literary Association' that would offer evening instruction to urban artisans and that would develop the three great means to social improvement: education, national industry, and arts and skilled crafts. The association's motto was to be 'À l'Avenir de la Patrie' (to the future of the motherland). He was also trying his hand at poetry. Taché received his medical diploma in 1844, interned briefly at the Quebec Marine and Emigrant Hospital, and set up in private practice in Rimouski. Acclaimed the MPP for Rimouski in the 1848 elections, he was a supporter of L.-H. Lafontaine and an energetic advocate of *la patrie*, reportedly going so far as to exclude all English imported items from his personal consumption and to dress in homespun. It was said to be Taché who fired on and drove off the arsonists who were attempting to raze Lafontaine's house during the 1849 Rebellion Losses riots.[7]

**Feudal Science in the Nineteenth Century**
Taché's first major Parliamentary initiative was to chair the 1849 Select Committee on the State of Agriculture in Lower Canada – perhaps his first direct experience both of the relevance of statistical knowledge in projects for social government and of the inadequacies of the existing statistical apparatus. Among other things, the committee attempted to measure the rate of emigration from Canada East, and its findings fuelled debate around census making in 1851. It was Taché who wrote the committee's report, in which he demonstrated his already developed ultramontane commitments and spelled out a political analysis and agenda that he would promote in later years. The future census maker was already actively promoting the placement of the people on the land and demanding interventionist measures to keep them there under the hegemony of the Catholic clergy. He would enlist statistical science and state power in support of this project.

Regretting 'the total absence of statistics of a recent nature,' the 1849 agriculture committee sent out a circular letter to members of the dominant groups with questions about agricultural societies, model farms, and the utility of using rural schools for distributing agricultural literature. The replies were distilled to present a critical analysis of the moral economy of agriculture in Canada East. This analysis concluded that Canada East's agricultural underdevelopment was not due to the quality of the soil or the nature of the climate, for both closely resembled those of Canada West while in terms of output its agriculture was more productive than that in many parts of Europe. Nor was the problem one of 'national character,' for the *canadiens* were the equals of any other people in terms of 'intelligence, health, dexterity, and strength,' while possessing 'in a greater degree perhaps than any other, that amiability and unaffected cheerfulness which contribute more than is commonly supposed to both health and happiness.' Where the *canadiens* suffered was 'in regard to political, and above all, agricultural education.'

Agricultural problems were held to be problems of practice and of the farmers' own conduct. They were caused, Taché argued, by 'the astonishing fertility of the soil ... by too great abundance; but, on the other hand, the lessons we have been taught by adversity will turn to our advantage.' Poor soils compelled farmers to innovate, Taché's analysis ran, but the rich virgin soil of Canada East had meant abundant wheat crops without the necessity of manuring. Farmers produced wheat intensively, which exhausted the soil, yet they raised no green crops to feed cattle to produce manure to replenish it. 'Abundant harvests had given a great number a taste for luxury' (that disfiguring materialist foe of Catholic morality), and had resulted in 'a large portion of our population being deeply in debt at the present day.'

Noticeable by its absence from the report by Taché, scion of a feudal family, was any criticism of landholding practices, or the seigneurial system, or class relations, or of the fact that a large share of the social product was earmarked to support the clerical establishment. Instead, he proposed to govern the conduct of farmers by creating a colonywide system of agricultural inspection, reporting, and instruction by officials appointed by the central government. The inspectors would educate the peasants in improved practices while reporting on agricultural conditions to the central authority. At the same time, he proposed that agricultural colleges be funded under clerical supervision. This was a state-forming project in that knowledge was to be centralized. It was also a governmental project, in a Foucauldian sense, though not a liberal one.[8]

Taché's acquaintance with questions of agricultural improvement and colonization – one of the main fields of population politics – was deepened in the following years. He was a regular member of the legislature's committees on agriculture and agricultural exhibitions, and was named to the first Board of Agriculture for Lower Canada, on which he sat for at least a decade. In the session before he resigned in 1856, he co-sponsored a Canada East Agricultural Improvement bill. Furthermore, at the height of the debates over abolishing the remnants of feudal relations of production in Canada East, Taché published one of the more concise, if politically conservative, plans for commuting seigneurial tenures. In it, he defended the seigneurial system as a colonization practice for a purely agrarian community, even while recognizing that it had to be removed as a barrier to the modern development of towns and railways. The debate over feudalism was inextricably bound up with matters of religious-ethnic pride. In Taché's view, feudalism had been good for the peasantry economically, spiritually, and morally, but the British conquerers had encouraged its degeneration by practising various kinds of encroachments and exactions on their own fiefs. These were not to be legitimated by compensation in Taché's scheme, which would gradually commute feudal obligations over a twenty-five-year period.

Particularly striking was the detailed account Taché gave of the numbers of inhabitants involved in feudal relations, of the capitalized value of their lands, and of the costs of commutation. He used statistical calculation to adjudicate courses of conduct in the plan, and did so with a degree of sophistication that made Hutton's comparison of the costs of wheat and potato production look like a schoolboy's exercise. Rational numerical calculation co-existed in Taché's work with a quasi-feudal paternalism and ultramontane social tutelage: a kind of feudal science in the nineteenth century.[9]

Taché served as Canada's commissioner to the 1855 Paris Exposition. From that experience, he produced a report on the colony's participation there, a prize-winning statistical pamphlet, and a series of newspaper articles for a domestic audience. His report was published as *Canada at the Universal Exhibition of 1855* (Toronto: 1856); his pamphlet, *Esquisse sur le Canada considéré sous le point de vue économiste*, was the compendium of statistical information about the colony judged to satisfy best the Executive Council's prize criterion of 'containing the most information, in the fewest words.' The *Esquisse* was a conventional piece of statistical description, much of it perhaps compiled by Taché's friend Stanislas Drapeau. Taché's manipulation of statistical information had sectional and sectarian overtones, reconfiguring the official 1852 enumeration returns to describe the colony as containing more French Canadians than people of any other origin and more Catholics than people of any other religious denomination. Taché described the French population as the most prolific the world had ever known, and made a point of insisting on the cultural and institutional differences between Canada East and West, strongly advising British immigrants to choose the latter. Emigrants from France, Belgium, and the French cantons of Switzerland would find themselves perfectly at home in Canada East.[10]

Taché's glimpses of the Paris proletariat reinforced his commitment to the ultramontane pastoralist, anticapitalist project. 'Let us consider ourselves fortunate in Canada to possess general comfort,' he said in one public letter, 'let us try to be content in our comparatively prosperous state ... and let us not chase after chimeras,' for it was clear that the problems of Europe came from what was in people's heads. 'Too many people there want to have it better without working and too many people believe themselves to be geniuses for whom bodily labour was not made.' Such beliefs were the source of 'political agitations and revolutions created by envy and by ambition ill-served by mediocrity or Sloth.' Taché made a brief attempt at a statistical classification of the French population for his readers' information.[11]

Strong opposition from the liberal Rouge party and from the *censitaires* for his pro-seigneurial position, combined with the poor impression created by his touristic letters from Paris and by his huge bill for expenses (£3,851.13.6), made it certain that Taché would not be re-elected to Parliament, and he resigned his seat in December 1856. At Bishop Bourget's invitation, he undertook to manage and edit the new ultramontane newspaper *Le Courrier du Canada*, launched in Quebec in February 1857 as a counter to the liberal press. He held this position until the end of October 1859, and from this fundamentalist pulpit, again propagated a social imaginary in which the Catholic *canadien* population distinguished itself on the historical stage as the world's most prolific. Yet he belonged to the pro-science wing of the ultramontane movement, which insisted on the importance of empirical science for promoting social progress. He argued, too, that the life of the colony was shaped by a continuing, but useful, struggle between British and French, anglophone and francophone, Protestant and Catholic. In the wake of the abortive 1858 Brown-Dorion liberal alliance, which seemed about to institute representation by population while preserving the Union of the Canadas, Taché was precocious in presenting a detailed plan for the confederation of the British North American colonies. He saw a federal form of government as the means to achieve his vision of French-Canadian survival even while accommodating demands for representation by population. While arguing that the struggle between 'the races' was a source of creative tension and progress, he was sharply critical of what he claimed to be the existing alien British and Protestant dominance in matters of state policy in Canada East.[12]

To take only one example, in March 1858 the *Courrier* reprinted what Taché described as an 'excellent article,' titled 'Agriculture and Government.' In it, the lack of agricultural improvement in and immigration to Canada East was attributed to its subordination to 'British' agricultural policies. Protestantism made the English suspicious of all higher authority; in contrast, for the French and Catholic 'race,' 'all good and all initiative for progress must come from on high.' It followed that while the policy of seeking agricultural improvement by subsidizing local agricultural societies and leaving them to their own devices might work in the west, it would surely fail in the east: a successful eastern agricultural policy had to be interventionist and *dirigiste*. 'Let the government instruct the farmers, guide them, protect them against themselves, against their own tendencies,' argued the piece. What was needed was not encouragement but 'coercive laws; in agriculture as in all the other positions of the social state the people must be enlightened as to its duties and its needs.' This principle was recognized in public education, where people were more or less forced to send their children to school: why, then, in agricultural practice should people not be forced to reforest the plains they had clear-cut? It was no attack on liberty to force people to do what was right. Taché commented that the two 'systems' of individualism and authority were in free competition in Canada and that the next quarter-century would demonstrate which was the greatest source of material comfort. As to progress in the arts and literature and in the greatness of nations, the matter had been decided: French superiority was evident in the examples of Alexandre, César, Charlemagne, Charles-Quint, Napoléon, and so on.[13]

Taché's contract with *Le Courrier du Canada* ended in October 1859, and he soon joined the Board of Inspectors of Asylums and Prisons, becoming its chair. Here again the scientific dimension of his religious fundamentalism was evident: Taché was a systematizer interested in bringing Canadian practice abreast of international trends. As a disciplined administrator, he attempted to standardize record-keeping practices both in the institutions subject to inspection and in the inspectoral reports themselves; such infrastructural work was clearly a precondition for improved statistical practice. He toured American prisons in search of innovation, and convinced the Executive Council that the board needed a library of international publications to keep up with its field. Taché used the statistical resources generated by the board to defend it against Liberal charges of mismanagement and extravagance; in the process he produced a comparative analysis of conditions and expenditures in Canadian and American public institutions.[14]

It was the complex mix of fundamentalist Catholicism, political paternalism linked to the seigneurial system, disciplined scientific and administrative expertise, engagement in political debate, and extensive practice in the making of representations of the nation, that made Joseph-Charles Taché such an interesting social activist and such an apt choice as official statistician. Census making, like nationalism, mobilized an imaginary of places, persons, and times, and much of Taché's work aimed at stabilizing such an imaginary. During his tenure on the Board of Inspectors of Asylum and Prisons, he helped found and manage *Les Soirées canadiennes: recueil de littérature nationale*, a magazine explicitly devoted to the creation of a *canadien* literature as a refuge and aliment for the popular imagination. Unlike many of his utilitarian-minded, English, Protestant contemporaries, for whom the popular imagination was a dangerous force that should be channelled toward the study of 'useful knowledge,' but also unlike many of his francophone literary contemporaries, who were contemptuous of popular literary forms, Taché authored popular, accessible literary 'legends' that were widely reprinted and durably influential.

For instance, in *Trois légendes de mon pays,* first published in 1861, Taché provided an exciting tale of pursuit, murder, vengeance, and subterfuge set during the wars between the Iroquois and Micmac nations in the earliest years of New France. Heroic Jesuit missionary work eventually led a younger generation of Micmacs to cast off the heathen, barbaric habits and irrational fears of their ancestors and to find salvation in the true Church – a fact that was to their terrestrial benefit, since in Taché's view, the aboriginal peoples were faced with assimilation or extinction. He would attempt to demonstrate this proposition scientifically in one of his reports on the 1871 census. While in his legends Taché did not allow preaching to get much in the way of the action, he was also clear about his objective, which was to fashion a *canadien* cultural memory through popular literature. He sought explicitly to create an alternative cultural trajectory to the one anchored in the liberal and romantic ideals of the French Revolution, an event that had produced the distorted life of contemporary France. 'We were born, as a people, out of the Catholicism of the seventeenth century and out of our struggles with a wild and indomitable nature,' he wrote. 'In no way are we sons of the Revolution and we do not need the expedients of modern romanticism to engage minds which believe and hearts which remain pure.'[15] The broad ethnic-national project that Taché announced in his literary work would come to guide his census-making activity.

### How and How Not to Conduct a Census: Taché's 1865 Memorandum

Taché began as deputy minister of agriculture on 11 August 1864 and quickly reorganized the moribund bureau at Quebec. He was to insist that all agencies under the board's supervision obey the letter of the law and adopt consistent administrative procedures. On 18 January 1865, he delivered a memorandum to the Board of Registration and Statistics, whose members were now his uncle Étienne-Pascal, his patron D'Arcy McGee, and William McDougall. Taché presented a detailed analysis of census making and a critique of past Canadian practice. He laid out an ambitious plan for reorganizing his department and for reconstructing and publicizing all statistics of population since the European invasion. The board accepted the bulk of his proposals, which would shape the activities of the department over the next fifteen years.

The memorandum provided the first systematic analysis of census making in Canadian administration. Taché pointed to four influences on the census:

> 1st The unity comprehensiveness and simplicity of the system adopted, and the sort of management by which it is put into execution.
> 2nd The social and family organization of the population, and its feeling as to the real or supposed advantages to be derived from exag[g]erating or underrating the numerical information asked of it.
> 3rd The fitness of those employed in the Collection of the Census returns.
> 4th The efficiency of the statistical Staff at head quarters.

Taché declined to speculate as to the relative weight of these factors in the fiasco of 1861, contenting himself with a satirical demonstration of the uselessness of the 'statistics' generated on that occasion. It is his satire that later writers, concerned with lionizing Taché as the statistical founding father, have found significant in the memorandum; but it was how Taché subsequently addressed the second of these four factors that distinguished him from his predecessors and from many of his contemporaries.[16]

He saw that statistical knowledge relied on the nature of social organization and on the interests of respondents. Such knowledge had to be adequate to its object and could be produced only with the aid of willing subjects: it was, in our terms, a reflexive knowledge, and this meant to Taché that consistent observation on the scale of a system of civil registration or of a census demanded public education and the disciplining of potential respondents. People had to be habituated to the making of consistent observations and convinced of the importance of so doing. As he would put it in 1867, 'when every one shall be convinced of the importance of such information, when the education of the public on this subject shall be nearly complete, it will then be possible to render perfectly regular a system which has already become a habit; there is no other way of proceeding.'[17] Clearly, the census was a governmental project in the Foucauldian sense, even if Taché did not reflect on the epistemological issues involved in generating knowledge on the basis of the prior configuration of the objects to be known and of the observations to be made. Yet unlike his predecessors, he was aware that such a prior configuration was a precondition for generating consistent observations, and his plans for the 1871 census show this.

Taché made six recommendations to the board for avoiding a repetition of past problems in census making. There must be 'a superior ordering and control[l]ing authority, possessed of the necessary power and prestige, and not embarrassed by minute legislation.' The board had failed in the past to satisfy its mandate to provide statistical information because it lacked sufficient administrative autonomy, and census making suffered because the law attempted to specify things (such as the precise enumeration period and the enumeration categories) that could only be determined according to particular local circumstances. There must be, next, 'one responsible and thoroughly competent managing officer,' and third, 'a regular permanent well chosen and properly paid staff of statistical clerks.'

Taché then urged that an interdepartmental statistical commission be created, to be chaired by the Minister of Agriculture. There should be a chief statistician who would command the authority to call together departmental deputies, the superintendents of education, the chairman of the Board of Prisons and Asylums, and the Auditor General whenever he thought it necessary to acquire information. Departmental and cabinet rivalries made this arrangement improbable. Taché argued further that effective census making required 'the temporary and occasional employment of men of science for the collection and arrangement of special statistics.' Drawing on the services of 'persons devoted to Statistical science not being in a position to accept the situation of permanent Departmental officers' was common in international practice, he claimed. In effect, these were thinly veiled arguments in favour of the department hiring Taché's friend Cyprien Tanguay, who was prevented by his clerical status from entering the state service directly. Taché's final consideration was that census enumerators should always be 'persons connected in some capacity with the public administration of affairs, and somewhat responsible to the Executive of the Country.' This last matter was not pressing; there was time yet before the next enumeration. Of more immediate concern was the organization of the office staff at Agriculture and Statistics.

Under McGee's proposed arrangements, Taché thought the board would have sufficient administrative autonomy, and he would himself serve as the 'responsible and thoroughly competent managing officer' of census matters until John Lowe took them over in the summer of 1870. What called for immediate attention was the staff complement. Taché claimed there were no competent statistical officers in the department (even though many clerks and one of the chief compilers employed on the 1861 census were still present). He urged that 'two permanent first class clerks' qualified in statistical matters be appointed immediately, that the internal administration of the department be reorganized, and that its extra clerks be fired. The additional salary costs for the two permanent clerks would be money well spent, for there was always statistical work to do, and in any case, their employment would mean that casual clerks would not be needed at census time.

## Building A National Monument

Taché ended his memorandum with a proposal for publishing a ten-volume statistical series, which would include corrected and annotated volumes on the 1852 and 1861 censuses, in addition to material from 'the earliest times' to the enumeration of 1871. This project was necessary because 'statistical science is above all a science of comparisons and proportions, and the longer the time and larger the figures, the more accurate the inferences and conclusions.'[18] Five volumes of this series would appear in the 1870s.

It is typical of Taché that he described his statistical project, including census making, as the creation of a 'monument.' This description was not offered lightly; 'monument' carries a very specific conception of statistics and the census as a governmental project. Taché's conception of monumentalism again underlines the insufficiency of previous accounts of his contributions – accounts which separate his practice of numerical statistics from his larger religious-national politics.

Although monumental facts and statistics rarely figure in it, a rapidly growing literature on the 'invention of tradition' and the politics of memory suggests that the making of monuments is an important tactic in social struggle, from the point of view both of state forming practices and of popular resistance to authority. Seen from above, pageantry and monumentalism imply, in H.V. Nelles's words, that 'through careful selection and deft balancing and by either avoiding or wilfully misrepresenting the unmentionable, history could be made to serve various present purposes.' As elements in the politics of hegemony, monuments identify and celebrate pasts. They commemorate. They configure memory and tradition. They figure in attempts to tie people to particular visions of their present and future. As what Cohn has called 'officializing practice,' making memory monuments helps posit the state, or church, or another social institution, as the repository of true history and social trajectory.[19]

Commemoration and celebration of the prolific past of the *canadiens* were central elements in Taché's ultramontane view of a people tied to its land, to its Catholic church, to its nationality, and to its genealogy as

Facts, Figures, and Fundamentalism 249

the flourishing progeniture of a handful of French Catholic men. Census making was situated on this terrain. Taché's projected 1871 census volumes were to be erected in public space and were to consecrate a particular vision of history and memory. As science, statistical monumentalism constructed series as a basis for comparisons. As political theatre, statistical monumentalism identified 'the people' and placed it in a historical trajectory. It is clear that Taché's published volumes have served as a basic reference for the truth of the past to generations of intellectuals and administrators, probably much more so than have most other kinds of Canadian monuments. Their factual character has tended to disguise their ideological character.

**The Mound Builders**
The Executive Council authorized the appointment of two permanent statistical clerks at an annual salary of $1,000 each in mid-March 1865 'in order to establish, and give vitality to the Statistical branch of the Department of Agriculture.' Taché hired William Henry Johnson and Stanislas Drapeau, and the same week, with McGee's authorization, named the abbé Cyprien Tanguay an external departmental 'attaché' at a monthly salary of $100 with expenses out of the contingencies.[20] Until the summer of 1870, it was Taché and these three men who worked on census questions. They studied past census-making practice in Canada and abroad. They also produced the larger statistical series into which the 1871 census results were to be inserted.

W.H. Johnson remains a little-known figure, and the surviving biographical information about him is both fragmentary and contradictory. Taché stated in response to an inquiry from the Civil Service Commission that Johnson had worked from 1857 as a sessional clerk in the Legislative Assembly before coming to Agriculture and Statistics. D'Arcy McGee had sufficient confidence in him to make him secretary to the 1868 interprovincial immigration conference. In July 1867, in describing the staff at Agriculture to his new minister and friend, T.C. Chapais, Taché wrote that 'the senior Johnson is a man of the greatest merit and Statistics needs him, as it does Drapeau and M. Tanguay.'[21]

**The Priest of the Lineages**
Taché's schoolmate Cyprien Tanguay (1819–1903) was an experienced statistician in Taché's understanding of the term. After ordination in the early 1840s, Tanguay's parishes were in the Rimouski area, where Taché was MPP. Tanguay had been interested in compilation and genealogical

investigation from his early childhood. The project that Taché convinced the government to support out of public funds was the reconstruction of a genealogy of the French-Canadian population from the first invasion – an ambitious effort that involved painstaking research in parish records and archival collections on both sides of the Atlantic. Tanguay's work was the basis for Taché's plan to include a history of the European population in his collection of census volumes, although his *Dictionnaire généalogique des familles canadiennes-françaises*, a multivolume effort that remained in use for a century after its first part appeared in 1871, was eventually excluded from the official series.[22]

Genealogy and chronology were central elements in the statistical projects pursued by Taché and his fellows. Tanguay was their leading and most prolific practitioner. His *Répertoire général du clergé canadien*, for instance, a 'complete table of all the priests who have served the church of Canada since its discovery,' presented a brief description of the establishment of the archdioceses and then a chronological list of bishops up to the present and of priests up to the British conquest. This work, which Tanguay described as 'a book of statistics,' offered 'a long list of martyrs, generous apostles, tireless missionaries and zealous friends of education.'[23] What it actually presented about clerics was their dates of birth, ordination, and death, with the clerical charges they held in between. There was, in fact, no description of anything substantive that any of them did: the book was a statistical monument in Taché's sense. It celebrated the religious past, glorified the clergy, and configured present authority figures as existing in a continuity.

For Taché, the making up of genealogy was central to the fabrication of French-Canadian nationality. In a strong sense, his 1871 census should be understood as a genealogical project. The genealogical practice he promoted was based on the tracing of patrilineal descent to the imaginary European country from which immigrants originated. This practice defined *canadiens* as the blood relations of individual men from a mythical place called France, and excluded everyone else in the world from the imagined *canadien* community.

The resources created by the genealogical project made it possible in principle for people to configure their social relations in ways other than those Taché sought to promote. For instance, the enduring set of records he created are still being used a century and a half later in efforts to reconstruct genetic heritages. Yet for Taché and Tanguay, the fact, for instance, that many 'French' men had sired children with aboriginal women did not make *canadiens* aboriginal people, nor aboriginal people *canadiens*, in any meaningful sense. The project similarly had no interest in using anything besides patrilineal descent to demonstrate the common membership of all in a larger community. Instead, it homogenized the places of European origin, conveniently neglecting the fact that for many immigrants, 'France' was an unstable entity at the time of migration, and that French was a language not spoken by many 'French' men. Paired to that other mythical construction – that the French were the 'world's most prolific people' – genealogy sought to tie people to a pastoral present under clerical hegemony. It fuelled an imaginary in which a handful of French men and their loyal spouses, sheltered under the Cross of the Lord and slaking their thirst in the Fountain of the Wisdom of the Church, pursued their historic mission of civilizing North America. Tanguay's genealogical project was a monumental undertaking.

It is worth remarking that the 'English' tangent of the project did not relate all English-speaking people to common male ancestors in a homogenized 'Britain.' The political struggles of the 1830s and 1840s in the colony had led to the defeat of attempts to construct a unitary 'British' Canadian identity. As one consequence of splitting 'Britain' into England, Ireland, Scotland, and Wales, the 'French' were now the largest nationality in Canada. In its concern with placing people in categories of national origin, the 1871 census was a totalizing project that worked a new economy of 'national' difference.

**The Colonizing Printer**

The other new 'statist' was Stanislas Drapeau (1821–1893). Drapeau left the Petit Séminaire in 1837 to become a typographer. In 1839, at age eighteen, he ran both *Le Fantastique* and *Le Canadien* while their editors were jailed. A variety of printing and publishing enterprises occupied him in the 1840s, including the production of the paper *L'Ami de la religion et de la patrie* (for which Joseph-Charles Taché was a Parliamentary correspondent), and the publishing of statistical compilations and an agricultural schoolbook. Drapeau was the business manager of the *Le Courrier du Canada* while Taché was editor. During this period he produced a manifesto in favour of rural colonization bearing the motto, 'Let us lay claim to the soil, if we wish to preserve our nationality.' The manifesto urged municipalities to pressure the central government to sponsor a serious colonization project in the St. Lawrence valley under the auspices of the Bureau of Agriculture. Drapeau urged that £100,000 a year for ten years be devoted to this cause under the supervision of two specially appointed colonization superintendents, arguing that the history of colonization showed that voluntary efforts alone could not succeed. He left *Le Courrier du Canada* early in 1859, moving to St-Jean-Port-Joli as the $4-a-day colonization agent for the Elgin-Taché road, and gaining some celebrity by organizing settlers' mutual aid societies.[24]

From his position as colonization agent, Drapeau produced his 593-page *Études sur les développements de la colonisation du Bas-Canada depuis dix ans: (1851 à 1861)*. This complex work contained a detailed description of the physical conditions in different sectors of Canada East where colonization was possible, accompanied by a series of maps (the latter produced in Crown Lands by E.E. Taché, one of Joseph-Charles's cousins, and Andrew Russell, both of whom would be enlisted by Agriculture and Statistics for the 1871 census effort). It offered statistical information about land, population, and production in the east, described how to organize a colonization society, and called for the creation of a separate colonization branch in Agriculture devoted to the eastern section.

Particularly important politically was Drapeau's claim that past censuses had presented a distorted picture of Canada East. The eastern section was far wealthier and more populous than they made it seem, and offered a much broader field for new settlement. His book corrected and supplemented the census returns of 1852 and 1861. It probably provided Taché with ammunition for his 1865 attack on past census practice, and it helped sustain the view among francophone politicians and intellectuals that past censuses were instruments of anglophone domination.

For example, the amount of land in the east was given in the 1861 census as 10,375,418 acres, while Drapeau claimed there were in fact 17,375,500 acres. According to the census only the unconceded lands in the old seigneuries were available for new settlement, and this was clearly an error. The census also presented a false picture of the wealth of people in the east. It calculated wealth per capita in terms of land values, but Drapeau added the value of agricultural implements and crops. His method gave a per capita wealth of $284.60, but he argued that a truer picture would include $749,268 for the value of ships constructed at Quebec and the huge sums of $11,012,253 from the timber industry and $12,647,048 for the products of manufactures, as well as some lesser sums. According to Drapeau, land values were underestimated by at least one-third in the 1861 census. Not only that, but crop returns were reported as being in bushels for the east when in fact they were in minots and should be one-eighth larger. In fact, in contrast to the image created by the census, between 1852 and 1861 the eastern population had had 'splendid results' in terms of growth, and the colony was developing rapidly.

Notwithstanding his demonstration of Canada East's remarkable wealth and progress in recent times, Drapeau argued that 'the future of the motherland' lay in agricultural colonization. He was not inconsistent in this. His numbers were meant to parry the attacks of those in the west who claimed that Catholicism and French culture retarded material prosperity and population growth. Yet to Drapeau the religious conservative, the consumption of luxury was demoralizing and could be discouraged through agrarian colonization, which would also give *Lebensraum* to the flourishing French population.

**Sodom and Gomorrah**

'Colonize!' Drapeau declaimed, 'it is to assure the conservation of our nationality; it is to reform morals, broaden the reign of civilization and make the country benefit from its works.' Agricultural colonization was protection from the degradation of urban, capitalist, and foreign luxury. 'Let luxury, that so hideous and deep wound of societies, be banned from the peaceful residence of the farmer, so that the homespun cloth made with the active hands of the mother of the family may be preferred to the cloth that comes from foreign places and which, often, becomes the occasion and the cause of the farmer's ruin.'[25] Drapeau almost certainly saw the post in Agriculture and Statistics as a base from which to pursue this broad, national, religious, and cultural political project.

Taché and Drapeau, authors of the first systematic census of Canadian industry, were avowed enemies of industrialization. For them, a strong population was a *rural* population engaged in domestic manufactures, and they would organize the 1871 census categories to demonstrate rural strength. Taché opposed one of the more foolish projects of the Agriculture Department, the encouragement of flax scutching and linen mills, not because labour-intensive industry made no sense in a country characterized by labour shortages, but because urban industry was demoralizing. As he put it in a letter to one linen-factory-promoting MPP, 'from the point of view of national habits and morals, it seems to me it would be infinitely more worthwhile to encourage domestic industry (I mean work done by the family in the house) than to open the door to the commercial manufacturing system which brings in its wake agglomerations of population, misery, the proletariat and above all demoralization.'[26] In the developing international division of labour, Canada's mission was to create an agrarian civilization, one strengthened by the technical and scientific advances of the age, but one free from the degrading tendencies of capitalist industrialization and free from the secular evils of postrevolutionary social philosophy.

French against English, Catholicism against Protestantism, conservativism against liberalism, agriculture against industry, the country against the city: for Taché, for the first two ministers under whom he served, and for at least part of his administrative team, the future of civilization was playing itself out in these antagonisms. Social investigation, official representations, and projects for reconstructing history and for creating literature were key forces in these struggles, in which the powers of science and of the state in alliance with the church were of central importance. The broad and variegated mandate of the Department of Agriculture and Statistics provided Taché with a great many opportunities to intervene in the battle. In his self-appointed task of fabricating a national identity, he would draw on his meticulously disciplined organizational skills and his appreciation for scientific observation. The 1871 census would be the apex of his efforts.[27]

**Statistical Excavations**

Taché began preparations for the multivolume census project even before Tanquay, Johnson, and Drapeau were appointed, seeking information from other jurisdictions about census matters.[28] His new employees set about collecting, reconstructing, and correcting all existing statistical and genealogical sources. Tanguay continued and extended his genealogical research. He devoted himself entirely to the work, going through all the parish records in Canada East/Quebec from the first European settlement. Claiming to have found 'numerous lacunae' in the early Canadian records, and with an anonymous patron willing to defray his expenses, Tanguay was granted leave in January 1867 to continue his research in Paris, where he tracked down duplicates of records lost or destroyed in Canada. Taché reported to the 1868 Civil Service Commission that 'no ordinary clerk could have accomplished what has been done, and what is being done by Mr. Tanguay, and no specialist could have done it, I think, for a smaller remuneration.' Tanguay, who worked mainly outside the department, was summoned to the Ottawa census conference in July 1870 and told to bring 'papers of parishes and statistics' with him. In 1871, Taché could boast that the fruit of Tanguay's research was 'a complete chain of documentary evidence for a period of 250 years' concerning the French population.[29]

Johnson and Drapeau worked on the statistics of Ontario and Quebec respectively; after Confederation, Johnson also searched out the maritime census records. The two men effected an enormous accumulation of knowledge at the centre of the state system. Their work involved a systematic assessment of existing statistical resources and the reconstruction of statistical series wherever possible. In anticipation of 1871, they engaged in extensive consultation with potential census organizers and administrators. They also worked at reconfiguring existing materials into more administratively useful and symbolically pleasing representations.

Taché's official instructions to Johnson for a research trip in the fall of 1868 illustrate the extent of the work. Johnson's brief was to spend two months in 'gathering all information as [to] the taking of the forthcoming Census, the best way of doing it in the most accurate and complete manner, and as to the class or classes of persons the most suitable for the collection of Census data.' He was to locate collections of 'general & special statistics, amongst others, Vital Statistics – Births deaths & Marriages[,] Inquests[,] Church Registers[,] Municipal Assessment Rolls[, and] Judicial Statistics.' He was to 'collect all such information as relates to the Emigration statistics connected with the history of the settlement of the localities visited,' and he was to 'take notes of all the information so gathered, and of the sources ancient and recent whereupon all such information can be derived, in order to lodge the same in the Records of this Department for immediate & future use.' Johnson spent two busy months visiting every county town west of Kingston, Ontario, some of them three times.[30] Stanislas Drapeau was similarly employed in Quebec, although detailed official instructions to him do not survive. Drapeau spent his time in late 1866 and early 1867 working in the archives of Laval University. By the end of 1869, Drapeau and Johnson had worked their way through all past Canadian censuses, up to and including that of 1852.[31]

These efforts at statistical reconstruction and at centralizing knowledge in the state system were extended to the Maritime provinces after Confederation, although it seemed for a time that Taché's grand project might be curtailed. There were ongoing denunciations in the press of his monumental vision of statistical knowledge; for instance, his Blue Book was attacked as 'receiving a stone where bread was promised' and denounced as 'a monstrous farce.' Taché was forced to defend his project against the probes of the Civil Service Commission and against the fiscal discipline exerted by its chair, John Langton. Taché feared that the appointment of the commission meant that 'it is to the most inveterate enemies of everything French, Catholic and Irish that we have been delivered.' In the summer of 1868, he was looking for another position in the expectation of losing his post.[32]

There was a debate over the department's attempt to centralize further the production of statistical knowledge by absorbing the Nova Scotia Board of Statistics, in part because as issuer of marriage licences, that body seemed to fall within provincial jurisdiction, while as registrar of vital events, its competence was federal.[33] Taché was alarmed to learn that there was no budget allocation for the Nova Scotia bureau in 1868–9. At the same time, the immigration and colonization budgets were slashed, and Taché believed that the Civil Service Commission was targeting French Canadians when it reduced the numbers of supernumerary clerks. As well, the commission demoted both Drapeau and Johnson. First-class clerks earning $1,000 and anticipating a salary increase in 1865, they smarted under the injustice of ranking as junior second-class clerks and still earning $1,000 in 1870. However, despite opposition from within and without the state system, Taché and his team survived the probes of the commission, and the department absorbed the Nova Scotia bureau.[34]

The work of statistical reconstruction and knowledge appropriation for the two Canadas was extended to the Maritimes. Of the twenty-one censuses conducted under British rule in Nova Scotia and New Brunswick, only five existed as printed papers from which W.H. Johnson had been able to create population abstracts in Ottawa. On 7 August 1871, Taché sent him to search for the records in local archives.[35] 'The archives are found!' Johnson telegraphed excitedly from Halifax on 6 September, requesting permission to engage a copying clerk immediately. Johnson uncovered a large and diverse amount of material, much of it in poor condition and incomplete. He urged that immediate steps be taken to preserve the originals and argued that since many of the documents were 'important to the country' and had been shipped from Quebec to Halifax during the War of 1812, the department should take steps to retain them. The absence of a continuous record of vital events showed that 'a stringent law for Births, Marriages and Burials is much required.'[36]

**Re-evaluating and Re-enumerating**
In response to immediate administrative needs, but also explicitly as a heuristic exercise in preparation for 1871, Taché, Drapeau, and Johnson 'corrected' the census returns from 1852 and 1861, and recompiled and reorganized the results. They evaluated critically the censuses conducted

in Upper Canada/Canada West from 1824 by comparing returns with other available information.[37] William Hutton's 1861 census made it impossible for the department reliably to determine the distribution of the seigneurial indemnities. It did not distinguish free and common soccage from seigneurial tenure in areas of Canada East where these were mixed, and changing municipal boundaries further complicated matters. Reworking this part of the 1861 census involved a partial re-enumeration, preparing 'on the spot, a list of the heads of families residing' in various localities in 1861, comparing this list with the surviving enumeration schedules, and then constructing a detailed account of changing parish and municipal boundaries over time. The resulting statement of administrative units in Canada East was published in the last pre-Confederation report of the Minister of Agriculture – the first complete inventory that the central government possessed of its own local units.[38]

Somewhere around this time, Taché concluded that the confused mix of *de facto* and *de jure* enumeration principles employed in 1852 and 1861 was unworkable. No account survives of the point at which, and the exact grounds on which, he decided to move to a strict *de jure* principle, but his field experiments with the 1861 census schedules took place at a time when it was clear that the 1871 census returns would directly determine Quebec's political representation. In any case, the kind of infrastructural work involved in remaking earlier censuses extended the administrative capacity of the state bureaucracy, and not only for census purposes. Taché's office was able to centralize aspects of knowledge production by breaking an earlier dependence on the local knowledge of particular individuals in administrative sub-units. This was particularly evident in his mapping operations.

**Laying out the Country in the Most Convenient Manner**
Taché's work on the seigneurial indemnity involved remapping the parishes of Canada East/Quebec. A key element in central control over the 1871 enumeration process in the other provinces was, similarly, territorial mapping. In Nova Scotia, in an attempt to generate usable maps, Taché enlisted the services of the secretary of the province's Board of Statistics, John Costley. The experiment was initially unsuccessful; however, it led to the seconding of Andrew Russell from the federal Crown Lands department for an ambitious census mapping operation. It was through the preparations for the 1871 census that the new federal government first generated systematic geographical knowledge of its

own administrative spaces – an elementary dimension of state formation and an infrastructural condition of systematic observation.

John Costley (c.1817–90), a Scottish immigrant who had taught in various classical schools and who had been principal of the well-known Pictou Academy from 1855, had been appointed in 1865 to administer Nova Scotia's progressive Registration Act, on which Taché would later attempt to base a national system of vital statistics. The act divided the province into registration districts, using the postal grid and the road system, and appointed a network of paid issuers of marriage licences and deputy registrars. These officials were offered free postage for reports to the board. In addition, any man wishing to marry had to pay for a licence, and the clergy could now only perform marriages for licensees. Anyone having a knowledge of such events was required to report births and deaths to deputy registrars within sixty days on pain of a fine, and Costley undertook to provide doctors with report books in which they could record the particulars of deaths. While Costley thought the act imperfect, it generated annual vital statistics superior to those available in the other provinces outside Quebec, and for that reason it interested Taché intensely.[39]

The two men seem not to have known each other before Confederation. Taché invited Costley to Ottawa in October 1868 to discuss whether he might 'devote some attention and some travelling for purposes connected with the forthcoming Census.' Illness prevented Costley from making that visit until the end of April 1869, when he spent ten days in the department. The costs of Costley's office and $3,000 for census preliminaries were now in the estimates of Agriculture and Statistics.[40] Between May 1869 and June 1870, Costley attempted to produce standard descriptions of electoral and registration districts in Nova Scotia. Taché wanted both detailed verbal descriptions of districts and skeleton maps that would show clearly their boundaries on the ground for the use of commissioners and enumerators. However, Costley found the work difficult because 'though the boundaries of some of the Districts have been nominally defined by Statute – there is in reality in many instances no written or printed description of these limits in existence – and they are to be had from a verbal account given by resident Officials.' He pointed out that the administration of the provincial territory was not organized on a geographically standardized administrative grid. 'Nova Scotia is not laid out in Square blocks, like Canada,' he commented, adding that 'much of it has never been laid out or surveyed at all.' Not only was there 'no modern reliable map of the Province on a large scale in existence,' but also 'the materials for constructing such maps ... are only to be had in the Crown Land Office, and are accessible, and ... can only be understood by its own officers, as no regular system has been followed in the management of that important Department.' Costley's circular letter to county surveyors revealed that it would cost $12 per county and eight or nine months' additional paid work to produce a skeleton map showing granted lands and lines of roads, and Costley would then himself have to travel around to locate such places. The Minister of Agriculture initially baulked at the expense of mapping Nova Scotia.[41]

In June 1870, after a visit to Halifax by Taché, a further visit to Ottawa, and three months' full-time work, Costley finished his descriptions of electoral districts. He had discovered that some areas were not even served by the registration system that he administered. More important, Costley argued for the electoral district as the major enumeration unit, given that 'the Counties are cut up into a great variety of arbitrary divisions, such as Townships – which generally included several Polling Districts or parts of Districts, Electoral Districts, Registration Districts, School Sections – and Poor Districts. All these differ from each other – and are liable without some distinct and definite guide to get mixed up and produce Confusion.' The electoral districts were easiest to identify, although their limits were altered by the legislature fairly often, something Costley thought would make comparisons between census periods difficult.[42]

Although they were handsomely printed on official blue paper, it was likely the *nature* of Costley's descriptions that made Taché push for a systematic remapping of the two Maritime provinces. While Costley could describe districts in Halifax in terms of street names, only knowledgeable local residents would have been able to find the boundaries of the rural districts he described and it was precisely this knowledge that Taché sought to centralize in order to command practices of observation and administration.[43] Agriculture and Statistics finally invited Crown Lands in Nova Scotia to bid on the preparation of provincial maps, with particular care to be taken to mark lines of roads. Samples were to be submitted for examination to Andrew Russell, one of the senior officers at federal Crown Lands seconded to Agriculture and Statistics as chief draughtsman.

One of the department's two New Brunswick census officers, J.G.G. Layton, was instructed to ship copies of all existing maps of that province to Ottawa, and Taché contacted the deputy surveyor general for other maps. Layton corresponded with the Surveyor General as well, seeking a list of parishes whose boundaries had changed since the 1861 census. As in the case of Nova Scotia, Agriculture and Statistics had 'the descriptions, in the Statutes but they refer to lots which are not laid down on' the department's existing maps.[44] The mapping operation was extended in Ontario and Quebec as well. Circular letters were sent to county registrars, electoral officers, prothonotaries, and other officers for the purpose of acquiring county, parish, and electoral district maps. The department called for its colonization agents to submit maps of lands granted and colonization roads. Andrew Russell and a team of draughtsmen travelled to Toronto for map-making purposes, and the large volume of correspondence reaching the department from the Ontario deputy superintendent of education suggests an attempt to map the limits of school districts. Already in August 1870, Taché was demanding delivery dates for lithographed maps in proof from the Quebec printer Desbarats.[45] Finally, when revisions to the Census Act extended its provisions to the North-West Territories and British Columbia, Agriculture and Statistics became responsible for dividing the new territories into provinces, districts, and subdistricts. All available maps, surveys, and exploration notes were sought in an effort to do so.[46]

Taché summarized this work for the 1870 departmental report: 'Every effort has been made to lay out the country in the most convenient manner possible.' Although 'everything had to be created; the territorial divisions had to be defined and described and mapped, from very irregular, and in many cases, very imperfect records,' his mapping of administrative space established and located units of investigation and analysis 'for future statistical purposes.'[47] During the 1852 and 1861 censuses the central authority had been heavily dependent on the local knowledge of largely autonomous officials in order to situate political subjects in space; now, through Taché's prior 'laying out of the country,' its investment in geo-administrative forms, the 1871 census put in place some of the territorial preconditions for the intensive administration of social relations and the practical extension of the governmentality.

**Legislation**
Preparations for the 1871 census began in earnest in 1865, well before census funds were included in the estimates. The estimates in turn contained census funds well before the 1870 Census Act was introduced. Most MPs had only the vaguest idea about the practicalities of census making. The only initial threat to Taché's plan was the 1869 demand by

the government of Prince Edward Island that an immediate census of all British North America be conducted in the context of ongoing discussions about extending the Canadian federation. The Minister of Agriculture, T.C. Chapais, to whom the island's demand was referred, pointed out that the 1860 Statistical Congress had endorsed the principle of a common census date throughout the British Empire and that censuses had been conducted in parts of Australia and in England, Ireland, Nova Scotia, New Brunswick, and Canada in 1861. Since 1871 was the next likely census year in the imperial country, the other British North American colonies should be encouraged to match it. Chapais did suggest one important alteration: the January enumeration date should be changed to coincide with the spring enumerations held in most other jurisdictions.[48]

The 1870 census bill was presented to Parliament by Chapais's successor as Minister of Agriculture, Christopher Dunkin, in early March of the same year. Dunkin insisted that 'the year 1871 might be emphatically characterized as a Census year,' since enumerations were taking place in many jurisdictions, and argued that the bill made it possible to appromixate practice in other countries. 'It was obvious,' he claimed, 'that this could not be done, if the law laid down anything like an iron rule as to the forms to be used or as to the precise time the information sought should be called for.' On these grounds, the bill removed census details from law and made them matters of administration (as Taché had urged in 1865). It 'left all these matters of detail to be decided on hereafter; and the more so, because such a course would also give the executive officer in charge of the matter more time to prepare those details, and modify them in accordance with what might be deemed desirable.'

Dunkin gave a brief account of the bill's origins, claiming that he, Dunkin (but of course in fact Taché), had studied census practice in all parts of the imperial state, in all colonies from which he could get information, and in the United States. The bill owed most to practice in the united Canadas, although its provisions concerning remuneration for census officials were primarily English. After explaining the main provisions of the bill, Dunkin concluded that the importance of the census 'could hardly be exaggerated; not only because our political system was based upon our population, but also because the correctness of our statistical information was of extreme importance, as showing the social character and position of the country, by which any changes might be made in harmony with the Constitution.'

The truncated reports of subsequent debate gave most attention to the reaction of Alexander Mackenzie. Mackenzie agreed that the bill should not attempt to spell out matters in detail, but argued that 'it was equally dangerous to be placing too much power in the hands of the Government, or centralizing too much the duties devolving upon certain Commissioners in the way indicated.' It was all very well not to specify a census day in the bill, but, as did many of his colleagues, Mackenzie had the murky idea that 'the personal Census should be taken upon one day, to avoid confusion arising from people changing residences.' Mackenzie had no clear conception of the census as an instrument for the government of population, with the partial exception that if it demonstrated the 'wealth of the country' then it might be used to 'encourage emigration.' For most members, the key question in the debate was asked by the Liberal Oliver Blake: Would there be a change in Parliamentary representation after the census? The prime minister answered in the affirmative.[49]

In committee later in March 1870, it was agreed that the precise census day could be left to the judgment of the census administrator, provided that it be no later than the first of May. Surviving reports of the committee discussions are highly abbreviated, but indicate that there was a lengthy debate over the proper enumeration principle. Only two positions in the debate were reported, which is insufficient to assess the extent to which MPs were aware of the stakes involved in different methods of distributing people in territory. A francophone member was quoted as claiming that 'the names of those temporarily absent should be included in the family to which they belong, as otherwise it would be unjust,' while Prime Minister Macdonald reportedly said that 'the correct principle was to take the names only of those who were actually at each place on a certain night.' It is not clear whether the first speaker was advocating a *de jure* enumeration method or a return to the practice of 1861, but Macdonald supported a *de facto* principle. Whatever the case, the Census Act effectively left the enumeration principle to the administrative discretion of the census organizer. The announcement that the 1871 census would be conducted on a *de jure* principle first appeared formally in the 1870 Annual Report of the Minister of Agriculture. Although he claimed that this principle was the 'best adapted' to Canada's circumstances, it would be naive to suppose that Taché was unaware of the likely consequences for the size of the population accorded to Quebec.[50]

The Census Act passed without any major modifications; thus, the legal framework for the enumeration was in place almost a year before the census date. A census amendment bill introduced in February 1871 extended the provisions of the act to the North-West Territories and to British Columbia, relaxed the requirement for an enumeration before 1 May in those cases, and accorded additional administrative discretion to the minister to order re-enumerations or additional inquiries in the case of incomplete information. Christopher Dunkin explained to members that the enumeration would likely take about three weeks in most cases, but that there were remote areas where it could not be so conducted and, given that 'in the numerous districts and sub-districts, it was hardly possible to avoid mistakes,' census officials needed to be able to conduct additional inquiries.

In response to the proposed amendments, William McDougall suggested sarcastically that all the clauses of the Census Act could be stricken except for the '*omnium gatherum*' clause now being suggested, a clause that seemed to make it possible 'to render valid anything that should be done' under the minister's authority. McDougall argued that alterations in established procedures should be declared by proclamation, not left to administrative fiat, because 'everything should be done open and above board that the people might see and know what was going on.' The potential for falsification in an undertaking that would determine Parliamentary representation could be avoided only if everything was done 'in the most open and frank manner possible.'[51] The practice of gazetting proposed changes was adopted, and the amendment bill passed the House on 7 March 1871.

'An Act respecting the First Census' (34 Vic. cap. XXI) thus accorded broad administrative powers to the Minister of Agriculture and to cabinet to determine most census matters, including the preparation of forms and instructions, the limits of the information to be sought, the procedures to be followed, and the period of census making itself, provided only that it take place before 1 May. The electoral division was chosen as the basic administrative unit for the enumeration, and the Minister of Agriculture was to appoint a commissioner for each such division. In contrast to the Canadian censuses of 1852 and 1861, the central government was now authorized to specify enumeration districts and to appoint enumerators, rather than the local census commissioners.

Commissioners were to ensure that enumerators understood what they were to do and that they were diligent in doing it. The enumerators were to visit every house in their districts; to ascertain carefully by personal inquiry all the information required of them and no other; to record that information and to attest to its accuracy. As in the past, the commissioners were to examine the enumerators' records, correcting them where necessary, and to send the certified returns to the Minister of Agriculture. The returns would be examined again by the minister before being submitted in tabular form to Parliament. The process between the return of the schedules to Ottawa and the preparation of the Parliamentary report was left entirely to administrative discretion.

The act provided for penalties for all parties to the enumeration for wilful wrongdoing, or for refusing to answer census queries or to answer them truthfully. It explicitly required all those in charge of both public and corporate records and documents to grant reasonable access to them to a commissioner, enumerator, or other person deputed by the Minister of Agriculture. In contrast to past legislation, the act allowed the minister to delegate juridical powers to census commissioners to conduct inquiries into any matter having to do with the execution of the census. It declared that letters from the minister or his deputy were *prima facie* authoritative documents and that the leaving of an enumeration schedule in the hands of a householder was tantamount to a legal instruction to complete it. These clauses were important extensions of the power of the central government, and made it possible in principle to counter some of the bases of resistance to past census inquiries. Finally, the act specified that the minister would determine the rates of pay for census officers, and repealed conflicting sections of past legislation.

**'Accurate Men' for the 'Stumbling Block Department'**
Taché had concluded from his study of past practice that the census effort required a team of experts. He did not need to read the critical editorial in the *Canada Free Press* that described his bureau as the 'Stumbling Block Department' and that called for the hiring of 'accurate men' in place of the extra clerks usually appointed under 'political influence' for census matters. A group of between thirteen and twenty men began to meet in the summer of 1870 to refine the census preparations. The mapping operation was in full swing, and Taché appointed a full-time census archivist.[52] This level of organization and planning was a far cry from the last-minute efforts of Crofton and Hutton for 1852 and 1861. The 1871 census staff officers, as they were called, included T.M. Daly, T.P. French, John Barwick, William Foster, and Dr John Beatty for Ontario; Joseph Anctil, E.-U. Piché, J.-A.-N. Provencher, George Weaver, and John Lowe for Quebec; John Costley and Amos Purdy for Nova Scotia; and Charles Everett and John G.G. Layton for New Brunswick.

John Lowe was quickly seconded to be Taché's deputy, then formally appointed departmental secretary and assistant deputy minister in February 1871.[53] Taché had argued in his 1865 memorandum that census officers should be men of social standing with some connection to the state system. Biographical information about some of the members of his team is fragmentary, but they met his criteria. They were experienced administrators and, perhaps, also intellectuals.[54] The Montreal staff commissioners, John Lowe and George Weaver, were particularly well connected socially and politically, although this fact did not prevent local government attacks on the 1871 Montreal census.[55]

The staff officers met collectively in Ottawa with Taché to consult with one another and plan census matters.[56] A first census conference was convened in July 1870. Many of the staff officers were incurring substantial travel expenses in the summer and early fall, well before their official appointments. By the late fall, a near-final draft of the census schedules had been produced. The schedules were probably tested in the field, for two compilers were hired in the summer of 1870 and travelled with the staff officers. After spending the month from mid-October to mid-November in Ottawa, John Lowe travelled on a 'special mission' to consult with the Toronto Board of Trade; soon after, he charged the department for a 'Sleigh and man 2 days in visiting industrial establishments.' It is likely he had draft schedules in hand. The detailed manual produced for the use of commissioners and enumerators contained samples of completed schedules and detailed instructions about recording conventions. This also suggests that field trials were conducted – a Canadian first.[57]

Taché's advance planning meant that the timelines for 1871 were far more relaxed than for past enumerations. The census districts were proclaimed officially on 1 December 1870, but the census commissioners were probably already in place; indeed, the New Brunswick staff officers left Ottawa in late September 1870 to prepare for meetings with census commissioners. Enumeration subdistricts were specified on 27 February 1871. Most enumerators had already been selected.[58] It would prove necessary to extend the enumeration time in a few remote areas, and there would be occasional complaints about the distribution of sample census schedules, but on the whole, Taché succeeded in avoiding the logistical problems that had undermined past enumerations.

**Centralized Printing**

The printing process was now centralized in the Queen's Printer in Ottawa, and specially watermarked paper was ordered. Proofs of the schedules were on hand five months before census day, in comparison to about six weeks in 1861. Taché was sharply critical of the proofs. He sent them back, scored with red correction marks and a veiled threat to the Printer. They might do 'for purposes of study and revision' in the department, but no errors of any sort could be tolerated in the final version. Indeed, Taché wrote, his minister was 'perplexed about printing and binding connected with the Census, as he is led to believe, from what has already occurred, that he can hardly calculate upon the capacity of the Government Contractor to do the work in the style and with the dispatch necessary. He directs me to say this for the simple reason that the Census work will be such that it will require to be made at the hour, in the manner wanted, and without any extra charges.' The printing contract was huge and lucrative. Most of it had been let to J.B. Taylor's Ottawa *Citizen*, although the Ottawa *Times* got some of the work. Taylor responded immediately to Taché's complaints, promising to redouble his efforts to prevent any possibility of error and insisting that he could execute the work.[59] Taché was organizing other logistical matters at least six months before census day as well, pushing Public Works for more office space, appropriating rooms near the Post Office department for the storage of schedules, and establishing a locked storage room for confidential material. As the enumeration began, he ordered forty custom-designed compilation tables and a large number of chairs.[60]

**Census Space**
In contrast to the situation in 1852 and 1861, and by virtue of the infrastructural work undertaken by Taché's statistical team, the census office now controlled the detailed definition of enumeration districts and was capable of producing cartographic representations of them. There were 206 census districts, numbered sequentially from west to east, each under the direction of a census commissioner. The central office defined the subdistricts, again numbering them sequentially. The electoral district was chosen as the unit for the census commissions, a choice that demonstrates the importance now accorded to determining Parliamentary representation. The subdistricts were townships in Ontario, parishes and townships in Quebec, parishes in New Brunswick, and polling districts in Nova Scotia. On the frontiers of settlement, the department was forced to define the subdistricts in terms of the boundaries of timber berths (leases). On average, there were about fifteen subdivisions in each district. There was no longer any talk of enumerators' turning left at 'Blueberry Cove' or going north at 'Amos Wiltse's

farm': census space was abstract space, described in such purely administrative terms as 'District 67, sub-district H part 2.'[61]

Of course, the census districts were not marked out on the ground: census enumerators had still to use their own knowledge to conduct the enumeration. Even so, the department's control over cartography facilitated its direction of the work and its control over expenditures. Commissioners were to be paid a lump sum of $50, $4 for every hundred families in their district, and a further sum of between $50 and $175 depending on the size of their districts, to a maximum of $4 for each day of service. Enumerators could no longer act as population entrepreneurs, because they were no longer paid by the name. Instead (with rural-urban differences), payment was decided according to a formula involving $3 per hundred families enumerated and $3 per eighteen measured miles of road travelled, with an additional $20 for conferring with and delivering papers to the commissioner, but to a daily maximum of $3. While some exceptions were made, these limits were enforced, and the census manager was able to use the census maps to verify claims for distance travelled. No one was paid for travelling the same road twice – a disciplinary measure meant to ensure a systematic, house-by-house enumeration and one made possible by the prior mapping of the Canadian territory for census purposes.[62]

**Setting Observational Protocols**

Taché's census planning worked in a remarkably systematic way to establish consistent observational protocols: this is partly what allows us to speak of the 1871 census as 'scientific.' The census staff officers worked through the schedules and procedures collectively and then travelled to their respective regions to conduct conferences with the census commissioners. The commissioners appointed their enumerators, with departmental approval, and then were to hold a conference with them to work through a very detailed enumeration manual containing sample schedules. Because the records have been lost or destroyed, it is not possible to say anything about the execution of such conferences. But it can at least be said that in contrast to 1852 and 1861, commissioners had the time and the explicit obligation to meet with and to instruct enumerators and that there were field officers in place to ensure they did so. The role of textual mediation was different in 1871 than in earlier years if we consider the census as action at a distance. On the one hand, the central authority relied less completely on textual mediation in its relations with commissioners and enumerators and more on direct personal contact.

On the other hand, infrastructural work made new kinds of textual controls possible, such as the centre's ability to trace out enumerators' routes on its maps.

Before the census day, every household was to receive a condensed form of the schedules, called 'the People's Schedules' in English and 'le tableau de famille' in French, so that the male household head could prepare his answers in advance. However, the material recorded on the enumeration schedules was to consist of responses to questions posed by the enumerator to the household head and entered by the enumerator on the spot. The department distributed a detailed census manual that included instructions and sample schedules. Repeated attempts were made in the manual, according to the logic of the *de jure* design, to ensure that people would be recorded in the enumeration district where they usually resided, and that products would be recorded where they were actually produced, and only there (with some rare exceptions). Considerable effort was devoted to reducing the discretionary powers of enumerators, despite the claim that 'an intelligent and well-trained Enumerator, will, in fact, generally speaking, know beforehand what are, as a whole, the conditions of every family in his division'(!!). Enumerators were not to make returns on the basis of their own 'local knowledge'; rather, they were to record answers to the census questions, which were to be addressed in full to each potential informant. The enumerators were told how physically to write in the schedule columns. In contrast to the earlier census efforts, which left such matters more or less to the discretion of enumerators, the 1871 manual specified a limited set of signs to be used for conveying information; enumerators were not to invent their own. They might use some discretion when designating religious denominations, so long as the main character of the denomination was indicated clearly, and their discretion was also called upon in making certain determinations about measures of output in forestry and fishing. But on the whole, Taché worked systematically to eliminate interpretive idiosyncracies.

**Census Standard Measures**

In the manual, definitional and metrological questions were addressed specifically and a serious attempt was made to invest the objects to be observed in standard forms using standard measures. A 'house' was defined in keeping with the work of the 1860 International Statistical Congress. A special set of 'census' concepts and measures was defined. Thus, a 'Census family' was composed of 'one person living alone, or of any number of persons living together under one roof, and having their food provided together.' Examples were given. A 'Census standard' measure was specified for recording saw logs, in the absence of uniform practice across the four provinces. A 'Census standard' barrel for recording fish was to contain two-and-a-half bushels or to weigh 200 lbs. Enumerators were to make calculations of reported quantities of these items in the standard measure, but in other matters of measurement they were simply to record respondents' returns as given. Thus, in the important matter of returns in *minots* or *boisseaux* in Quebec, they were simply to note these; compilers would do the conversion. The hay crop could likewise be given in bundles or tons; compilers would make the conversion. Terms such as 'quintal,' 'toise,' and 'board measurement' were given specific meanings. Sons following fathers' occupations were to be identified as such, although no age limits were specified. Women were not to be attributed an occupation unless doing something other than household work. Taché allowed the multiple reporting of occupations according to the answers given to enumerators, although the latter were to take care to inquire after the existence of manufacturing and other industry when questioning farmer informants.

Enumerators were explicitly instructed to limit themselves to the census queries. The 'date of operations and remarks' column included on their first schedule, and the 'remarks' columns on their other schedules, were to be used only for recording their daily progress and for noting special difficulties in getting information. There was no space here for discursive accounts of the district or its people, conditions, and concerns: 'in general, enumerators should not have resort to explanations.' Enumerators were to do no addition and to make no calculations of figures. All sheets were to be returned to the commissioner and by him to the department in their original portfolio. If errors were made, the entries were to be lightly crossed out in ink in such a manner as not to render them illegible. No corrected or copied schedules were to be returned in place of the originals, and while commissioners were to go over the schedules and to remedy obvious errors, evidence of the corrections was to be visible on the schedules as submitted. In short, Taché and his team effected the transition from 'literary' to 'numerical' statistics through systematic efforts to stabilize observational and recording protocols, to circumscribe tightly the interpretive discretion of enumerators, and to banish discursive accounts of social relations.

Related to this transition was the assertion of firm control over census returns by the central authority. Taché was clearly aware of past political debates drawing on partial census returns and perhaps also of their effects on the compilation process. Enumerators were to allow no one to see their completed schedules, nor were they to reveal to anyone the information in them. Commissioners and enumerators were explicitly forbidden to release partial returns. As the census manual put it, 'The Commissioners and Enumerators are forbidden to give any synopsis of the result of the Census, or any part thereof, to any one. Partial communication of information is calculated to produce mischief, if not to mislead, and may be made subservient to purposes totally unconnected with the Census, and detrimental to it. The result will be given by the Department in a careful and comprehensive manner, at the earliest possible period.'[63]

**Scheduling Population**
The power of observational texts is related to their physical and textual organization as such. Taché attended closely to such matters. The 1871 census schedules were about half the size of those produced in 1861, and easily contained in a portfolio, which provided enumerators with a writing surface. They were printed on one side of sheets of good-quality paper: in contrast to some past efforts, ink did not leak through to obscure entries on the reverse of schedules, and pens did not plough through the schedules themselves. Taché made it simpler for enumerators and compilers to negotiate the schedules by providing a reference system that tied entries on later schedules (with the exception of the industrial) to entries on the first schedule. If they could follow their instructions (which were complex), enumerators would no longer have difficulty carrying entries from one schedule to the next. The repetition, or further specification, of some items of information on different schedules introduced a workable control device for commissioners and compilers.

It is not germane to my argument to present an exhaustive examination of Taché's nine schedules, but a brief account is pertinent. They were titled, in order of completion, 'Nominal return of the living,' 'Nominal returns of the Deaths within the last 12 months,' 'Return of Public Institutions, Real Estate, Vehicles and Implements,' 'Return of Cultivated Land, of Field Products and of Plants and Fruits,' 'Live Stock, Animal Products, Home-made Fabrics and Furs,' 'Return of Industrial Establishments,' 'Return of Products of the Forest,' 'Return of Shipping and Fisheries,' and 'Return of Mineral Products.' The schedules contained over 200 columns. Yet while the scope of the 1871 inquiries was considerably broader than that of the earlier censuses, those inquiries were not distinguished by the general nature of the intelligence sought. Returns of births, marriages, and deaths, and accounts of property holding, of agricultural and industrial products and production, and of fishing, forestry and mining, had all been sought in 1861. The key innovations lay elsewhere.

There were three. The first – the specifying of observational and reporting protocols – has already been discussed.[64] The second was a conceptual reorganization of social relations that put an end to some of the main sources of confusion in 1852 and 1861. Third, the multiplication of schedules made possible a more systematic division and classification of information during the enumeration, and made the later work of correlation simpler and more fruitful, in a Queteletian spirit.

Taché severed the enumeration from its origins as a tool for assessing the value of men's property. The census was a statistical inquiry and as such 'directly connected with the science of Government; which presupposes a general knowledge of the wants and capabilities, the defects and advantages, numerically presented, of the population and the country.' With the exception of the census of industrial establishments, 'where, as a general rule, a simple enumeration of quantities and kinds would not give an accurate or intelligible result,' enumerators were not to inquire into property values: 'Enumerators are not assessors, and cannot be made to act as such.' In any case, past experience showed that such valuations 'must always be set down as given by each interested party' and hence would be unreliable. In sum, the census was not an assessment instrument.

**Sending People Back to the Countryside**
Taché abandoned the confused mix of *de facto/de jure* principles through which census officers in 1852 and 1861 had tried to replicate the enumeration template recommended by the imperial government and the Statistical Congress. He adopted a strictly *de jure* census design that eliminated the main sources of the multiple recording of names. The manual described the project as aimed at 'the population legally *domiciled* within the territory of the Dominion, and including all persons who may be temporarily absent from their place of abode.' Each person was to be 'registered in the province and particular locality in which their home, family dwelling, or place of abode is situate, although they may happen to be in other parts of the Dominion ... or in foreign parts' on census day. The point was repeated emphatically: 'all living members of

one family are to be registered as being present at the family abode, unless they are settled in homes of their own or have left the country with intention not to return.'

In the absence of a developed national system of civil registration, it is difficult to imagine a stronger statement of the *de jure* principle. Taché described the census repeatedly as an exercise in 'registration': people were not 'counted' (assigned a numeral) or 'enumerated' (mentioned one by one) but 'registered' (set down authoritatively in an official list). In other words, they were tied officially to a particular locale within an electoral district. Taché's enumeration principle promoted his pastoralist vision of population by returning both urban migrants and immigrants to the United States to the countryside if they had not married and established independent households – or indeed, if informants were hoping they might return. Given that representation in the House of Commons was to be determined by the census's returns of population and that Quebec was particularly subject to rural outmigration, it must have been obvious to Taché that the *de jure* principle was likely to increase the number of seats accorded to Quebec in general and to rural districts within that province in particular.

At the same time, the principle made it a straightforward matter for enumerators to assign people to a single normal place, and Taché's justification for selecting it was technical rather than religious or political. The manual provided a clear system for dealing with the 'floating population' – servants, people in hotels, in boarding houses, on board ship, and in public institutions, people with separate places of work and residence, and so forth — that alleviated many problems encountered with earlier census designs. This system led to considerable debate after the fact, but it immobilized people in a manner that observers could replicate, and made it easier for compilers to count them.

Finally, Taché overcame the failure of the earlier censuses to specify a workable protocol for rendering the relations among property, proprietors, and territory. In earlier censuses, property relations could not be captured by the administrative space of the enumeration process, nor could they be contained in it. It had been left to enumerators and commissioners to decide whether to report in a given district all the property and production of a given proprietor, wherever it was located, or to report only that property and production located in the enumeration district. In consequence, the earlier censuses either multiplied the numbers of proprietors across districts while underreporting their holdings as individuals, or multiplied property held in the district by reporting everything people owned as if it were situated there. Confusion was increased because commissioners and enumerators were left to decide whether to report agricultural production as marketable surplus or as total production.

The 1871 enumeration introduced a schedule that reported the total amount of property held by individuals wherever it was situated, and a number of other schedules that tied property and different kinds of production to specific locales. Production was now to be reported as total output, with no distinction between items for domestic consumption and marketable surpluses. William Hutton's attempt to specify a distinction between rural and urban production was jettisoned. Property as such stood out much more clearly as a conceptual entity, as a social institution, and as a potential object of government, even as Taché muddied the distinction between production for sale and production for use. The enumeration both attached property to individuals and spaces and detached it from them, thereby increasing the variety of possible governmental reconfigurations of these objects and relations.

The schedules were also designed to generate a usable set of vital statistics in the absence of a national system of civil registration. The first two schedules – the nominal returns of the living and dead – sought to identify people by age and sex and to indicate those born, married, or having died during the year. Multiple textual controls were introduced. Births were to be indicated by the month of birth, and the ages of those under one year were to be given as a fraction of twelve. The religion, age, sex, occupation, and place of residence of those reported as having died was to be given – a replication of the information contained on the return of the living. The month of marriage was to be specified. Infant deaths were to be indicated, as were the deaths of those recently married. Taché also sought an indication of cause of death.

The design and instructions by no means eliminated interpretive and conceptual difficulties; but taken together, they underline the scientific character of the 1871 census. The 1871 effort involved the application of carefully considered, well-articulated, and thorough observational protocols by an efficiently equipped body of observers, to a set of reasonably well-defined objects and relations. Taché and his team had done the infrastructural work necessary to extend their conclusions about past census making into the field. These characteristics of the census project make the ways in which it configured its objects of knowledge clearly accessible to observation and critique. They are not only accessible to those interested in historical sociological investigation; they were the subjects of contemporary debate and conflict, as the following chapter demonstrates.

Chapter 8

# The 'Pur Sang' Census

On 3 April 1871, more than 2,800 well-equipped and at least partially trained enumerators took to the field in the four Canadian provinces. Despite occasional complaints, one of them in Parliament, that the 'People's Schedules' had not been distributed beforehand, the surviving enumeration schedules show most enumerators at work continuously from the enumeration date until mid-May.[1] The bulk of the manuscript enumerators' books were in the compilers' hands soon after, and a formal report of the population totals was made to cabinet in mid-October. The returns quickly provoked heated debates that led to partial re-enumerations. Taché's configuration of social relations would become official and authoritative, but only after considerable debate and conflict.

It was the overcoming of logistical problems, the clear definition of the object of inquiry, the specifying of clear observational protocols, and the systematic limitation of the interpretive discretion of enumerators that distinguished the 1871 enumeration from those which preceeded it. The contingent at work in the census districts and subdistricts was much as it had been in 1861, with a number of the same men serving in both years. Once again it was farmers, artisans, minor civil servants, merchants, notaries, and so on – men (there were no women) with various levels of literacy – who conducted the enumeration. The census design and instructions worked to reduce substantially the discursive content of the completed schedules. Where enumerators made comments, the prior specification of observational protocols and the physical organization of the schedules meant that most of them could simply be disregarded by compilers. Commissioners' reports were censored by departmental officials to remove objectionable 'allusions.'[2] Other comments served their intended purpose of guiding decision making during the compilation process. In such conditions, 'numerical' facts about population were easily extracted from the perceptions of enumerators and the reports of informants, while the practice of 'literary' statistics was relegated to the margins.

### 'This woman has no hands!'

Still, in the nature of the case, the official reading of the schedules remained selective and disciplinary, aimed as it was at producing useful facts for a specific version of the 'science of government' and for Joseph-Charles Taché's fundamentalist religious imagination. This reading was indifferent to many of the things that had impressed enumerators. It reworked some of their perceptions and reports to produce its statistical account: like those which preceeded it, it codified observations; it made facts rather than simply 'collecting' them. Unlike earlier efforts, however, it made up the facts scientifically.

It is easy to see things enumerators thought worthy of note in their districts that held no interest for compilers and census managers: the existence of twins and newborn infants; people who did not marry and thus lived in 'Batchelor's Hall' or 'old Woman's Hall'; the 'adopted' and the 'iligamast' (illegitimate) child; the blind woman who could read the 13th Psalm on a book with raised letters; women separated 'in body and goods' from their husbands; women and men abandoned by their spouses; the man who seemed to be 'unfit for work' although he was quite young; or fifty-nine-year-old Elizabeth Cosgrove, 'said by her neighbours to have seasons of unsoundness as to her mind.' Census managers had no interest in twenty-nine-year-old Mary Goddine, even if she caused a New Brunswick enumerator to marvel: 'This poor woman cannot walk and was born without hands, she sews with her mouth. I saw a large quilt – patch-work – made by this poor woman without hands, I was told that she cut the Patches, & threads her own needles.' Mary Goddine became indistinguishable from other single women in her age group, and it was also of no concern to census officers that 'the Hansons ... live[d] like Indians or like the *ancient* Britons' and survived 'by shinglemaking & days labour.' It was no longer a fact of moment, as it had been in 1852, that 'South Burgess is a Hilly Country abounding in Islands and lakes Difficult to Travel but Rich in Minerals.'

These were local matters, not what the manual called 'matters of leading importance to the whole Dominion.' Local matters could not generally be subjected to statistical translation; or better, they were not matters that figured in any political project emanating from the central government. One could imagine, for instance, some extension of William Farr's concern for using the census as a medical survey, which would have categorized people by the bodily appendage with which they worked habitually, or by the absence of bodily appendages.[3] In such a category system, Mary Goddine would have appeared in the 'mouth worker' category, or in the 'has no hands' category, and one might further imagine some governmental project aimed at individuals like her. The 1871 census embodied no such political interest, hence people like Mary Goddine could not form part of a totalizing moment, and so could not figure in the domain of government that the census project was seeking to delineate. The 1871 enumeration literally confined them, with other local particularities, to the margins of inquiry.

'Matters of importance to the whole Dominion' resulted from knowledge-producing practices that abstracted general features from local particularities. The latter were flattened in the process. Practices of abstraction constructed a new economy of sameness and difference in which particularity became variation from the standards prevailing in constructed categories. Such is the logic of 'modern' statistical practice, and as a practice of state formation, census making in 1871 defined both a field and a set of objects of rule. It is striking that Taché could claim so confidently to be defining nationally important knowledge. The contrast is particularly sharp with the assumption made twenty years earlier by Walter Crofton that local observers would be the ones to define what it was important for the central government to know. The contrast marks a heightened development of the administrative powers of state and the extension of the hegemony of state agencies over collective representations. Taché's claimed right to define what it was important to know did not go unchallenged, and the manual urged enumerators repeatedly to appreciate that conditions, features, and products of great importance to a locality or region might be much less significant in the context of the country as a whole. Yet Taché was placed to make and defend such a distinction between the national and the local in ways that neither of his predecessors had been.

As for the enumerators, even in the circumscribed domain allotted to them they were necessarily interpreters as well as recorders. They understood their instructions in a variety of ways. Some had dubious skills of literacy, a phonetic command of orthography, or difficulty in keeping their entries in the approved order. They left lines blank, forget to list husbands and wives together, and occasionally missed a house and had to return to it. They found it difficult to distinguish shops from manufacturing establishments, were confused about the use of the special 'census standard' measures, and used their own occupational nomenclatures. They created extra work for compilers, compensating them only with brief flashes of levity, as when one gave 'Hupencoff' [Whooping Cough] as a cause of death. Still, even the least competent enumerators using Taché's design produced schedules that compilers could mine for facts.

Not one of the least competent was Samuel Young, the enumerator for part of Yonge Township in Leeds County, Canada West, in 1861, whom we heard earlier grumbling about having to get his information from women. He was back at it in 1871, his district now called 67-e and forming part of the electoral district of South Leeds, although its geomorphology was unchanged. Young filled in his schedules, on the whole, in the approved manner and offered little commentary, reporting nothing substantive about the enumeration process beyond the fact that he was rained out on 27 April. Evidently, $3 a day was enough to keep him from grousing about his pay.

He used some of the categories and made some of the same attributions in 1871 as in the earlier year, but these were easily standardized by compilers. For instance, his reports of religious denominations included 'R Catholick' and 'no Church,' both of which he used in 1861, and 'Presbyterian,' an entry that provided less detail than called for by his instructions. He was aware of this lapse, for he noted in the margin beside one such entry, 'I was told Presbetarian and he nor I dont [know] what else to put him.' The first two usages were easily translated by compilers into the official religious categories, and someone, likely a compiler, added a 'C' before each of Young's entries for Presbyterians, thereby translating them as well.[4] The new census design eliminated the main causes of the multiple counting of names. Individuals who can be found more than once in 1861 were returned once only in 1871. Chauncey Bellamy, the Leeds County farmer-miller who in 1861 was enumerated as resident both on his farm (in one township) and at his mill (in another), now appeared only at his farm (although he had been rechristened 'Chancy').

Enumerators followed the logic of the *de jure* design to enumerate people who had left the country, although some distinguished those absent temporarily from those established elsewhere. For instance, a New Brunswick enumerator in a border district (179-o-1) listed people who were 'in woods across the line' and 'in the woods in the U States with a large party of men,' but did not return others who seemed to have moved there permanently, writing instead beside the spouse's name, 'husband lives in US.' In contrast, the enumerator for part of North Crosby Township in Leeds County, Ontario (dist. 67-h-2) marked 'in U.S.' beside the names of a number of people on his schedules. His district was some distance from the American border. People returned as resident in other districts were described in such terms as 'lately domiciled here.' Those reassigned to their 'permanent' homes cannot usually be identified now unless enumerators chose to make some comment on them, but the tendency of Taché's census to return emigrants to Canada and urban residents to the countryside is evident on the face of the census schedules. In a period of rural-urban migration and of emigration from the agricultural districts of Canada East to the New England factory states, the *de jure* method replenished the French-Canadian countryside.

**Official Results and the Compilation Process**
Officials at Agriculture and Statistics expected the 1871 census to indicate that the population of the four Canadian provinces had surpassed 4 million, from the 3.1 million reported in 1861. Such expectations had been nurtured by the press, and the department's secretary and census manager, John Lowe, was himself directly implicated in raising them. His *Year-Book and Almanac of British North America for 1867*, based on information compiled by Arthur Harvey of the Finance Department, had claimed that Ontario and Quebec had received more than 100,000 immigrants in the five years ending in 1865. 'A great increase' had 'undoubtedly taken place in the population of all the larger cities,' and Montreal, with a mere 90,000 people according to the 1861 census, with its suburbs was now estimated to contain 'nearly 130,000 souls.' By 1871, Lowe's publication was claiming that almost 200,000 new immigrants had settled in Canada in the 1860s. Taché wrote to an American correspondent after the enumeration was underway that the census would show there to be about 4 million people.[5]

Officials were shocked when the tabulation of returns indicated a population of less than 3.5 million. The 1871 return for Quebec, at 1,186,340, was a minuscule 75,000 more than that of 1861, suggesting both an enormous outmigration from the province and the complete failure of the immigration and colonization projects. It was so politically embarrassing to the Minister of Agriculture, Christopher Dunkin, a Quebec MP, that he resigned the day before the results were presented to the Privy Council. Rumours flew about Taché's imminent removal from office.⁶ The ministry was perplexed. 'The census figures have been given to the Privy Council,' wrote Lowe to Taché on 26 October 1871, 'and they are dreadfully disappointing. They don't know what to do with them and hesitate to make them public. Many – in fact most – of the old counties show a positive *decrease* and in many cases a very large one. The increase that there is, is principally in the *new* counties.'⁷ Council refused to allow publication until the results were retabulated using county boundaries in an attempt to disguise the magnitude of the population shortfall in electoral districts. Lowe himself corresponded with his Montreal commissioner George Weaver about plans for 'preparing the public mind' for the disappointing results, and he had reason to do so, for the department was soon subjected to blistering public attacks.⁸

Charles Tupper, President of the Privy Council, investigated the possibility that the population returns might be the result of compilation errors. In an exhaustive defence of the compilation process, Lowe insisted that the population for each enumeration subdistrict was compiled independently twice, by two different compilers who were prevented from communicating with each other. If their totals agreed when inspected by a supervisor, they were accepted as accurate. If they disagreed, a third compiler did a recount, and if he came to a total that agreed with that of one of the first two, the erring compiler was set to discover his own error. Supervisiors kept population subtotals secret from compilers, so 'the mode of compiling the figures of the population was of a nature to secure absolute accuracy.'⁹

Earlier, Lowe had written a detailed description of the compilation process to enable George Weaver to counter the fears of Montreal Protestants that Taché and his Catholic friends would manufacture false returns of religious denominations. 'With regard to forms of *compilation*,' Weaver was assured, 'these will *not* be left to the compilers. Printed headings will be given to them; and they will have their precise work set out for them, day by day as they proceed.' They would follow a system: 'First there is to be the *correction*, [now] all completed, and after that the compiling of the *population*. After the population is compiled then will come the compilations of *Religions* &c.' Lowe insisted that his office would '*not* leave the headings of compilation of the *Religious Denominations* to the compilers,' but instead would 'give them printed headings,' themselves to be 'the result of Departmental action, in which there is a full measure of Protestant influence, with a Protestant Minister. The compilers will not have authority to change a single entry. They will have no discretionary powers. They must take what they find.' Lowe reminded

Weaver that the '*discretionary power* lay in the correction; and you were yourself at the head of that' for the Montreal returns.[10]

In response to queries from Arthur Harvey, Lowe insisted that Harvey could 'rest assured that we have got the *true population* and that it has been *carefully compiled.*' If there was any error, it was one of over-enumeration, for the department might 'have taken four or five thousand servant girls twice over.' Harvey was invited to come to Ottawa to inspect the compilation process if he wished, but as far as Lowe was concerned, the census results showed that the country had been 'deluding itself' on the basis of the erroneous returns from the 1861 census – an argument on which he would expand in the ensuing debate.[11]

Taché and Lowe were on solid ground in their insistence that great care had been taken in the compilation process. Five of the census staff officers who had prepared the enumeration remained as supervisors, and competence was a criterion for the selection of compilers. While the distribution of compilerships was unambiguously a matter of political patronage, controlled mainly by G.-É. Cartier, most of the appointments were recommendations made by Lowe on the basis both of the applicants' political loyalties and of their fitness for the work. For example, 'among those from Montreal is Mr. George Glackmeyer,' wrote Lowe to Cartier, 'a brother of Mr. Charles Glackmeyer, the City clerk, and a relative, I believe, of the Duvernays. At any rate he is a blue of the blues, and I believe that his appointment would be agreeable to many of your friends. He has particular fitness for the place. He speaks and writes both languages, and he has aptitude for figures which is wanted.' People who proved incompetent could not rely on their political connections for protection or promotion. In one case, Lowe wrote to the Maritime politician S.L. Tilley, who had been attempting to promote a certain Mr Knowles, that Tilley's client was 'not even a good second-class compiler, in that he is inaccurate and will persist in going his own way.' In the course of his refusal to promote Knowles, Lowe revealed that there was a competence-based hierarchy in the compiling rooms, with four 'first class compilers whose duties are to assist the four chief compilers' earning $2.50 a day, while second-class compilers made $2.[12]

The manuscript schedules themselves support claims that care was exercised in the compilation process; a number of checks and controls were in place beyond those described above. For example, as a control for population totals, at the end of the personal returns for each enumeration district, compilers made a list of blank lines and then matched the number of lines completed with the number of males and females returned. They were meticulous about it. For instance, they corrected the report of the enumerator in district 179-i who claimed '15 blank lines left in this schedule by mistake,' finding that there were in fact seventeen.

In district 68-a, the west ward of the town of Brockville, the compiler found a person reported twice and did not count him, writing on the schedule 'Reg[istered]d as repetition by Mr Layton.' No similar attempts to control double-counting had been made by compilers in either 1852 or 1861. In the 1871 compilation, people who seemed to have been returned at their place of work were traced to their 'normal' place of residence and counted only once; other suspect entries about individuals led to further investigation. For example, in district 190-m in Annapolis County, Nova Scotia, the enumerator made a minor error in entering surnames. The enumerator was to list surnames first, but he recorded the name of Harris Prentis's nineteen-year-old son not 'Prentis, Stanley' but rather 'Harris, Stanley.' This entry made it appear that Stanley Prentis's younger siblings were also called Harris, but then it was unclear in what household they lived. 'What does this mean are they all boarders?' asked the compiler in the margin. Further inquiry revealed the cause of confusion, and the compiler corrected it on the schedules. For another example, incomplete information about a foundry and flour mill in Longueuil village (district 188-c-2) led the compiler to make this marginal notation: 'Not taken off. Information written for.'

This level of detail work is remarkable, and if it were of any possible interest to anyone, these examples could be multiplied. Despite occasional disciplinary initiatives directed at the compilers – for 'reading newspapers in the Census room, during office hours,' for example – they cannot be accused of sloppiness or carelessness.[13] The scientific character of the enumeration process was replicated in the compilation process. However, care in compilation did *not* mean that compilers only took what they found: schedules were 'corrected' to make them fit the compilation grid, and it sometimes proved difficult to make them fit consistently.

**Whose Science? Which Science?**
The debate resulting from the publication of the 1871 census returns centred on the relative merits of *de facto* and *de jure* enumeration principles, the technical quality of the enumeration and compilation processes, and the resulting population totals. What did not figure in it were the ways in which even systematically generated, scientifically organized

accounts of population and social relations made particular kinds of substantive determinations. These scientific accounts characterized, categorized, identified, and specified people in their social relations as they translated them into numerical form. They constructed official representations of the nation and its people, industries, and conditions of life. The fact that these representations were worked up scientifically according to systematically applied protocols does not alter their cultural, political-economic, religious, and ethnic overdetermination.

As we have seen, the manual introduced a number of 'census standards,' ranging from measures of logs to definitions of 'the family.' National metrological uniformity did not yet exist, and these 'standards' were not measures employed by census informants. Rather, they were ordering devices that made it possible to translate informants' accounts into forms considered useful for the 'science of government.' Their existence should discount attempts to evaluate the 'accuracy' of the census on the basis of a correspondence theory of truth. Insofar as they were governmental instruments, the imposition of them was a political project. This is not to argue that all these attempts to rework the world into statistical categories issued in clear projects of government, nor even that the categories involved worked well in the field. Yet through the application of a particular technology of knowledge, the census delimited a terrain on which political and administrative projects could be situated, and it created a set of resources that could potentially be mobilized in their pursuit. Interestingly, 'census standards' that were not mentioned in the manual were mobilized in the course of the 'correction' and compilation of the manuscript schedules. Some of these were decided in advance of the enumeration and were likely imparted to enumerators in conference with their commissioners. Others seem to have been responses on the part of census managers to events that emerged in the enumeration process.

**Statistical Cows, Cloth, and Canadians**
Seabury Scovil, the farmer who enumerated part of the electoral district of South Leeds, Ontario (dist. 67-f), wrote a number of marginal comments on his schedules about the measurement units he employed, most of which were later heavily scored out. On his second page, he noted that 'all parties owning cows are supposed to mek 100lbs of Butter from each cow and where returns are not made in accordance with that parties have sold their milk.' The comment must have been alarming to census managers, demonstrating as it did that Scovil had not asked informants

the relevant question about butter production, but had instead invented a standard cow. The compiler (J.P. Taylor) went through Scovil's butter returns, substituting new figures for those reported. Scovil's total return of 101,600 lbs. was reduced to 66,151 lbs., and individual cows in his subdistrict were not allowed to produce more than 75 lbs. of butter annually. The same operation was performed on the butter returns for all other subdistricts under this census commission. Here, the census managers produced an alternative 'census standard' cow using their own criteria to rework that employed by enumerators. However, the attempt to discipline cows in the compiling rooms was made inconsistently. Cows in Annapolis County, Nova Scotia, for instance, were forced to reduce their butter production, while those in Brockville, Ontario, were allowed to produce as much as 200 lbs. each.

Handloom weaving presented interesting difficulties for enumerators and compilers, and it is remarkable that the quantity of cloth produced by textile factories was not reported in the completed 1871 census volumes. The published account did not make it possible to compare the relative productivity of household and factory industry in this area. It should be recalled that Taché, as Canada's commissioner to the 1867 International Exposition in Paris, was himself involved in the contemporary debate over whether small manufacturing and domestic industry would prove itself superior to factory industry in the future of civilization. Taché and his fellow agrarian colonizers repeatedly pronounced that women's domestic hand production of cloth played a civilizing role, and argued against urban manufacturing. According to the broad definition of an industrial establishment in the manual, which read 'any establishment ... where materials are manufactured, made up, changed or altered from one form into another, [f]or sale, use, or consumption, is an industrial establishment,' farmhouses containing a loom were industrial establishments. Most likely, Taché was designing an industrial census aimed at demonstrating the strength of domestic industry – a key element in his project for an agrarian Catholic French Canada.

Yet the product of handloom weaving created reporting difficulties. On the one hand, the activity seemed to coincide with the definition of an industrial establishment, which meant it should be reported on the industrial schedule 6. On the other hand, the manual instructed enumerators that 'home-made fabrics are to be kept distinct from those made in cloth and linen factories,' which implied that they were to be returned on schedule 5, 'Home-made fabrics and furs.' According to Kris Inwood and Phyllis Wagg, enumerators in Ontario and elsewhere were divided as to how to return the *product* of individual looms. One distinction seemed to be the quantity of cloth available for sale. Yet the looms themselves appear on the industrial schedules, with handloom weavers returned as if they were capitalists, owning means of production, paying themselves wages, and producing commodities, even if the product was consumed domestically. The published returns eventually showed a Quebec producing five times as much home-made linen as the other provinces combined and about 40 per cent of the national total of home-made woollen cloth. On the other hand, because the quantity of factory-made cloth was not reported, contemporary analysts could not judge whether factories were more productive than households. Of the country's 270 reported woollen factories, 233 were in Ontario.[14]

Applying the definition of 'industrial establishment' led to other peculiarities; for example, painters working to order, tailors working up cloth furnished by others, and butchers owning their own shops and cutting meat for retail sale were all struck off the industrial schedules by compilers. Taché and his team had refined the categories for industry and agriculture, but these would remain ambiguous, given the absence of well-articulated projects for governing the industrial economy, the survival of transitional forms of production, and the agrarian project.

Other constructions of census standards could be mentioned, but given Taché's political interests and the nature of the contemporary political debate, a brief examination of the construction of national 'origins' will suffice to carry the argument that systematic, 'scientific' observation and politically laden identifications are not mutually antagonistic. For a century-and-a-quarter after Confederation, the census allowed no one to be a Canadian, and it was Taché who initiated this convention. The 'Nominal Return of the Living' schedule for 1871 contained two relevant columns, one dealing with 'Country or Place of Birth,' the other with 'Origin.' The manual told the enumerators that the place-of-birth column 'explains itself; and the entry must be made by writing such information as "England," "France," "Germany," "O," "N.S.," &c, as the case may be.' In contrast, the instruction for 'Origin,' was one of the few in the manual that was internally contradictory: 'Origin is to be scrupulously entered, as given by the person questioned; in the manner shown in the specimen schedule, by the words English, Irish, Scotch, African, German, French, and so forth.' The census plan created 'census standard' origins, and 'Canadian' was not among them.

In practice, enumerators were torn between entering respondents' answers in the 'origins' column and entering one of the census standard nationalities. Some respondents clearly declared their origin to be 'Canadian,' and others declared themselves 'American,' yet neither entry was acceptable. Enumerators, likely on the instructions of their commissioners, and the compilers after the fact, scratched out such entries and made an attribution of origins according to the census standard. The results seem best understood as part of Taché's concern for demonstrating the flourishing condition of French Canadians. Such attributions of origins required a number of contortions on the part of compilers and enumerators. In Kingston, Ontario (dist. 66-I), for example, the enumerator reported that Lewis Geraldi and his wife and children had been born in Ontario. The children were named 'John,' 'Minnie,' 'Cecilia,' 'Abertha,' and so on. Mr Geraldi became a census 'Italian'; his wife, a census 'Scot'; and his children, all census 'Italians.' Francis Rondin's family (dist. 66-f) was treated in a similar way, with the patriarch and the Ontario-born children defined as 'Italian,' but his wife as 'Irish.' The patriarch's origin was attributed to children even in households headed by women.

Samuel Young, the enumerator for district 67–e, entered 'Canadian' in the origins column of his schedules for many people. His entries were scratched out and 'Irish' was substituted for them in a different hand. Young was uncertain about what to do with fifty-nine-year-old Ira Mallory. Mallory was reportedly born in Ontario; Young entered his origin as 'US' but added this marginal note: 'This man told me as far as he knew his fathers people came from Ireland.' The compiler made Mallory a census Irishman. Elsewhere, when enumerators were unable to make an entry in the origins column, compilers made an attribution, apparently on the basis of surnames. The Pankhursts (dist. 67-a-2), 'origin unknown,' became 'English,' as did many others (e.g., dist.67-h-2). In the Maritime provinces, attempts by enumerators to give 'N.S.' or 'N.B.' were altered to one of the standard nationalities (e.g., dist.179-o-1; 190-m).

In Quebec, in contrast, people became 'census French' if either their mother or their father was born in Quebec. In St-Paschal-de-Kamouraska (dist. 165-i), Daniel Hatton was returned as a forty-six-year-old Catholic, born in Ireland, and married to a *québecoise*. Their children were named Mary, Jane, Laure, John, and Edward, and were all returned as 'census French.' Timothy and Alvina O'Leary from the same district, whose father, James, was born in Ireland and whose mother, Josephine, was born in Quebec, were also made into 'census French.' This sort of practice was followed consistently in this province, but not in the others.

These constructions of 'origins' were not measures of what we would call cultural 'assimilation.' There is no less reason for us to assume that the Grimaldi children from Kingston spoke English than that the Hatton children in the depths of rural Quebec spoke French. The point is that the Grimaldis did not become census 'English'; the Hattons *did* become census 'French.' 'Origin' was attributed on the basis of the paternal line outside Quebec; but inside Quebec, people became census 'French' if either parent was of 'French' origin. These attributions were extensions of Taché's reworking of the genealogical project underlying the census. This project defined people living in Canada as patrilineal descendants of standardized transatlantic populations, and situated them in more or less differentiated 'national' categories. Given Taché's concern for demonstrating the prolific character of his *canadiens*, prospering under the French language, rural industry, and Catholicism, this way of rendering 'origins' was politically useful, as was his aggregation of 'Catholics' and his disaggregation of 'Protestants' in the religious census. The 'French' and 'Catholics' became the most numerically important elements in the population of Canada. It should be recalled that the representativeness of Parliament before 1867 had been attacked by francophone intellectuals on the grounds that there were proportionately fewer francophones and Catholics in Parliament than in the country as a whole. Taché's constructions were not contested in the debate that followed the publication of the census results, and would provide fuel for religious fundamentalism and ethnic nationalism in Quebec.

**The Pure-Blooded Frenchman's Census**
The 1871 population totals were sent to newspaper editors on 7 November and published immediately thereafter. The press, anglophone as well as francophone, greeted the results with incredulity bordering on outrage. In Montreal, *La Minerve* translated an outspoken editorial from the Toronto *Globe* that claimed the *de jure* design was consciously intended by the government to harm the interests of Ontario. Official social science was attacked on the grounds that it was incompatible with other, superior methods of knowing population. The *Globe*'s editor, in a common reaction, pointed to 'what everyone knew' about the level of immigration to Ontario, and about house construction and the growth of towns, as well as to the contrast anyone could see between the condition of the Upper Canada of 1861 and the Ontario of 1871, to insist that the census return was simply absurd. *La Minerve* considered the returns of population sufficiently provocative that it published them in a pamphlet edition.[15]

The most systematic attack on the 1871 census was published in the *Canadian Monthly and National Review*, by Arthur Harvey, a fellow of the Royal Statistical Society and former statistical clerk in the Department of Finance who had been involved in compiling census returns for 1861.[16] There was likely a residue of interdepartmental rivalry in his attack. Harvey was obviously not convinced by John Lowe's assurances about the compilation process, and his published attack on the census was a complex and curious mixture of myth-making, chauvinism, and serious social analysis, in which he examined competing census designs critically before demanding a general check census.

Harvey began by repeating the myth that the 1861 census 'was taken in one day; and the *de facto* population, that is the population actually there, was assigned to each house, village, county, city.' The 1871 census, in contrast, counted the people who by right should be in a locality, and hence it was not necessary to execute it in a day, even though a common day was taken as a reference point. Harvey wrote, chauvinistically, that the *de facto* principle prevailed in northern Europe, 'where ... whatever is most practical is best,' while the *de jure* principle was favoured by the 'Latin peoples,' with whom 'whatever is logical and theoretically right is sought to be carried out.' Of course, the Minister of Agriculture was a lawyer from Quebec, learned in the Roman law, 'which there mystifies the unwary litigant,' and his deputy minister was 'a French Canadian, *pur sang*.' So, claimed Harvey, the census principles were 'foreign to the genius of the people of Ontario' and to the other provinces but 'cognate to that of the people of Quebec.'

Harvey admitted that the census design had not been meant to do injustice to any province – 'the moral character of the officials concerned is too high' – but at the same time he claimed 'there is no reason why the enumeration should not be taken both of the *de facto* and the *de jure* populations, at the same time.' Doing so would mean 'the one [method] would be useful check upon the other.' As matters stood, the census had been conducted by hordes of 'untrained men,' and the lengthy period between the enumeration and the publication of results made it impossible to undertake verification measures. Still, maintained Harvey, such (unnamed) checks as had been made had shown the census figures to be an underenumeration, and some cities, towns, and villages were 'repudiating them with indignation.'

Harvey argued that the *de jure* principle worked best in provinces like Quebec and Nova Scotia, where systems of civil registration were in place, and that it was in those places that the census totals were likely most accurate. Such provinces gained by the census method. Carelessness on the part of enumerators still meant that 6 to 7 per cent of the population had been missed in those two provinces, and in Ontario the error was likely to be greater. Indeed, Harvey estimated, a correct enumeration would have returned another 300,000 people outside Quebec and Nova Scotia. Oddly, he did not point explicitly to the electoral consequences. Perhaps he was not sufficiently sharp to understand that what was at issue was the method employed for tying bodies to political spaces, or perhaps he and his readers took that issue for granted. Whatever the case, he did not attack Taché's department directly for boosting the electoral fortunes of Quebec. His claims about ethnic-national prejudices and his call for a return to the methods of 1861 offered little engagement with the scientific issues. Part of the problem was that Harvey, like many other commentators, was shocked as much by the low population totals as by the distribution of inhabitants within the country. This double-preoccupation muddied the lines of debate somewhat.

Harvey allowed that even an incorrectly conducted census gave 'useful indications of social movements to which we should be awake.' First among these was the rapid growth of cities caused by the railway boom and the growth of manufacturing. In fact, he wrote, the *de jure* principle likely understated the degree of urban growth, for it reassigned many city residents to rural areas and did not capture the transient population. 'The travellers staying at hotels, the young lads at schools and boarding houses, the servants in families,' Harvey protested, 'all these are referred to their homes, which are chiefly in the country, while foreigners passing through the Dominion who are not enumerated at all, are almost altogether in cities and towns.'

In a reasonably novel analysis, Harvey separated the census returns for counties in both Ontario and Quebec into four categories according to period of settlement and geographical location. He then claimed that most old, settled rural areas in Ontario were undergoing slight population increases and that those in Quebec were suffering important population declines. The fastest-growing parts of these provinces were the newly settled agricultural lands. An important policy question arose for Harvey: if old settled regions were indeed losing population, was it due to a lack of capital for needed improvements? If so, then perhaps public investment in underdraining the land was required. Was it preference for new land? If so, a policy of opening new lands for settlement by railway construction should be pursued to prevent emigration. If the latter policy was pursued, at least the government could rest assured that population movement would be directed to the new territories, because population 'will not go southward. It will keep, if not on the same parallel of latitude, as near to it as possible; emigration movements always do so.'

The returns from Quebec were especially puzzling to Harvey for they seemed to call into question established 'Malthusian laws.' The old counties seemed to have lost 7 per cent of their population, but how could that be when 'almost every house, looks like a rabbit warren, for young'? Even if 40,000 men had been killed in the American War, even if thousands had immigrated to New England, it would hardly have made an impact on a population of 'such fecundity as that of Quebec.' Harvey had no explanation to offer, but his findings raised the spectre of a far-reaching fertility decline that meant Canadians would be 'doomed to ultimate extinction' and 'fundamentally dependent upon immigration.' Such a condition would prevent Canadian political independence from developing and would cause the country to remain 'a mere pigmy beside a giant.' If the population figures were in fact accurate, if Canada was 'a comparatively stationary instead of a rapidly progressive country,' then immediate steps had to be taken to colonize the new lands to the northwest. But this policy would be costly and risky; it was not one to undertake without better assurances that the census findings were accurate.

Thus Harvey returned, in the final sections of his paper, to criticize again the execution of the 1871 census, appealing 'to what everyone knew.' While governmental officials were certain the census was accurate, he insisted 'almost every one of us knows of some persons omitted' from it. And how could it be otherwise? The census-making system in North America as a whole was full of faults. It attempted too much. It was a discontinuous undertaking: every decade a new group of 'unskilled, untried and hastily appointed persons' set out on census work, and people had no memory of any previous census to aid them in providing census information. 'Men of all stations' naturally resented 'revealing their private affairs,' and as a result, the censuses were erroneous. Even the Americans got it wrong, claimed Harvey!

In short, the census should be restricted to a count of population; other information should be sought through a system of civil registration. In deciding the important policy questions facing the country, the 1871 census results should not be acted upon until they were verified. Harvey urged the appointment of four special commissioners, to include Taché and John Costley, to supervise an immediate check census.

Such a check would satisfy the country. If the contentious returns were allowed to stand, 'there will be political agitations, and a tendency to relapse from the healthy national bearing we have been hopefully assuming into the old, dead, inglorious, Colonial listlessness.'[17]

**The Statist Replies**
Styling himself a disinterested 'statist,' Taché responded to Harvey's critique in 'The Canadian Census of 1871,' defending the project in detail before examining its implications.[18] People were disappointed at the population totals, according to Taché, because 'prophets and their believers' had been assiduously creating 'wild expectations' about population growth, some of them going so far as to claim authoritatively that the country contained 4,707,751 people. The same thing had happened in the United States, although there people 'have had the good disposition to accept with dignity the unwelcome truth.'[19]

Harvey's suspicions about the 1871 population totals were based on false anticipations created by exaggerated rates of growth reported in past censuses. 'The rate of increase of one period,' Taché pointed out, is 'no criterion whatever of the rate of increase of the next period.' The rates of Canadian population growth in 1841–51 and 1851–61 were themselves dramatically different and showed 'the fallacy of calculations based on a mere geometrical progression.' Taché took Harvey to task for repeating the myth that the 1861 census had been taken in a day: this claim was sufficient to 'delude the prejudiced portion of the public,' but the facts were that the 1861 census took as long to complete as that of 1871, although the country was much smaller. It was taken neither under the *de facto* nor under the *de jure* system 'but without system.' It was 'made to include both the *present* and *absent* of every family; thereby making a double entry of all the fluctuating population.' It gave exaggerated results, and the 1852 census, taken in the same way, had had the same consequence. Thus, past perceptions of rapid increase were flawed, and present claims about a rapid falling off of growth rates were exaggerated.

Taché declined to enter into a discussion of a 'transcendental nature' about the relative genius of the Latin and Teutonic peoples, 'being rather inclined to restrict [him]self to facts and to arguments derived therefrom,' but it was simply not the case that the choice of enumeration method expressed national character. The 'latin' government of France employed the *de facto* enumeration method, while the *de jure* principle had been employed by the Americans in 1870. Nor was it the case that the so-called checks to which Harvey appealed in questioning the returns were a reliable measure of the 1871 enumeration. The assessors' returns made in Ontario shortly before the census showed a population lower than that subsequently enumerated. Taché claimed to know of only two enumerations taken since the census, one in St. Mary's, Ontario, the other in the border town of St. John's, Quebec, and both had been executed 'under preconceived ideas and with the avowed purpose of showing the Census at fault.' Nine months after the 1871 census gave it a population of 3,120, the re-enumeration of the town of St. Mary's found a total of 3,178: a clear vindication of the census itself. The St. John's re-enumeration was not to be trusted: it found hundreds of people beyond the 3,022 returned in 1871, a clear indication of exaggeration. It was taken by 'agents not legally responsible, under sectional influences, at work, amongst a population, at the time actuated by an intense spirit of locality and almost pledged to procure a higher figure than the Census.' Furthermore, no record was kept in St. John's of the names of those enumerated, and 'an enumeration made without writing in the name of every person is admitted to be, by all authorities, under all circumstances, a questionable piece of statistics.'

In fact, the St. John's check census results were particularly worrisome for Agriculture and Statistics. Well before Harvey's attack was published, John Lowe, George Weaver, and Christopher Dunkin had considered organizing a third St. John's enumeration; and in December 1871, Lowe was sending Weaver information to feed to the press in an effort to discredit the claims about people being omitted in 1871. Lowe urged Weaver to 'go quietly to work' on the matter, and later assured him that the people in the St. John's asylum, likely returned twice as residents of the asylum and of the town in the check census, had been assigned to their homes in the 1871 census.[20]

Thus, after rejecting as 'simply ludicrous' Harvey's claim that the Nova Scotia enumeration was more reliable than that in the other provinces, Taché returned again to defend the 1871 enumeration against the re-enumeration that had been made in St. John's. Harvey criticized the *de jure* method, Taché wrote, because it did not count people at school, in hotels, or temporarily in the cities, or foreigners in transit. But 'what is the object of an enumeration of the population of a country?' Was it to crowd 'the largest possible figures on paper,' or was it to know the real strengths and weaknesses of the country? 'If, to the real population of a frontier town were added (as a local operation has done) the few hundreds, travellers, strangers and foreigners, who gather there, will it be a greater producer or consumer, or a greater bulwark against invasion?'

Surely not! On the contrary, such a proceeding would 'mislead the administration and induce the country to calculate upon a fictitious strength.' In the end, there was no difference in the population totals yielded by a correctly executed census taken by either method. The *de jure* method had been chosen in Canada, as in the United States, 'as being the better in view of special difficulties of organization, of the immense extent of territories and of federal political institutions.'

In his attempt to interpret the significance of the census results and to discuss their political implications, Taché continued to justify the 1871 enumeration and to push for his statistical projects. It was clear that there had been a decline in the growth rate of the Canadian population, but, he claimed, very disingenuously, 'men who had spent time in analysing the movements of our population were prepared for a result which has taken by entire surprise a large portion of our public.' It was clear in the past decade that 'immigration permanently settling in the country' had become 'a mere nothing,' while there was 'a considerable emigration' from all four provinces, but especially from Quebec, to the United States. People were moving in response to the high wages created by the American Civil War and by the abolition of slave labour. It would indicate 'a very unhealthy state of the public mind' to ignore such facts.

Taché claimed that Harvey effectively admitted these conditions to be the case in his musings about population movement, and also that he took an unnecessarily gloomy view in suggesting that Canada would disappear without a steady influx of European immigration. The American 'emigrating mania is curing itself' and would continue to do so 'as long as the rate of wages finds its ordinary level,' while in Canada 'the fecundity of our families, on the whole, is not impaired.' Population growth was about 1 per cent annually in all provinces except Quebec, a province acknowledged 'picturesquely' by Harvey to be 'renowned for its extraordinary fecundity.' Indeed, if any province had been hard done by in the census, it must have been Quebec.

Taché concluded by congratulating Harvey for his insistence that the country needed a system of civil registration, and used this opening to advertise his genealogical project and to repeat once more his arguments about the remarkably prolific Catholic population. Indeed, claimed Taché, his department's investigations showed that if there had been no emigration from Quebec, the Catholic population there alone at the end of 1870 would have numbered 1,183,557 'plus a number equal to the grand total of the Catholic immigration from the beginning.' Untroubled by invoking speculations similar to those he had denounced on

Harvey's part, Taché affirmed that 'the triumph of truth over delusion, popular infatuation and local prejudices, if retarded, cannot be for ever prevented.' The 1871 census was the only authoritative, official account; its results must stand.

## Defending the 1871 Census

Both before and after Taché's exchange with Harvey, the Department of Agriculture and Statistics worked to defend the 1871 census results and to counter public criticism. One important forum for this was Lowe's *Year Book and Almanac* for 1872, published sometime late in 1871, at the end of which Lowe tacked a discussion of census returns for the United States, Britain, and Canada. Lowe had gathered ammunition for this defence in part from Thomas White, Jr., the Peterborough County commissioner for the 1861 census, whose *Exhibit of the Progress, Position and Resources of the County of Peterboro, Canada West,* reported an alternative compilation of the county's 1861 census results. White had told Lowe that his 'compilation differed from the official compilation, in that the latter added in both the *absent and the present* in the actual population.' Lowe was eager to find a copy of 'the only thing extant' that could 'show the difference which that kind of compilation will make in one county' – the more so as 'it has a very important influence on the comparisons of population' between census periods. White's method of compilation gave a county population total of 23,249, in contrast to the 24,631 reported in the press. Counting absentees twice had inflated the reported number of inhabitants, in this case by about 5.6 per cent.[21]

Lowe's tactic in defending the 1871 census results was to compare decennial growth rates in Canada with those in Britain and the United States and then to speculate on why they differed. Britain's population had grown by 8.6 per cent, Canada's by 12.79 per cent and that of the United States by 22.52 per cent. But of course everyone knew there was a massive emigration from Britain and a massive immigration to the United States that undercut growth rates in the former and swelled those in the latter. In fact, the 1870 census showed almost one-seventh of the American population to have been foreign born; if the emigration from Britain 'had been retained at home,' it would have 'doubled the rate per cent' of British growth.

While greater than that of Britain on its face, the reported Canadian growth rate was an underestimation because one of its terms was the 1861 census results. That census could only be described by the word '*exaggeration*,' because 'the enumerators were paid so much for every name they put down on their books ... and the temptation to swell both population and payment at the same time was altogether too great.' Lowe claimed to 'have proof of cases in which this was done,' and to this source of exaggeration had to be added double-counting during compilation. It would be too time consuming and laborious ever to determine the exact degree of overenumeration, but in Peterborough County, counting the absentees twice showed that the official population report was '5½ per cent exaggerated.'

Now, Lowe continued, if one assumed that the 1861 results were exaggerated to this extent, the decennial growth rates leading up to 1871 'would make a very near approach to those presented by the returns from the United States.' Lowe made this claim simply by adding 5.5 per cent to the decennial growth rate – a peculiar piece of reasoning, but one that raised Canada's rate to 19.35 per cent and Ontario's to 22.85 per cent, respectable figures indeed! The growth rates were likely even higher because 'a correction of error based simply on one glaring form, is not sufficient to account for all the exaggeration of 1861.' After all, the livestock of the county of Waterloo in 1861 was valued at $10 million more than it actually was, an enormous error that swelled the reported value for the province as a whole by 20 per cent.[22]

Despite their confident public defence of the 1871 census results and of the larger project of which they formed part, Taché and Lowe were clearly taken aback by the low population totals. The results raised doubts about the intelligence generated by the statistical system as a whole, and pushed the department into more sustained reflection on population matters. After W.H. Johnson and Stanislas Drapeau produced abstracts of past enumerations, William Kingston, one of the census clerks, was put to work making sense of the 1871 population totals for Ontario. Kingston's effort is an early example of demographic modelling, even if its objective was to evaluate the quality of the existing statistical system in defence of the 1871 census.

Kingston wrote that the average growth rates for the population of New France across twenty-one enumerations between 1700 and 1750 had been 2.58 per cent. If one assumed that the population of immigrants to Ontario from Great Britain and Ireland, whose members were 'generally very prolific,' grew at a manifestly low annual rate of 2 per cent, by the official count such immigrants should have increased Ontario's population between 1861 and 1871 by 208,053. Now, the census gave Ontario a population in 1871 of 1,620,850. Subtracting the 'result of immigration' (208,053) meant that the native Ontario population in 1871 was 1,412,797.

The 1861 census had reported 1,396,091 for Canada West. In other words, according to these returns the native population had increased by 16,706 over ten years, 'a decennial per centage of only *1.2*, and an annual percentage of *less than two tenths of one percent*, or less than *2 in 1000* which is manifestly absurd.' Another way of working the same returns suggested that if the 1861 census and the immigration returns were reliable, there were about 207,000 people missing from Ontario.

Kingston concluded, 'it appears evident from this that the immigration returns were altogether too great; or that the Census of 1861 was too great; or very probably both were in excess of the facts; either way, the result seriously affects the late Census, by exciting anticipations in the public mind that *were not*, and *could not* be, obtained.'[23] Kingston's work may have given Taché and Lowe solace, convincing them that their census represented population 'accurately,' but it did not stop the attacks on the census from those who drew on other forms of evidence to estimate population and who were interested in configuring social relations differently. In the late winter of 1872, Agriculture and Statistics faced a particularly serious challenge in the guise of a second enumeration of Montreal. Quite apart from anything else, the debates around the 1871 census returns and the Montreal re-enumeration prevented Taché and Lowe from pursuing other initiatives planned for the summer of 1871, such as the sanitary census of Canadian cities and the attempt to push for a national civil registry.[24]

**The Montreal Check Census**

In December 1871 the Montreal City Council determined to conduct a 'check census' in an effort to correct what a majority of its members saw as the obviously erroneous returns of population provided by Agriculture and Statistics. Taché's management of the department had been receiving bad press in Montreal well before the 1871 census results were published. The opposition *Gazette* had attacked the department's immigration policy, describing Taché as enjoying an 'undisturbed and sleepy incumbency' out of which the Minister of Agriculture, Christopher Dunkin, had not had the decisiveness to awaken him. It was as promising 'to post letters on business to the Parish Pump as it would be to send them to the Department over which Mr Taché presides,' and in immigration 'no practical result can be hoped for from the present managers of the Department.'[25]

When the pro-government Ottawa *Times* objected to these charges, the *Gazette* returned with more detail. Much had been looked for from

Taché when he was appointed, given that he was a man 'of considerable literary culture,' and 'statistics were to be specially attended to by him.' But 'the mysterious hints of a good work going on, eventuated at last in a blue book, in which the numbers, nationalities, and salaries of employees of the civil service were stated! This effort at "statistics" seems to have exhausted the genius of the Doctor.' Since that time, he had done nothing, if one discounted rumours about a volume of figures about the country prior to the Conquest said to be in the works. The editor suggested that 'to purely literary men this forthcoming marvel of statistical genius, will possibly be of value,' but it was of no practical use. 'Indeed, the only statistics of any importance with which the country has been favoured since Dr. Taché's appointment have come from another department, that of Finance.' Taché's lack of interest in promoting immigration, especially English-speaking immigration, was again assailed.[26] The Montreal *Herald* claimed that whatever the Department of Agriculture did was 'so mysterious that nobody seems to have yet been able' to discover it. In the domain of agricultural statistics, the Department had produced no information on its own.[27] These criticisms, especially the *Gazette's* denigration of literary statistics and statistical monuments, with praise for statistics of 'practical value,' rehearsed the attacks on *de jure* and the support for *de facto* census designs taken up by Arthur Harvey.

The 1852 census had reported the population of Montreal to be 57,715; that of 1861 gave 90,323. Many people believed the city's growth rate between 1861 and 1871 to have been at least as great as in the preceding decade and looked for a population of as much as 150,000. Yet the 1871 census gave the total as 107,225. *La Minerve* agitated for the taking of a second census, and other papers supported the project. It was evident, *La Minerve* claimed, that the census was seriously defective. There were many cases of notable Montreal families having been omitted, and if the enumerators had been lax in the best-known streets, they must have been 'less scrupulous in the slums, where there is a considerable agglomeration of population.'

Some of the indications of negligence were clearly spurious and stemmed from a misunderstanding of census procedures. For instance, *La Minerve* repeated again the fact that enumerators had not collected the census forms left at people's houses as an example of incompetence, failing to distinguish the 1871 enumeration proper from the information leaflets distributed beforehand.[28] Nonetheless, after some debate a majority of City Council claimed that the 'late census of this city has not been taken in such a way as to give general satisfaction,' and moved on 13 December 1871 to appoint a committee to consider ways to carry out its own census of population.[29]

The correspondence of Agriculture and Statistics points to other sources of contention surrounding the enumeration of Montreal that do not seem to have been discussed in the press but that may, even so, have formed a subtext for the public attacks. Commissioner George Weaver had concerns about the compilation process stemming from a heated debate over ethnic and religious bias in the Montreal enumeration. Only the department's response to Weaver survives, but John Lowe defended the department against charges of pro-Catholic bias. Whatever Taché's own loyalties, Protestant enumerators were disproportionately represented in Montreal, and the two clerks Weaver employed to correct the schedules were a Protestant minister and an avowed Orangeman.[30]

Also, the department was dissatisfied with the work of J.J. Curran, one of Weaver's fellow Montreal commissioners. Curran was slow in delivering the census schedules, and when he did deliver them, they were incomplete and had to be returned to him. Weaver insisted on seeing manuscript schedules from delayed districts to assure himself they were not being rigged. As well, Curran fired one of his enumerators for incompetence and then attempted to avoid paying the man for the work he had done. Fragmentary surviving correspondence points to difficulties Curran's enumerators encountered in reporting on the Grand Trunk Rail Road shops, with hints of opposition to government snooping from the company's management. Finally, the enumerator W.B. Lambe, active in the central city, made a great deal of noise about his pay, claiming that his work was exceptionally difficult because there were many businesses and industries in his district, while he was poorly paid because there were few resident families. A special case was made to allow Lambe $4 a day under the table.[31]

Despite all this, the Montreal enumeration was probably done at least as carefully as those conducted anywhere else, and perhaps more so. Indeed, the department took the unusual step, while the enumeration was underway, of acquiring copies of the city's *Livre de renvoi* (i.e., the official assessment document) from the Cadastre Office, likely to serve as a check on the thoroughness of the enumeration. Because the enumerators routinely recorded street names and house numbers on their schedules, missing or multiplied entries could be detected. In fact, in later debate about life and labour in working-class Montreal, researchers have retraced the enumerators' routes through the city and have compared their reports with the surviving housing stock. Because of the established urban infrastructure, census managers working at a distance had a means of measuring the thoroughness of the coverage of the city.[32]

**Multiplying Montreal**

To bolster the suggestion that the 1871 enumeration was erroneous, *La Minerve* attacked it using other methods for determining population, claiming these were superior to official social science. The paper estimated the city's population by applying multipliers to various indicators; the resulting estimates were all higher than the 1871 return. If one took the number of houses constructed in the decade since 1861 and assumed that eight people lived in each, Montreal's population would be 112,323. But this was a low estimate. From the level of water consumption, it was evident that there were more people than formerly living in older houses in the city. Using water consumption as a guide, there must be 147,461 people in Montreal. Alternatively, using the increase in the tax rolls, Montreal had 159,962 residents; using the water tax instead, it had 141,563. Or again, given that the number of electors had almost doubled in the preceding decade, with no change in the conditions of the franchise, Montreal must have a population of 166,856. Of course, the paper remarked, 'it may be that these figures are not of an algebraic precision,' but they certainly showed that the last census could not offer 'the guarantees of exactness in respect to the population of Montreal that it ought.' A final and absolutely low estimate was then offered: 122,934. *La Minerve* also claimed that a second enumeration conducted in 'the little city of St. John's,' whose population was only a few thousand, had discovered over five hundred people missed by the federal enumerators.[33]

A majority of City Council was enthusiastic about the project of a second census and reported that 'the people of Montreal were alive to the necessity of putting the city in its true position.' Montreal was suffering 'materially in many ways from the false presentation' given in the official census, and there were plenty of volunteers willing to do the work of enumeration. It was suggested that the city water collectors could distribute census schedules, which could be returned by the first of February.[34] The committee appointed to consider how to make the census decided instead that the city assessors were best placed to conduct it. The census was to be a nominal one, conducted on the *de facto* principle and giving information about sex and religion. Council appropriated $2,000 for the effort on 24 January 1872.[35] Injunctions to cooperate with enumerators were read from the pulpits of city churches on Sunday, 4 February, and the enumeration began on Monday, 12 February. Four days later, the enumerators reported having taken 18,000 names, and people were said to be cooperating fully. More promising, 'they have verified that several of the houses at which they presented themselves had not been entered by the government enumerators last spring.'[36] The city, it seemed, would soon be vindicated.

### The Department of Agriculture and the Check Census

The events in Montreal were followed closely by Lowe, who was managing the department while Taché fought off another attack of carbuncles. Lowe was in regular contact with George Weaver, and spent two days with him in Montreal early in January 1872 conducting a special census inquiry. Immediately after the appointment of City Council's first census committee, Lowe contacted him again. He wished especially to be informed whether the enumerators were to 'take the *names*,' noting 'unless they do this, it will be no census.'[37] As a control on Montreal's enumerators, Lowe instructed Weaver to calculate the average number of people returned per family. The department's records showed '*over six to a family*' in St-Antoine's ward, and Weaver was to 'take any time; or any means to check this.'[38] Weaver's report that the city enumerators were finding fewer large families than had their federal counterparts encouraged Lowe to suggest that the check census would return a lower population, but he remained concerned that the enumeration would not be done fairly. Weaver was instructed both to see that 'the *additions* are not made to give any improper increase to the population' and to 'let the corporation know you act on your own responsibility.'[39]

### Results of the Check Census

*La Minerve* scooped the other Montreal newspapers by reporting the results of the check census on 9 March, four days before they were officially reported to City Council: 'We believe that it puts the population, inside the city limits at 118,000.'[40] Four days later, the census committee was more precise: 117,865, compared with 107,225 in the 1871 census.

The council meeting at which this figure was delivered was acrimonious, with councillors denouncing and defending the enumerators. When Councillor Kennedy claimed that the census couldn't be correct because he himself had not been enumerated, Councillor Loranger reminded him that notices had been printed in the press calling on all heads of families who had been missed to present themselves to be counted. Loranger was then able to show that Kennedy had indeed been returned, but under another name. Councillor Loranger knew several other men who claimed to have been missed but who later found they had in fact been reported by someone else. The debate reached its zenith when Alderman Simard cited, as proof that confidence should be reposed in the enumerators, the fact that he had himself given them 'lists of those living in certain of his houses.' To this, Alderman Bastien responded that if Simard's behaviour had been often repeated, it 'would serve to shake his confidence in the census completely.'[41]

In any case, City Council's census committee reported that the enumerators had been careful and diligent in their work and the air went out of the census balloon with a sigh: 117,000 was rather less than 166,000. Still, the committee attempted to put a happy face on the results, remarking that the increase, 'although falling somewhat short of the expectations that were entertained is not however unwelcome and the impetus which the several large public improvements and interprises [sic] now in Store, are likely to produce, the Citizens may look to the future with confidence and anticipate a still more favorable result in the next decade.'[42] The official report further softened the low population return by suggesting that an additional 2,000 heads of families worked in Montreal but lived outside the city limits – an addition of perhaps 20,000 people. Still, not all members of council were mollified. As far as Alderman McGavran was concerned, for instance, 'Councillor Loranger had rather underestimated the persons living outside the limits *who might properly be considered* as forming part of the population of the city.' A better estimate would mean that Montreal's population was in fact as much as 160,000.[43]

McGavran's position notwithstanding, the press, earlier certain that the federal census had been poorly done, now set about reconciling the census results with new accounts of what everyone knew. Montrealers had been entertaining false hopes about the size of their city. 'The disappointment respecting the results of our census,' editorialized the *Herald*, 'is due more to exaggerated expectations than to circumstances inherent in the nature of things ... Every one who has had occasion to compare popular calculations with ascertained numbers is aware of the tendency to excessive multiplication, which is always present.' Not only were there many people working in the city who lived outside it, but – now echoing the official line of the Department of Agriculture – the 1852 and 1861 censuses were probably overenumerations. In any case, even the American census showed a smaller population than people expected.[44] *La Minerve* added its own nuance: people were disappointed by the returns because they were in regular contact with others who worked in the city but lived outside its walls. Naturally, they believed such people to be Montrealers, but they couldn't really be counted as such in a census.[45]

The check census had been an attack by the municipal government, with press support, on the authority of Agriculture and Statistics to construct collective representations of social relations in Montreal. City council and the press had mobilized alternative statistical resources to counter the claims produced by the federal government through what were still novel techniques of social scientific inquiry. Council and the press championed a view in which official representations could be assessed in terms of 'what everyone knew.' Counting and calculating continued to coexist uneasily.

After the second enumeration, the press continued to draw a distinction between what it was supposed everyone knew, experienced, or could decipher, on the one hand, and on the other hand, official representations based on social scientific inquiry (i.e., Taché's matters of national importance). They contrasted two competing visions of where people belonged, were situated, and could properly be considered to live: a vision based on common sense, memory, and with whom one regularly came in contact; and a vision based on placement in terms of administrative boundaries. After the check census, the press in Montreal came to argue that the administrative vision was, if not the only 'true' or 'accurate' one, at least reasonable in its own terms. The sense people had of who was a Montrealer, this part of the social imaginary, stood in need of correction. The challenge to the social imaginary offered by official social science – the claim that there existed a reality accessible through social scientific inquiry and different from 'what everyone knows' – was a particularly significant result of the Montreal census controversy. Interestingly, there was no comment in this debate on the implications of a lower-than-expected census result for the place of the city and region in the electoral system, beyond some oblique remarks about Montreal not getting its due. But the check census helped solidify the federal agency's claims that it was able to define the domain in which 'matters of national importance' were situated.

**Contesting the Results**
The City Council and the press in Montreal were able to console themselves with the discovery of about 10,000 more citizens than the 1871 census had counted and the fact that thousands more people lived just

outside the city limits. The same cannot be said for the Department of Agriculture. A difference of this magnitude was seen by Lowe and Taché as a serious compromise of their census, and they expected criticism in Parliament. They refused to accept the results of the check census. The suggestions made by Lowe's Montreal agent, George Weaver, to account for the different findings were dismissed. Even before Weaver reported the results, Lowe had been insisting that the '*difference in the mode of taking the Census* will not make anything like 10 per cent,' if enumerators had done their work accurately.[46]

Weaver managed to get the census results to Lowe by 1 March, well before they were presented to City Council, and Lowe and Taché immediately began analysing them. 'The *difference* of the two modes of taking the Census would not amount in figures to 7,800,' Lowe insisted, 'and we believe there is exaggeration in the *check* census.' Its source was clear: 'If you ask simply the question who *slept* in a house on a given night, those who are *temporarily absent* will about make up for the strangers *temporarily present* and the two ends will meet. – certainly there w[oul]d not be a difference of nearly 7 per cent.' On the other hand, 'if the question was asked *both ways* ... the difference might be made.' As with the censuses of 1852 and 1861, it seemed to Lowe that the Montreal check census counted transients twice, and he instructed Weaver to find some cases where this kind of double-counting had been done, again urging great secrecy. 'Try your best to establish *one* or *two clear cases*,' he wrote. 'Go very quietly to work on this; and don't alarm them. We rely upon your shrewdness and discretion, and it is of immense public importance to expose error in this matter. Never mind any expense. Get a few ... places where you think there has been either error or fraud. Then it may be well to find out how many names *they allege* we did not take; and test the truth of that statement.'[47]

Weaver was maladroit. He used Lowe's name, to the latter's great chagrin, in an attempt to get more information about the check census. He also proposed an alternative explanation for the census findings: a real increase in population demonstrated by the construction of 1,060 buildings in Montreal in 1871, of which 908 were houses. This was an important departure from the decennial average of 534. '*Clap-trap*,' responded Lowe, demanding that Weaver send a complete copy of the census so that he and Taché could find the errors in it.[48] At this point, the department's correspondence about the check census disappears, but it may well have been Lowe who fed information to city councillors to counter claims about people who had been omitted.

For a time, Agriculture and Statistics was faced with a competing account of Montreal's population. The president of the Montreal Board of Trade could write in 1873 that 'according to the Census of 1871, the population of the city within the nine wards was 107,245, a subsequent proof-enumeration giving 117,865, – while the contiguous suburbs (which are practically a part of the city) include a population of about 23,000. The aggregate population is, therefore (say) 140,865. The increase in the city proper since 1861 was 26,706, or 29.29 per cent; – the increase in city and suburbs being 38,398, or 37.79 per cent.'[49] But the Board of Trade was engaged in bravado: its claims about population influenced neither the political representation of the city nor its share in public monies. The census was no longer primarily an advertising tool; it had become a scientific administrative instrument. The authority of the official account grew in the course of the next decade, and Taché's published report of the development of the Canadian population displaced its competitors: it became 'made science.' No one now remembers the Montreal check census; no contemporary historian of Montreal has paid any attention to it. Those interested in knowing the number of inhabitants in Canada in earlier years routinely consult Taché's published census volumes, firm in the belief that the authority of the state is a guarantee of their truthfulness.

**Unveiling the Monument**
Between 1873 and 1878, Agriculture and Statistics produced five volumes of reports on the 1871 census, a collection of official statistics that rivalled international practice in sophistication and complexity.[50] Thousands of copies were printed and widely distributed. Much of the material generated through the 1871 enumeration was presented in tabular form, aggregated and disaggregated in a variety of ways. In true Queteletian fashion, the department produced a great many comparisons. The abstraction 'population' was configured as numbers of individuals in the territory as a whole and in different sections of it. It appeared through the articulation of characteristics such as age, occupation, origin, religion, and so on. It acquired a history, through comparisons with the numbers given in past censuses, as well as a trajectory, through a detailed reconstruction of the 'movement' of those defined as French Catholics. The identifying characteristics of one of its elements, 'centenarians,' were probed in great detail, and the status of the claims of named individuals to be 'centenarians' was examined. Taché devoted a considerable section of Volume VI to an examination of what he

considered to be the inevitable decline of the aboriginal population, arguing that hunting and gathering as a mode of production demanded access to large land masses and posed technical limits to population size. Assimilation was held to be inevitable for aboriginals as white expansion continued.

Taché's interest in fundamentalist religion, pronatalist politics, and agrarian civilization, which had shaped both his engagement with the census project and the ways in which it tied people to territory and identity, were 'black-boxed,' becoming part of the project's invisible infrastructures. Taché became the disinterested 'statist,' concerned only with ensuring that the contribution Canada had to offer to science was presented clearly and concisely. The *de jure* enumeration principle was significant only because it was the most efficient method for large and federated territories. The social conflicts in which the project as a whole had been embedded, and the challenges to its authority, were nowhere mentioned. Canada's statistical statue was pristine.

The reports pointed to the thoroughness and efficiency of the census-making operation. Its numbers and tables constituted a well-bounded field in which 'statists' could labour to understand the fundamental phenomena of 'population.' The availability of the maps and related materials used in the effort was indicated for anyone wishing to conduct more minute investigations. Still, the 'Canada' presented in Taché's reports could be disaggregated in ways pleasing to him. Quebec was 78 per cent French and 86 per cent Catholic. Even in the new federation, the French Canadians were the single most important group by origins – 32 per cent of the total, trailed by the Irish at 25 per cent and the English at 21 per cent. French Catholics, research in Volume V demonstrated, were to be met with everywhere in North America, and readers were referred to the abbé Tanguay's genealogical dictionary for a more detailed demonstration of their heritage.

At the same time, the published census volumes continued to present the discredited population totals returned by the censuses of 1852 and 1861 as authoritative. Taché wished to present statistical series and did not have the means or, perhaps, the authority to rewrite the representations he had so often denounced. They remain part of the official version of Canada's population. Still, Taché's statistical commemoration made many comparisons, delineated many new statistical objects, and created many possibilities for purchase on social relations.

In sum, the team working under Taché's meticulous direction organized the first scientific census of the new national state, Canada. The systematic application of clearly defined observational protocols, to well-defined objects of observation, by a trained corps of observers, throughout a delimited territory, with reports compiled and abstracted by disciplined workers, using consistent decisional rules, yielded an internally coherent image of social relations. The marginalization of the interpretive discretion of observers in the course of the enumeration, the removal of descriptive accounts, the absence of discussion of correction, emendation, and attribution during compilation, and the expurgation of explicit political discussion from the official reports – all of these contributed to the scientific image of the results. All traces of science-in-the-making were erased in the census reports themselves and, at some time, in Agriculture and Statistics itself. The voluminous correspondence files concerning census planning and execution were later destroyed, leaving later researchers, like this one, to scratch away at fragmentary and suggestive reports. Certified by the authority of the existing regime, the census's facts about Canada became reliable resources for an array of governmental projects. They defined a domain of rule and populated it with objects of rule, and thereby extended the administrative capacity of state and disciplined political subjects.

Conclusion

# Administering the 'Knowable Community'

The 1871 census produced the first scientifically organized configuration of the 'population of Canada.' Through the disciplined and imaginative labour of the team of intellectuals, administrators, and state servants directed by Joseph-Charles Taché, the capacities of the state system were extended dramatically. While in earlier decades other administrative projects, such as public education, had centralized relations of administrative command and government, the census effort pushed matters further. In conjunction with projects for specifying a national money, reforming weights and measures, extending practices of inspection, and (later) codifying the law, census making was a constitutive element in the formation of the Canadian state. The 1871 census specified a domain of rule, created a set of political capacities, and laid the basis for the elaboration of a wide variety of political projects.

The field or domain of population emerged out of investment in statistical forms and infrastructural work. The domain of population was demarcated as the field of 'matters of national importance.' The people contained in it were defined practically as equivalently subordinate to administrative authority. The space of population was the administrative space that resulted from 'laying out the country' in numerically sequential units. The domain was coterminous with the physical space of the national territory, but it reorganized that physical space in administratively pertinent forms. The field acquired both a history and a trajectory, worked up as genealogy and as the civilizing mission of Europeans in North America.

Capturing 'matters of national interest' numerically, as the census did, involved investment in forms – that is, the codification of social relations and activities and the specification of protocols for their observation and

## Conclusion: Administering the 'Knowable Community' 307

recording. 'Census standard' measures abstracted from the qualitative diversity of objects of observation to render them subject to quantification, and quantification in turn yielded 'things which stay together,' that is, actionable objects. The possibilities for the emergence of actionable objects were increased in Canada especially after 1871, because systematic social observation first stabilized many different aspects of social relations and then, as a monumental undertaking, made many comparisons among them.[1]

Investments in forms are theoretical preconditions for practical interventions, in the physical as much as in the administrative sciences. Such practical interventions depend also on the 'infrastructural work' that makes it possible practically to connect what Anderson calls 'the feverish imaginings' of administrators and scientists with the world outside the office and laboratory.[2] The transition from theoretical to practical scientific intervention is similar in the physical and social scientific laboratories.

Investing social relations in forms works to specify and stabilize manipulable objects, representing them in ways that offer practical purchase for intervention. Such investments relieve scientist-administrators of the debilitating and immobilizing necessity of continually questioning the ontological status of the field of intervention. They also sustain the normally realist attitude of everyday practice that makes it possible to problematize objects within the taken-for-granted confines of the field.[3]

The scientific and administrative fields depend equally on mundane infrastructural work, both for producing knowledge and for executing projects of mastery. As Bruno Latour has put it, infrastructural work makes it possible to make of the world outside the laboratory a world inside the laboratory; the same is true for the world in and outside the office or bureau.[4] Work in the social laboratory depends on incorporating objects of investigation in administrative structures of greater or lesser complexity and solidity. Censuses are made, not taken. Observations are of the opinions of informants who have been incorporated into administrative structures. Systematic observations depend on the prior generation of common understandings of the purposes of inquiry, of the objects to be observed, and of the manner in which they are to be observed. To that end, observers and informants must have been subjected to a minimal degree of prior discipline; they may resist or prove to be recalcitrant.

In mid-nineteenth-century census making, fitting social relations into the spaces of an enumeration grid depended on the execution of what was, for the time, the highly complex and demanding labour of coordination, transport, printing, packing, distribution, and collection. The internal coherence of observational practices depended directly on logistical considerations, and also on systematic inattention to aspects of social relations not invested in statistical forms.

Successful investments in forms and successful infrastructural work banish investments and intrastructures themselves to the realm of the obvious and commonsensical. Statistical objects and practices are 'black-boxed'; that is, their dependence on particular investigative modalities ceases to be visible. Objects and practices that emerge out of the work of classification, codification, and theoretical formation come to be taken as commonsensical elements of the scientific or administrative domain.

As Philip Corrigan and Derek Sayer remind us, the fabrication of common sense is a politically laden process on which the legitimacy of regimes depends.[5] Remaking common sense is part of the cultural revolution associated with state formation, in which census making, in relation to modern states, has played an important role. That there exists an order of reality, 'matters of national importance,' which agencies of the state can know, but which is different from and not accessible by what 'everyone knows,' is a radical political claim. In class-divided societies, this claim can sustain the existence of the illusory community in the interests of which agencies of state and political parties justify their political projects. This is a claim about meaning-making, but not one that excludes in any way attention to conduct.[6]

I am not making a romantic claim of the sort that seeks to hold up the purity or superior ontological status of 'experience' against the 'artificial' or 'ideological' character of statistical knowledge forms. For instance, some dimensions of the movements of the world economy, the administration of health care, and the consequences of environmental pollution cannot be grasped in politically pertinent ways without the aid of such forms of knowledge. Yet statistical knowledges are conditioned by the materiality of the social relations they attempt to appropriate; they are historically specific knowledges that are adequate to particular kinds of social objects and, by implication, inadequate to others. In his elegant analysis of the development of English literature, Raymond Williams argues convincingly, that the emergence of statistical knowledges is necessarily connected to the expanding boundaries of 'the knowable community,' boundaries pushed outwards by the growth of commodity production and exchange and by state administration. As Williams put it,

> The statistical mode itself, which to Dickens and other early Victorian humanists had seemed destructive and hateful, was a necessary response to

a civilisation of this scale and complexity. It is hardly surprising that the statistical mode in modern social investigation began effectively in Manchester, in the 1830s: it is part of that version of the world. But without it, nevertheless, much that needed to be seen, in a complicated, often opaque and generally divided society, could not, as a basis for common experience and response be seen at all.[7]

Statistical modes of knowing are particularly capacious for appropriating expansive, but also increasingly formally equivalent, social relations. Yet they appropriate such social relations from what Williams calls a particular kind of 'identifying position': one that operates from above and beyond, that creates a new economy of sameness and difference in which variation is deviation. Such modes of knowing create their own representational problems, an example from this book being the matter of 'the woman with no hands,' who was not a matter of 'national importance.' As Williams puts it, 'the problem of the knowable community is then, in a new way, a problem of language': of how to speak of the grounded and rich particularities of social lives in a world of increasingly dominant large abstractions.[8]

Yet the problem is more complex than this way of posing it suggests, for official statistical forms, and social scientific concepts more generally, are invasive of such grounded particularities. The rising regime of statistical knowledge-power, of which census making is a key element, is parasitical on other ways of configuring and apprehending social relations and conditions. Census making is not in any simple sense the *taking* of things as they are; in an important sense it is the *making* of things to be taken. Social relations must be organized minimally by the census-making process if they are to be appropriated and translated into numerical form. Typically, the results of census making are fed back into administrative processes, where their fabrication of social relations acquires a firmer material existence. This circular process has been described by Hacking as 'dynamic nominalism,' although we should remember that the subjects of it are not passive. Official classifications and categorizations may be opposed or subverted as well as embraced.[9]

'Statistical thinking' and making up population partake of a novel regime of knowledge-power, one that grew increasingly dominant culturally in the middle decades of the nineteenth century, well before its mathematical foundations were laid. As Theodore Porter has put it, 'the demands [statistical ways of knowing] placed on people to classify things so that they could be counted and placed in an appropriate box on some official table, and more generally its impact on the character of the information people need to possess before they feel they understand something, are of the greatest interest and importance.'[10]

Census making and the statistical knowledges it sustains shape the field of intervention for administrative science and for political debate and opposition. Large-scale, systematic social observation gives access to orders of phenomena that transcend, but that may also determine, social relations in localities. In liberal democratic regimes, which are torn between intensive administrative domination and the preservation and extension of individual liberties, and in which the results of the investigation of large-scale regularities are more or less public knowledge, systematic observation creates scientific resources.

These resources are not exempt from the influences directing their creation, but neither are they entirely subordinate to them. They may be taken up by groups and individuals whose interests are quite different from those which guided their initial production, and reconfigured and enlisted in pursuit of projects not anticipated by (or even positively repugnant to) the initial purposes of observation. Access to statistical knowledges may create heightened possibilities for enlightened individual self-mastery. Yet the regime of statistical knowledge-power also extends dramatically the possibilities for political domination. The bulimic character of knowledge-producing agencies threatens to drown political subjects in an ocean of information. Abundance itself is a form of censorship.[11]

At the same time, matters of 'local interest' are relegated to the lower levels of the hierarchy of political knowledge. The novel forms of generality created when social relations are configured as population substitute new forms of particularity for matters of local interest. The numerical subdivision of the domain of population, and the creation of new objects of knowledge through cross-tabulation and other mechanisms for ordering and scaling census observations, cause new regularities to emerge. In the early regime of statistical knowledge of population, locality figures typically as deviation and variation from observable regularity. It serves as the target of administrative technologies that focus on optimization and risk management.

To assess the practical impact of statistical knowledge forms, then, we must attend both to the investments and infrastructural labours on which they depend, and to the diverse, competing, and potentially antagonistic projects on behalf of which such knowledges are taken up. We must attend to the ways in which meaning-making, selves, and self-understandings are transformed and specified. We must also attend to the distributions of resources for knowledge production and manipulation that make it possible for hegemonic groups and social classes to impose identifications on others against their struggles of resistance.

**Symbolic Government?**
To a certain extent, Michel Foucault's examination of 'governmentality,' which posits that population is the main object of rule in modern societies, is instructive for the investigation of census making, especially insofar as it suggests that we triangulate our investigations around sovereignty, discipline, and government. Census making does involve the assertion of sovereign authority. Imperial powers typically assert their authority to create inventories of newly conquered territory and resources. Insurgent bureaucracies interested in intensively administering social relations must establish and enforce equivalencies that make it possible to categorize and hence to locate relevant administrative objects. In class-divided societies, population can be analysed as the domain of universality.

Census making is also a disciplinary activity in the Foucauldian sense. It involves applying a grid to social relations, and tying human beings and their social relations and activities to particular identities. It involves the disciplinary techniques of partition and inscription, whereby objects and relations are laid out in tabular form, and ranked and ordered into 'cases,' and thus subjected to new forms of administrative legibility. 'Normalizing judgment,' which seeks to regulate objects and relations by containing them within a specified range of variation, is evident in such census-making practices as those which reassign human beings to what are considered to be their 'normal places.'

Finally, census making is clearly caught up in projects for the 'conduct of conduct,' in commands and exhortations to 'go here, now; do this, then; understand yourself and your destiny in this way.' These projects of government do not originate solely in the state system; they may emerge outside it and then attempt to invest it, as in the case of ultramontane Catholicism. Projects of government may also originate in the interest that individuals or groups develop in mastering their own social circumstances or in construing imaginaries of their own histories. Census making contributes to the formation of a new field of government, defined as matters of national importance, and multiplies the knowledge resources contained in this field. These resources are commonly public knowledge and may, in principle, be enlisted in many different governmental projects.

Foucault did not himself use the concepts implied in a 'governmentality' approach to investigate any empirical phenomenon, at least not in detail. The approach has been developed by other writers, who have interpreted it in a variety of ways. The limitations of some of these interpretations seem fairly clear, especially those which propose to focus on the articulations of 'rationalities' and 'technologies' of government. Such a focus deprives historical sociology of many of the elementary conceptual resources it requires to come to grips with concrete historical development. Most immediately, this way of posing questions of political power contains no analysis of institutions and structures. It banishes from analysis any notion of political capacities and their accumulation or concentration in the institutions of a state. Its theoretical 'problem-space' deprives political theories and political philosophies of their concrete historical conditions of emergence. It causes most of the real historical intellectuals and administrators who grappled with these theories and philosophies to disappear. It tends to present political rationalities as internally coherent and consistent. It presupposes a frictionless connection between the rationalities of government and the technologies of government that realize them (despite the insistence on the incompleteness of government). 'Governmentality,' I suggest, presents a set of conceptual abstractions that are useful for orienting some dimensions of inquiry, but it may also be used to problematize the making up of population in ways that do not allow us much purchase on the messy, inchoate, incoherent, and antagonistic practices and processes of census making. In its refusal to engage systematically with state formation, it 'naturalizes' population, ignoring the fact that it is a category of state.

I wish also to stress that while Foucault's work enabled us to gain invaluable insight into the positivity of power, against conceptions of power as repression, it did so at the cost of the ritual and symbolic dimensions of rule. In his *Discipline and Punish*, Foucault argued that with the rise of capitalism the spectacular, festive excesses of torture, characteristic of feudal regimes, were displaced by routinized practices of discipline, whose perfect model was Bentham's panopticon. He followed the same line of argument in *The History of Sexuality* (Volume 1) and related texts, in drawing the distinction between juridico-discursive and bio-political modes of power. For instance, 'as exercized in societies of the feudal type, power functioned, *grosso modo*, by means of signs and exactions. Signs of loyalty to the lord, rituals, ceremonies, and exactions of goods through taxation, pillage, the chase and warfare. Beginning in the 17th and 18th centuries, we find a power which begins to be exercised through production and the provision of services. It becomes a matter of deriving productive services from individuals in their material existence.'[12] As in many of Foucault's texts from this period, change in the form of power is a by-product of changes in the mode of extraction of surplus labour. But ritual and ceremonial elements of power were displaced from the analysis never to reappear. This displacement is doubly problematic.

It is problematic as a reading of some of the key texts on which Foucault's work relies. For example, 'speak to the eyes if you wish to move the heart ... the emblematic robes of the inquisition may be usefully applied to criminal justice. An incendiary clothed in a robe of pictured flames, would offer to every eye the image of his crime, and the indignation of the spectator would be fixed by the image of the offence. A system of punishments accompanied by emblems appropriate as far as possible to each offence, would have an additional advantage. It would furnish allusions to poetry, to eloquence, to dramatic authors, to ordinary conversation.'[13] The passage is Jeremy Bentham's, the promoter of the 'perfect machine of power.' For Bentham, there was no disjuncture or break between the festive and the disciplinary, between the routine and the ritualistic. The adequacy of punishment to crime is, in part at least, pictoral. Spectacle is an integral part of disciplinary power.

The displacement of the ritual, symbolic, and ceremonial deprives researchers of the means necessary to understand elements that remain central to the operation of relations of domination and exploitation in modern societies. Constructions of statistical monuments, struggles over social meanings and memories, antagonisms around social destinies, are opaque to a governmentality approach. So is the kind of fundamentalist Catholic pastoral implicated in census making when a politics of 'each and all' is paired to a fundamental antagonism to liberalism and capitalist luxury.[14]

Finally, and perhaps most important, if my analysis of population as an imaginary of proper places is correct, the investigation of political administration in a liberal mode of government must attend first, not to concerns with 'governing things as they are' or with 'governing too much,' but rather with the practical specification of how things are to be so that they may be ruled.[15]

## The Population of Canada

Census making in mid-nineteenth-century Canada was inextricably bound up with social struggles and antagonisms around ethnic-linguistic, religious, and political destinies, although little scholarly attention has been devoted to this. Social historians have used census data as black-boxed resources for addressing particular empirical questions, sometimes uneasily but on the whole without systematically considering how their sources actually emerged.

This book has shown that the rich 'manuscript' Canadian census records compiled before 1871 were based on unregulated observational protocols applied to ill-defined objects. What survives as 'manuscript' records is usually the product of several reworkings of what enumerators learned from informants in the field. In such field encounters, common interests and understandings often did not prevail. The surviving manuscript material was 'corrected' and 'reduced to uniformity' by census administrators. However well-intentioned these people were, they usually left no means for later researchers to reconstruct the criteria they employed in transforming enumerators' recordings of informants' reports.

Except in those cases where it is possible to reconstruct observational and post-observational protocols, modern-day researchers should not have any confidence in the scientific character of the official aggregate returns. The mid-nineteenth-century censuses remain rich sources for historians and historical sociologists, but they are ill-suited to provide quantitative evidence for examinations of large-scale social patterns. That they are often the best available source is a thin justification for relying on materials that were generated so haphazardly.

The book also suggests that scepticism is in order in the face of the commonly repeated claim that nineteenth-century census enumerations failed to register the presence of large numbers of inhabitants of the enumerated territory. The evidence suggests that mixed *de facto* and *de jure* enumeration principles resulted in the multiple recording of names of inhabitants. Compilation practices ensured that the numbers given as the aggregate population included such multiply recorded names. It follows that care should be taken to avoid confusing artefacts of the modalities of census investigations with empirically existing social relations. Even the most consistently executed census of population depends on a particular imaginary of human beings in virtual time and space. It disciplines empirical social relations in order to capture them in the confines of its grid.

The 1871 census of Canada, in contrast to those which preceded it, is a model of nineteenth-century social scientific observation, and a fascinating instance of the nesting of feudal paternalism in scientific rationalism. There was nothing of this degree of sophistication taking place elsewhere in Canada in the period – not in the few universities, not in capitalist enterprise, not in the activities of private associations, and not elsewhere in the state system. The 1871 census was experimental social science that profited from extensive investigation of prior census-making practice. It involved heuristic exercises intended to chart the limitations of past efforts, field trials of enumeration schedules, extensive training of officials, and remarkable infrastructural work and formal investments. Its 'manuscript' materials may reliably be seen as original transcriptions of informants' disciplined accounts. Corrections in the field and after the fact remain visible on the census schedules themselves.

**Calculating Canadians**

It is remarkable as well that this scientific effort was tributary to a fundamentalist Catholic national-ethnic-linguistic imaginary, one that enlisted state power and rational social-scientific practice against Protestant liberalism and urban, capitalist luxury and demoralization. The political utopia promoted by Joseph-Charles Taché left Protestants and anglophones to pursue perdition with all the enthusiasm at their command. The destiny of francophone Catholics was to cultivate the land under the social, political, and religious hegemony of the clergy, to multiply, and to civilize the North American continent.

The census was one tactic in a larger strategy for constructing a franco-Catholic nationality by establishing a cultural *cordon sanitaire*. French Canadians would flourish in the countryside, safe from the infections of the liberal capitalist cities. Colonization projects would allow for growth in their numbers. In Taché's own version of the project, a French-Canadian literature would provide wholesome food for the imagination, and education in scientific agriculture would provide the basis for economic comfort, with the surplus product supporting the clergy. Even his version, however, contained an insistence on the stupefaction of the masses; agricultural routine would substitute for rational appreciation of religious ethics. Peasants could not be trusted to guard themselves against the dangers of the city; they were not to be delivered unto temptation.

Versions of this oppressive project reverberate through Canadian history over the last two centuries. Able to dominate their opponents from the mid-1850s onwards, conservative state-church alliances shaped the destiny of the great majority of French Canadians for more than a century. These alliances survived the Second World War, despite rising opposition, only to implode dramatically with Quebec's 'Quiet Revolution' of the early 1960s. The latter displaced the Catholic church, transformed ethnic nationalism into a civil religion, and pulled the frontiers of the imagined national community back to those of the boundaries of the would-be sovereign Quebec provincial territory.

Taché's 1871 census provided resources for the fundamentalist project. It reassigned migrants to the countryside and bolstered the electoral fortunes of Quebec. It performed part of the ideological work that undepinned ultramontane claims about the close relationships among Catholicism, agrarianism, and ethnic-national survival. It foretold extinction for aboriginal peoples who did not adopt Christian civilization. At the same time, the census's sustained refusal to allow informants to identify themselves as 'Canadians' worked to limit the emergence of an alternative civic nationalism. This refusal created a condition under which 'the Canadian population' could appear as an administrative abstraction laid on top of identities defined otherwise – a fundamental feature of nationalist identity politics as fought out in contemporary Quebec.

Perhaps most remarkable is Joseph-Charles Taché's success in embedding his political project deep in the foundations of a Canadian statistical monument. By casting his politics of population in the mould of scientific fact, Taché ensured that they would continue to bear witness as seemingly neutral numbers.

# Notes

**Introduction: The 'Eyes of Politics'**

1 Libby Schweber, 'L'histoire de la statistique, laboratoire pour la théorie sociale,' *Revue française de sociologie* 37(1), 1996: 107–28. See also Max Weber, *Economy and Society* (Berkeley and Los Angeles: University of California Press, 1978), II: 972, 'the "intensity" of the administration, that is, the assumption of as many tasks as possible by the state apparatus for continuous management and discharge in its own establishment.'
2 Margo J. Anderson, in *The American Census: A Social History* (New Haven, Conn.: Yale University Press, 1988), provides the most extensive monographic treatment. Most of those who work with empirical questions for which census data are evidence have been content with more guidelike accounts; among the best of these is Edward Higgs, *Making Sense of the Census: The Manuscript Returns for England and Wales, 1801–1901*, Public Record Office Handbooks No. 23. (London: HMSO, 1989). See also M. Drake, 'The Census, 1801–1901' in E.A. Wrigley, ed., *Nineteenth-Century Society: Essays in the Use of Quantitative Methods for the Study of Social Data* (Cambridge: Cambridge University Press, 1972): 7–46; Jacques Dupâquier and Michel Dupâquier, *Histoire de la démographie. La statistique de la population des origines à 1914* (Paris: Librairie Académique Perrin, 1985); and D.V. Glass, *Numbering the People: The Eighteenth-Century Population Controversy and the Development of Census and Vital Statistics in Britain* (Farnborough, Hants.: Saxon House, 1973).
3 On American debate, see Margo J. Anderson and Stephen E. Fienberg, *Who Counts? The Politics of Census-Taking in Contemporary America* (New York: Russell Sage Foundation, 1999); Harvey M. Choldin, *Looking for the Last Percent. The Controversy over Census Undercounts* (New Brunswick, N.J.: Rutgers

University Press, 1994); and Kenneth Draga, *Sampling and the Census: A Case against the Proposed Adjustments for Undercount* (Washington: The American Enterprise Press, 1999). Recent Canadian debate has surrounded census categories such as 'same sex spouse,' as opposed to sampling and enumeration technique; this reflects the different role of the census here. I am not writing in support of the critique of a sample survey. See also Michel Foucault, *Discipline and Punish* (New York: Pantheon, 1979).

4 Sylvana Patriarca, *Numbers and Nationhood: Writing Statistics in Nineteenth-Century Italy* (Cambridge: Cambridge University Press, 1996); but compare Jean-Pierre Beaud and Jean-Guy Prévost, 'La forme est le fond: La structuration des appareils statistiques nationaux (1800–1945),' *Revue de synthèse* 4e S.4 1997: 419–56.

5 It would be impossible to be exhaustive, but see among others Patricia Cline Cohen, *A Calculating People: The Spread of Numeracy in Early America* (Chicago: University of Chicago Press, 1982); Michael J. Cullen, *The Statistical Movement in Early Victorian Britain* (New York: Harvester, 1975); Theodore Porter, *The Rise of Statistical Thinking 1820–1900* (Princeton: Princeton University Press, 1986); *Trust in Numbers. The Pursuit of Objectivity in Science and Public Life* (Princeton: Princeton University Press, 1996); Mary Poovey, *Making a Social Body: British Cultural Formation, 1830–1864* (Chicago: University of Chicago Press, 1995); and Nikolas Rose, 'Governing by Numbers: Figuring out Democracy,' *Accounting, Organizations and Society* 16, 1991: 673–92.

6 See Bruce Curtis, *True Government by Choice Men? Inspection, Education and State Formation in Canada West* (Toronto: University of Toronto Press, 1992); see also 'The State of Tutelage in Lower Canada, 1835–55,' *History of Education Quarterly* 37(1), 1997: 25–43.

7 Cited in Patriarca, *Numbers and Nationhood*: 41. The preceding account is overly schematized, but I have worked out the dimensions of the transition more fully elsewhere. See Curtis, 'Administrative Infrastructure and Social Enquiry: Finding the Facts about Agriculture in Quebec, 1853–4,' *Journal of Social History* 32(2), 1998: 309–28; 'Mapping the Social: Jacob Keefer's Educational Tour, 1845,' *Journal of Canadian Studies* 28(2), 1993: 51–68; and 'Révolution gouvernementale et savoir politique au Canada-Uni,' *Sociologie et Sociétés* XXIV, 1992: 169–179. For the point about masses of material, see Bruce Curtis, 'Selective Publicity and Informed Public Opinion in the Canadas, 1841–1856,' *History of Education Review* 27(1), 1998: 1–19; and 'Official Documentary Systems and Colonial Governance: Towards Colonial Autonomy in the Canadas,' *Journal of Historical Sociology* 10(4), 1997: 389–417. On cultural transformation, see Cohen, *A Calculating People*; and Porter, *Statistical Thinking*.

8 See for instance, Max Weber, *Economy and Society: An Outline of Interpretive Sociology* (Berkeley: University of California Press, 1978), I: 551–6; and Robert K. Merton, *Science, Technology and Society in Seventeenth Century England* (London: Fertig, 1970).
9 M.C. Urquhart, 'Three Builders of Canada's Statistical System,' *Canadian Historical Review* 68(3), 1987: 414–5; R.H. Coats, 'Beginnings in Canadian Statistics,' *Canadian Historical Review* 27, 1946: 114. David A. Worton, in *The Dominion Bureau of Statistics: A History of Canada's Central Statistical Office, 1841–1972* (Montreal and Kingston: McGill-Queen's University Press, 1998), devotes only a very few pages to the period before 1871, does not mention Walter Crofton at all, and cites only a printed document by William Hutton, whom he does not identify.
10 I am thinking especially of Evelyn Bossé, *Joseph-Charles Taché: Un grand représentant de l'élite canadienne-française* (Québec: Éditions Garneau, 1971).
11 E.A. Wrigley, ed., *Identifying People in the Past* (London: Edward Arnold, 1973): 1.
12 Michael B. Katz, *The People of Hamilton, Canada West. Family and Class in a Mid-Nineteenth-Century City* (Cambridge: Harvard University Press, 1975): 8–10.
13 See the discussion in the introduction to Franca Iacovetta and Wendy Mitchinson eds., *On the Case: Explorations in Social History* (Toronto: University of Toronto Press, 1998).
14 I detail some of the important exceptions to my remarks here in Bruce Curtis, 'On the Local Construction of Statistical Knowledge: Making up the Census of the Canadas, 1861,' *Journal of Historical Sociology* 10(4) 1994: 416–34.
15 The first wave of the accuracy literature did yield some work – for instance, Alan A. Brookes, '"Doing the Best I Can": The Taking of the 1861 New Brunswick Census,' *Histoire sociale/ Social History* 9, 1976: 70–91; and regarding methodology, David P. Gagan, 'Enumerator's Instructions for the Census of Canada 1852 and 1861,' *Histoire sociale/ Social History* 8(16), 1974: 355–65. For an additional recent account of census making, see Patrick A. Dunae, 'Making the 1891 Census in British Columbia,' *Histoire sociale/ Social History* 31 (62), 1998: 223–41.
16 On the metric system, see Witold Kula, *Measures and Men* (Princeton: Princeton University Press, 1986); and Bruce Curtis, 'From the Moral Thermometer to Money: Metrological Reform in Pre-Confederation Canada,' *Social Studies of Science* 28(4), 1998: 547–70. On the Bureau de Statistique, see Marie-Noëlle Bourguet, *Déchiffrer la France. La statistique*

*départementale à l'époque napoléonienne* (Paris, 1988), and 'Décrire, Compter, Calculer: The Debate over Statistics during the Napoleonic Period,' in Lorenz Krüger et al, eds., *The Probabilistic Revolution. Vol. 1: Ideas in History* (Cambridge: MIT Press, 1990): 305–16; Stuart J. Woolf, 'Towards the History of the Origins of Statistics: France, 1789–1815,' in J.-C. Perron and Stuart J. Woolf, eds., *State and Statistics in France 1789–1815* (Amsterdam: Harwood Academic Publishers, 1984): 81–194. For Milan, see Olivier Faron, 'L'ordre statistique: Sur l'usage politique d'un registre démographique à Milan au XIXe siècle,' *Revue d'histoire moderne et contemporaine* 36, 1989: 586–606.

17 Ian Hacking, 'Biopower and the Avalanche of Printed Numbers,' *Humanities in Society* 5, 1982: 279–95; 'flood' from Porter, *Statistical Thinking*; 'cult' from Woolf, *State and Statistics*.

18 Alain Desrosières, 'How to Make Things'; see also 'Comment faire des choses qui tiennent: Histoire sociale et statistique,' *Histoire et Mesure* 4(3/4) 1989: 225–42.

19 John Powell, *Statistical Illustrations of the Territorial Extent and Population, Rental, Taxation, Finances, Commerce, Consumption, Insolvency, Pauperism, and Crime of the British Empire. Compiled for and Published by Order of the London Statistical Society*, 3rd ed. (London: Effingham Wilson, 1827).

20 See Lucy Brown, *The Board of Trade and the Free-Trade Movement, 1830–42* (Oxford: Clarendon Press, 1958): 76ff. Brown claims that the branch was formed before the societies, giving the lie to claims that the latter were at the origins of statistical practice in England; see also M.J. Cullen, *The Statistical Movement in Early Victorian Britain* (Brighton: Harvester, 1975). On the statistical societies, see T.S. Ashton, *Economic and Social Investigations in Manchester, 1833–1933. A Centenary History of the Manchester Statistical Society* (1934; reprint, Brighton: Harvester Press, 1977); David Elesh, 'The Manchester Statistical Society: A Case Study of a Discontinuity in the History of Empirical Social Research,' *Journal of the History of the Behavioural Sciences* 8, 1972: 280–301, 407–17; V.L. Hilts, '*Aliis exterendum*, or, the Origins of the Statistical Society of London,' *Isis* 69, 1978: 21–43; and Council of the Royal Statistical Society, *Annals of the Royal Statistical Society, 1834–1934* (London: The Royal Statistical Society, 1934).

21 For English census making, see M. Drake, 'The Census, 1801–1901' in Wrigley (Ed.), *Nineteenth-century Society*: 7–46; Glass, *Numbering the People*; and Higgs, *Making Sense of the Census*.

22 For more on Kennedy, Shattuck, and the American Statistical Association, see Anderson, *American Census*; James H. Cassedy, *American Medicine and Statistical Thinking, 1800–1860* (Cambridge, Mass.: Harvard University Press, 1984); and Cohen, *A Calculating People*.

23 Dupâquier and Dupâquier, *Histoire de la démographie*, 229ff; for the later period, see Éric Brian, 'Statistique administrative et internationalisme statistique pendant la seconde moitié du XIXe siècle,' *Histoire et mesure* 3/4, 1989: 201–24.
24 The Rawson-Quetelet link is detailed in Jean-Pierre Beaud and Jean-Guy Prévost, '"Back to Quételet,"' *Recherches sociologiques* 2, 1998: 83–100. For the office of Civil Secretary, see Bruce Curtis, 'Official Documentary Systems and Colonial Governance: Towards Colonial Autonomy in the Canadas,' *Journal of Historical Sociology* 10(4), 1997: 389–417.
25 For a detailed overview of the fourth Congress, see William Farr, ed., *Report of the Proceedings of the Fourth Session of the International Statistical Congress, Held in London July 16th 1860, and the Five Following Days* (London: HMSO, 1861); see also Martha Vicinus and Bea Nergaard, eds., *Ever Yours, Florence Nightingale: Selected Letters* (London: Virago 1989): 207, for her contributions to the Congress, and, more generally, F.B. Smith, *Florence Nightingale: Reputation and Power* (London: Croom Helm, 1982). A popular topic at the Paris Congress in 1855 was criminal statistics; see Congrès international de la statistique, *Rapport sur la statistique des établissements pénitentiaires* par M Paul Bucquet (Paris: Boucha-Huzard,1856).

**1: Making up Population**

1 Benedict Anderson, *Imagined Communities: Reflections on the Origin and Spread of Nationalism*, 2nd ed. (London: Verso, 1991): 166.
2 See Michel Foucault, *Discipline and Punish: The Birth of the Prison* (New York: Pantheon, 1979).
3 The example is from George Emery's *Facts of Life: The Social Construction of Vital Statistics in Ontario, 1869–1952* (Montreal and Kingston: McGill-Queen's University Press, 1993); see also his 'Ontario's Civil Registration of Vital Statistics, 1869–1926: The Evolution of an Administrative System,' *Canadian Historical Review* 64(4), 1983: 468–93.
4 Such representations may be theoretical in a weak sense, but as Ian Hacking puts it, 'We represent in order to intervene, and we intervene in the light of representations.' See *Representing and Intervening: Introductory Topics in the Philosophy of Natural Science* (Cambridge: Cambridge University Press, 1983): 31.
5 As Anderson and Fienberg show in *Who Counts?* sampling is seen as particularly vulnerable to partisan political manipulation in the United States; see also Alain Desrosières, 'The Part in Relation to the Whole? How to Generalise. A Prehistory of Representative Sampling,' in M. Bulmer et al., eds., *The Social Survey in Historical Perspective, 1880–1940* (Cambridge: Cambridge

University Press, 1991): 217–44; and especially the suggestion that checks on the 'accuracy' of the census can best be done before it is undertaken in William N. Hurwitz, Morris H. Hansen, and Leon Pritzker, 'The Accuracy of Census Results,' *American Sociological Review* 18, 1953: 416–23.

6 Dupâquier and Dupâquier, *Histoire de la démographie*: 92–3. The multiplier was 28.35 times the number of live births.

7 Stephan Fuchs, 'The New Wars of Truth: Conflicts over Science Studies as Differential Modes of Observation,' *Social Science Information* 35(2), 1996: 307–26.

8 B. Latour, *Science in Action: How to Follow Scientists and Engineers Through Society* (Milton Keynes: Open University Press, 1987). For an accessible and comprehensive overview of Latour's work, see Steven C. Ward, *Reconfiguring Truth: Postmodernism, Science Studies and the Search for a New Model of Knowledge* (Lanham, Md.: Rowman & Littlefield, 1996).

9 For an elaboration and illustration of 'investment,' see Bruce Curtis, 'Social Investment in Medical Forms: The 1866 Cholera Scare and Beyond,' *Canadian Historical Review* 81(4), 2000; Alain Desrosières, 'How to Make Things Which Hold Together: Social Science, Statistics and the State,' in P. Wittrock, B. Wagner, and R. Whitley, eds., *Discourses on Society. The Shaping of the Social Science Disciplines* (Dordrecht, 1991): 195–218; *La politique des grands nombres: Histoire de la raison statistique.* (Paris: La Découverte, 1993); Ian Hacking, *The Taming of Chance* (Cambridge: Cambridge University Press, 1990); and Laurent Thévenot, 'Rules and Implements: Investment in Forms,' *Social Science Information* 23(1), 1984: 1–45. Thévenot's initial formulation is not particularly clear, but the concept of investment in forms has been absorbed by the science studies literature.

10 See especially Bruno Latour, 'Visualization and Cognition: Thinking with Eyes and Hands,' *Knowledge and Society: Studies in the Sociology of Culture Past and Present* 6, 1986: 1–40. See also 'The Impact of Science Studies on Political Philosophy,' *Science, Technology and Human Values* 16, 1991: 3–19; and *We Have Never Been Modern* (Cambridge, Mass.: Harvard University Press, 1993).

11 For more on infrastructural work, see Geoffrey Bowker, *Science on the Run: Information Management and Industrial Geophysics at Schlumberger, 1920–1940* (Cambridge: MIT Press, 1994): 52–4, 167.

12 Paul Starr, 'The Sociology of Official Statistics,' in William Alonso and Paul Starr, eds., *The Politics of Numbers* (New York: Russell Sage Foundation, 1987): 33–47.

13 The official compendium used by a generation of Canadian economic historians, K.A.H. Buckley and M.C. Urquhart, *Historical Statistics of Canada*

(Toronto: Macmillan, 1965) makes such a claim about the 1852 and 1861 censuses; and the assumption about 'underenumeration' reappears, for instance, in Gordon Darroch, 'Small Fortunes and Rural Middle-Class Formation in Nineteenth-Century Rural Ontario,' *Canadian Historical Review* 79(4), 1998: 621–59, where we read, 'We know that underenumeration was relatively high in all nineteenth-century censuses' (p. 639). I argue in the body of the book that such views are questionable for Canada, although I do not propose that there is a 'true' population number that censuses reveal more or less well.

14 Quoted in Margo J. Anderson and Stephen E. Fienberg, *Who Counts? The Politics of Census-Taking in Contemporary America* (New York: Russell Sage Foundation, 1999): 42.

15 For instance, John W. Adams and Alice Bee Kasakoff, 'Estimates of Census Underenumeration Based on Genealogies,' *Social Science History* 15(4), 1991: 527–43; Donald A. DeBats, 'Hide and Seek: The Historian and Nineteenth Century Social Accounting,' *Social Science History* 15(4), 1991: 545–63; F. Furstenberg, D. Strong, and A. Crawford, 'What Happened When the Census Was Re-done: An Analysis of the Recount of 1870 in Philadelphia,' *Sociology and Social Research* 63, 1979: 475–503; Caren A. Ginsberg, 'Estimates and Correlates of Enumeration Completeness: Censuses and Maps in Nineteenth-Century Massachusetts,' *Social Science History* 12(1), 1988: 71–86; Peter R. Knights, 'Potholes in the Road of Improvement? Estimating Census Underenumeration by Longitudinal Tracing: U.S. Censuses, 1850–1880,' *Social Science History* 15(4), 1991: 516–26; D.H. Parkerson, 'Comments on the Underenumeration of the U.S. Census, 1850–1880,' *Social Science History* 15(4), 1991: 509–15; J.B. Sharpless and R.M. Shortridge, 'Biased Underenumeration in Census Manuscripts: Methodological Implications,' *Journal of Urban History* 1, 1975: 409–39; R.H. Steckel, 'Census Matching and Migration: A Research Strategy,' *Historical Methods Newsletter* 21, 1988: 52–60; and 'The Quality of Census Data for Historical Inquiry: A Research Agenda,' *Social Science History* 15(4), 1991: 579–99; and P.M. Tillott, 'Sources of Inaccuracy in the 1851 and 1861 Censuses,' in E.A. Wrigley (Ed.), *Nineteenth-Century Society: Essays in the Use of Quantitative Methods for the Study of Social Data* (Cambridge: Cambridge University Press, 1972): 82–133.

16 Desrosières in 'How to Make Things' does point out that state power lies between the establishment of equivalences inherent in statistical knowledge, but he does not pursue this observation. Anderson in *Imagined Communities* and Patriarca in *Numbers and Nationhood* attend to identity formation. Starr in 'Official Statistics' writes of a form of tribute. See also

Norbert Elias, 'The Retreat of Sociologists into the Present,' in Volker Meja et al, eds., *Modern German Sociology* (New York: Columbia University Press, 1987): 150–72.

17 Philip Abrams, 'Notes on the Difficulty of Studying the State,' *Journal of Historical Sociology* 1(1), 1988: 57–84; Philip Corrigan and Derek Sayer, *The Great Arch: English State Formation as Cultural Revolution* (Oxford: Blackwell, 1985); Bruce Curtis, 'Moving beyond the Great Abstraction: Abrams and Foucault on the State and Government,' *Les cahiers d'histoire* 17(2), 1997: 9–18; 'Reworking Moral Regulation: Metaphorical Capital and the Field of Disinterest,' *Canadian Journal of Sociology* 22(3), 1997: 303–18; 'Taking the State Back Out: Rose and Miller on Political Power,' *British Journal of Sociology* 46(4), 1995: 575–89; Mitchell Dean, *Critical and Effective Histories: Foucault's Methods and Historical Sociology* (New York: Routledge, 1994); and Lorna Weir and Mariana Valverde, 'Struggles of the Immoral: Preliminary Remarks on Moral Regulation,' *Resources for Feminist Research* 17(3), 1988: 31–4.

18 The essay circulated in a variety of versions before appearing in *Folk* 26, 1984: 25–49. Widely reprinted, it appears in B.S. Cohn, *An Anthropologist among the Historians and Other Essays* (Delhi: Oxford University Press, 1985): 224–54.

19 B.S. Cohn, *Colonialism and Its Forms of Knowledge: The British in India* (Princeton: Princeton University Press, 1996): 1–17; see also B.S. Cohn and Nicholas Dirks, 'Beyond the Fringe: The Nation State, Colonialism, and the Technologies of Power,' *Journal of Historical Sociology* 1(2), 1988: 224–9.

20 Mitchell Dean, in *The Constitution of Poverty: Towards a Genealogy of Liberal Governance* (London: Routledge, 1991): 33, notes Foucault's mistaken interpretation of population in the eighteenth century, but does not pursue this critique. The bibliography of 'govermentality' is expanding rapidly. By way of example, see Robert Castel, 'From Dangerousness to Risk,' and Colin Gordon, 'Governmental Rationality: An Introduction,' in Graham Burchell et al, eds., *The Foucault Effect: Studies in Governmentality* (Chicago: University of Chicago Press, 1991): 281–98; 1–51; and Lorna Weir, 'Recent Developments in the Government of Pregnancy,' *Economy and Society* 25(3), 1996: 373–92. For more critical accounts, see George Steinmetz, *Regulating the Social: The Welfare State and Local Politics in Imperial Germany* (Princeton: Princeton University Press, 1993); and Pat O'Malley, 'Risk and Responsibility,' in A. Barry et al, eds., *Foucault and Political Reason* (London: UCL Press, 1996): 189–207.

21 Michel Foucault, 'Governmentality,' in Graham Burchell et al, eds., *The Foucault Effect: Studies in Governmentality* (Chicago: University of Chicago Press, 1991): 98.

22 Michel Foucault, 'Les mailles du pouvoir,' in *Dits et écrits*, Tome IV (Paris: Gallimard, 1994): 182–201; quotations at 193–4, my emphasis. All translations from the French in the book are mine. This fascinating and little-known text credits Karl Marx's *Capital*, Volume II, with the discovery of the essential nature of power in modern society and absolves him from charges of state determinism in his analysis!

23 Michel Foucault, *Résumé des cours, 1970–1982* (Paris: Juillard, 1989): 104.

24 Michel Foucault, 'Governmentality': 101.

25 See, for instance the essays in the special issue of *Economy and Society* 22(3), 1993, many of whose themes are reprised in Barry et al, eds., *Foucault and Political Reason*. Among those sceptical of discontinuity are Barry Hindess, 'Liberalism, Socialism and Democracy: Variations on a Governmental Theme,' and Alan Hunt, 'Governing the City: Liberalism and Early Modern Modes of Governance,' in *Foucault and Political Reason*: 65–80; 167–88. See also O'Malley et al., 'Governmentality, Criticism, Politics.' The empirical case presented in Henry E. Lowood, 'The Calculating Forester: Quantification, Cameral Science, and the Emergence of Scientific Forest Management in Germany,' in Tore Frängsmyr et al, eds., *The Quantifying Spirit in the 18th Century* (Berkeley: University of California Press, 1990): 315–42, may appear quaint, but the demonstration that cameral science produced the abstraction 'the standard tree' and that forestry practice remade real forests in terms of it is theoretically significant. Conceptually, there is not much distance between this abstraction and Quetelet's 'average man,' who is central to the government of population.

26 For the quote, see Peter Miller and Nikolas Rose, 'Governing Economic Life,' *Economy and Society* 19(1), 1990: 1–31; also, Bruce Curtis, 'Taking the State Back Out: Rose and Miller on Political Power,' *British Journal of Sociology* 46(4), 1995: 575–89.

27 For instance, Dean, in *Critical and Effective Histories:* 180, notes the incoherence, and charitably presents Foucault as grappling with the problem of the state, but then proceeds to write of the state as an actor. It is not as if Foucault had to invent an analysis of the state from scratch!

28 Foucault describes his 'governmentality' lectures as his attempt to make sense of the state in the revealing 'Méthodologie pour la connaissance du monde: comment se débarrasser du marxisme,' *Dits et écrits* (Paris: Gallimard, 1994), III: 595–618; the remark about the king's head is in *The History of Sexuality, Volume 1* (New York: Random House, 1978): 88–9; the argument is repeated in the English context by Nikolas Rose and Peter Miller, 'Political Power beyond the State: Problematics of Government,' *British Journal of Sociology* 43(2): 173–205. For a telling critique of the ab-

sence of a theory of administration in Foucault, see Mark Neocleous, *Administering Civil Society: Towards a Theory of State Power* (London: Macmillan, 1996); unfortunately, Neocleous offers an instrumentalist view of the state that is not helpful.
29 M.T. Clanchy, *From Memory to Written Record: England, 1066–1307* (London: Edward Arnold, 1979); 'Literacy, Law, and the Power of the State,' in CNRS et L'École française de Rome, *Culture et idéologie dans la genèse de l'état moderne* (Rome, 1985): 25–34; and Corrigan and Sayer, *Great Arch*; Dupâquier and Dupâquier, *Histoire de la démographie.*
30 Karl Marx, *Capital*, vol. 1 (New York: International Publishers, 1967).
31 Cases where it is blocked as a practice until much later are also revealing; see for instance A. Kim Clark, 'Race, 'Culture' and Mestizaje: The Statistical Construction of the Ecuadorian Nation, 1930–1950,' *Journal of Historical Sociology* 11(2), 1998: 185–211; Roger Owen, 'The Population Census of 1917 and its Relationship to Egypt's Three 19th Century Statistical Regimes,' *Journal of Historical Sociology* 9(4), 1996: 457–72; and Lisandro and Perez, 'The Political Contexts of Cuban Population Censuses, 1899–1981,' *Latin American Research Review* 19(2), 1984: 143–61.

**2: The First Experiments**

1 See Brian Young, 'Positive Law, Positive State: Class Realignment and the Transformation of Lower Canada, 1815–1866,' in A. Greer and I. Radforth, eds., *Colonial Leviathan: State Formation in Mid-Nineteenth-Century Canada* (Toronto: University of Toronto Press, 1992): 50–63; on the insurrection generally, see Allan Greer, *The Patriots and the People: The Rebellion of 1837 in Lower Canada* (Toronto: University of Toronto Press, 1993).
2 Philip Lawson, 'A Perspective on British History and the Treatment of the Conquest of Quebec,' *Journal of Historical Sociology* 3(3), 1990: 253–71.
3 Bruce Curtis, 'The Canada "Blue Books" and the Administrative Capacity of the Canadian State, 1822–67,' *Canadian Historical Review* 74(4), 1993: 535–65; 'Official Documentary Systems and Colonial Government: From Imperial Sovereignty to Colonial Autonomy in the Canadas,' *Journal of Historical Sociology* 10(4), 1997: 389–417.
4 John Garner, *The Franchise and Politics in British North America 1755–1867* (Toronto: University of Toronto Press, 1969): 92–104. I follow his account closely here.
5 It is beyond the scope of my concerns to deal with the inequities produced by the disenfranchisement of women and those who did not meet the property qualification.

6 *Le Canadien*, 4, 6, 13 May 1840; my use of newspaper accounts throughout is informed by the multivolume André Beaulieu, Jean Hamelin, et al. (Eds.), *La presse québécoise. Des origines à nos jours* (Québec: PUL, 1985).
7 Reprinted in *Le Canadien*, 6 May 1840.
8 Their duties had been extended by Upper Canada *Statutes* 59 Geo. III cap.7, although the act doesn't mention population returns.
9 Upper Canada, *Statutes*, 4 Geo. IV c.7.
10 J.L.H. Henderson, ed., *John Strachan: Documents and Opinions* (Toronto: McClelland and Stewart, 1969); G.W. Spragge, 'Elementary Education in Upper Canada, 1820–1840,' *Ontario History* 43(3), 1951: 107–22.
11 The original text of the report is copied in National Archives of Canada (NAC) CO42/476, 2 March 1841, with the census section pp. 64ff. Macaulay applied multipliers to population figures to estimate tea tax.
12 Upper Canada Legislative Assembly, *Sessional Papers*, 13$^{th}$ Parl. 5$^{th}$ sess., 'Report of Select Committee on Population Returns,' 1839.
13 Lower Canada, *Statutes*, 6 Will. IV cap.40: 'such Census shall be confined to the mere enumeration of the inhabitants without distinction of age or sex, or any distinction whatever.'
14 Lower Canada, *Statutes*, 1 Geo. IV c.I: 'An act for ascertaining the population of the several counties in this province and for obtaining certain Statistical information therein mentioned.' Notice that the county as an administrative unit had a precarious existence.
15 NAC CO42/476, 2 March 1841.
16 For example, NAC RG17 A I 2, May to Belleau, 1 April 1862, has the chief census clerk in Registration and Statistics informing the Minister of Agriculture that 'the population of Upper Canada in 1841 was ascertained by Census to be 465.367. Hence it would follow that the population for Lower Canada in 1841 was 624.633.' J.-C. Taché's official reconstruction, *Census of Canada. 1665 to 1871. Recensements du Canada. Statistics of Canada. Statistiques du Canada. Volume IV* (Ottawa: J.B. Taylor, 1876), gave the figures 487,053 for Canada West in 1842 and 697,084 for Canada East in 1844.
17 NAC RG4 A1 vol. 604, Prothonotary, Montreal district to Murdoch, 14 March 1840; Prothonotary, Quebec district to Murdoch, 30 March 1840.
18 For instance, NAC CO42/662 no. 84, Michell to Buckingham, 12 June 1867, enclosing Johnson to Meredith, 31 May 1867. Johnson, the chief statistical clerk at Agriculture, explains that there are no indexes to the civil registers and that to find an individual one must know the religious denomination and parish involved. This example is quite late, but there are others in the 1840s where a Canadian governor is asked by an imperial official to locate a particular individual immigrant.

19 *Le Canadien*, 3 December 1841; see also, *La Minerve*, 19 July 1841.
20 For the attempt to make the district councils work in the Eastern Townships, see J.I. Little, *State and Society in Transition: The Politics of Institutional Reform in the Eastern Townships, 1838–1852* (Montreal and Kingston: McGill-Queen's University Press, 1997): 125–50.
21 *La Minerve*, 13, 29 December 1842; 5, 9, 16 January; 18 November, 1843; *Le Canadien*, 18 May 1843. See also NAC CO42/504 no. 23, Bagot to Stanley, 18 February 1843, with the results of Dr Douglas's enumeration of the Gaspé; RG1 E1 Canada State Book B, 7 March 1843, cabinet's refusal to enforce the law; and Canada State Book C, 1 April 1844, refusal to pay enumerators.
22 *Le Canadien*, 20 September 1843.
23 NAC CO42/513 no. 26, Metcalfe to Stanley, 27 January 1844.
24 Parliament of Canada, Legislative Council, *Journals*, 18 November 1843. 'Serious attention was paid to the proposed schedules by a special committee of the Legislative Council, which suggested amendments and improvements.' No account of the discussions in council has survived. In their instructive analysis of changing census age categories, Beaud and Prévost suggest that there are Malthusian echoes here. See Jean-Pierre Beaud and Jean-Guy Prévost, 'Models for Recording Age in 1692–1851 Canada: The Political-Cognitive Functions of Census Statistics,' *Scientia Canadensis* 18, 2, 1994: 136–51.
25 See J.-P. Beaud and J.-G. Prévost, '"Back to Quételet,"' *Recherches sociologiques* 2, 1998: 83–100, and Bruce Curtis, 'Official Documentary Systems,' for more on Rawson's time in Canada. For Quetelet, see, for instance, Bibliothèque Nationale Française, m794, for a work dated c.1827 on vital statistics, and M.A. Quetelet, *A Treatise on Man and the Development of his Faculties* (Edinburgh: Chambers, 1842), reprinted in *Comparative Statistics in the 19$^{th}$ Century* (n.p.: Gregg International Publishers, 1973). For the library, Gilles Gallichan, *Livre et politique au Bas-Canada, 1791–1849* (Québec: Septentrion, 1991).
26 For the connection between the English census and medical government, see Edward Higgs, 'Disease, Febrile Poisons, and Statistics: The Census as a Medical Survey, 1841–1911,' *The Social History of Medicine and Allied Sciences* 43, 1991: 465–78; and more generally, John M. Eyler, *Victorian Social Medicine: The Ideas and Methods of William Farr* (Baltimore: The Johns Hopkins University Press, 1979).
27 See 7 Vic. cap.XXIV, 'Acte pour faire le recensement des habitans du Bas-Canada, et pour obtenir certains renseignements statistiques y mentionnés.'
28 *Le Canadien*, 19 February 1844. The complete list of fifty-two commissioners' appointments was gazetted on 1 March 1844.

29 Signed 'un commissaire' in *La Minerve*, 29 February 1844; reprinted in *Le Canadien* 4 March 1844.
30 *Le Canadien*, 18 March 1844.
31 *Le Canadien*, 15 April 1844.
32 Reprinted from *L'Artisan* in *Le Canadien*, 28 June 1844. Note that the enumerator reported his crop yields in 'minots anglais.'
33 *Le Canadien*, 17 June 1844.
34 *Le Canadien*, 3 June 1844.
35 *Le Canadien*, 14 June 1844; curiously, the figure is exactly what the Board of Registration and Statistics would cite in 1849.
36 *Le Canadien*, 6 December 1844; notice the continuing variations in estimates. Taché's official version in 1876 gave 697,084 for 1844 compared to 487,053 for 1831.
37 *La Minerve*, 26 December 1844.
38 Legislative Council of Canada, *Journals*, 'Report of the Select Committee on the Lower Canada Census Returns,' 25 March 1845; reprinted in *Le Canadien*, 9 April 1845.
39 Legislative Assembly of Canada, *Sessional Papers*, Appendix D, 1846. 'Recapitulation by Districts and Counties, of the Returns of the Enumeration of the Inhabitants of Lower Canada, and of the Other Statistical Information Obtained in the Year 1844 ...'
40 For the census figure, see *Census of Canada*, Volume IV (Ottawa, 1876), which contains a summary of nineteenth-century census returns. For a detailed summary of 1844 returns, see Parliament of Canada, Legislative Assembly *Journals*, Appendix D, 1846. For the administrative use of the 1844 returns, see Legislative Assembly, *Debates*, 22 February 1849.
41 NAC RG1 E7 vol. 25, submissions of 25 January 1847. The schedules were not radically different, although some categories had been altered.
42 NAC RG1 E1 Canada State Book F p. 314, [25?] January 1847; Canada State book G p. 141, 15 July 1847; Province of Canada, Legislative Assembly *Journals*, 'Return to an address calling for copies of circulars to wardens on the taking of a periodical census,' Appendix YY 1847. *Le Canadien*'s notes on the proceedings of the legislature for 17 July 1847 had the cryptic remark, 'Some explanations which explained nothing about the flagrant disobedience on the part of the government of one of the clauses of the census act.'
43 See Bruce Curtis, 'Selective Publicity' and 'Canada "Blue Books."'
44 For this reason, the manuscript 1848 enumeration schedules were not consumed in the 1849 Parliamentary fire.
45 11&12 Vic., c.XIV, 'An Act for Taking the Census of this Province, and Obtaining Statistical Information Therein,' proclaimed 28 July 1847.

46 John M. Eyler, *Victorian Social Medicine: The Ideas and Methods of William Farr* (Baltimore: The Johns Hopkins University Press, 1979); Samuel Finer, *The Life and Times of Sir Edwin Chadwick* (New York: Franklin, 1970); and 'The Transmission of Benthamite Ideas, 1820–50,' in Gillian Sutherland, ed., *Studies in the Growth of Nineteenth Century Government* (London: Routledge and Kegan Paul, 1972): 11–32; R.J.W. Selleck, *James Kay-Shuttleworth: Journey of an Outsider* (Essex: Woburn Press, 1994).
47 I have examined Ryerson's initiatives in this regard in detail in 'From Class Culture to Bureaucratic Procedure,' in *True Government*: 174–92.
48 W.A. Langton (Ed.), *Early Days in Upper Canada. Letters of John Langton from the Backwoods of Upper Canada and the Audit Office of the Province of Canada* (Toronto: Macmillan, 1926): 217–8; 231; for more on how Crofton's employment was disguised in the Parliamentary accounts, see Bruce Curtis, 'Comment dénombrer les serviteurs de l'état.'
49 Legislative Assembly of Upper Canada, *Sessional Papers*, paper 26, 1836, gives 15 May 1835; *Sessional Papers*, Public Accounts, 1837, gives 1 July 1835; NAC RG1 E13, 1837, gives 1 July 1835. The first source concerns when Crofton began receiving his pay, the other two his official appointment. Legislative Assembly of Upper Canada, *Sessional Papers*, School Reports 1839–40, repeats the Trinity College claim; the *Sessional Papers*, Public Accounts, 1840, gives the £100. The TCD university archivist says no list of registrants was kept for the period; Crofton does not appear among those taking a degree. Dora E. Wattie, *Cobourg 1784–1867*, Vol. II (n.d. typescript, Cobourg Public Library), seems to be in error in claiming that 'in 1838 W.C. Crofton resigned from the Grammar School.'
50 NAC CO42/476, 2 March 1841, for the Macaulay quote; for the rest, see what follows.
51 The pamphlets were 'Erinensis,' *Sketches of the Thirteenth Parliament of Upper Canada* (Toronto: Rogers and Thomson, 1840); and 'Uncle Ben,' *A Brief Sketch of the Life of Charles, Baron Metcalfe* ... (Kingston: Atheneum, 1846). For the newspaper work, see Cobourg *Star*, 18 August 1841; see also 21 July 1841; Percy L. Climo, *Early Cobourg* (Cobourg: privately printed, 1985), p. 111; reprinting an advertisement in Cobourg *Star*, 4 June 1845; and Cobourg *Star*, 3 & 17 September 1845. See Archives of Ontario (AO) RG2 C6C, clerk of police, Cobourg to Education office, 28 March 1844, for the appointment of Crofton as town school superintendent. For Crofton's attempt to promote Cobourg as a site for the provincial normal school, see David Calnan, 'Postponed Progress: Cobourg Common Schools 1850–1871,' in J. Petryshyn, ed. *Victorian Cobourg: A Nineteenth Century Profile* (Belleville: Mika Publishing, 1976): 192. The appendix to this article is likely in error in

describing Crofton as school inspector from 1842, unless he was acting by local arrangement, for the position existed in the School Act in towns only from 1844 to 1846. With respect to pay, NAC RG19, vol. 1925, no. 816, 12 April 1844, shows a warrant for Crofton in the amount of £55.19.8; I think it is an annual payment.

52 For the communications leading up to the manuscript, see AO, RG2 C6C, Crofton to Jameson, 30 August 1842; C1 vol. 1, Richardson to Crofton, 3 September 1842; then Crofton to Harrison, 7 September 1842, with (MSS) *Thoughts on Education in Three Letters Respectfully Addressed to the Right Honorable Sir Charles Bagot Governor General of B.N. America* by Walter Crofton. For the official response to him, AO RG2 C6C, Murray to Harrison, 13 September 1842; for the text of the Tory-authored Education Commission Report, parts of which Crofton cited, see J.G. Hodgins, ed., *The Documentary History of Education in Upper Canada* (Toronto: L.K. Cameron, 1894–1912) III: 252–83.
53 NAC RG1 E1, Canada State Book F, p. 138, minute of 2 December 1846; Harington's description of the work is attached.
54 Curtis, 'Canada "Blue Books,"' and NAC RG1 E13, the Blue Book for 1846. On Cayley, see Paul Cornell, 'Cayley, William,' *Dictionary of Canadian Biography* (Toronto: University of Toronto Press, 1982) XI: 165–7.
55 NAC RG1 E1, Canada State Book H, 8 December 1847.
56 NAC RG1 E1, Canada State Book H, p. 360, 5 April 1848.
57 NAC RG31, Census Field, census returns, 1848.
58 *La Minerve*, 24 January 1848.
59 *La Minerve*, 27 January 1848.
60 NAC RG31 vol.1307, 'Instructions To Persons appointed to take the Census under 10 & 11 Vic. Chap. 14,' 29 December 1847.
61 NAC RG31 Census returns, Augusta Township, Johnstown District, 1848, Garret Doyle, Prescott, 22 May 1848; South Gower township, Johnstown District, John Gray, 22 May 1848.
62 NAC RG31 Census returns, John Elliott, Wolford Township, Johnstown District, 30 May 1848; Jacob Smith, Elizabethtown Township, Johnstown District, 8 August 1848.
63 NAC RG31 Census returns, Jacob Smith, Elizabethtown Township, Johnstown District, remarks on pages 24, 32, 40, 72, 128, 144, 168.
64 NAC RG31 Census returns, J.W. McCarthy, Town of Prescott, Johnstown District, 27 June 1848.
65 What was counted in the occupations column was typically checked off by the compiler; women's occupations weren't. Some sheets show someone other than the enumerator making entries. See for instance, NAC RG31

Census returns 1848, Walter Whelan, North Crosby Township, Johnstown District, 20 June 1848, where someone other than Whelan has written 'Squatter' beside many names. RG31 vol.1307, Office of Registration and Statistics, Montreal, 14 May 1848, for the circular. No correspondence from the municipal clerks survives in state paper collections.
66 *Le Canadien*, 14 March 1848.
67 *La Minerve*, 1 May 1848.
68 *La Minerve*, 2 December 1849; Montreal *Gazette*, 13 February 1850.
69 NAC RG31, vol. 1307, Office of Registration and Statistics, 26 October 1849; Bureau d'enrégistrement et de statistiques, Toronto, 7 Mai 1850.
70 *Le Canadien*, 18 July 1851.
71 *Debates*, 5 June 1851.
72 Legislative Assembly, *Debates*, 'Reply to an Address to the Governor General Calling for List of Localities in LC Where the Census Was Taken out in Accordance with 10 & 11 Vic. c.14,' 26 June 1851.
73 *Le Canadien*, 1 August 1851. A report in the same paper on 8 October 1851 gave the results of the religious census for Canada West as 799,847.
74 NAC RG1 E13, 'Population,' in the Blue Book for 1847.
75 NAC CO42/552, no. 127, Elgin to Grey, 20 September 1848; a congratulatory reply is RG1 E1, vol. 120, no. 295, Grey to Elgin 10 November 1848. Notice CO42/557, no. 6, Elgin to Grey, 27 January 1849, which encloses a printed Tabular Statement of property values, houses, lands, mills, population, and so on under the assessment acts by year from 1825 to 1848. Here the 1848 population is given as 717,560.
76 *La Minerve*, 8 February 1849.
77 Province of Canada, Legislative Assembly, *Sessional Papers*, Appendix B, 1849, Board of Registration and Statistics, Appendix to First Report, 1849. See also, NAC RG1 E1, Canada State Book J, p. 510, 1 December 1849, in which the bill of £400 is presented from the Queen's Printer for printing for the board.
78 They were published regularly as Parliamentary papers. See, for example, Legislative Assembly of Canada, *Sessional papers*, Appendix III, 1846.
79 On Porter, see Lucy Brown, *The Board of Trade and the Free-Trade Movement, 1830–42* (Oxford: Clarendon, 1958): *passim*. G.R. Porter, David Ricardo's brother-in-law and a founding member of the London Statistical Society, headed the statistical branch at the Board of Trade and so was one of Crofton's English counterparts. Brown shows that Porter could not command reliable statistical reports on a national scale on most subjects in this period either, but the English statisticians agitated for change in this area. Crofton had access to English materials but did not take up their examples.

80 Hincks wrote: 'The object of this publication is to place before the Government and people of England ... the actual financial position of one of the most important colonies of the empire, and to give to those who take an interest in the subject, and especially to capitalists, some idea of the extent of its resources, the rapid increase of its wealth, the stability of its institutions, and the perfect reliance which may be placed on its ability and determination to fulfil all its pecuniary engagements.' Francis Hincks, *Canada: Its Financial Position and Resources* (London: James Ridgway, 1849): 1.

81 Legislative Assembly of Canada, *Debates*, 22–4 January 1849; the quotation is from 24 January.

82 The report was in print and despatched to England by 10 April; see NAC CO42/558, 10 April 1849.

83 He is actually reported to have said 'le recensement fait, il y a quatre ans,' but he must have meant 1844.

84 All quotations in the preceeding sections are from Legislative Assembly of Canada, *Debates*, 20 March 1849.

85 Legislative Assembly of Canada, *Debates*, 21 March 1849.

## 3: Numbering Names

1 See M. Drake, 'The Census, 1801–1901,' in E.A. Wrigley (Ed.), *Nineteenth-century Society: Essays in the Use of Quantitative Methods for the Study of Social Data* (Cambridge: Cambridge University Press, 1972): 7–46; and D.V. Glass, *Numbering the People. The Eighteenth-Century Population Controversy and the Development of Census and Vital Statistics in Britain* (Farnborough: Saxon House, 1973): 114–17.

2 See, for instance, Nikolas Rose, 'Governing "Advanced" Liberal Democracies,' in A. Barry et al, eds., *Foucault and Political Reason* (London: UCL Press,1996): 37–64; but in Rose's account, rationalities of government do not perhaps lead directly to technologies of government.

3 The circular is contained in NAC RG7 G1, vol. 121, Grey to Elgin, 20 January 1849.

4 Elgin to Grey, 4 January 1849, in Sir A.G. Doughtey (Ed.), *The Elgin-Grey Papers 1846–1852* (Ottawa, 1937) I: 281. 'Mr. Hincks has also the honour to enclose a table giving a portion of the Statistical information relating to Upper Canada which has been Compiled with great care by Mr. Croften who has charge of the Blue Books. This information may be interesting to Earl Grey. at a time when Colonization is so much discussed.' See also William D. Reid, *Marriage Notices of Ontario* (Lambertville, N.J., Hunterdon

334  Notes to pages 95–104

House, 1980), from the *Toronto Patriot* of 10 May 1849. 'At St. George's Church, Montreal, on 25<sup>th</sup> inst. [*sic*], W.C. Crofton, to Elizabeth Miriam, second daughter of the late Dr. Edward John Dudderidge, Fenchurch Street, London. (Rev. W. T. Leach).'

5  For the discussions in council about the purge, see NAC RG1 E1, Canada State Book J, 521–3, 1 December 1849.
6  Doughtey, *Elgin-Grey Papers* I: 785, Elgin to Grey, 7 January 1851.
7  Legislative Assembly of Canada, *Debates*, 5 June, 13 June, 6 August 1851.
8  Legislative Assembly of Canada, *Debates*, 13 June 1851. The commissioners or superintendents would get $2.50 a day, and the enumerators a rate that would vary in keeping with the difficulty of their task. See also *Debates*, 17 June 1851, for the report on the places where the census had been taken successfully in Canada East in 1848. It seems that at some point, Lord Elgin intervened on instructions from Lord Grey to have the initial proposition for a census in 1860 changed to 1861; see NAC RG7 G1, vol. 127, no. 620, Grey to Elgin, 14 July 1851.
9  Legislative Assembly of Canada, *Debates*, 2 and 7 July 1851. The amendment suggests that the government had intended to follow the English practice to omit information about religious affiliation.
10  Legislative Assembly of Canada, *Debates*, 6 and 8 August 1851; 14 and 15 Vic., cap. XLIX.
11  *Le Canadien*, 23, 27 June 1851.
12  *Le Canadien*, 18 July 1851.
13  *Le Canadien*, 25 July 1851.
14  Few records survive. Crofton did not control commissioners' appointments: these were matters of political patronage. He seems to have had a high degree of administrative autonomy, however, with appeals being made to Morin or Francis Hincks when Crofton proved incompetent or confused.
15  The press did encourage participation, well in advance. See, for instance, *La Minerve*, 23 and 24 December 1851; and *Le Canadien*, 26 December 1851. But as in NAC RG31, vol. 1298, commissioners Pouliot and Labelle were proposing measures to give some notice of the enumeration.
16  No account survives of the size of the clerical contingent at the board before the compilation process began. As we shall see, even then the employees were described by Crofton as day workers.
17  NAC RG31, vol. 1298, L.A. Olivier, Berthier, to A.-N. Morin, 7 November 1851. Olivier was consulted on 1 October about the appointment, but complained he had heard nothing about it since.
18  See Canada *Gazette*, 8 November 1851, for the initial appointments, and 3 January 1852 for the appointment of François Vézina in place of the

deceased commissioner for the city of Quebec, Joseph LeFebvre. Even this did not slow matters down, for the urban schedules had been distributed and Vézina was familiar with the process. Note that the other material in this and the following section, unless otherwise indicated, is from NAC RG31, vol. 1298, a register containing transcribed (and occasionally original pasted in) incoming correspondence from the commissioners to the Board of Registration and Statistics. The volume also contains occasional transcribed correspondence between third parties and odd copies of outgoing correspondence.

19 Canada *Gazette*, 20 December 1851; 3 January 1852. Of the thirty-one for whom I have found information about occupations, nine were merchants of various kinds, six were barristers, four were insurance company agents (who would have travelled around their counties), two were doctors, and one was a coroner; of the state servants, six were municipal clerks, two were Crown Lands agents, and one was the Chamberlain of Toronto.

20 NAC RG31, vol. 1298; the clerk has jumbled the correspondence together in transcribing it; I've reconstructed Waters's account.

21 They were the commissioners for Beauharnois, Champlain, Drummond, Leinster, Ottawa, Rimouski, Rouville, St-Hyacinthe, Saguenay and Terrebonne counties.

22 No reply survives, but Drummond was enumerated by township and part-township.

23 NAC RG17, vol. 1298; there was one case of overlap on the boundary between the city of Quebec and its suburbs.

24 Narcisse Larue's visit is mentioned in Vézina's correspondence in the Quebec section and Larue's contact with Charles Belle in the Montreal County section of NAC RG31, vol. 1298.

25 A partial return of enumerators is in Province of Canada, *Sessional Papers* Appendix T.T. 1852. Several counties are missing, and some commissioners simply submitted an account for so many names, not indicating their enumerators. See also, Appendix C, 1853–4, 'First Report of the Secretary of the Board of Registration and Statistics on the Census of the Canadas for 1851–52': 1.

26 Province of Canada, *Sessional Papers*, Public Accounts, 1851. Also, NAC RG19, vol. 1927, warrant of 10 May 1852, where the board's total printing and stationery bill from November 1851 to March 1852 apparently amounted to the modest sum of £287.7.7. More printing money may have been coming out of the board's large contingent funds. Notice also, in vol. 1928 for 1853, that William Hutton claimed an additional £574 to defray the printing bill; however, this may have been for the bound census reports.

27 NAC RG17, vol. 1298; there is a first direct contact between J.-C. Taché and the census-making process here, for Heath had consulted him about the estimated population of the county. Crofton did not manage to respond.
28 See NAC RG17, vol. 1298; Félix Lemaire for Deux-Montagnes, for instance, ordered 500 French and 400 English personal schedules and 125 French and 100 English agricultural schedules on 3 December 1851. On 26 December, he received 650 French and 100 English personal schedules and 180 French and 40 English agricultural schedules. Henri Garon for Kamouraska regretted that the agricultural schedules sent to him were 'in English, for it will expose some of the enumerators to several errors'; he must have received more schedules in French, for as in NAC RG31, Census field 1852, Kamouraska co.; while only partial returns survive, the agricultural schedules are in French.
29 See NAC RG31, Census field 1852, Lambton County; very few returns survive, and the collection contains hand-ruled schedules but none on 1850 forms.
30 All this is transcribed in NAC RG31, vol. 1298, but as in many other sections of this volume, the clerk has been extremely sloppy.
31 Montreal *Gazette*, 14 and 21 January 1852; *La Minerve*, 19 March 1852; *Le Canadien*, 9 and 12 January, 19 March 1852.
32 For instance, the Rimouski commissioner, John Heath, noted that there was an important export market for eggs in his county, most of them going to Montreal; quoted in *Le Canadien*, 27 March 1852.
33 See Bruce Curtis, 'Moral Thermometer,' on metrological history.
34 In the absence of a copy of the 1852 instructions in the census field, NAC RG31, I follow David Gagan's reproduction in 'Enumerator's Instructions for the Census of Canada 1852 and 1861,' *Histoire sociale/Social History* 7(14), 1974: 355-65; with additional comments from RG 31, vol. 1298. I have uncovered no surviving set of instructions to urban enumerators.
35 Including, I think, the capacity to consult with individual enumerators to determine the decisional rules they applied in placing people in different categories.
36 Also here in NAC RG31, vol. 1298, is John Kirby, Hamilton commissioner, to Crofton, 8 January 1852, pointing out that he is distributing the slips that arrived on the 6th but anticipating that it will be tedious to collect them, 'so many being ignorant of the Forms, they will have to be filled in by the enumerators.'
37 Again, still in NAC RG31, vol. 1298, Larue asked 'as to Column 30, the age and cause of death are asked for? And I don't see where to enter their names.' No response from Crofton survives.

38 This is the Board's clerk's transcription.
39 See Bruce Curtis, *True Government* 154–64, for a description of the network in which Shenston was involved; and David G. Burley, 'Shenston, Thomas Strahan,' *Dictionary of Canadian Biography* (Toronto: University of Toronto Press, 1990), XII: 967–8.
40 NAC RG31, vol. 1298. Shenston was quite a literate person; the errors here are almost certainly those of the transcription clerk. A notation follows this letter indicating that there was other correspondence in which Crofton proposed to reply to Shenston, but I have not been able to find it.
41 The point is repeated by one of Cox's enumerators, who is quoted in NAC RG31, vol. 1299, a volume containing transcribed and translated comments by enumerators taken from the schedules for Canada East.
42 See Province of Canada, *Sessional Papers*, Appendix T.T., 1852, for the claims and allowances; NAC RG1 E1, Canada State Book M, 21 October 1852, p. 547. McLaren is the only one I've seen who managed to get pay for the agricultural schedules.
43 NAC RG17 vol. 2416, petition, 18 December 1852. Morin describes his enormous district in detail.
44 Unless otherwise indicated, quotations in this section are from NAC RG31, vols. 1298 and 1299. The latter volume contains transcribed, translated, and sometimes pasted in comments from enumerators. Here I am quoting the commissioner, Horace Horton.
45 NAC RG17, vol. 2416, certified 7 June 1852, letter with McCargar's accounts.
46 NAC RG31, Census field 1852, Orford twp, Kent co., comment on schedule 9; repeated later in the run.
47 NAC RG31, vol. 1299, for the quotation, and Province of Canada, *Sessional Papers*, Appendix T.T., 1852, for the pay.
48 NAC RG31, Census field 1852, Warwick twp, Lambton co., comment on 1$^{st}$ agricultural schedule; note also his p. 19, where he lists three farms for W. Thompson. Some enumerators report, others don't; for example, in Upton twp, Drummond co., pork is given in cwts; in St-Denis in Kamouraska co. the enumerator does not specify.
49 NAC RG31, vol. 1299; clerk's translation. Note that this enumerator returned fowl, 'about fifteen hundred couples a year but this number should not be considered because he is not half of what he should be.' See also Census field 1852, Russeltown twp, Beauharnois co., 24 February 1852, remarks of Fisher Ames, enumerator, regarding agricultural returns, p. 88: 'Tenant lately moved on. Knows nothing about crop'; p. 95: 'Just moved on Knows nothing about the Crops.'

50 NAC RG31, Census field 1852, St-Jean, city of Quebec, no. 215; personal schedules, Kamouraska co., p.3ff.
51 NAC RG31, Census field 1852, city of Hamilton, p. 37.
52 NAC RG31, Census field 1852, Bellechasse co., enumerator's remarks on p. 78 dated 6 March 1852.
53 NAC RG31, Census field 1852, Plympton twp, Lambton co.
54 NAC RG31, Census field 1852, Bellechasse co., district of St-François-de-la-Rivière-Sud, commissioner's remarks at the start of the run; Thibaud on p. 5. Note birthplaces are by parish; someone has added 'En Canada' in the margin.
55 NAC RG31 Census field 1852, parish of St-Remi, Huntingdon co., p. 148. Notice that Mégritte writes 'St Remi' in every cell of 'Residence if out of limits.'
56 NAC RG31 Census field 1852, Chatham town, Kent co., schedule 22; notice that the miller, J. Sanderson, on schedule 44 'said he was unprepared to give any account as to cost and produce.' On schedule 85 Shipley also returns the commissioner, Alexander Knapp, as boarding in the Royal Exchange Hotel.
57 NAC RG31, vol. 1298.
58 NAC RG31, Census field 1852, parish of St-Roch, city of Quebec, nos. 1182-3; see also no. 287, where D. Garnon's claim to be a 'journallie' was annotated 'House of Illfame.'
59 Nothing for London, Kingston, or Toronto; very fragmentary runs for Bytown, Quebec, and Montreal.
60 NAC RG31, Census field 1852, no. 39 St-Jean, city of Quebec; Montreal no. 337.
61 NAC RG31, Census field 1852, city of Quebec, St Roch, nos. 2636, 2640; St-Jean, nos. 123, 125, 129, 253; 'brun' for Croteau likely meant dark brown hair and eyes as in 'un beau brun.' For Toronto, RG31, vol. 1298.
62 NAC RG31, Census field 1852, Montreal, St-Laurent ward, long autograph description by Renaud dated 14 February 1852. It is too tedious to do the count in most places to find out what proportion of schedules resulted from self-enumeration, but one can see that in other cities the enumerators filled in the majority of the schedules. For instance, in Bytown, where Robert Farley did much of the town, householders regularly made their mark on the sheets completed in the enumerator's hand.
63 NAC RG1 E1, Canada State Book M., pp. 63-4; committee report of 14 March 1852.
64 NAC RG31, Census field 1852, Frontenac co., is missing. There are some examples elsewhere. See Plympton twp., Lambton co., where all the col-

umns are reproduced on a perfectly clean and regular hand-ruled run. Note that this is where the commissioner proposed to use 1850 schedules if those for 1852 did not arrive. Also, city of Montreal, Montreal General Hospital, is on hand-ruled sheets. The possibilities for variation here concern especially sheets produced by the enumerators themselves in the field.
65 For instance, Heath for Rimouski, *Le Canadien*, 27 March 1852; Varin for Huntingdon, *La Minerve*, 23 April 1852; Olivier on Berthier, *La Minerve*, 19 May 1852; Bonneville on Dorchester, *Le Canadien*, 2 and 4 June 1852.
66 NAC RG31, vol. 1298, the exchange between Pouliot and Crofton of 14 February 1852: 'I have the right to demand access to parish and school registers, &c., but have I that of asking each curé what his Salary is in tithe &c and can I insist in this matter'? 'You cannot force these Gentlemen to give you such an account and you should not insist upon it.'
67 NAC RG31, vol. 1298, for Moynahan; RG17 vol. 2416, 5 July 1852 for Irving's suggestions for an improved enumeration method. See also nd 1852, commissioner's [?] remark on Russell county abstract, 'Seven Persons were returned "Protestants" which are included in the column C. of S. and one family "Methodists" enclued in the column W.M.' I don't wish to exaggerate the Moynahan example, but the board was overriding the enumerator's account after the fact, and denominational strength was a contentious issue.
68 NAC RG31, Census field 1852, Upton twp., Drummond co., commissioner's comments at the end of the agricultural run.

**4: Calculating Canada in the 1850s**

1 The act creating the bureau wasn't passed until November; as I show below, the clerks were at work before the passage of the act. Re space: on 16 October 1852, for instance, the Executive Council considered a request for funds from Cameron for 'the expense of washing and cleaning rooms for the Statistical Offices and the Bureau of Agriculture'; see NAC RG1 E1, Canada State Book M., 544–5, and RG1 E7, vol. 38, both of the date mentioned.
2 Province of Canada, Legislative Assembly, *Sessional Papers*, Appendix C, 1852–3.
3 On the religious returns, see the Montreal *Gazette*, 29 March and 2 April 1852, and *La Minerve*, 2 April 1852; on boosterism, see *Le Canadien*, 10 March 1852.
4 T.S. Shenston, *The Oxford Gazeteer; Containing a Complete History of the County of Oxford from Its First Settlement* ... (Hamilton, 1852).

340   Notes to pages 136–40

5 *La Minerve, Le Canadien*, 7 July 1852.
6 *Le Canadien*, 21 July 1852.
7 See the widely used return in J.-C. Taché's benchmark *Census of Canada 1665–1871. Statistics of Canada*, Volume IV (Ottawa: J.B. Taylor, 1876).
8 *Le Canadien*, 21 July 1852, for instance, where the editor argued that Canada East's population growth from natural increase was probably nearly as great as that of the west, and that immigration was responsible for the difference.
9 P.-J.-O. Chaveau, *Charles Guérin. Roman de Moeurs Canadienne* (Montréal: Guérin, 1973): 359–65; the quoted passages are at 364 and 365. Much of the thrust of this interesting work is an argument in favour of scientific agriculture, colonization, and religion.
10 J.-C. Taché, 'Des provinces de l'Amérique du Nord et d'une Union Fédérale,' *Courrier du Canada*, 7 August 1857.
11 Particularly visibly in the Charitable Corporations debate of 1853, where George Brown and Joseph Cauchon debated the relative moral condition of the two 'races.' See *Debates*, 24 February, 9 March 1853.
12 John Garner, *The Franchise and Politics in British North America* (Toronto: University of Toronto Press, 1969): 96. Space precludes comment on alterations to the franchise in this period and attempts at constructing a voters' register.
13 The best copy is in NAC RG17, vol. 2416, from Robert Onselande in Wentworth County, dated 14 January 1852; see also RG17 1, J.O. Arcand to A.-N. Morin, 14 March 1852.
14 For example, NAC RG17, vol. 2326, bound responses to 'Circular of Agricultural Queries from the Minister of Agriculture,' 1858–61.
15 For Cameron's biography, see Margaret Coleman, 'Cameron, Malcolm,' *Dictionary of Canadian Biography* (Toronto: University of Toronto Press, 1972): 124–9. Coleman does not make the connection between Cameron's resignation and the ministry's support for Ryerson's School Act. I have detailed it in *True Government*: 82ff. Notice that J.O. Coté, *Political Appointments and Elections in the Province of Canada from 1841 to 1865*, 2nd ed. (Ottawa: Lowe-Martin, 1918), repeatedly gives the date of Cameron's chairmanship as that of the ministry, 28 October 1851. In fact, Cameron was sworn as a member of council on 5 March 1852; see NAC RG1 E1, Canada State Book M, 8; see also *Debates*, 29 April 1853, where Brown claims that Cameron was receiving his ministerial pay from 4 January 1852.
16 The claim was made in Parliament by the opposition; see, for instance, *Debates*, 29 April 1853. It was also picked up in standard works like J.M.S.

Careless, *Brown of the Globe* (Toronto: Macmillan, 1958). This has meant that only J.E. Hodgetts, in his *Pioneer Public Service: An Administrative History of the United Canadas, 1841–67* (Toronto: University of Toronto Press, 1955), has attended seriously to the Bureau of Agriculture as an administrative entity, although he offers no detailed account of the bureau's activities. A less dismissive account of the bureau's origins is in Lillian F. Gates, *After the Rebellion: The Later Years of William Lyon Mackenzie* (Toronto: Dundurn Press, 1988): 196ff.

17 Michael Piva, *The Borrowing Process: Public Finance in the Province of Canada, 1840–1867* (Ottawa: University of Ottawa Press, 1992). Hincks's policy is described at length in NAC CO42/552, no. 151, Elgin to Grey, 20 December 1848.

18 See Legislative Assembly of Canada, *Sessional Papers*, 'Report of M. Cameron, Esquire, Commissioner Appointed to Inquire into the State and Management of Customs, in Upper Canada, Laid before the Legislative Assembly, Friday, 27th October, 1843.'

19 Curtis, *True Government* 82–4.

20 A flood of temperance petitions began to reach Parliament in early 1849, and the first of several select committees on temperance was established on 23 January. Cameron participated in the 1850 select committee that drafted a temperance bill, subsequently lost at second reading in July. As temperance lodges sprang up in many parts of Canada West, Cameron again promoted a bill, this one aiming to copy the Maine Temperance Act for Canada. The bill was hotly debated in September 1852 and again in March 1853, with Cameron, on the latter occasion, decrying the fact that 'immorality is at the present moment sustained by law' and drawing upon comparative statistics to support his case. In April, this bill was given the six months' hoist. See Legislative Assembly of Canada *Journals* and *Debates*, 23 January 1849; 31 May, 28 June, 23 and 29 July, 6 August 1850; 5 and 26 June, 1 August 1851; 7 and 28 September 1852; 21 March, 13 April 1853.

21 *Debates*, 20 August 1852.

22 *Debates*, 25 August 1852.

23 NAC RG1 E1, Canada State Book M: 170–1, 10 May 1852, which also contains a memorandum of 15 December 1851 on the subject from John Young, the public works commissioner.

24 NAC RG19, vol. 1927, 30 June, 9 July 1852; RG17 AI 2, Cameron to Sewell, 2 July 1852; MG30 E96 6, Hutton to Anna Hutton Ponton, 3 October [1852]. See also *Debates*, 1 December 1852, where Hincks deflects Chabot's demand to know if the 'new Department of Agriculture and Statistics' had

342  Notes to pages 143–7

been organized. Hodgetts, *Pioneer Public Service*, consistently dates the formation of the bureau from 1853, despite the fact that even the act that created it passed on 10 November 1852.

25 NAC RG17 AI 2, Cameron to P.E. Leclaire, 2 July 1852. See also Cameron to A. Cameron, President, Agricultural Society, Frontenac, Lennox and Addington, 6 July 1852; and Cameron to M.G. Hall, President, Agricultural Society, Lanark, 15 July 1852. This is official correspondence before the official creation of the office, and for SSK readers an obvious attempt at enrolment.

26 *Debates*, 5 October 1852.

27 *Debates*, 5 and 22 October 1852. Murney signed the letter of support that Crofton presented to Council to appeal his final dismissal, as did such other opponents of the bill as Joseph Cauchon and Harmanus Smith; see NAC RG1 E1, Canada State Book U, 6 September 1859, p. 332.

28 *Debates*, 22 October 1852; 6 November 1852. 16 Vic. cap.XI, 'An Act to provide for the establishment of a Bureau of Agriculture, and to amend and consolidate the Laws relating to Agriculture,' was proclaimed 10 November 1852.

29 As he wrote to his mother, 'the Roman Catholic religion is a great *Retarder* of Progress especially where there is little of the leaven of Protestantism in free thought and action mixed in the mass'; Hutton to his mother, 25 June 1853, in G.E. Boyce, *Hutton of Hastings: The Life and Letters of William Hutton, 1801–1861* (Belleville: Hastings County Council, 1972): 185.

30 The essays are reproduced in Boyce, *Hutton of Hastings*, an invaluable source. For Hutton as school inspector, see Curtis, *True Government*; also Wesley B. Turner, 'Hutton, William,' *Dictionary of Canadian Biography* (Toronto: University of Toronto Press, 1976) IX: 404–5, with a list of other publications; Crofton did say that rising crime rates pointed to the ill effects of abandoning flogging, but this was a rare claim.

31 Legislative Assembly of Canada, *Sessional Papers*, Appendix FFFF, 1853–4; for a description of the work, see NAC MG30 E96 6, Hutton to Anna (Hutton) Ponton, 10 September 1852.

32 NAC MG30 E96 6, Hutton to Anna (Hutton) Ponton, nd 1854 [the Sunday after Hincks's resignation]; there are 'some errors in the Census as to Presbyterians & Methodists not being properly classified but these errors were all published about 4000 copies of them six months before I became Secry I am trying to include the errors in the "errata" at the close of *second vol*... but I know the different kinds of Presbyterians were not properly taken & never can be correct. I can only give them as they are returned to

the office & hope to be able to do that if I have time – The number of Presbyterians *as a whole* is correct but not the subdivisions.'
33 Legislative Assembly of Canada, *Sessional Papers*, Appendix C, 1853–54, 'First Report of the Secretary of the Board of Registration and Statistics on the Census of the Canadas, for 1851–52,' 15 August 1853 [hereafter 'First Report']: 7.
34 NAC RG17 A 1, Morin to Cameron, 26 March 1853, copied to Crofton, with Crofton to Morin, 28 March 1853. A note of caution: Crofton added in this response to a demand for an official account of the staff, 'In short I am the only Permanent Officer,' three days before his ouster by Hutton. Hutton knew about it well beforehand; see MG30 E96 6, Hutton to Anna Hutton Ponton, 16 and 17 March 1853. Perhaps Crofton was dissembling to bolster his own position. See also RG4 B75, Board of Registration and Statistics, pay lists for November and December 1852; many of these clerks stay on at Agriculture, and Evelyn Campbell will become acting secretary after Hutton's death. The lists are signed by Crofton and that for December by Cameron; RG31, Census field 1852, Orford twp., Kent co., the initials of 'DR' who wrote 'Done' on the last of the agricultural schedules correspond to none of the eleven clerical names.
35 See, for instance, NAC RG17, vol. 2416, census accounts, Stanstead County, submitted 26 March 1852. Crofton has gone through them line by line, and signs an approval for payment 21 June 1852, countersigned by the Receiver General, 22 June 1852. Some of the addition has also been done by the Deputy Inspector General, Joseph Carey.
36 NAC RG1 E13, the Blue Book for 1851; RG31, vol. 1299; Peter De Guise (1810–60) is the likely candidate, on the pay list in this period, since he did the translation work under Hutton.
37 NAC RG1 E1, Canada State Book P, 2 March 1855, pp. 21–2. See also *Le Canadien*, 1 April and 25 May 1853, for reports of Crofton at work on tabular returns and mention of something showing distribution of francophone population in Canada West (the map?).
38 First Report; he got the number of columns on the personal and agricultural schedules wrong, but no matter – it was still lots of work.
39 It is impossible to estimate the number of those 'out of place' returned more than once without actually recompiling the returns, not all of which survive. Hutton later gave the death returns as 19,449 – that is, about 1.1 per cent of the enumerated population.
40 For instance, NAC RG31, Census field 1852, Bellechasse County, District 2, Notre-Dame-de-l'Assomption-de-Berthier-en-Bas. The enumerator listed

occupations such as 'épouse, fille, fils, mendiant, rentier, rentière'; the compiler did not check off any of the women – thus, for example, he checked off 'rentier' but not 'rentière.' Again, in St-Michel-de-Bellechasse, the compiler did not even check off 'maîtresse d'école.'

41 For instance, NAC RG31, Census field 1852, Dorchester County, Parish of St-Elzéar, where the compiler places an 'X' in the age column for married partners.
42 First Report: 8–10.
43 First Report: 6, 10.
44 First Report: 30: 'In the four Eastern Townships, the Land was estimated in acres and the Grain in bushels. In all the others the arpents have been converted into acres, and the minots into bushels.'
45 Legislative Assembly of Canada, *Sessional Papers*, Appendix C, 1854–55, 'Second Report of the Secretary of the Board of Registration and Statistics on the Census of the Canadas for 1851–52' [hereafter 'Second Report]: 30–33.
46 Second Report: 41–5.
47 Second Report: 38–40.
48 Compare Mary Poovey, *Making a Social Body: British Cultural Formation, 1830–1860* (Chicago: University of Chicago Press, 1995).
49 First Report: 36.
50 First Report: 38–40.
51 Second Report: 19.
52 A medical man, for instance, might have called for tieing rates of death to occupations or to the sanitary condition of towns; cf. Higgs, 'Census as a medical survey.' Alternative models existed for Hutton, but colonial needs and his own interests confined the census largely to an agricultural survey. Hutton did not raise the charged questions of ethnic and denominational destinies.
53 NAC RG31, vol. 1299, J.B. Commeault to A.J.O. Arcand, 12 February 1852.
54 First Report: 41.
55 See Curtis, 'Administrative Infrastructure,' for a detailed analysis of one of Cameron's projects, the investigation of agricultural conditions in the Quebec city district.
56 His manuscript of the lectures, about 130 autograph pages headed 'comd Novr 10th 1852,' is in NAC MG30 E96 6. Despite his warnings about exaggerated accounts to which intending immigrants were exposed, Hutton's lectures are remarkably puffy, full of rags-to-riches stories. They presumed that settlers would come to Canada West.
57 NAC MG30 E96 6, Frances Hutton to Anna (Hutton) Ponton, 3 October 1853.

58 NAC MG30 E96 6, Frances (McCrea) Hutton to Frances Hutton, 17 June 1854; Boyd, *Hutton of Hastings*, 191, Hutton to his mother, 6 July 1854. As well, the commissioners recently named in preparation for the colony's participation in the 1855 Paris Exhibition had announced a competition for the three best essays on Canada, and Hutton set to work on a submission.
59 NAC MG30 E96 6, Hutton to Anna (Hutton) Ponton, nd September 1854. Notice that in NAC RG17 AI 2, 26 March 1853, Hutton's correspondence was already headed 'Bureau of Agriculture and Statistics.' His was probably an accurate description of the clerks, at least of Donald McLeod, whose handwriting was as shaky as his orthography. McLeod was a Hincksite political organizer and was paid from 1855 to stay home, which suggests that the bureau after Cameron was a patronage station. See, for instance, NAC RG17 AI 2, Campbell to L. Burwell MPP, 14 September 1863: 'From the date of his first appointment Mr. McLeod was unable from age and infirmity to perform efficiently the duty assigned to him and his absences were frequent and of long duration. At no time during his tenure of Office were his services adequate to his remuneration.'
60 NAC MG30 E96 6, Hutton to Anna (Hutton) Ponton, nd September 1854.
61 Legislative Assembly of Canada, *Sessional Papers*, Appendix II, 'Hon. Mr. Cameron's Report,' 20 August 1854.
62 NAC RG1 E7, vol. 41, submission of 20 February 1855; discussed in RG1 E1, vol. 77, Canada State Book O, 20 February 1855: 668–72. Earlier, MacNab had recommended the publication of a volume of transactions; see RG17 AI 2, MacNab to Executive Council, 22 January 1855. See also Legislative Assembly of Canada, *Sessional Papers*, Appendix SSS, 1855, where the functions of the bureau as a whole and of each functionary individually are given; McLeod is reported as earning £200. See also NAC MG30 E96 6, Hutton to Frances Hutton jr., 29 March 1855: 'the Council adopted my report *immediately* Sir All[an] and I get on swimmingly together & have a most excellent understanding.' Hutton's staff was to be as follows: Evelyn Campbell as chief clerk at £300; N. Laurent as French-language second clerk in charge of patents and patent models at £250; Pierre DeGuise as third clerk at £225; and the hapless Donald McLeod as fourth clerk at £200. Hutton noted that McLeod had recently had a salary increase to £250 and recommended that if McLeod were allowed to retain this amount, his successor should have only £200.
63 *Debates*, 16 May 1855.
64 See NAC RG17 AI 2, 21 March 1859, statement of bureau personnel to be moved to Quebec with their families. McLeod is listed but didn't move.
65 These arrangements degenerated into venality and corruption. With the

knowledge of Sir C.P. Roney, Canadian immigration agents sold through tickets to the United States on commission; see for instance, NAC RG17 AI 2, Hutton to Clemoux, to Buchanan, 14 July 1857.

66 NAC RG17 AI 2; for a description of the policy, based on 16 Vic. c.159 sec.14, Hutton to Savage, 23 February 1856; for the appropriations, see Hutton to Clerk of the Legislative Assembly, 7 August 1860; for Macdonald's concerns, see Gates, *After the Rebellion*: 283.

67 On speculation, see NAC MG30 E96 6, Hayes to Hutton, 13 April 1860. On the Camden-to-Madawaska road, the bridge over the Madawaska was repeatedly destroyed by timber cutters, for whose log booms it was an obstacle. Hutton had to deal with the question repeatedly, starting with RG17 AI 2, Hutton to lumber merchants, Hutton to Perry, 14 June 1856. The first reconstruction, as in Hutton to Gibson, 17 October 1856, cost £273 of public money, but the saga dragged on. For a recent novelistic treatment of settlement on the Canadian Shield, see Jane Urquhart, *Away* (Toronto: McClelland & Stewart, 1993).

68 In this regard see NAC RG17 AI 2, 1 August 1857, a notice of the first meetings of the BAMs in Toronto and Montreal on the 25$^{th}$, with a description of membership and functions.

69 The patents, published as the 'Encyclopaedia of Practical Knowledge' in 200 volumes, are offered to the colony in NAC RG7 G1, vol. 137; see Labouchere to Head, 24 December 1855. In RG17 AI 2, Hutton to Executive Council, 7 March 1856, there is a long discussion of the English patents and of arrangements for displaying the patent drawings that Charles Lindsey had made for the bureau at the 1855 Paris Exhibition. The arrival of the English material, loose, is announced in RG7 G1, vol. 141, Labouchere to Head, 15 April 1857. The Canadian patent publication plan is RG17 AI 2, 'Memorandum on publishing specifications and drawings of inventions,' 19 November 1857. In Hutton to Laurent, 13 May 1857, Hutton disciplined the patent clerk, N.F. Laurent, for making out the applications for those seeking patents himself during office hours.

70 See Bruce Curtis, 'Canada "Blue Books."'

71 NAC RG17 AI 2, Hutton to Hicks, McFaul, Whittier, Hodgins, and Keeler, 27 March 1856; and to Pilgrim, to Price, 21 November 1856. Later attempts include Hutton to Handyside, 21 September 1859; and to Devine, 7 October 1859. On the agricultural societies, see Hutton to Crowe, 12 February 1857. For the quote, see Hutton to Campbell, 5 February 1858.

72 NAC RG17 AI 2, Hutton to Hewson, 30 December 1856; see also Hutton to Beasley, 23 April 1856.

73 NAC RG17 AI 2, Hutton to Macdonald, 29 April 1856; in Hutton to Cartier, 15 May 1856, the returns are nonetheless provided for the legislature.
74 The prothonotaries frequently sent their returns to the bureau and sought payment; Hutton did not know what to do with them and suggested they be sent elsewhere. See, for instance, NAC RG17 AI 2, Hutton to Burroughs et Fiset, 22 March 1858; same to same, 22 March 1859.
75 NAC RG7 G1, vol. 130, Pakington to Elgin, 24 November 1852. 'My attention has been called, to the mutilated state of many of the Registers of Births, Marriages, and Deaths, kept in the different Parishes and Towns in the Colonies; and I should be glad of your assistance in devising some plan for their better preservation, and at the same time, for making a reference to them more convenient for persons residing in this Country ... I should wish you to Report to me, on the best mode of giving effect to the object which I have in view. The Returns should be sent to me annually at this Office.'
76 *Canada Free Press*, 29 March 1856; Montreal *Witness*, 14 February 1857. This was the second call for a good system of registration from the *Witness*; see also 23 August 1854.
77 NAC RG17 AI 2, Hutton to Cartier, 9 May 1856; reprinted with some responses to the circular as Legislative Assembly of Canada, *Sessional Papers*, Appendix 19, 1856. The bureau's conviction that the existing arrangements were useless is repeated in RG17 AI 2, Hutton to McVity[?], 15 December 1856; Hutton to McAllister, 24 September, 4 October 1858.
78 See Emery, 'Civil Registration'; medical assistance at hospital births, and at deaths, and the effective licensing of marriages, and then the interest created by things such as welfare state benefits, had first to be in place.
79 NAC RG17 AI 2, Hutton to Hough, 23 September 1857.
80 *Debates*, 12 May 1856; notice also the remarks of the racist MPP for Kent, E. Larwill, on columns dealing with race in the census.
81 NAC RG17 AI 2, Hutton to Roney, 14 February 1857.
82 NAC RG1 E13, the Blue Book for 1855, 'Population' section, reprints a letter from Hutton dated 12 May 1856; he had promised Macdonald, RG17 AI 2, Hutton to Macdonald, 29 April 1856, 'in a few days I shall be able to give you a very close approximation to the Population of every County & Township in Ca. West taken by the school Trustees for School purposes.'
83 NAC RG17 AI 2, Hutton to Chauveau, 25 June 1856; see also same to same, 22 February 1856, by telegraph, 'Children between five and sixteen form a full third of the population and the increase since the Census (four years) is one fourth of that number.' It is not clear which 'census of the people'

Hutton was writing about; notice, however, that urban enumerations were reported in some places in 1855; for one report, Stratford *Weekly Beacon and Perth County General Intelligencer*, 9 February 1855.

84 NAC RG17 AI 2, Hutton to Fontlangue, 5 July 1856; Hutton to Gourlay, 14 November 1856.
85 NAC RG17 AI 2, Hutton to Chauveau, 2 January 1857.
86 NAC RG17 AI 2, Hutton to McCann, 15 September 1857; Hutton to clerk of legislature, 12 September 1859.
87 *La Minerve*, 'La Population du Canada,' 23 December 1859. How Hutton decided that the female population aged 18–60 was equal the male, and why one should multiply this sum by four to get the total population, he did not explain.
88 NAC RG17 AI 2, Hutton to Chauveau, 21 December 1859; Hutton to Ryerson, 28 December 1859.

**5: Setting up the Sectarian Census**

1 Gates, *After the Rebellion*, shows that the 'double-shuffle' was possible because the 1857 Reform of Parliament Act required new incoming ministers to go to election, but not ministers changing their posts. The Brown-Dorion alliance had to appeal to the country after losing a vote, but a reconstructed conservative coalition could and did take office without the necessity of an election.
2 *Globe*, Reports of speech by Brown, 20 September, 1860; 'French Canada,' 18 September 1860; 'The Census,' 18 October 1860; 'What Is Coming,' 24 October 1860; 'Papal Troops for Lower Canada,' 29 October 1860; 'Protestant and Catholic,' 6 November 1860.
3 *Globe*, 'The Real Question at Issue,' 5 December 1860; 'Political Crisis,' 5 January 1861.
4 *Le Canadien*, 28 February 1860.
5 *La Minerve*, 16 October 1860; Brown had indeed done what was charged; his lame response is in the *Globe*, 6 November 1860.
6 *La Minerve*, 30 June 1860.
7 *Le Courrier du Canada*, 5 August 1860.
8 *La Minerve*, 7 December 1860.
9 NAC RG17 AI 2, Hutton to Edwards, 30 November 1860; to George Lanigan, 26 October 1860.
10 *La Minerve*, 4 January 1861; *Courrier du Canada*, 7 January 1861.
11 *Globe*, 9 January 1861.
12 *Courrier du Canada*, 16 January 1861; *Le Canadien*, 21 January 1861.

13 St. Mary's *Weekly Argus*, 31 January 1861.
14 *La Minerve*, 14 March 1861.
15 NAC RG17 AI 2, Hutton to Hough, 11 July, 23 September 1857.
16 NAC RG17 AI 2, Hutton to Secretary of State, Maine, 17 March 1855; to Donnally, 17 November 1855; to de Bow, 22 May 1860; to Kennedy, 6 June 1860.
17 NAC RG17 AI 2, Hutton to Barclay, 28 March 1857; Hutton to Ross, 25 February 1859. See also 22 Vic. cap.32, 'An Act respecting the Board of Registration and Statistics, and the Census and Statistical Information,' which also specified the second Monday in January 1861 as the next census date; see Schedule A.
18 NAC RG7 G1, vol. 150, Newcastle to Head, 31 January, 10 February 1860.
19 See NAC RG17 AI, 2, Hutton to Alleyn, 28 February 1860; to Vankoughnet, 5 March 1860; and to Sherwood, 14 April 1860, where Alexander Cambie was sent from Agriculture to the Receiver General's office on census duty. For the quotation, see to [Langton?], 4 May 1860, where the census is estimated to cost 50 per cent more than that of 1852. See also Hutton to Cook, to Marsh, to Ryerson, 2 June 1860. In Hutton to Kemp, 24 October 1860, Hutton sent an extract from the instructions to enumerators with respect to religion and offered to incorporate practical changes Kemp might make. Also see Hutton to Richd. Nettle, L' Anse-St-Jean, Saguenay, 5 June 1860. The proposal was for returns of quantity and value of dried, salted, and fresh fish; the schedules omitted the value column.
20 NAC RG1 E1, Canada State Book V, pp. 262–3, 19 June 1860; see also the copy in CO42/623, no. 72, 21 June 1860, which includes the notification sent to William Farr of Galt's nomination. As in RG19, vol. 1932, 22 June 1860, we see $400 advanced to Galt for expenses.
21 NAC RG17 AI, 2, 'Private,' Hutton to Galt, 20 June 1860; same to same, 22 June 1860 with a large package of material on the census, including a 'copy of the contemplated changes to be made in the ensuing Census.'
22 See *Report of the Proceedings of the Fourth Session of the International Statistical Congress, Held in London July 16th 1860, and the Five following Days* (London: HMSO, 1861); Henry Yule Hind, *British North America: Reports of Progress, Together with a Preliminary and General Report on the Assinniboine and Saskatchewan Exploring Expedition Made under Instruction from the Provincial Secretary, Canada* (London: Eyre and Spottiswoode, 1860); and O.D. Skelton, *The Life and Times of Sir Alexander Tilloch Galt* (Ottawa: Carleton University Press, 1966). W.L. Morton, in *Henry Yule Hind, 1823–1908* (Toronto: University of Toronto Press, 1980), suggests politely that Hind's statistical compendium borrowed heavily from other people's work. On Delany, see R. Blachett, 'In

350   Notes to pages 179–81

Search of International Support for African Colonization: Martin R. Delany's Visit to England, 1860.' *Canadian Journal of History* 10(3), 1975; and Paul Gilroy, *The Black Atlantic: Modernity and Double Consciousness* (Cambridge: Harvard University Press, 1993).
23 *Proceedings*, p.150. In any case, the delegates had not managed to consider two other matters of interest to Hutton, the 'Forms of Record and General Plan to be followed in the publication of Facts ascertained at the Census enumerations' and the 'Principal Numerical Ratios which it is desirable to calculate and publish on the occasions of Census taking.' They did insist on the necessity of an enumeration in one day, or where this was not possible, with reference to the same day; and did insist on the importance of a plan of civil registration to bolster the census.
24 NAC RG7 G1, vol. 152, Lewis to Head, 14 and 22 August 1860.
25 NAC RG17 AI, 2, Hutton to Queen's Printer, 10 October 1860; to Alleyn and Registration and Statistics, 10 October 1860; to S.B. Foote, *Chronicle*, 16 October 1860; to Editor, the *Leader*, 18 October 1860; to the *Spectator*, Hamilton, 19 October 1860; to Augustin Côté, *Journal de Québec*, 20 October 1860; to Alleyn, 24 October 1860; to Beaty, the *Leader*, 31 October 1860; to Gillespie and Robertson, the *Spectator*, 31 October 1860; Campbell to Price, 12 November 1860.
26 NAC RG17 AI, 2, Hutton to Beaty, the *Leader*, 19 November 1860; RG17, vol. 2418, Hutton to Gillespie & Robertson, the *Spectator*, 24 November 1860.
27 NAC RG17 AI, 2, Hutton to Côté, 20 October 1860; here Hutton invites a tender for a list of material and adds 'All translated & printed in the French language.' Note also Hutton to Kemp, 19 November 1860. The translations were far from perfect, with the commissioners' instructions containing such Anglicisms and grammatical errors as: 'Dans le cas où quelqu'un de vos énumérateurs se montreraient incapables ...'
28 NAC RG17, vol. 2418, John Beatty, 14 January 1861.
29 The Census and Statistics Act of 1859 specified that a letter of notification from the board was sufficient authority for a commissioner to act, so the fact that their official commissions arrived only the last week in December in most cases did not slow them down. The official appointments were decided in Council the last week of November; see, for example, NAC RG17, vol. 2418, Macdonald to Sherwood, 27 November 1860.
30 NAC RG17 AI, 2, Hutton to John Eden, Crown Lands Agent, Gaspé Basin, 4 August 1860; to James Beatty, 29 November 1860.
31 For instance, NAC RG17 AI, 2, Hutton to B. Pouliot, 31 July 1860; Hutton to Cayley, 1 September 1860: 'there cannot be a doubt but that the nomi-

Notes to pages 182–5  351

nees of those members who were invited to nominate will be appointed to the office unless some serious objection is made by the Board.'
32 NAC RG17, AI, 2, Hutton to Winram, 10 April 1860; Hutton to Neville, 10 July 1860; Hutton to Ross, nd July 1860; Hutton to Neville, 28 July 1860; Hutton to Alleyn, 27 October 1860; RG19, vol. 2083, roster of employees for the census, December 1860; June 1861. The fact that there are no other clerks besides A.J. Cambie at work on census matters before November suggests that he and Hutton devised all the forms and instructions.
33 NAC RG17 AI, 2, Hutton to Parent, 20 November 1860; Hutton to Alleyn, 21 November 1860; John Garner, *The Franchise and Politics in British North America* (Toronto: University of Toronto Press, 1969): 109–17.
34 NAC RG17 AI, 2, Hutton to 'Upper Canada' census commissioners, 25 November 1860.
35 NAC RG17, vol. 2418 [misdated in a different colour ink], 4 December 1860, report of A. Macdonald Lockhart, Haldimand co., where mention is made of Hutton's 'private instructions'; also RG31, Census field 1861, Algoma District, which contains a transcribed Hutton to Carney, 10 December 1860, with personal instructions for enumerating 'Indians' and 'Shantymen'; RG17, vol. 2418, October 1860, 'Instructions aux Commissaires du Recensement.' I have found no English copy. See also RG31, Census Field 1861, Algoma District, which contains a copy of 'Instructions to Enumerators,' Quebec, November 1860.
36 NAC RG17, vol. 2418, McDougall, Russell co. commissioner, to BRS, 14 January 1861, pencilled notation in Hutton's hand; ditto on Bishop, Wolfe co. commissioner, to BRS, 14 January 1861; AI 2, Hutton to Hope, 4 January 1861. 'I have not time to write – The Census keeps me at the stretch'; MG30 E96 6, Hutton to Anna (Hutton) Ponton, 17 February 1861; Frances McCrea Hutton to Anna (Hutton) Ponton, 28 February 1861.
37 22 Vic. cap. 33, sec. 16; A common source of complaint as the enumeration unfolded in Canada West was that villages and towns weren't provided with self-enumeration sheets. For instance, in the *Globe*, 16 January 1861, a correspondent from Yorkville village complained, 'Not a paper for the Census has been left in this village'; in the Stratford *Weekly Beacon*, 18 January 1861: 'Through some bad arrangements, enumerators seem not to be supplied with schedules, and consequently they are going about from house to house asking the requisite information.' NAC RG17, vol. 2419, J.W. Walsh, 27 December 1860: 'Some of my enumerators contend that the Act does not require in rural districts that the Enumerators should make a double tour ...'
38 NAC RG17, vol. 2419, Thomas White, 17 January 1861.

39 NAC RG17, vol. 2419, N.S. Appleby, 5, 15 January 1861.
40 NAC RG17, vol. 2418, James Beatty, 15 December 1860; 10 and 14 January 1861.
41 Legislative Assembly of Canada, *Sessional Papers*, no. 23, 10 April 1861, 'Report of the Minister of Agriculture of Canada': 'A misapprehension of these duties has caused a very undeserved censure on several of the commissioners and enumerators through the public press ... In all cases the work has been much better done when the information was collected personally, and written down by the enumerator himself, as very many of the citizens put various interpretations on the headings, and fill them in so as to render the enquiry fruitless, or cause much trouble to the commissioners and enumerators in correcting their erroneous answers.' In RG31, Census field 1861, town of Cobourg, town of Belleville, the schedules are those used in rural areas, but consider the town of Simcoe, where S. Fuller seems to have started by allowing members of the elite to fill in their own entries on the rural schedule.
42 NAC RG17, vol. 2420, John Beatty, Cobourg, 30 April 1861.
43 NAC RG17, vol. 2419, William Gunn, Kincardine, 16 April 1861.
44 NAC RG17, vol. 2419, Jarvis to Hutton, 12, 31 December 1860; 10, 11, 16 January 1861.
45 NAC RG17, vol. 2419, Solyme Bertrand, St-Mathias, 9, 20, 31 December 1860.
46 NAC RG17, vol. 2419, P. Labelle, St-Vincent-de-Paul, 2 January (two letters), 4 January (two letters) 1861.
47 NAC RG17 AI, 2, Hutton to Chauveau, 28, 30 May 1860; to Jas. C.Z. Kennedy, census superintendent, Washington, 5 June 1860.
48 NAC RG17, vol. 2418, 'Instructions aux commissaires du Recensement.'
49 NAC RG17 AI, 2, Hutton to commissioners, London, Kingston, and Hamilton, Canada West, 29 November 1860; and RG17, vol. 2417, Charles Waters, Prescott County, 2 January 1860 (misdated; should read 1861): 'the Latitude allowed in Extending the Enumeration Districts, where ever it is found absolutely necessary is a great relief ...'; vol. 2419, 2 February 1861: 'it was fortunate that I was allowed to extend the Number of souls to "800 or Even 1000" ...'
50 NAC RG17, vol. 2418, Leary to Hutton, 9 December 1860; vol. 2419, Gunn to Hutton, 18 December 1860; White to Hutton 17 January 1861.
51 NAC RG17, vol. 2418, John Beatty, 15 December 1860.
52 NAC RG17, vol. 2418, A. Macdonald Lockhart, [misdated 4 December 1860].
53 On the feminization of teaching, see Curtis, *Building the Educational State.* 253.

54 NAC RG17, vols. 2419–20, Holmes to Hutton, 5, 17, 20, 26 December 1860; 3, 19, 28 January 1861. Marginal note in Hutton's hand in pencil on 12 January: 'send him what he wants.'
55 For the Crown Lands map, NAC RG1 E7, vol. 49, 22 June 1858; the plan had emerged out of an attempt to chart timber berths. For some of Hutton's other involvements with producing maps, see RG17 AI 2, Rolph to Hamling, 27 May 1854, on the railway map; Hutton to Council, 12 November 1855; to Wilcocks, 4 April 1857; to Commissioners of National Education, Dublin, 7 September 1860; there are others. On the Geological Survey, Hutton to Logan, 5 January 1860. See also Suzanne Zeller, *Inventing Canada: Early Victorian Science and the Idea of a Transcontinental Nation* (Toronto: University of Toronto Press, 1987).
56 NAC RG17, vols. 2419–20, Holmes to Hutton, 28 January 1861; Holmes was the appointee of the racist MPP Edwin Larwill. Also, Vidal to Hutton, 7 December 1860, 6 May 1861; Vidal revealed that 'the enumeration of the Indians was a very troublesome and difficult work. The Enumerator, David B Wawanosh, is the head Chief and performed his duty well – The Bosanquet Reserves are 35 miles from Sarnia – his home – and Walpole Island is 25 miles in the opposite direction.'
57 NAC RG31, Census field 1861, Dorchester twp., Middlesex co., enumerator's complaints about Oneidas on Agricultural, p. 2. See, for instance, Charlotteville twp., Norfolk co., District 1, and Kamouraska, District 16, p. 124, for typical sloppy enumeration of people marked 'Ind.' See also RG17, vol. 2420, Charles L. Martigny, 17 May 1861, re: claims extra pay for interpreters used to enumerate Algonquins and Iroquois.
58 NAC RG31, Census field 1861, Algoma District; all of the above correspondence, with forms and estimated returns, is copied at the start of the Algoma run.
59 NAC RG17, vol. 2419, Charles Waters, 2 February 1861; for more on the contentious issue of the enumeration of the black population, see Michael Wayne, 'The Black Population of Canada West on the Eve of the American Civil War: A Reassessment Based on the Manuscript Census of 1861,' *Histoire sociale/Social History* 28(56), 1995: 465–85,
60 NAC RG17, vol. 2418, A. Macdonald Lockhart, 6 December 1860 (misdated; should read 1861).
61 NAC RG17, vol. 2418, Francis Clemow, 14 January 1861.
62 NAC RG17, vols. 2418–19, Hugh McDougall, 4, 21, 23 January, 6 February, 18 March 1861.
63 NAC RG17, vols. 2417–19, Charles Waters, 4, 8, 18, 19, 22, 26 January, 2 February, 12, 22 April 1861.
64 NAC RG17, vol. 2418; Increase Bullock, 6 February 1861, discovers that an

354   Notes to pages 196–201

enumerator called away on business gets someone else to do it. Notice the two maps of districts drawn by Bullock in this file.
65 NAC RG17, vol. 2418, John Barker, 4 April 1861.

## 6: The 'Reality of Representation'

1 He rearranged some enumeration columns and added a number of others on both the personal and agricultural schedules. The 1861 personal schedules grew to 60 columns from 41 in 1852, and the agricultural schedules to 69 columns from 56. The urban self-enumeration schedules now contained 60 columns as well, in contrast to 43 in 1852. Physically, the schedules had become much larger and more cumbersome, but the board did not deliver on its promise to provide enumerators' books in which they could be carried and protected.
2 No copy has survived, but it is announced in *La Minerve*, 24 January 1861.
3 Lengthy debates at the Statistical Congress had concerned the urban/rural divide; the French delegates were especially eager to mobilize the concept that the 'moral density' of social relations changed qualitatively with a population of around 5,000.
4 On normalizing judgment, see Foucault, *Discipline and Punish.*
5 Desrosières, 'How to Make Things Which Hold Together,' stresses that the establishment of such equivalences in statistical matters is a result of state power; on representation, see Hacking, *Representing and Intervening.*
6 It is instructive to consider relations in Hutton's own household, as in Boyce, *Hutton of Hastings*, where William travels frequently, Joseph is away at school, the daughters visit friends and relations and receive their friends and relations, transient workers are hired at harvest time, and others stay more regularly.
7 NAC RG31, Census field 1861, Algoma District; copy of Hutton to Carney, 1 December 1861.
8 NAC RG17, vol. 2420, John Beatty, Cobourg, nd 1861.
9 NAC RG31, Census field 1861, Kamouraska co. Districts 15 and 17; District 6, Chambly co., pp. 122–3. The logic of my argument precludes an interest in any exhaustive attempt to track down multiple entries, which is fortunate, for the practical challenge is considerable. I did take four counties, Chambly, Kamouraska, Leeds, and Norfolk, make a detailed list of those returned as non-residents, and then attempt to track them to their 'normal residences,' but only as a heuristic exercise to understand the work that would have been required of compilers in reassigning people. With some reasonably defensible inferences, many of those whose normal residence

was in the same county can be tracked in this way – about half. But people are mobile across county boundaries. Information returned about what are likely identical individuals varies from one enumerator to another. Enumerators were not consistent in the amount of information they offered about those out of place, and many did not give a 'normal residence.'

10 The best source for 1861 census instruments, which seem not to have been collected elsewhere, is at the outset of the Algoma District census run: NAC RG31, Census field 1861, Algoma District.
11 NAC RG17, vols. 2419–20, Holmes to Hutton, 3 January 1861, first draws Hutton's attention to it.
12 A good example is the returns for Chambly County: NAC RG31, Census field 1861, Chambly County.
13 NAC RG17, vol. 2418, 'Instructions aux Commissaires du Recensement.'
14 NAC RG17, vol. 2419, Solyme Bertrand, St-Mathias, 9, 20, 31 December 1860. I don't think he quite got it: he seems to have assumed that enumerators would enter nothing for strangers in the sex column, so including strangers in the household columns would cause a problem. In practice, the problem was the inverse: entering information for transients in the sex column and then not including them in the household columns. Perhaps Bertrand's imprecision allowed the board to disregard his warning.
15 NAC RG17, vol. 2418, White's instructions are in Kintrea to BRS, 18 January 1861.
16 NAC RG17, vol. 2419, P. Labelle, Laval, 23 février 1861; William Gunn, Bruce County, 26 February 1861. Gunn wanted fifty names on each sheet.
17 NAC RG17, vol. 2419, John Leary, Huron County, 15 March 1861.
18 NAC RG17, vol. 2419, Alexander Vidal, Sarnia, 19 March, 6 May 1861. For examples of treatment of deaths, see NAC RG31, Census field 1861, St-Onésime-d'Ixworth, Kamouraska co., p. 7; most Kamouraska enumerators did not count the dead in their totals; some did. See District 2, Bastard twp., Leeds co., where Alis Corrs and Josia Johnston are among the living dead.
19 NAC RG31, Census field 1861, West Ward Brockville, Leeds co.; the enumerator understood the heading to mean *married during 1860* and sometimes noted 'none in 1860.' Nicholas Willoughby for Leeds twp., Districts 2 and 3, Leeds co., gave the year people were married. David Gagan's *Hopeful Travellers: Families, Land, and Social Change in Mid-Victorian Peel County, Canada West* (Toronto: University of Toronto Press, 1982), draws on the work of one enumerator who returned the year people were married in arguments about life cycle and family strategies.
20 For example, NAC RG31, Census field 1861, District 4, Wolford twp., Grenville co., where Morris McFadden, William Bush, Margaret Smith, and

Catherine Durell are to be one year old and are not reported in the births column. James Kelly is to be one at his next birthday, except that he is dead. He is counted as among the living in the other census columns. In Kamouraska co., District 3, p. 9, Marguerite Dionne is to be ½ at her next birthday.
21 The enumerators may simply not have used the column. See the early debate, Harvey Graff, 'Literacy and Social Structure in Elgin County, Canada West: 1861,' *Histoire sociale/Social History* 6, 1973: 25–48; H.J. Mays and H.F. Manzl, 'Literacy and Social Structure in Nineteenth Century Ontario: An Exercise in Historical Methodology,' *Histoire sociale/Social History* 7, 1974: 331–45.
22 NAC RG31, Census field 1861, Elizabethtown twp., Leeds co., James B. Powell, p. 32; Geo. P. Wight, Yonge twp., District 3, p. 73; Nicholas Willoughby, Leeds twp., District 3, their orthography.
23 NAC RG31, Census field 1861, Toronto, St Andrew's ward, no. 267; this respondent also writes 'Cannot tell' in the column dealing with the amount invested in his business.
24 NAC RG17, vol. 2419, William Gunn, Bruce co., 26 February 1861; vol. 2420, John Beatty, Cobourg, nd 1861.
25 NAC RG31, Census field 1861, Districts 2 and 3, Leeds twp., Leeds co., comments on p. 59, pt. 2; his orthography.
26 NAC RG17, vol. 2419, Solyme Bertrand, St-Mathias, 9, 20, 31 December 1860.
27 NAC RG17, vol. 2420, John Beatty, Cobourg, 30 April 1861; vol. 2419, John Leary, Huron co., 4 January 1861; Thomas White, Jr., Peterborough, 17 January 1861; Simon Johnston, Dundas, 5 February 1861.
28 NAC RG17, vol. 2419, Thomas White, Jr., Peterborough, 17 January 1861; vol. 2420, David White, Woodstock, 'Notice to Enumerators,' 17 January 1861; RG31, Middlesex County census returns, 1861, p. 105, sheet 2, note from enumerator to commissioner: 'Having found the Orchards in my Division under crop I included them in the column for crops. David McKenzie. Enumerator'; Leeds County census returns 1861, Leeds twp., Districts 2 and 3, enumerator's comments: 'There being no Collum for Meadows I was obliged to put the Meadow and pasture in the same Collum although it canot be denied that Hay is a crop.'
29 NAC RG17, vol. 2418, 18 January 1861; see also R.M. McInnis, 'Perspectives on Ontario Agriculture, 1815–1930' in D.H. Akenson, ed., *Canadian Papers in Rural History* Vol. VIII (Gananoque: Langdale Press, 1992): 17–128.
30 NAC RG17, vol. 2420, J.O. Bastien, 7 January 1861; see also his 10 January 1861, where he notices the typographical error in the enumerators' instructions.

31 NAC RG31, Census field 1861, Middlesex co.; see for example the agricultural census sheet no. 41, where the enumerator has returned one person who held one acre, and another who held no land but had some livestock.
32 NAC RG31, Census field 1861, remarks on agricultural run, Edwardsburgh twp., District 6, Grenville co.
33 NAC RG31, Census field 1861, Leeds co., Canada West, Kitley personal p. 42; agricultural, p. 67; Yonge personal, p. 67. Bellamy was forty-three years old in Kitley but forty-two years old in Yonge.
34 For the distinction between representational and conventional measurements, see W. Kula, *Measures and Men* (Princeton: Princeton University Press, 1986).
35 NAC RG17, vol. 2418, Kintrea to Hutton, 11 April 1861.
36 NAC RG31, Census field 1861, District 1, Artemesia twp., Grey co.; compilers tended to read down columns, not across rows. See also Huron and Kent County, Ward 3, Stanley twp., where Henry Pollock used agricultural as personal sheets, and comments, 'I did not use some parts of the sheets for what they were marked out – Yet I had to apply them for Census list as I had not sheets enough for that purpose.' In the RG31 collection, these personal returns are catalogued as agricultural returns, since they are on agricultural sheets. One wonders what the compilers did with them. Another set is to be found in the Middlesex County agricultural census, pp. 106, 110–11, with the enumerator's remark, 'I had been under the obligation of taking this sheet for the personal for Carlisle not having any other.'
37 NAC RG17, vol. 2419, P.R. Jarvis, Stratford, 12 December 1860.
38 NAC RG17, vol. 2420, Dawson Kerr, 4 March 1861.
39 NAC RG31, Leeds co., Elizabeth twp., District 3, John Young's comments, 20 February 1861, last sheet in the run; Yonge twp., District 2, comments on p. 43.
40 NAC RG17, vol. 2419; enumerators' letters included in Gunn to Board of Registration and Statistics, 16 April 1861. These men were pleading for extra pay, but similar reports arrived from all over the colony.
41 Legislative Assembly of Canada, *Sessional Papers*, no. 23, 1861, 'Report of the Minister of Agriculture of Canada.'
42 NAC RG17, vol. 2420, W.W. Holmes, 18 March, 22 April, 6, 23 May 1861.
43 NAC RG17, vol. 2419, Rev. H. Richardson to Chas Alleyn, Provincial Secretary, 25 January 1861.
44 NAC RG31, Census field 1861, Joliette co., comments on p. 477, District 7, by Dézil, by Crépeau at the end of the agricultural sheets.
45 NAC RG31, Census field 1861, Huron and Kent county, Stanley twp., Ward

3, Henry Pollock's comments on p. 2; RG17, vol. 2419, enumerators' comments in Gunn to Board of Registration and Statistics, 16 May 1861.
46 NAC RG17, vol. 2419, P. Labelle, 26 March 1861.
47 NAC RG17, vol. 2420, Isiah Wright, 24 June, 1 August 1861; William Dickinson, 1, 15 July 1861.
48 NAC RG31, Census field 1861, Yonge twp., Leeds co., District 2, agricultural census, remarks on final sheet. Young's hesitation about female informants might carry more weight if his enumeration of his own land had been internally consistent.
49 NAC RG17, vol. 2420, John Jarvis, 17 March 1861; Bouchard and Wright are included in vol. 2419, Charles Le Brun, nd March 1861, census accounts.
50 NAC RG31, Census field 1861, enumerators' remarks. For the pork grease, London twp., and Deleware twp., Middlesex co.; he signs 'H.R.E.' on both. For the threshing, Deleware twp., Middlesex co., p. 345, pt. 2. In RG17, vol. 2418, John McDougall, 31 December 1861, the enumerators' list is given. McDougall calls Cradmore 'Deadman' and gives the name of the person quoted here as 'Henry Rollins' for Deleware; there is no one with such initials for London twp. McDougall knew the enumerators very slightly and there may have been a turnover.
51 NAC RG17, vol. 2420, Cassidy to Gunn, enclosed with Gunn's accounts.
52 NAC RG17, vol. 2419, Thomas White, Jr., 8 February 1861; RG31, Census field 1861, Edward D. Buchner's comments on Middleton twp., Norfolk co., District 2, p. 43, pt. 2. The majority of the large numbers of men at work in the woods in this county are counted at least twice on the schedules. Since many farmers took their teams to the woods and hauled for different camps, they may appear more than twice.
53 NAC RG17, vol. 2420, Charles Waters, 22 January 1861; vol. 2418, John Leary, 18 February 1861; RG31, Census field 1861, North Dorchester twp., Middlesex co., p. 63 agricultural census.
54 NAC RG17, vol. 2418, Increase Bullock, 2 March, 4 May 1861.
55 NAC RG17, vol. 2419, David Morrow, 5 March 1861.
56 NAC RG17, vol. 2418, James Kintrea, 11 April 1861; he does not say what the 'errors' were; vol. 2419, S.B. Fairbanks, 2 February, 23 April 1861; N.S. Appleby, 18 March, 10, 17 April 1861; Jacob Hespeler, 26 March 1861.
57 NAC RG17, vol. 2419, P. Labelle, 23 February, 4 March 1861.
58 NAC RG17, vol. 2419, John Leary, 18 February, 15 March 1861.
59 NAC RG17, vol. 2419, William Gunn, 26 February, 2, 9 April 1861; Gunn shipped the original sheets to the board after he sent in his corrected copies. Unfortunately, none of the original schedules has survived, and I have also been unable to find the memorandum he mentions about some

of the columns. See also vol. 2420, James McDougall, 16 March 1861, adding *inter alia* 'some of the Enumerators have not described their Enumeration Districts, this in some cases would be very difficult to do, as the boundaries of many of the wards are very crooked.' RG31, Census field 1861, West Williams twp., Middlesex co., agricultural census, p. 94, pt. 2.
60 NAC RG17, vol. 2418, John Beatty, 2 March 1861; vol. 2420, nd 1861; R.M. McInnis, 'Perspectives on Ontario Agriculture, 1815–1930,' in D.H. Akenson, ed., *Canadian Papers in Rural History* (Gananoque: Langdale Press, 1992) VIII: 17–128, assumes that Canadian women did not do field labour in agriculture.
61 NAC RG31, Census field 1861, Algoma District, 'Memoranda' from Richard Carney, 18 April 1861, at beginning of run.
62 NAC RG31, Census field 1861, L'Islet County. For example, District 4, St-Aubert-du-Portjoli personal returns; District 1 of the parish of L'Islet, agricultural returns.
63 *La Minerve*, 7, 9, and 14 February; 2, and 14 March. In the latter the enumerator complains of the absence of a space for reporting poultry and eggs on the schedules. Also, *Weekly Beacon*, 8 February; Chatham *Argus*, 18 February; *Le Courrier du Canada*, 18 February 1861; NAC RG17, AI 2, Hutton to Wilcocks, 22 March 1861.
64 Notice *Le Canadien*'s two articles, 20 and 22 February 1861, with different totals for Quebec and warnings about which returns one should believe; see the *Argus* of 18 April for rivalry between Stratford and St. Mary's; and for Jarvis, see *Weekly Beacon*, 12 April 1861.
65 *Le Courrier du Canada*, 20, and 22 February, 1 March 1861.
66 *La Minerve*, 21 May 1861.
67 *La Minerve*, 21 March 1861.
68 *La Minerve*, 2 May 1861.
69 *Le Courrier du Canada*, 6 May; *La Minerve*, 14 June, 12 October; *Le Canadien*, 16 October; *Le Courrier du Canada*, 11 December 1861.
70 *Le Canadien*, 17 January 1862; also, *La Minerve* 18, and 25 January 1862.
71 The clerical contingent can be traced through the lists of warrants in NAC RG19, vols. 2083–9. Regarding accommodation, RG17 AI 2, Campbell to Alleyn, 26 July 1861, mentions two people without chairs; this even after Council had accepted the department's pleas for extra space in RG1 E1, Canada State Book W, 13 June 1861; note that the compilation process is estimated here to take two years. For Finance's share, RG17 AI 2, Eventurel to Bureau, 13 April 1863; Campbell to Harvey, 15 April 1863. There is a dispute about his pay, and Harvey is J.-C. Taché's most vocal critic around the census of 1871.

72 For the ages, see the partial list in NAC RG17 AI 9, 13 April 1866, where those still in government service are enrolled in the militia; for Byrne and also perhaps O'Brien, AI 2, Hutton to Ross, nd July 1860; for Willoughby, AI 2, Memorandum dated 8 March 1862; Belleau to Council, 'Que le Gouvernement avait droit d'utiliser les services du réclamant dans l'un ou l'autre des departments [sic] lorsqu'il était à son service'; also, RG19, vol. 2088, p. 193. Willoughby died soon after his work as inspector, although the cause is unknown; a month's gratuity was paid to his widow.

73 NAC RG17 AI 2, Hutton to Buchanan, 17–19 April 1861: 'It appears our Population will not exceed 2.5 million.' Also, McGee, 1 May 1861, commenting on the 2$^{nd}$ report of the Emigration Committee; to Hope, 3 May 1861. His last letter in the series is dated 11 May 1861. On Hutton's illness, Campbell to Donaldson, 23 May 1861. On Finden, ANQ, fonds Famille Langevin, P134, Taché to Chapais, 18 July 1867.

74 For disciplining the clerk, NAC RG17 AI 2, May to Laurent, 19 November 1861; for the rest, Evanturel to May, 23 September 1862; Memorandum to Council, 20 January 1864; and RG1 E7 vol. 62, 17 February 1864. Documents accompanying May's claim for extra pay include not only his resignation letter and statement of past work, but the only surviving copies of the circulars he prepared for the department.

75 NAC RG31, Census field 1861, for instance, Chambly co., St-Bruno p. 206; District 2, village of Longueuil; Boucherville sheets 2 and 4 graffitum and drawings of bottles in the deaths column, a girl's face and a goat in the school attendance; Yonge twp., Leeds co., District 3, p. 66, has 'hi randy dandy ho' and several drawings; there are many others.

76 No description survives of what they did; I am interpreting control marks on the schedules, but notice, for instance, NAC RG31, Census field 1861, St-Pierre, Quebec city (or any other urban run), sheet totals at the foot of columns 1, 8 and 9, 14–20; running totals for the District at the foot of 3 and 4. Chambly co., Dist. 8, paroisse de Boucherville, running totals at the foot of 8 and 9, 14–19.

77 It is somewhat speculative to suggest that compilers were responsible for such changes as that noted for Simcoe; commissioners could have made such alterations or in some cases the enumerators. Still, the changes made it possible for the compilers to do their work and the ink looks like theirs. I have made no attempt to be exhaustive, and the argument doesn't depend on an exhaustive treatment. For my examples, NAC RG31, Census field 1861, Charlotteville twp., Norfolk co., District 3, p. 55; Kamouraska co., parish of St-Pacôme, p. 335; parish of Ste-Anne-de-la-Pocatière, pp. 203–9, where the first totals excluding 'residence out' are scratched and the

transients counted; Chambly co., parish of Chambly, *passim* for added occupations; RG17, vol. 2421, Wm Dickinson, 25 February 1862; RG31, Census field 1861, Oxford twp., Grenville co., District 1, personal and agricultural census. There are no marks of correction.
78 NAC RG17, vol. 2420, Chauveau, 11 December 1861; Michael Wayne, 'The Black Population of Canada West on the Eve of the American Civil War: A Reassessment Based on the Manuscript Census of 1861,' *Histoire sociale/Social History* 28(56), 1995: 465–85.
79 NAC RG31, Census field 1861, Ste-Anne-de-la-Pocatière, Kamouraska co., p. 238; also p. 235, 'un cultivateur' who owns a large 'moulin à scie.'
80 NAC RG31, Census field 1861, Bastard twp., Leeds co., District 3, agricultural and personal returns; for instance, Lyddy Haskins.
81 NAC RG31, Census field 1861, parish of Longueuil, Chambly co., pp. 241, 247, 249, 253, 263. Hurteau enumerates himself in Chambly, District 2, p. 203; see also Townsend twp., Norfolk co., District 4, where women 'farmers' are checked.
82 *Census of the Canadas*, Vol. II, no. 13, Upper Canada – Return of Mills, Manufactories etc. (Quebec 1864); NAC RG31, Census field 1861, Leeds twp., Leeds co., p. 15. There were five melodian makers listed on this sheet, although three of them were aged six, three, and two years respectively.
83 On pushing the compilers, NAC RG17, AI 2, Campbell to McNider, 7 January 1862 (misdated; should read 1863). For the requests for copies, Campbell to Charlton, 26 February 1862; to Godley, 19 August 1862; to Kennedy, 25 September 1862; to Graham, 26 September 1862; With regard to printing, 'Tenders for Printing Census,' 24 August 1861; Campbell to Foote, 26 November 1862; Evanturel to Council, 11 December 1862; Campbell to Hunter and Rose, 4 July 1863; Campbell to Foote, 23 December 1863.
84 NAC RG17, vol. 1663, copy of an address from the Legislature calling for a return of population for each township entitled to a share of funds under the 1859 Seigneurial Amendment Act. Less important, the petition of a Quebec County municipal official to dispense with the French language in his township, on the grounds that the majority were English speaking, was denied with reference to the census AI 2, Evanturel to Council, 29 October 1862; also vol. 2417, where other departments of government seek returns for various administrative purposes.
85 *La Minerve*, 19 March 1861.
86 Reprinted in *La Minerve*, 30 April 1861.
87 For Chauveau's remarks, NAC RG17, vol. 2420, Chauveau, 6 June, 11 December 1861; Rameau's work was *La France aux colonies. Études sur le*

*développement de la race française hors de l'Europe* (Paris: A. Jouby, 1859); Rameau remained involved in these questions for several decades, publishing a sharp attack on the treatment of French Canadians in the 1891 census, at which time he was honorary president of the St-Jean-Baptiste Society; see *Le recensement de 1891. Ses inexactitudes et ses altérations au point de vue français* (Paris: Imprimerie Chaix, 1894).

88 *Le Canadien*, 3 March; *Le Courrier du Canada*, 5 March 1862.
89 *Le Canadien*, *Le Courrier du Canada* 20 May 1864. The Canadian papers are picking up a debate that was conducted in the *London Canadian News* and *L'Économiste Française*, which I don't follow further here.
90 No detail survives about the Parliamentary committee, but it is mentioned in NAC RG17 AI 2, Campbell to Lindsay, 25 January 1864. John Langton, *The Census of 1861; A Paper Read before the Literary and Historical Society of Quebec, 2nd March, 1864.* (Quebec: Hunter, Rose & Co., 1864).

## 7: Facts, Figures, and Fundamentalism

1 For examples of changing position, see P.B. Waite, ed., *The Confederation Debates in the Province of Canada/1865* (Toronto: McClelland and Stewart, 1963); and Joseph Cauchon, *L'union des provinces de l'Amérique britannique du nord* (Québec: A. Coté et Cie., 1865). The BNA Act suggested that each province, except where it would have fewer commons seats than senate seats, be allocated its share by taking the population of the whole dominion from the 1861 census, dividing it by the number of seats, and then, disregarding fractions, by dividing the population of each province by the number so obtained to determine its number of seats. A formula for dealing with the remainder was offered.
2 Province of Canada, *Sessional Papers*, no. 4, 1863, 'Annual Report of the Minister of Agriculture and Statistics ... for the Year 1862.'
3 Province of Canada, *Sessional Papers*, no. 32, 1864, 'Report of the Minister of Agriculture and Statistics for the Year 1863.'
4 McGee was Minister of Agriculture until Confederation, when he was replaced by T.C. Chapais. For McGee's biography, Isabel Skelton, *The Life of Thomas D'Arcy McGee* (Gardenvale: Garden City Press, 1925), and Robin B. Burns, 'McGee, Thomas D'Arcy,' *Dictionary of Canadian Biography* (Toronto: University of Toronto Press, 1976) IX: 489–95. Little is said about McGee's reorganization of government.
5 NAC RG1 E7, vol. 59A, February 1863, Thomas D'Arcy McGee, 'Report on Origins of The Public Departments.'
6 I echo J.-G. Nadeau's assertion that Taché deserves to be better known; see

his 'Taché, Joseph-Charles,' *Dictionary of Canadian Biography* (Toronto: University of Toronto Press, 1990) XII: 1012–16
7 ANQ Fonds Taché, p. 407.5, g110; 407.5, g96–7. I draw heavily in this section on Nadeau, 'Taché, Joseph-Charles'; and Evelyn Bossé, *Joseph-Charles Taché: Un grand représantant de l'élite canadienne-française* (Québec: Éditions Garneau, 1971). Neither pays particular attention to Taché the statistician.
8 All quotations are from Legislative Assembly of Canada, *Sessional papers*, Appendix TT, 1850, 'Report of the Special Committee on the State of Agriculture in Lower Canada' (translation). It is worth noting in the appendix to the report William Evans's critique of the agricultural inquiries in the 1848 census schedule.
9 For the plan, Joseph-Charles Taché, *The Seigniorial Tenure in Canada, and Plan of Commutation* (Quebec: Lovell and Lamoureux, 1854); for committee memberships etc., Province of Canada, Legislative Assembly, *Debates*, 31 August 1852; 14 September 1854; 27 February 1855; *Sessional Papers*, Appendix J, 1851; Canada *Gazette*, 19 February 1853.
10 J.C. Taché, *Esquisse sur le Canada considéré sous le point de vue économiste* (Paris: Bossange et Fils, 1855).
11 ANQ P407-5, no. 119, letters of 29 May, 26 July 1855. There is no mention anywhere of the 1855 Statistical Congress, and Taché employed none of its categories.
12 On the ultramontanes, see Nive Voisine, 'L'ultramontanisme canadien-français au XIXe siècle,' in Nive Voisine and Jean Hamelin, eds., *Les ultramontains canadien-français* (Montréal: Boréal Express, 1985): 67–104. For the plan for federation, Joseph-Charles Taché, *Des provinces de l'amérique du nord et d'une union fédérale* (Québec: J.T. Brousseau, 1858).
13 *Le Courrier du Canada*, 8 March 1858.
14 NAC RG19, vol. 1932, 21 May 1860; RG1 E1, Canada State Book W, p. 366, 23 September 1861; the board subscribed to *The Lancet*; *La revue penitentiaire des institutions préventives*; *The American Journal of Insanity*; *Annales d'hygiène publique et de médecine légale*; *The Psychological Journal*; and *Annales médico-psychologique*. Taché also reorganized the quarantine regulations at Grosse Île and was employed in various capacities not strictly in the board's mandate, such as reporting on the agricultural college at Ste-Anne; see Canada State Book W, p. 458, 23 October 1861; RG1 E7, vol. 60, 22 April 1863; also, *Report of the Board of Inspectors of Asylums, Prisons, etc., for the Year 1863* (Quebec: Hunter, Rose & Co, 1864), and Joseph-Charles Taché, *The Board of Inspectors of Prisons and Hospitals and Its Accusers* (Quebec: Morning Chronicle, 1864). Notice that Taché was also one of the Canadian commissioners to the 1862 London Exhibition and that John Beatty, a fellow

commissioner, would serve as one of the 1871 census managers; see NAC RG17, vol. 1663.
15 Joseph-Charles Taché, *Trois légendes de mon pays, ou l'évangile ignoré, l'évangile prêché, l'évangile accepté* (Montréal: Librairie Beauchemin, 1917 [1861]); also, Graham Parker, *The Beginnings of the Book Trade in Canada* (Toronto: University of Toronto Press, 1985). For the contrast with the official politics of literature in Canada West, see Bruce Curtis, 'Curricular Change and the Red Readers: History and Theory,' in R. Clarke, I. Goodson, and G. Milburn, eds., *Reinterpreting Curriculum Research: Images & Arguments* (London: Althouse; Sussex: Falmer, 1989): 41–63; '"Littery Merrit", "Useful Knowledge", and the Organization of Township Libraries in Canada West, 1840–1860,' *Ontario History* 78 (4), 1986: 284–312; and 'The Speller Expelled: Disciplining the Common Reader in Canada West,' *Canadian Review of Sociology and Anthropology* 22(3), 1985: 346–68.
16 Both Hodgetts, *Pioneer Public Service*, and Warton, *Dominion Bureau of Statistics*, do so, clearly to claim that nothing significant happened before Taché.
17 Parliament of Canada, *Sessional Papers*, no. 42, 1869 (written in 1867).
18 NAC RG17, vol. 2415, 18 January 1865.
19 Foucauldian studies of government, by contrast, have had little to offer to the investigation of mnemonic practices, perhaps because these are ritualized rather than routinized practices. For the quote, H.V. Nelles, 'Historical Pageantry and the "Fusion of the Races" at the Tercentenary of Quebec, 1908,' *Histoire sociale/Social history* 29(58), 1996: 391–415, at 395. Allan Greer's analysis of struggles around militia officers' maypoles is one useful treatment of the politics of monuments; see his *The Patriots and the People*, and Cohn, *Colonialism and Its Forms of Knowledge*, for 'officializing practices.' See also Dorothy Noyes and Roger D. Abrahams, 'From Calendar Custom to National Memory: European Commonplaces,' in Dan Ben-Amos and Liliane Weissberg, eds., *Cultural Memory and the Construction of Identity* (Detroit: Wayne State University Press, 1999): 77–98; Mary Gergen, 'The Social Construction of Personal Histories: Gendered Lives in Popular Autobiographies,' in T.R. Sarbin and J.I. Kitsuse, eds., *Constructing the Social* (London: Sage, 1994): 19–44; Raphael Samuel, *Theatres of Memory* (London: Verso, 1994); Nicholas Rogers and Adrian Shubert, 'Spectacle, Monument, and Memory,' *Histoire sociale/Social History* 29(58), 1996: 265–74; John Urry, 'How Societies Remember the Past,' in Sharon Macdonald and Gordon Fyfe, eds., *Theorizing Museums* (Oxford: Blackwell Publishers/The Sociological Review, 1996): 45–65; and Richard Werbner, 'Smoke from the Barrel of a Gun: Postwars of the Dead, Memory and Reinscription in Zimbabwe,' in

Richard Werbner, ed., *Memory and the Postcolony: African Anthropology and the Critique of Power* (London: ZED Books, 1998): 71–102.

20 For the appointments, NAC RG17, vol. 4, W.H. Lee to Taché, 15 March 1865; Johnson to Taché, 17 March 1865; Drapeau to Taché, 18 March 1865, *inter alia*: 'J'accepte la situation qui m'est offerte, malgré que le salaire en soit moins élevé que celui de ma présente charge d'Agent de Colonisation.' Both men would later complain bitterly that they were promised they would earn $1,200 after a few months; the Civil Service Reform kept them at $1,000 after they expected $1,440. RG17 AI 2, Taché to Tanguay, 13 March 1865.

21 The remark suggests that there were two Johnsons, although only one appears anywhere in the records of Agriculture and Statistics. Taché described him as sixty-two years old in 1868, although the 1871 census enumerator for Ottawa (District 77-d-2, p. 70) returned him as a fifty-four-year-old civil servant, an Englishman, and a Congregationalist. Perhaps the census enumerator made a slip of the pen, writing fifty-four instead of sixty-four; Johnson's wife was said to be fifty-eight. On the other hand, the compilers had examined the census return closely, noting in the margin, 'one son of Johnson not recorded'; see also Province of Canada, *Sessional Papers*, no. 3, 1867 (the Blue Book for 1865); NAC RG17 AI 2, Taché to Langton (as civil service commissioner), 24 June 1868; and ANQ Fonds Famille Langevin, loc. 3A07–3406A, Taché to Chapais, 18 July 1867. The junior Johnson does not appear to have been George, who organized the census of 1891, although a look at George Johnson's work is rewarding. See especially the state-of-the-art demonstration of graphical statistical representation prepared for the Royal Jubilee, George Johnson, *Johnson's Graphic Statistics* (Ottawa: np, 1887).

22 Noël Bélanger, 'Tanguay, Cyprien,' *Dictionary of Canadian Biography* (Toronto: University of Toronto Press, 1995) XIII: 1094–7; and Mgr Cyprien Tanguay, *Dictionnaire généalogique des familles canadiennes-françaises*, Vol. 1, (Montréal: Sénécal, 1871). Having one's family tree reconstructed was a popular initiative on the part of the petty bourgeoisie in Quebec quite early, and one that created employment for genealogists, many of whom copied out information from Tanguay for individual clients. In NAC RG17 AI 2, Taché to Langton, 21 November 1868, Taché defended Tanguay's work at length to the Civil Service Commission.

23 L'Abbé C. Tanguay, *Répertoire général du clergé canadien par ordre chronologique depuis la fondation de la colonie jusqu'à nos jours* (Québec: Darveau, 1868): 1–2. Tanguay's introduction claims we'll hear about the contemporary priests,

'friends of colonization who, for about a quarter century, breviary and axe in hand, have not feared to confront the depths of the forest to mark out the lines of colonization,' but he seems not to have got to this part before publication. A discussion with Ollivier Hubert helped clarify my take on the genealogical project in what follows.

24 Elzéar Lavoie, 'Drapeau, Stanislas,' *Dictionary of Canadian Biography* (Toronto: University of Toronto Press, 1990) XII: 269–73; NAC RG1 E1, Canada State Book T, p. 509, 29 January 1859; p. 626, 30 March 1859; Canada State Book U, pp. 612–3, 1 February 1860. Drapeau's account books while road agent are in ANQ Fonds Taché, P-1000–597 3A192605A. For the schoolbook, see Province of Canada, Legislative Assembly, *Debates*, 6 October 1852; 13 April 1853; *Appel aux municipalités du Bas-Canada. La colonisation du Canada envisagée au point de vue national* (Quebec: Lamoureux, 1858); for Drapeau in the 1871 census, District 77–d-1, p. 5.

25 *Études sur les développements de la colonisation du Bas-Canada depuis dix ans:(1851 à 1861). Constantan les progrès des défrichements, de l'ouverture des chemins de colonisation et du développement de la population canadienne française.* Par Stanislas Drapeau. Agent de colonisation et promoteur des 'Sociétés de Secours,' etc. (Québec: Typographie de Léger Brousseau, 7 Rue Buade, 1863).

26 NAC RG17 AI 2, Taché to Robitaille, 4 February 1865.

27 To take only two cases beyond the census, consider Taché's *Memorandum on Cholera, Adopted at a Medical Conference Held in the Bureau of Agriculture, in March, 1866.* (Ottawa: Bureau of Agriculture and Statistics, 1866), where he used the cholera scare to agitate for statistical observation, temperance, moderation, and the avoidance of public amusements. Again, one wonders how Taché interpreted his role as Canadian representative to the Paris Exhibition of 1867, where the organizing commission described the event as a means of settling 'some of the most important questions of present day, namely, the changes which are being made in the organization of labour in great factories, the struggle which is going on between great and small industries, and the destruction or preservation of family, or home labour'; quoted in NAC RG17, vol. 7, Cardwell to Administrator of Canadian Government, 21 December 1865.

28 NAC RG17 AI 2, Taché to Daly, 2 November; to Newton, 26 November 1864; to secretaries of other British North American colonies, 4 January 1865.

29 NAC RG17, vol. 4, Tanguay to Taché, 16 March 1865; vol. 13, Tanguay to Taché, 4 January 1867; AI 2, Tanquay to Langton, 21 November 1868; AI 2, Cambie to Tanguay, 24 January 1867, the trip should 'add to the stock of

information you are preparing for the Department'; vol. 39, Tanguay to Taché (telegram), 25 July 1870, with pencilled notation; Parliament of Canada, *Sessional Papers*, no. 64. 1871.
30 NAC RG17 AI 2, Taché to Minister of Finance, 15 September 1868, with official instructions to Johnson. Vol. 25, Johnson to Taché, 17 November 1868, contains Johnson's detailed expenses and places visited.
31 Province of Canada, Legislative Assembly, *Sessional Papers*, no. 5, 1866, 'the antecedent statistics of the Province ... have been laboriously worked up, by Mr. Stanislas Drapeau, for Lower, and Mr. W.H. Johnson, for Upper Canada. Mr. Drapeau's researches extend to the first founding of Quebec in 1608 ...' Parliament of Canada, *Sessional Papers*, no. 80, 1870. NAC RG17 AI 2, Cambie to Drapeau, 24 January 1867, 'you are to remain in Quebec until further orders, prosecuting your statistical researches there.'
32 *Canada Free Press*, 12 May 1866; ANQ Fonds Famille Langevin, loc. 3A07–3406A, Taché to Chapais, 8 June 1868.
33 Parliament of Canada, *Sessional Papers*, No. 2A, 1872, for a discussion of the issue and for Taché's remarkable distinction between statistics as a federal matter and 'social *status*' as a provincial matter.
34 ANQ Fonds Famille Langevin, loc. 3A07–3406A, Taché to Chapais, 2 June 1868; NAC RG17, vol. 38, Drapeau and Johnson to Dunkin, 27 June 1870; Drapeau to Dunkin, 4 July 1870. The two had just learned that Andrew Russell had been appointed to the department to do the maps for the census at a salary of $1,800, and since they'd been told they'd be working on the project too, they sought a similar salary. Taché's defence of the department's work and of the general plan for a statistical system in the wake of the commission's inquiries can be found in Parliament of Canada, *Sessional Papers*, no. 76, 1867–68.
35 NAC RG17 AI 2, Taché to Johnson, 7 August, 'the object of your mission will be to obtain access to the archives of the above mentioned Provinces with permission to make up the Résumé of the Censuses which cannot be got at Ottawa.'
36 NAC RG17, vol. 51, Johnson to Taché, 7 September (telegram and lengthy letter); 13, and 16 September; vol. 54, 24 November 1871, shows that the clerk hired to copy things is still at work after almost three months.
37 No description of the decisional rules they employed in 'correcting' and 'recompiling' survives, but a consequence is that Taché's official census volumes typically give different returns for some categories from those in the census reports of 1852 and 1861. Taché's figures tend to be preferred by researchers; few people attend to the competing configurations of knowledge that are at issue.

368   Notes to pages 257–9

38 Province of Canada, Legislative Assembly, *Sessional Papers*, no. 42, 1867; also, no. 5 1866, where Taché writes: 'A very useful revision of the published Census of 1861 and that of 1852, by comparison with the original documents in our possession, has been made; while it displays an amazing quantity of errors in both ... the labor serves to educate those employed upon it, for the taking hereafter of a full and accurate Census.' NAC RG17, vol. 30, Langton to Taché, 14 June 1869.
39 NAC RG17, vol. 16, Costley to Chapais, 29 July 1867. Enclosed are the registration reports for 1865 and 1866, both of which reproduce the Registration Act; *Registration Report, Together with Copy of Amended Registration Act and Directions to Issuers of Marriage Licenses, Deputy Registrars, and Medical Men* (Halifax: Compton & Co., 1866). The financial and coercive clauses of the act likely made it more effective than the 1847 Census and Statistics Act. Biographical information is from a helpful private communication from Allan C. Dunlop of the Public Archives of Nova Scotia.
40 NAC RG17 AI 2, Taché to Costley, 21 October; 5, 11 November 1868; 16 January 1869; RG17, vol. 25, Costley to Taché, 9 November 1868; vol. 26, Costley to Taché, 11 January 1869, explaining that he suffered from an aneurism in his thigh and was too ill to travel, but would come when he could 'as the proposed work is one in which I am much interested'; vol. 28, Costley to Taché, 25 March 1869 and 9 May 1867 (misdated; should read 1869); AI 2, Taché to Minister of Finance, 24 March; 10 May 1869.
41 NAC RG17, vol. 30, Costley to Taché,13 July; vol. 32, 5 October 1869.
42 NAC RG17 AI 2, Cambie to Costley, 29 September; 13 October 1869; vol. 38, Costley to Taché, 6 June 1870; nd June 1870.
43 NAC RG17 AI 2, Taché to Minister of Finance, 19 July 1870; for Costley's descriptions, vol. 33, Costley to Taché, 2 November 1869; his description of electoral District 2 in Queen's County read: 'Electoral District No. 2 commences at the sea shore of Blue Berry Cove where the highway from Blue Berry to the South West Cove of Port Medway leaves the Pudding Pan Road, and by the farm of Edumund Darrow at said Blue Berry Cove; thence along the said road to the South West Cove, until passing Blue Berry Lake and the Wagner Farm, or the Farm lately occupied by Henry Wagner, of Blue Berry Lake, deceased; thence running in a direction nearly north 22° west, to Grodes' Falls on the Medway River about eight miles from Mills' Village; thence following the said Port Medway River north-westerly to the north-west line of the said Township; thence by the said Township line south, 58° west, crossing the Brookfield Road to the Liverpool River at Hemlock Point, so called; thence southerly and easterly along the said Liverpool River through Milton to Bristol; thence easterly along the shore

of Sandy Cove and Herring Cove to the eastern head of the Harbor of Liverpool; and thence along the sea shore of Beech Meadows, Broad Cove, and Eagle Head, to Blue Berry Cove, and the place of beginning of No. 2, in which is included Coffin's Island.'

44 NAC RG17 AI 2, Taché to Crown Lands department, Halifax, 22 July 1870; to Emigrant Agent, Saint John, 23 July 1870; Costley to Hendry, 25 July 1870; Taché to depty. Surveyor General, 26 July 1870; Taché to Indes, 1 August 1870, with correspondence between Layton and Indes.

45 NAC RG17, vol. 2423, Census Diaries; entries for 29 August; 13, 30 September; 7, 14, 16, 26, 29 October; 4, 5, 12, 29 November; 5 December 1870; AI 2, Taché to Butter, 4 August; Taché to Minister of Finance, 4 August, where there are now six employees doing piece work, some of them copying maps; Taché to Desbarats, 9 August 1870.

46 NAC RG17 AI 2, Dunkin to Richards, 28 April 1871.

47 Parliament of Canada, *Sessional Papers*, no. 61, 1871.

48 NAC RG17 AI 2, Chapais to Council, 14 April 1869.

49 Dominion of Canada, *Parliamentary Debates* [hereafter *Debates*], Third Session 1870, 8 March 1870.

50 *Debates*, 29 March 1870; Parliament of Canada, *Sessional Papers*, no. 64, 1871: 'The system, which after very careful consideration, has been adopted, is that which is known among Statists as the *population de droit* or *de jure*; that is the legal or domiciled population, as being best adapted to the circumstances of the Dominion.'

51 Dominion of Canada, *Debates*, 3 March 1871.

52 *Canada Free Press*, 29 June 1869, and *inter alia*, 'Our neighbours will also learn that universal suffrage is not an inseparable condition of development and that progress can take place under semi-monarchical as well as under purely republican institutions.' The official reports put the team at thirteen, but this excluded Taché, Drapeau, Johnson, and Lowe at least, as well as people in other departments, such as Andrew Russell.

53 John Lowe (1824–1913) was born in England and educated privately there, coming to Canada in 1841. He worked as a reporter and shorthand writer until entering into the publishing business, sometime after marrying Minnie Chamberlin in 1852. The Lowe-Chamberlin partnership acquired the Montreal *Gazette*, and after a brief stint as editor of the Toronto *Colonist*, Lowe was its senior editor until it went bankrupt shortly before he joined Agriculture and Statistics. Brown Chamberlin was then MP, and it was with him that Lowe lived while in Ottawa. After Confederation, the federal government ceased to produce an annual Blue Book: probably with Taché's active cooperation, Lowe and Chamberlin took over what became the

*Canada Year Book* as a private enterprise. Their main contributor in the 1867 effort was Arthur Harvey from the Finance department, the man who would lead the attacks on the 1871 census results. Lowe carried on the work after joining Agriculture and Statistics, although Christopher Dunkin as Minister of Agriculture instructed him to remove his name from the title page as editor for 1872. Lowe acquired a huge tract of land in the Northwest Territories and operated a model farming community. He replaced Taché as deputy agriculture minister in 1888 and was involved in the 1891 census before being forcibly retired in 1895; see especially NAC MG29 E13 3, John Lowe papers. This source contains departmental and personal correspondence lumped together. It is invaluable for the 1871, 1881, and 1891 censuses. Note that Lowe was extremely well connected to the Montreal politicians, and actively organized electoral matters while working as a civil servant. He shared horticulture with them as a pastime. When Lowe's daughter Annie died in October 1871, he could no longer stand to live in his Côtes-des-neiges house. Closing house meant distributing his interesting plants, including rare spruce trees and a variety of gooseberry and blackberry bushes. Sir G.-É. Cartier, who controlled many of the patronage appointments in the Macdonald government, including compilers' jobs, was one recipient, Christopher Dunkin another. See also Gwynneth C. Davies, 'Lowe, John,' *Dictionary of Canadian Biography* (Toronto: University of Toronto Press, 1998) XIV: 666–8.

54 John Beatty, for instance, was a professor at Victoria College, president of the Cobourg Mechanics' Insitute and of the Upper Canada Board of Arts and Manufactures, a census commissioner in 1861, and one of Taché's fellow commissioners to the 1862 London Exhibition. T.P. French was the long-serving Ottawa District colonization and emigrant agent whose emigration pamphlets had been widely distributed by William Hutton. John Layton was Crown Lands Surveyor for Northumberland County, Chatham District Police Magistrate, and also the immigration agent. Charles Everett (1828–1909), partner in a large Saint John import and export company, had been one of two chief compilers for the 1861 New Brunswick census, under the direction of S.L. Tilley, and had chaired the Board of Assessors. He would be elected to Parliament in 1885 and was described in an obituary as a 'master of finance.' Amos Purdy (1825–c.1902) was a merchant and sawmiller who served as Cumberland County MLA from 1867 to 1871. Eusèbe-Ubalde Piché (1824–1894) was a lawyer with *rouge* party connections and had been the Berthier County MPP from 1858 to 1861.

A dash of excitement was added by the presence of the young J.-A.-N. Provencher (1843–1887), whose uncle had preceded Taché's brother as

Bishop of St-Boniface. After he was defeated in the 1867 elections as a Conservative candidate, Provencher edited *La Minerve* before becoming secretary to William McDougall, lieutenant-governor of the recently acquired North-West Territories. Provencher had just returned from the Red River colony, whose annexation by Canada McDougall had despatched him to proclaim. Provencher had been arrested and imprisoned by the Métis before managing to flee to the United States; see Kenneth Landry, 'Provencher, Joseph-Alfred-Norbert,' *Dictionary of Canadian Biography* (Toronto: University of Toronto Press, 1982) XI: 716–17; notice that Provencher's presence on the team clarifies the gap in Landry's account for 1870–1: 'Provencher presumably went back to central Canada.'

55 Weaver was on the managing committee of the Montreal Mechanics' Institute and had been a member of the Lower Canada Board of Arts and Manufactures, whose president was Brown Chamberlin, John Lowe's brother-in-law and partner in the Montreal Printing and Publishing Company. Weaver was also one of the founding members of the Montreal Sanitary Association, a broadly based organization that sought to reform urban infrastructures and the personal habits of citizens. The association enlisted Taché in an attempt to follow up the 1871 population census with a sanitary census of Canadian cities. For more on the Sanitary Association, see Bruce Curtis, 'Social Investment in Medical Forms: the 1866 Cholera Scare and Beyond,' *Canadian Historical Review* 81(4), 2000.

56 I have found only fragments of the considerable departmental census correspondence. Census diaries show that between 1 August 1870 and 22 May 1871 there were 2,650 incoming and 1,278 outgoing census letters and 1,446 personal memoranda, of which only a list survives. The department's accounts show official dates of engagement of census personnel and payments to them. There is little formal discussion of census matters beyond that contained in John Lowe's personal papers and in published documents. For the diaries, NAC RG17, vol. 2423; vol. 55 nd 1871 has a communication to Langton concerning census accounts; RG31, vol. 1249 is the account book for 1871.

57 NAC MG29 E18 7, 31 December 1870.

58 NAC RG17 AI 2, Cambie to Parent, 15 November 1871, for a list of census orders-in-council.

59 NAC RG17 AI 2, Taché to Queen's Printer, 7 December 1870; vol. 42, copy of Taylor to Queen's Printer, 9 December 1870.

60 There had been some earlier steps. In February 1868, in anticipation both of the census and of the new patent law, the Minister of Agriculture, T.C. Chapais, was seeking six additional rooms for his department. In late

August 1868, Taché made his first formal application for census funds, and census monies began to flow more rapidly in the following months. NAC RG17 AI 2, Chapais to Public Works, 29 February; Taché to Langton, 29 August 1868, for $500 'expenses on account of preparing the forthcoming census'; Taché to Minister of Public Works, 24 October 1870; Dunkin to same, 21 November 1870; Taché to Braun, 29 November 1870; to Braun, 3 April 1871, an order for 'the making of 40 little tables 3 feet by 1 foot and 8 ft. as well as 45 chairs for the census compilers.' Notice that these would make it possible to lay out each run of nine schedules end to end.

61 The 'part 2' points to the small measure of discretion allowed commissioners in dividing subdistricts if it proved necessary. In such a case, the enumerator was to write a brief topographical description of the subdivision, such as 'concessions 1 to 6, North Crosby Township.'

62 For instance, NAC RG17 AI 6, Lowe to J.F. Lafrain (?) MP, 13 May 1872, concerning a constituent's claim: 'A careful measurement has been made on a map, of the mileage that has been allowed him, which has shown that if there were any error at all in the allowance, it was in his favour ... Mr. Smith's mileage has been settled on the same principle as that of all other Enumerators, and with the same care ... no allowance is made for twice going over the same road. The length of the road itself only is measured.' The policy with respect to exceptions is in MG29 E 18, 7, 31 December 1871. RG17, vol. 2423, shows the pay rates officially announced by OIC the second week in February.

63 'Manual Containing "The Census Act", and Instructions to Officers Employed in the Taking of the First Census of Canada, 1871' reproduced in Parliament of Canada, *Sessional Papers*, no. 64, pt. 19, 1871 [hereafter cited as *Manual 1871*], quotation at p. 129; the material in this section is drawn from the *Manual 1871* and accompanying documents unless otherwise indicated.

64 Taché not only sought to instruct potential informants about how to answer, by distributing the 'People's Schedules,' but also secured the cooperation of sections of the press in publicizing the enumeration. For instance, *Courrier du Canada*, 27 March 1871; *La Minerve*, 3 April 1871.

## 8: The 'Pur Sang' Census

1 Dominion of Canada, *Debates*, 11 April 1871: 1019–20.
2 For instance, NAC RG17 AI 6, Lowe to Piché, 2 August 1871. None of the original commissioners' reports seem to have survived. In this case, Lowe gets one of the Montreal staff officers to tell a commissioner to remove material from his report because it might be asked for in Parliament.

3 Higgs, 'Disease, Febrile Poisons, and Statistics,' argues that Farr's occupational categories were guided by a medical logic that related disease to the materials with which people habitually worked.
4 NAC RG31, Census field 1871, District 67-e, South Leeds, Ontario; p. 7, personal.
5 *Year-Book and Almanac of British North America for 1867* ... (Montreal: Lowe and Chamberlin, 1866): 18–19; *The Year Book and Almanac of Canada for 1872* (Ottawa: James Bailiff, 1871): 164; and NAC RG17 AI 2, Taché to Leverson, 3 May 1871.
6 NAC MG29 E18 3, Lowe to Taché, 26 October 1871; notice that these totals were somewhat fluid, with the published Quebec total later given as 1,191,516.
7 NAC MG29 E18 3, Lowe to Taché, 26 October 1871.
8 NAC MG29 E18 3, Lowe to Taché, 2, 14 November 1871; Lowe to G.W. Weaver, 8 November 1871.
9 NAC MG29 E18 7, Lowe to Tupper, 15 November 1871
10 NAC RG17 AI 6, Lowe to Weaver, 18 September 1871; there is more going on in this letter, to which I return later in the chapter.
11 NAC MG29 E18 3, Lowe to Harvey, 20 November 1871.
12 NAC MG29 E18 3, Lowe to Cartier, 26 June; to Dunkin, 23 August 1871; RG17 AI 6, Lowe to Sexton, 14 August; to Tilley, 28 October 1871.
13 NAC MG29 E18 7, Lowe to chief compilers, 21 August 1871.
14 NAC RG31, Census field 1871, for instance in 68–d-1 and d-2; the production totals have also been altered on the industrial schedule; *Census of Canada*, Vol. 3, for the yards of home-made linen and woollens and for the return on the wool industry; Kris Inwood and Phyllis Wagg, 'The Survival of Handloom Weaving in Rural Canada Circa 1870,' *Journal of Economic History* 53(2), 1993: 346–58; also, Janine Grant and Kris Inwood, 'Gender and Organization in the Canadian Cloth Industry, 1870,' in Peter Baskerville, ed., *Canadian Papers in Business History*, Vol. 1 (Victoria: The Public History Group, 1989): 17–32; Janine Roelens and Kris Inwood, '"Labouring at the Loom": A Case Study of Rural Manufacturing in Leeds County, Ontario, 1870,' in D.H. Akenson, ed., *Canadian Papers in Rural History*, Vol. VII (Gananoque: Langdale Press, 1990): 215–36.
15 *La Minerve*, 'Le Recensement,' 22 November 1871.
16 Arthur Harvey, 'The Canadian Census of 1871,' *Canadian Monthly and National Review* 1(2), 1872: 97–104.
17 All citations in the preceeding section are taken from Harvey, 'The Canadian Census of 1871.'
18 Unless otherwise indicated, what follows comes from J.-C. Taché, 'The Canadian Census of 1871. Remarks on Mr. Harvey's Paper published in the

February Number of "The Canadian Monthly,"' *Canadian Institute for Historical Microfilms*, reproduction. 'Statist' was the preferred term for those engaged in the science of statistics; it seemed to have more cachet to practitioners than 'statistician.'
19 Margo Anderson, *The American Census: A Social History* (New Haven: Princeton University Press, 1988): 89, on the contrary, shows that in the United States there were repeated demands for recounts in many cities after 1870, and that several were conducted.
20 NAC RG17 AI 6, Lowe to Weaver, 16, and 27 December 1871.
21 NAC MG29 E18 3, Lowe to White, 14 November 1871; Thomas White, Jr., *An Exhibit of the Progress, Position and Resources, of the County of Peterboro,' Canada West, Based Upon the Census of 1861; Together with a Statement of the Trade of the Town of Peterborough* (Peterborough: T. and R. White, Printers, 186?): 44. White thought the main source of the difference was that seasonal lumber workers were counted twice.
22 *The Year Book and Almanac of Canada for 1872* (Ottawa: James Bailiff, 1871): 234–8.
23 NAC MG29 E18 7, nd 1872, 'Remarks on the Recent Census of Ontario and the Immigration Statistics during the Decade from 1861 to 1871,' marked 'Mr. Kingston.'
24 For the sanitary census, Bruce Curtis, 'Social Investment in Medical Forms'; the plan for national statistical reform, NAC RG17, 51, Costley to Dunkin, 4 September 1871.
25 Montreal *Gazette*, 'Immigration,' 3 October 1871.
26 Montreal *Gazette*, 'The Department of Agriculture,' 7 October 1871; Arthur Harvey had been the Finance Department's statistician.
27 Montreal *Herald and Daily Commercial Gazette*, 'Agricultural Improvement,' 6 December 1871.
28 *La Minerve* 'Le Recensement,' 2 December 1871. In 'Le Recensement,' 27 March 1871, Taché's old newspaper, *Le Courrier du Canada*, had explained the procedures in detail before the enumeration.
29 City of Montreal Archives (CMA) Administration Municipale (ADM), 2–Conseil Municipal, 2–Procès Verbaux, 13 December 1871: 69–70.
30 NAC RG17 AI 6, Lowe to Weaver, 18 September 1871.
31 NAC RG17 AI 6, Lowe to Curran, 26 June, 10, and 15 July 1871; to Piché, 6 July 1871; to Weaver, 26 September 1871, and notice that the enumerator claimed 'he ought at least be paid for the preliminary work $20 – he says he distributed the People's Schedules'; to Weaver [concerning Lambe], 16 December 1871; MG29 E18 3, to Lambe, 16 December 1871, 13, and 25 January 1872; AI 6, to Lambe, 23, and 25 January 1872.

32 NAC RG17 AI 2, Lowe to Sicotte, 17 April 1871; RG31, Census field 1871, District 106-c-7, for example, p. 77; Gilles Lauzon, *Habitat ouvrier et revolution industrielle: Le cas du village St-Augustin* (Montréal, 1989).
33 *La Minerve*, 'Le recensement de Montreal,' 15 December 1871.
34 Montreal *Herald and Daily Commercial Gazette*, 14 December 1871; the mayor seems to have doubted the city had the authority to conduct a second enumeration.
35 CMA, ADM, 2–Conseil Municipal, 2–Procès Verbaux, 24 January 1872: 94–6; Montreal *Gazette*, Montreal *Herald and Daily Commercial Advertiser*, 25 January 1872; *La Minerve*, 31 January 1872.
36 *La Minerve*, 'Le Recensement,' 16 February 1872.
37 NAC RG17 AI 6, Lowe to Weaver, 16 December 1871; MG29 E18 3, Lowe to Weaver, 9 February 1872. The receipts for Lowe's January visit are nd January 1872. Taché had repeated attacks of carbuncles in the fall, winter, and early spring of 1871–72 and took refuge in Kamouraska, where he underwent a 'ventouse.' Lowe's correspondence suggests that Taché was hiding his condition from his wife Françoise; see MG29 E18 3, Lowe to Taché, 2 November 1871, 'your wife has sent to the office for news about you.'
38 NAC RG17 A I 6, Lowe to Weaver, 19 February 1872.
39 NAC RG17 A I 6, Lowe to Weaver, 24 February 1872.
40 *La Minerve*, 'Le Recensement,' 9 March 1872.
41 Montreal *Gazette*, 'City Council'; *La Minerve*, 'Rapport du Recensement'; Montreal *Herald and Daily Commercial Gazette*, 'City Council,' 14 March 1872.
42 CMA ADM 2–Conseil Municipal, 2–Procès Verbaux, 12, 13 March 1872: 155, 167, 262–3, 272.
43 Montreal *Gazette*, 'City Council,' 14 March 1872; my emphasis.
44 Montreal *Herald and Daily Commercial Gazette*, 'Census Taking,' 15 March 1872.
45 *La Minerve* 'Rapport du Recensement, 14 March 1872.
46 NAC RG17 A I 6, Lowe to Weaver, 24 February 1872.
47 NAC RG17 A I 6, Lowe to Weaver, 1 March 1872.
48 NAC RG17 A I 6, Lowe to Weaver, 6 March 1872; see also same to same, 8 April 1872; MG29 E18 7, Weaver's statement of number of houses constructed in Montreal, nd 1872.
49 Wm. J. Patterson, *Statements Relating to the Home and Foreign Trade of the Dominion of Canada: Also, Annual Report of the Commerce of Montreal for 1872.* (Montreal: Gazette Printing House, 1873): 34.
50 The volumes can be found in Parliament of Canada, *Sessional papers*, beginning with Volume I in 1873.

## Conclusion: Administering the 'Knowable Community'

1 Laurent Thévenot, 'Rules and implements: investment in forms,' *Social Science Information* 23(1), 1984: 1–45; Alain Desrosières, 'How to Make Things Which Hold Together: Social Science, Statistics and the State,' in P. Wittrock, B. Wagner, and R. Whitley, eds., *Discourses on Society: The Shaping of the Social Science Disciplines* (Dordrecht, 1991): 195–218.
2 Benedict Anderson, 'Census, Map, Museum,' in *Imagined Communities: Reflections on the Origin and Spread of Nationalism,* 2nd ed. (Princeton: Princeton University Press, 1991).
3 In this regard, see the debate, S. Fuchs and S. Ward, 'What is Deconstruction and Where and When Does It Take Place? Making Facts in Science, Building Cases in Law'; Ben Agger, 'Derrida for Sociology? A Comment on Fuchs and Ward'; S. Fuchs and S. Ward, 'The Sociology and Paradoxes of Deconstruction: A Reply to Agger,' *American Journal of Sociology* 59, 1994: 481–500, 501–5, 506–10.
4 B. Latour, *Science in Action: How to Follow Scientists and Engineers through Society* (Milton Keynes: Open University Press, 1987).
5 Philip Corrigan and Derek Sayer, *The Great Arch: English State Formation as Cultural Revolution* (Oxford: Basil Blackwell, 1985).
6 Mitchell Dean's interesting and frequently insightful critique of moral regulation suggests that such is the thrust of the approach; I disagree, and take up the matter of symbolism and ritual below. Dean also separates radically the personal and the political. See '"A Social Structure of Many Souls": Moral Regulation, Government, and Self-government,' *Canadian Journal of Sociology* 19(2), 1994: 145–68.
7 Raymond Williams, *The Country and the City* (New York: Oxford University Press, 1973): 222.
8 Williams, *Country and the City*: 171.
9 Ian Hacking, 'Making Up People,' in T.C. Heller et al, eds., *Reconstructing Individualism: Autonomy, Individuality, and the Self in Western Thought* (Stanford: Stanford University Press, 1986): 222–36.
10 Theodore Porter, *The Rise of Statistical Thinking, 1820–1900* (Princeton: Princeton University Press, 1986): 11.
11 See Oscar J. Gandy, Jr., *The Panoptic Sort: The Political Economy of Personal Information* (Boulder: Westview Press, 1993); Lorna Weir, 'Recent Developments in the Government of Pregnancy,' *Economy and Society* 25(3), 1996: 373–92.
12 Michel Foucault, 'Entretien avec Michel Foucault,' *Dits et écrits* (Paris: Gallimard, 1994) III: 153; compare 'Interview with Michel Foucault,' in

Michel Foucault, *Power/Knowledge: Selected Interviews & Other Writings, 1972–1977* (New York: Pantheon, 1980): 125.
13 Jeremy Bentham, *The Theory of Legislation* (London: Routledge & Kegan Paul, 1931): 399–400.
14 In this regard, Bernard Cohn, 'Cloth, Clothes and Colonialism,' in *Imperialism and Its Forms of Knowledge: The British in India* (Princeton: Princeton University Press, 1996).
15 On governing too much, see Michel Foucault, *Résumé des cours. 1970–1982* (Paris: Julliard, 1989): 112–3.

# Index

Abbott, Edward, 227
Abrams, Philip, 36–7, 42
action at a distance, 31–2, 103, 267–8
Adams, Levi, 125
Agricultural Societies Act (1851), 142
Anctil, Joseph, 264
Anderson, Benedict, 26, 307
Annes, Ezra, 104
Appendix to the Report of the Board of Registration and Statistics (1849), 84–91, 95
Appleby, N.S., 185, 218
Archambault, Louis, 106

Barker, John, 195–6
Barwick, John, 264
Bastien, J.O., 209
Beardsell, the Rev. W.C., 121
Beatty, Dr John, 185, 186, 190, 201, 206, 219–20, 229, 264–5, 370n54
Beaud, J.-P., 57
Belleau, N.F., 226
Bentham, Jeremy, 312–13
Bertrand, Solyme, 187, 203, 208
black boxing, 23, 30, 35, 304, 314
Blake, Oliver, 262

Blouin, A.N., 127
Blue Book, 15, 48, 67, 74, 75, 84, 95, 134, 148, 157,162–6
Board of Agriculture for Lower Canada, 142
Board of Agriculture for Upper Canada, 142
Board of Registration and Statistics, creation of, 66–7
Bouchard, Joseph, 216
Boulton, W.H., 144
Bourget, Msgr Ignace, 174, 243
Boyd, Thomas, 210
British North America Act (1867), 144–5
Brown, George (MPP and editor), 140, 143, 166, 171–5, 223
Brown, George G. (census enumerator), 126
Bruneau, F.-P., 62
Buchner, Edward D., 216
Bull, William, 213
Bullock, Increase, 209, 217
Bureau of Agriculture, creation of, 238–9
Burwash, William, 212
Byrne, E., 225

380  Index

Cambie, A.J., 160
Cameron, Malcolm, 140–2, 147, 156–8
Campbell, Evelyn, 226
Canada East Municipal Act (1845), 65
Canada East Municipal Act (1847), 81
Carney, Richard, 193–4, 220
Caron, Henri, 120
Cartier, G.-É., 280
Cassidy, William, 214, 216
Catholicism, ultramontane, 8, 11, 243, 311, 315
Cauchon, Joseph, 144
Cayley, William, 70, 74, 121, 148
census acts: of 1824 in Upper Canada, 51–2; of 1831 in Lower Canada, 53–4; of 1841, 55–6; of 1843, 56–9; of 1847, 66–9; of 1851, 95–101; of 1859, 176; of 1871, 263–4
census making: and aboriginal population, 48, 54, 60, 108–9, 127, 192–4, 245, 303–4; and accuracy, 4, 16, 33–4; and conflict and resistance, 4, 27–8, 60–1, 126–7, 215–17; in contemporary historiography, 13–16; and cultural domination, 60, 97, 252; and economic advertising, 9, 12, 153; and genealogy, 250–1; as a medical project, 58, 94, 155, 276; methods of: *de facto*, 19, 26–7, 262, 278, 287, 290; –, *de jure*, 26–7, 262, 268, 271–2, 287, 290, 304; –, nominal, 19–20, 22, 44–5, 93; and monumentalism, 248–9, 251; and overenumeration, 135, 199–201, 204, 227; and property relations, 12, 13, 118–19, 163–4, 209–11, 271–3; and religious allegiance, 52–3, 74, 94, 97, 131–2, 150, 205–6, 222; and underenumeration, 17, 33, 116
Census of 1842, 55–6
Census of 1844: execution of, 59–62; Legislative Council Committee Report on, 62–3; results of, 62
Census of 1847, abandonment of, 64–6
Census of 1848, 75–81
Census of 1850, 83
Census of 1852: appointments of commissioners, 103–5, appointments of enumerators, 109–10; categories of origin, 120–1; compilation of schedules for, 146–50; conditions of work of enumerators, 123–9; corrections of schedules, 130–3; double-counting, 119–20; duties of commissioners, 101–2; duties of enumerators, 102; enumeration districts, 105–9; instructions for completion of schedules, 114–17; printing and supply, 110–13; reports of commissioners, 135–6; reports on, 151–5; results of, 221–5; schedules for, 113–14
Census of 1861: appointments of commissioners, 181–2; appointments of enumerators, 194–6; –, instructions to, 182–4; compilation of schedules for, 225–30; conditions of work of enumerators, 211–17; and corrections of schedules, 217–21; definition of enumeration districts, 188–92; failure to map districts for, 191–2;

incoherence of schedules, 201–2, 207–9; instructions for completion of schedules, 201–11; logistical difficulties in, 184–8; modelling of social relations for, 199–200; printing and supply, 179–81; reports on, 230–3; results of, 221–5; and women as informants, 214–15

Census of 1871: compilation of schedules for, 278–86; definition of enumeration districts, 266–7; duties of enumerators, 269; interpretations by enumerators, 275–8; legislative debate, 260–3; mapping for, 257–60; printing and supply, 265–6; reconstruction of past practice in anticipation of, 254–7; reports on, 303–5; results of, 286–92; staff officers for, 264–5

Census of 1872. *See* Montreal Check Census

centralization of knowledge, 4, 7, 12, 35, 66–7, 78, 94, 144–5, 254–60

Chadwick, Edwin, 69

Chapais, T.C., 249, 261

Chauveau, P.-J.-O., 89, 137–8, 167–8, 170, 189, 228, 231

Child, Marcus, 106, 124

civil registration. *See* vital statistics

Clear Grit party, 9, 95, 140–5

Clemow, Francis, 194

Coats, R.H., 14

Cohen, Elizabeth Cline, 7

Cohn, Bernard, 37–8, 308

Commeault, J.B., 155

Corrigan, Philip, 36–7, 44, 308

Costley, John, 257–9, 264

Côté, Augustin, 179

Cox, Edumund, 106, 121, 123, 130, 132

Cradmore, Abdiel G., 216

Crofton, Walter Cavendish, 15; biography and political opinions, 70–4; and Blue Book, 75, 84, 95, 162–3; and compilation of 1852 census returns, 148; criticism of in Parliament, 144; and enumerators' pay, 124; and organization of 1852 census, 101–3; and political crisis of 1849, 94–5; and relations with Hincksite commissions, 112, 121–2, 139

Curran, J.J., 297

Daly, T.M., 264–5n

Delany, Dr Martin, 178

Desrosières, Alain, 31–2

Dézil, Louis Isaaë, 213–4

Dickinson, William, 227–8

discipline, 26, 33, 246, 275, 283, 307

District Councils Act (1841), 65

Doyle, Garret, 79

Drapeau, Stanlislas, 239, 251–3, 254–6

Draper, W.H., 74

Dunkin, Christopher, 261, 263, 278, 291, 370n53

Dupâquier, Jacques, 29, 44

Dupâquier, Michel, 29, 44

Durham, John George Lambton, first Earl of, 20, 49

dynamic nominalism, 308

Edwards, William, 174

Egan, John, 107

Elliot, William, 111

Elliott, John, 79

## 382  Index

Evanturel, François, 236
Everett, Charles, 264–5, 370n54
Eyre, Thomas, 109

Fairbanks, S.B., 218
Farr, William, 21, 58, 69–70, 92–4
feudalism. *See* seigneurial system
Finden, S.S., 182, 225
Foote, S.B., 230
Foster, William, 264
Foucault, Michel, 4, 26, 41–5, 311–3
French, T.P., 264, 370n54
Fuchs, Stephan, 30

Gagné, J.-B., 128
Galt, A.T., 178
Garner, John, 139
General Register Office, 21–2, 69–70, 92–3
Gourlay, Robert, 14, 168
governmentality, 4, 38–45, 74, 79, 93, 152–5, 224, 241, 246, 260, 311–13
Gramsci, Antonio, 43
Gray, John, 79
Grenier, Louis, 107, 119–20
Gunn, William, 186, 190, 203–4, 206, 219

Hacking, Ian, 31, 309
Harington, T.D., 65, 67, 74, 75
Harvey, Arthur, 230, 280, 287–90
Heath, John, 107, 111, 130
Heffernan, Thomas, 105, 110
Hespeler, Jacob, 218
Hincks, Francis, 88, 96–7, 112, 140–1, 145, 147, 160
Hind, H.Y., 178
Hindess, Barry, 40
Holmes, William W., 190, 192, 213
Hough, F.B., 165, 176

Howard, Matthew, 119
Hunt, Alan, 40
Huot, Charles, 124
Hurteau, P.E., 229
Hutton, William, 15, 134, 145–7; and assessment returns, 163–4; and Blue Book, 157, 162–6; and departmental amalgamation, 159–60; failing health, 184; illness and death, 226; reactions to logistical problems, 184; seeks to attend Statistical Congress, 178; and use of population multipliers, 166–70, 172–3; and vital statistics, 164–5

identifying position, 308
infrastructural work, 32–3, 35, 82, 105, 307, 315
intensive administration, 3, 7, 18, 35, 134, 260, 310, 311, 317n1
International Statistical Congress, 11, 20–2, 176–9
investment in forms, 15, 24, 26, 30–1, 58, 78, 260, 306–7
Inwood, Kris, 283–4
Irving, Aemelius, 120, 121, 125, 131–2

Jackson, G. (MPP), 166
Jarvis, John, 187, 191, 215
Johnson, W.H., 239, 249, 254–6
Johnston, Simon, 208
Jordan, John, 112

Katz, M.B., 15–16
Kay-Shuttleworth, Sir James P., 69
Kennedy, J.G.G., 20
Ketcheson, Elijah, 126
Kingston, William, 294–5
Kintrea, James, 218

Kirby, John, 104
Knapp, Alexander, 104, 108–9, 112
knowable community, 308

Labelle, Pierre, 187, 214, 218
Labranche, Jacques Olivier, 201
Lafontaine, L.-H., 89, 239
Lambe, W.B., 297
Landon, W.H., 121
Langton, John, 70, 234, 255
Larocque, Msgr, 174
Larue, André, 107–8
Larue, Nazaire, 107, 120, 132–3
Latour, Bruno, 30–2, 307
Laurin, J., 89
Layton, J.G.G., 259, 264, 370n54
Leary, John, 190, 204, 217, 218–19
Leclaire, P.E., 142
LeFebvre, Joseph, 118
Letellier, Luc, 237
local knowledge, 78, 102, 107, 267–8
Lockhart, A. Macdonald, 190, 194
London Statistical Society, 20–2, 47, 57, 58
Lowe, John, 247, 264–5n, 278, 291, 293–4, 301–3, 369n53
Lower Canada Agricultural Society, 142

Macaulay, John, 51, 54, 72
Macdonald, John A., 140, 161, 166, 262
Mackenzie, Alexander (MP), 262
Mackenzie, W.L., 144, 160
MacNab, Sir Allan, 157
McCann, H.W., 169
McCargar, Milo, 128
McCord, Andrew, 104
Mcdonald, Donald, 104–5
McDonald, William, 130

McDougall, Hugh, 194–5
McDougall, James, 219
McDougall, William (MP), 245, 263
McGee, T.D., 156, 235, 237–8, 245
McKie, William, 217
McLaren, John, 124
McLeod, Donald, 160
McLeod, James, 212
McNider, Thomas, 182, 225
made science, 17, 30
Marx, Karl, 44
Masson, L.-H., 108, 111
May, Henry, 226, 236–7
Mégritte, Narcisse, 128
Meilleur, J.-B., 56, 70
Merritt, W.H., 96, 143
metrological issues, 8, 114, 197–8, 211, 215, 268–9, 282–6
Miller, Peter, 42
Montreal Check Census, 295–303
Morin, A.-N., 101, 107, 121, 148
Morin, Isidore, 124
Morris, William, 74
Morrow, David, 217
Moynahan, Dennis, 131
Murney, Edmund, 144

Nelles, H.V., 248
Nettle, Richard, 178
normalizing judgment, 4, 198, 311

Olivier, L.A., 106, 110
Ouellet, Odulphe, 229

Papineau, D.-B., 74
Papineau, L.-J., 88–91
Paris, John, 110
Piché, E.-U., 264, 370n54
Piva, Michael, 141
political representation, 6–7, 9–10,

48–50, 88–91, 136–7, 166, 171–5, 221–5, 236
Pollock, Henry, 214
population: as category of state, 25, 105; as configuration of social relations, 24, 37, 197; discovery of, 4, 38–45; and territory, 26
Porter, Theodore, 309
Pouliot, Barthélemy, 131
Powell, James B., 205–6
Powell, John, 19
Prévost, J.-G., 57
Provencher, J.-A.-N., 264, 370n54
Purdy, Amos, 264, 370n54

Quetelet, L.-A.-J., 19–21, 57, 68, 92, 176

Rameau, François-Edmé de St-Père, 232–3
Rawson, Rawson W., 20–1, 57–8, 64
Read, David, 53
Rebellion Losses Riots (1849), 9, 88, 91, 94, 240
Regnaud, Victor, 129
Report of the Select Committee of Agriculture in Lower Canada (1849), 240–1
Report on the Affairs of British North America (1839), 49, 237
Report on Government Departments (1863), 237–8
Representation Act (1853), 139
representation by population. *See* political representation
Robinson, Charles, 109, 120–1
Rolph, John, 140, 157
Romagnosi, Gian Domenico, 7
Roney, Sir C.P., 166–7
Rose, Nikolas, 42

Ross, John, 145, 156
Russell, Andrew, 252, 257, 259, 260
Ryerson, Egerton, 70, 170

Sayer, Derek, 36–7, 44, 308
school monies, 10, 47, 173
Schweber, Libby, 3
science in the making, 17, 30, 305
sectional conflict, 46, 49, 85, 87–91, 97–8, 120–1, 134, 136–9, 166–7, 171–5, 222–4, 233, 235, 242, 254
seigneurial system, 6, 8, 64–5, 241–2, 244
Select Committee on Population Returns (1839), 52–3
Shattuck, Lemuel, 20
Shenston, T.S., 121–2, 132
Sherwood, Henry, 66
Shipley, James, 128
Sloan, D.G., 124
Smith, Harmanus, 143
Smith, Henry, 96
Smith, Jacob, 79–80
Smith, James, 74
social imaginary, 5, 11, 12, 13, 24, 27, 137–9, 192
sovereignty, 5, 10, 12, 32, 36, 42
Star, John, 125–7
Starr, Paul, 33
state formation, 8, 17, 36–8, 79, 308; and matters of national importance, 275–6, 308
statistical internationalism, 17–22
statistical translation, 13, 17; and feudal relations, 64–5
statistics: as abstraction, 132–3; and conduct, 158; and feudal relations, 64–5; and hierarchy of knowledge, 310; literary and numerical, 5, 14, 71, 135, 269; and multipliers, 91,

166–70, 296, 298; and political centralization, 7; and popular recreation, 7
Strachan, John, 52
Street, T.C., 143
Sydenham, Lord. *See* Thomson, Poulett

Taché, Msgr A.-A., 239
Taché, E.E., 252
Taché, Sir É.-P., 239, 245
Taché, J.-B., 239
Taché, Joseph-Charles: and analysis of census making, 245–9; biography and opinions, 238–45; and Civil Service Commission, 255–6; in contemporary historiography, 13–15; criticism of in press in Montreal, 295–6; and cultural politics in 1871 census, 285–6, 315–16; and defence of 1871 census, 290–3; and genealogy, 250–1; and monumentalism, 248; and reaction to, 1852 census results, 138–9; and reorganization of Agriculture, Registration and Statistics, 247–8
Tanguay, Cyprien, 239, 247; biography and activities as genealogist, 249–51; and preparations for, 1871 census, 354
Taylor, J.B., 266
Thévenot, Laurent, 30–1
things which hold [or stay] together, 18, 31, 307
Thomson, Poulett, 20–1, 54, 147
Tilley, S.L., 280

Tupper, Charles, 279
Turcotte, J.-E., 144

Urquhart, M.C., 14

Vézina, François, 107
Vidal, Alexander, 192, 204
Viger, Jacques, 60
vital statistics, 10–11; under the act of 1847, 68–9, 164–6; in census of 1861, 205, 233–4; in Lower Canada, 54; in Upper Canada, 52

Wagg, Phyllis, 283–4
Waters, Charles, 104–5, 194–5, 216–17
Wayne, Michael, 228
Weaver, George, 264–5, 279, 291, 297, 299, 301–3, 375n55
weights and measures. *See* metrological issues
White, David, 203, 208, 211
White, Thomas Jr., 185, 208, 216, 293
Wight, George P., 206, 210
Wight, James, 215
Williams, Raymond, 308–9
Willoughby, George, 225
Willoughby, Nicholas, 206
Wiltse, Amos, 266
Winter, Peter, 123
Worton, David, 14
Wright, W.R., 142
Wrigley, E.A., 15

Young, John, 212
Young, Samuel, 215, 277, 285